DIVINE SPEECH

EXPLORING THE QURAN AS LITERATURE

NOUMAN ALI KHAN
SHARIF RANDHAWA

Edited by
Abdullah Budeir

Limited Edition

Bayyinah Institute
1701 Euless Blvd,
Euless, TX 76040
www.bayyinah.com

For comments/questions contact us at divinespeech@bayyinah.com

ISBN: 978-0-9977150-3-3

I would like to dedicate this book to my parents, Afrina and Kausar Ali Khan, whose undying love, encouragement, support and prayers have been the most invaluable treasure of my life.

Nouman Ali Khan

Table of Contents

About the Authors

Nouman Ali Khan was recently listed among the top 500 most influential Muslims in the world. He is the CEO of Bayyinah Institute and through it he has been furthering the cause of Qur'an awareness and Arabic education throughout the world. With a social media following in the several millions, Ustadh Nouman continues to leverage his worldwide reach to promote a better understanding of the Qur'an based on rigorous research yet easy to understand language. He has already completed a video translation of the entire Qur'an and is now dedicated to completing an exhaustive explanation over the course of the next few years. He respectfully asks for your prayers in order for him to complete this mission.

Sharif Randhawa graduated from the Bayyinah Dream program in 2014 and serves as a researcher and writer for Bayyinah Institute. He is currently pursuing studies in the field of Near Eastern Languages and Civilizations, with a focus on the literary and historical study of the Qur'an and its relationship to Jewish, Christian, and other Near Eastern traditions of Late Antiquity. His interests also include philosophy of religion and Islamic intellectual history.

Acknowledgements

There are a number of people to whom I owe thanks for encouraging or helping me with my part in the authorship of this book.

First among them is my dear teacher, Ustadh Nouman Ali Khan, who boldly placed his confidence in me in requesting me to co-author this book with him. When I was in my mid-teens, it was through his online videos and podcasts that I first acquired a sense of what makes the Qur'an "divine speech," producing in me an unquenchable longing to dive further into its depths. Being his student in the Bayyinah Dream class of 2014 was the start of a wonderful journey for me, and I hope that this book is the first of many to come as a result. I owe him more than I can possibly express in words. While the task he has entrusted me with is a formidable one, I hope I have done a fair job in putting into words some of what he has taught me.

Professor Neal Robinson kindly provided a valuable critique of a late manuscript of this book, and also provided me his valuable friendship, mentorship, and encouragement. His pioneering study, *Discovering the Qur'an: A Contemporary Approach to a Veiled Text*—which is the most influential and frequently cited work of scholarship on the Qur'an by a single author in English—was another major factor in making me realize how profound and sophisticated a text the Qur'an is, and which convinced me to devote my life to its literary and historical study. I will never forget my rich and stimulating exchanges with him about Qur'anic studies, Biblical studies, and sundry other topics, and I hope there will be more in the future.

In addition of course to Ustadh Nouman, Abdullah Syed and Misbah Sheikh supervised my work, and also handled the administrative aspects of this book's publication. Ahmad Azlan Shamsuddin designed the graphics found inside this book, which include a map of the world of early seventh-century Arabia and the diagrams of ring composition in the Qur'an. Shaykh Jawad Beg graciously provided references for prophetic traditions and other classical Arabic resources cited in this book. Innumerable readers also provided beneficial feedback for various chapters, several of whom I would like to mention by name. Two dear friends of mine, Taha Soomro and

Shaykh Hammadur Rahman Fahim, read manuscripts of the entire work and provided beneficial feedback. Adil Tobaa offered a very helpful critique of chapter 10, bringing some explanatory gaps to my attention and leading me to rewrite significant portions of it to make it more lucid. Abdullah Budeir, Shaykh Sohaib Saeed, and Dr. Atif Imtiaz, and Nameera Akhtar offered valuable comments and corrections to the final manuscript. I am also honored that Shaykh Dr. Mohammad Akram Nadwi read through a late manuscript of this work.

Last but not least, my parents, Tariq and Maureen Randhawa, have provided me their loving support throughout this journey. I dedicate my part in this book to them.

Sharif Randhawa

Foreword

For more than five hundred years, the Qur'an remained virtually unknown in the West. The first European translation was into Latin in 1143. It was commissioned by Peter the Venerable, the Abbot of Cluny, to help Christians in their ongoing struggle to "reconquer" Muslim Spain, and it bears the title *Lex Mahumet Pseudoprophete* ("The Law of Muhammad the False Prophet"). Fast-forward a further five centuries to 1649. In that year, the Qur'an at long last appeared in English thanks to Alexander Ross, another Christian clergyman. Ross's version is based on a French translation published by Du Ryer two years earlier. The preliminary matter contains some interesting observations, for instance that the author "frequently maketh God to speak in the plural in a stile (*sic*) that is not ordinary." However the volume ends with Ross's own "Needfull Caveat or Admonition" in which he dismisses the Prophet as "the great Arabian imposter" and calls the Qur'an "a gallimaufry of errors." You probably won't find the word gallimaufry in your dictionary. It means a dish made of odds and ends of leftovers.

Many more translations are available today, including a few by non-Muslims less prejudiced than Ross. Nevertheless at the popular level, non-Muslim perceptions of the Qur'an have barely changed. It is widely assumed that Muhammad was an imposter who feigned revelation, that he was influenced by one or more Christian heretics from whom he acquired erroneous views, and that his book is essentially a law code. Moreover those who try to read it in translation usually give up in despair. Not only is the style "not ordinary," its 114 "chapters" have no obvious structure and seem not to be arranged in any meaningful order. In the words of Thomas Carlyle, the nineteenth-century essayist, the Qur'an seems to be "a confused jumble."

Muslim readers of course know better. Or do they? In one respect they are at a distinct advantage. They realize from hearing the Qur'an recited in Arabic that it is sublimely beautiful and that much is lost in translation. They grasp instinctively that it is highly structured. They may also be aware that only two hundred or so verses out of over six thousand deal specifically with regulations for the Muslim community. Nevertheless, because the Qur'an is the principal root of jurisprudence, most of the traditional commentaries were written by jurists who took an atomistic approach to the text, examining the meaning of individual words, phrases or verses, and rarely discussing matters of style and structure.

In recent years, there has been a silent revolution in Qur'anic studies in Western academia. To be sure, one still encounters a few non-Muslim scholars whose stance is aggressively polemical, some of whom have adopted a radical revisionist approach to early Islamic history. One also encounters the occasional Muslim scholar who gives the impression that the definitive meaning of the Qur'an is enshrined in medieval commentaries. Nevertheless, the majority of specialists based in Western universities now take the Qur'an much more seriously as a text in its own right and draw on developments in linguistics and literary theory to shed new light on its meaning and structure. The authors of this slim volume have done an immense service to non-specialist readers by summarizing recent research in language that they will find both accessible and appetizing.

Neal Robinson

Preface

The study of the Qur'an[1] has captured my imagination since 1999. As I made headway into the field, one realization that most impacted me was that its study means different things to different people. For example, the Islamic scholarly tradition devoted to analyzing the text of the Qur'an, called the *tafsīr* tradition, can itself be broken down into several genres. In past centuries, there have been scores of scholars who focused on documenting the earliest commentaries of the Qur'an. Other scholars grappled with its legal implications for Islamic civilization. Yet others dove into its philosophical and theological underpinnings. The list goes on and on.

Although I am an eager student of all of these genres, what has captivated me above all else is the study of the Qur'an aimed at highlighting its literary beauty and linguistic marvel. This is certainly a technical subject, and one must dive deep into Classical Arabic to really be able to get a taste of what it is about. Moreover, Classical Arabic itself is an ocean that has an incredibly intricate system of grammar and morphology (the way words are formed) and a spellbinding variety of rhetorical devices (neat tricks to say stuff in much cooler ways). As I dove into this field, I arrived at two further conclusions:

1. That this study is also multifaceted. While one group of scholars and researchers will argue that a feature such as the Qur'an's language or word choice is its defining literary feature, another will claim that it is something else, such as its use of various literary techniques, or its fascinating coherence and structure.
2. That the insights from the literary and linguistic analysis of the Qur'an are mind-blowing, yet so often their power is lost on most people because the research is just way too technical.

---

1 The word "Qur'an" is also commonly spelled and pronounced "Quran." It is also sometimes spelled "Koran," especially in older English publications, though this spelling is a less accurate representation of the Arabic and is becoming less commonly used.

After taking a leap of faith, I founded the Bayyinah Institute in 2005, dedicated to sharing the beauty of the Qur'an with the world and providing students an education in Classical Arabic. In the early years of this institute, I used to teach a weekend long seminar called "Divine Speech," offering a glimpse into the literary and linguistic marvel of the Qur'an. I conducted it nearly a hundred times over in different communities across the United States, Canada, Europe, and even Malaysia. The overwhelming success and ecstatic feedback from the Divine Speech seminar helped to propel Bayyinah Institute beyond not only my expectations, but my wildest imagination. Hundreds of students have graduated from our Arabic immersion program, hundreds of thousands have attended our various seminars around the world, and millions are following our work online. I consider this book, which is based in part on that seminar and is our first publication, yet another major milestone along this adventurous journey.

With the help of my dear student Sharif Randhawa, who has inspired me perhaps more than I have ever inspired him, this book is an attempt to put something together in light of the two conclusions I spelled out above. Firstly, it is aimed at highlighting unique and interesting literary qualities of the Qur'an from many different points of view. Secondly, it is an attempt to simplify and make digestible what is otherwise only accessible to expert audiences. To put it simply, this is a book about what makes the Qur'an a fascinating read for the rest of us.[2]

Nouman Ali Khan
Founder and CEO of Bayyinah Institute

2 Readers who have any questions or constructive feedback about this book are welcome to email us at divinespeech@bayyinah.com.

Notes for the Reader

Notes on Style, Format, and Use of Arabic Words

This book is primarily intended for non-specialists in Qur'anic studies, including readers who have little prior knowledge of Islam or the Arabic language. While Arabic words inevitably do occur throughout this book, as well as a few English literary and grammatical terms, we have done our best to remove any obstacles this might pose. The reader is only required to familiarize himself with the small handful of key Arabic and English terms that are introduced in **bold**—the majority of which are explained in the first chapter. These terms reappear in the "Glossary of Arabic Terms" and the "Glossary of English Terms" at the end of the book for easy reference.

Arabic words that do not occur in bold but that are instead *italicized* do not need to be remembered over the course of the book, but usually only serve to illustrate immediate examples of literary nuances in the Qur'an. For example, in a discussion in one chapter, we compare three words for "praise" in Arabic, *ḥamd*, *madḥ*, and *thanā'*, to observe the subtleties implicit in the Qur'an's use of *ḥamd* over its near-synonyms. The reader does not have to familiarize himself with these words outside the context of that specific example. In some cases, the mention of an Arabic word in italics merely serves as extra information, especially for aspiring students of Arabic or Qur'anic studies, but can otherwise be ignored without expense. For example, we will refer to the **suras**[3] of the Qur'an by the English equivalents of their titles in Arabic, but will also indicate the Arabic title in parentheses. Similarly, we may sometimes note the Arabic term for a concept in italics, while otherwise adhering to its English equivalent.

The Arabic language contains a number of consonants that do not exist in the English language (such as *ḥ kh*, *ṣ*, *ḍ*, *'*, *gh*, *ṭ*, *ẓ*, and *q*), as well as a differentiation

3 A sura is a distinct portion or section of the Qur'an, often, but somewhat misleadingly, characterized as a "chapter." A fuller explanation of this term will be provided in chapter 1, "An Introduction to the Qur'an."

between long and short vowels (ā vs. *a*, *ī* vs. *i*, and *ū* vs. *u*). The reader is not required to know how exactly to pronounce these sounds, though we have provided a table below for more information on pronunciation. In the case of Arabic personal names (like Muhammad or Abdullah), city names (like Mecca or Medina), words that have become part of English usage (like Qur'an or Hijra), or select words that are used repeatedly over the course of this book (like sura or Fatiha), we have simply used a standardized English spelling, without using italicized font or special characters.

Throughout the book, translations of the Qur'an are either our own, or have been adopted from M.A.S. Abdel Haleem, *The Qur'an: A New Translation* (New York: Oxford University Press, 2005), though frequently with modifications.

The following abbreviations are used later in this book:

v. = "verse" vv. = "verses"	s. = "sura" ss. = "suras"	d. = "died," used to indicate the year of a person's death

Upon the mention of the name of a prophet, especially Muhammad, Muslims customarily say the benediction "may peace be upon him," and may even record this in abbreviation or in full in the case of written text. However, to keep this book as user-friendly as possible, we will not write out this benediction, but simply offer this note as a reminder to Muslim readers.

The Structure of This Book

This book begins with an introductory chapter (chap. 1, "An Introduction to the Qur'an"), which presents general knowledge about Islam, the Qur'an, and the Arabic language; this equips the reader with the necessary background knowledge for the rest of this book, and for any further studies of Islam or the Qur'an. This chapter includes a basic summary of Islam and the key themes of the Qur'an; a description of the historical context of the Qur'an in pre-Islamic Arabia and in the prophetic career of Muhammad (peace be upon him); some points about the Arabic language; and a few of the Qur'an's basic literary features. Unavoidably, this will be the longest and most content-packed chapter of the book. However, it will also be extremely rewarding for non-Muslim and even Muslim readers who desire a succinct but comprehensive overview of these topics.

Following this, the book divides roughly into two halves. The first half (chaps. 2–8) consists of a study of some of the "micro" literary features of the Qur'an, and focuses on individual words, sentences, or small passages. This covers the beauty, precision, and subtlety of the Qur'an's word choice (chap. 2,

"Word Choice"), its ordering of words in a sequence (chap. 3, "Word Order"), its unexpected shifts in person, number, and tense (chap. 4, "Grammatical Shifts"), and its use of Arabic stylistic and grammatical devices (chap. 5, "Other Subtleties of Style and Grammar"). These are followed by studies of figurative language and imagery in the Qur'an, including its use of similes, metaphors, idioms, and parables (chap. 6, "Figurative Language and Imagery"), and of the purposes and meanings of oaths, a common literary device in the Qur'an (chap. 7, "Divine Oaths"). This half of the book concludes with a study of how precise word choice and grammatical arrangement contribute to the richness and beauty of one of the opening verses of the Qur'an (chap. 8, "'All praise is due to God, the Lord of all peoples'").

The second half of the book (chaps. 8–14) consists of a study of some of the "macro" literary features of the Qur'an. In addition to providing a look at some aspects of storytelling in the Qur'an (chaps. 9 and 10, "Storytelling I" and "Storytelling II"), this part of the book largely concerns the topic of the literary coherence and structure of the suras of the Qur'an: how they form distinct and unified wholes and how their structure is integral to their beauty and meaning. This includes studies of coherence and structure within the sura (chap. 11, "The Coherence and Structure of the Sura"), symmetrical "ring" patterns in the Qur'an (chap. 12, "Symmetry in the Qur'an"), the composition of the second, and longest, sura of the Qur'an (chap. 13, "The Coherence and Structure of Sura 2, *The Cow*"), an investigation into whether the suras are arranged in a meaningful order in the scripture as a whole (chap. 14, "The Order of the Suras"), and a study of the word choice, grammatical arrangement, imagery, coherence, structure, and placement of the first sura of the Qur'an (chap. 15, "Sura 1, The Opening"). The entire book is concluded with a brief postscript.

The chapters of this book are written with a sense of progression of scale: from the level of individual words, to that of phrases, to sentences, to passages, to stories, to short suras, to long suras, and finally to the Qur'an as a whole. Nonetheless, should the reader wish to skip ahead to a chapter of particular interest, or read them out of sequence, he should generally be able to do so with little trouble. There are, however, a few exceptions. Chapter 1 is crucial for the reader who has little prior knowledge of the Qur'an, Islam, or the Arabic language. The introduction to chapter 9, "Storytelling in the Qur'an I," serves as an introduction to both chapter 9 and chapter 10, "Storytelling in the Qur'an II." Finally, chapters 13-15, which focus on the topic of coherence, depend to some extent on the concepts introduced in chapter 11, "The Coherence and Structure of the Sura," and chapter 12, "Symmetry in the Qur'an."

At the end of the book we have included a number of resources for interested readers. Among them is an appendix on jihad or fighting in the

Qur'an. Since the topic appears occasionally in Qur'anic citations in this book, and given the many misconceptions surrounding the issue, we felt that a brief treatment of it would be in order for readers interested in more information. There are also glossaries of Arabic and English terms used in this book and recommendations for readers interested in further literary study of the Qur'an in English.

Arabic Pronunciation Guide

The accurate pronunciation of Arabic words is not necessary for the purposes of this book. Nonetheless, the following tables offer a guide for readers who would like to have an idea of how to pronounce the sounds represented in English transliteration by special characters (such as ʿ, *ā,* and *ṣ*) or letters used in ways otherwise not familiar in English (such as the *q* in *qiyāma* or the *kh* in *khālid*).

The Arabic language has three "short" vowel sounds, which are always unstressed:

English transl.	Arabic symbol	Description
a	◌َ	A short '*uh*' sound as in '*but*'
i	◌ِ	A short '*i*' sound as in '*sit*'
u	◌ُ	A short (unstressed) '*u*' sound as in '*tuition*'

These vowels also have "elongated" forms, which are always stressed. These are transliterated with special characters (*ā, ī,* and *ū*) in English to distinguish them from the short vowel sounds:

English transl.	Arabic symbol	Description
ā	◌َا	An '*ah*' sound as in '*spa*' or '*rock*'
ī	◌ِي	An '*ee*' sound as in '*see*'
ū	◌ُو	A stressed '*u*' sound as in '*student*' or '*school*'

Arabic also has two diphthongs, sounds formed by the combination of two vowels into a single syllable:

English transl.	Arabic symbol	Description
aw	◌َو	An '*ow*' sound as in '*house*' or the German '*sauerkraut*'
ay	◌َي	An '*ay*' sound as in '*day*' or '*great*'

Arabic also has a number of consonants that are indicated in English transliteration by special characters or by letters or letter combinations used in specialized ways. Most of these sounds do not have precise equivalents in English:

English translit.	Arabic symbol	Description
'	ء	A glottal stop, like the catch in the voice when pronouncing '*uh-oh!*'
dh	ذ	The '*th*' sound in '*that*' (opposed to in '*thin*')
ḥ	ح	Like '*h*,' but articulated while constricting the muscles in the throat used for swallowing, like the '*j*' in some dialects of Spanish
kh	خ	Like the '*ch*' in the Scottish English '*loch*' or in the Yiddish '*chutzpah*'
'	ع	Like ', but articulated by pressing the muscles in the throat used for swallowing, like a "strangling" sound
gh	غ	Like a "gargling" sound, as in the French '*r*' in 'Paris'
ṣ	ص	Like '*s*' articulated with a raised and tensed tongue
ḍ	ض	Like '*d*' articulated with a raised and tensed tongue
ṭ	ط	Like '*t*' articulated with a raised and tensed tongue
ẓ	ظ	Like the '*th*' in '*this*' articulated with a raised and tensed tongue
q	ق	Like '*k*,' but articulated by clicking the back of the tongue against the very back of the mouth, where the uvula is, as when imitating the '*caw caw*' sound of a crow

A hyphen is used to represent the attachment of a prefix or suffix to a word, such as with the definite article *al-* ("the") in *al-bayt* ("the house"), the prefix *wa-* ("and") in *wa-kataba* ("and he wrote"), or the suffix *-hu* ("him") in *ra'aytu-hu* ("I saw him"). The hyphen does not indicate a pause in pronunciation, but on the contrary indicates that that joined elements should be pronounced smoothly as if they were a single word, such as "*albayt*," "*wakataba*," and "*ra'aytuhu*" respectively. The hyphen is merely written to distinguish the prefixes and suffixes from the base word, for the convenience of some readers.

Besides representing the glottal stop, the apostrophe symbol (') is used—preceded by a space or dash—to mark the place of a letter that is omitted due to the merging of two words, known as elision. For example, in the phrases *wa-'ktub* ("and write") and *fī 'l-bayt* ("in the house"), the apostrophe represents the omission of the vowels *u* and *a,* respectively. Like the hyphen, the apostrophe does not indicate a pause in pronunciation, but is simply a written device to mark where two separate words or word elements elide; the words or word elements joined by an apostrophe should be pronounced smoothly as if they were a single word, such as "*waktub*" or "*filbayt,*" respectively.

CHAPTER 1

An Introduction to the Qur'an

Islam is the world's second largest faith, with more than 1.5 billion followers: about one fifth of the world's population. It is a monotheistic faith, a member of the same Abrahamic tradition as Christianity and Judaism. Yet, unlike the other world religions, Islam is not named after a particular person, place, or group of people, but rather after a timeless concept. The word "**Islam**" is Arabic for "submission"—that is, to the will of God. The word "**Muslim**," referring to an adherent of Islam, comes from this word. It literally means "one who submits" to God.

The basic message of Islam is embodied in the first half of the testimony of faith, *lā ilāha illā 'llāh*, which can be translated as, "There is nothing worthy of worship except God". Muslims believe that this basic idea captures the very purpose of existence, and represents the core message of all prophets or messengers that God has sent to humanity. The second half of the testimony of faith, *muḥammadun rasūlu 'llāh*, "Muhammad is the messenger of God" follows from this. Muslims regard the Prophet **Muhammad** as the last prophet and messenger of God, following the likes of Noah, Abraham, Moses, Jesus, and many other Biblical prophets. To Muslims, Muhammad was a model and teacher of how to worship God and live the sort of life that pleases Him.

At the center of Islam is its holy scripture, the **Qur'an**. Following the Torah of Moses, the Gospel of Jesus, and countless other revelations, Muslims view the Qur'an as God's final revelation to humanity, and in fact His very speech. The Qur'an was revealed in the Arabic language to the Prophet Muhammad in the years 610 to 632 CE, primarily in the cities of **Mecca** and **Medina**, in the western Arabian Peninsula. Arabic is a Semitic language, which means that it is closely related to Hebrew, the language of the Jewish Bible or Christian Old Testament. It is especially close to Aramaic, the spoken language of Jesus and of formative Judaism.

For Muslims, as well as many non-Muslims, the impact of the Qur'an derives from both its message and its astounding literary and rhetorical power and beauty. (**Rhetoric** is the art of eloquent and effective speech, with a focus on its persuasive, aesthetic, and emotional impact.) This power is primarily conveyed in the oral recitation of the Qur'an (the very word *qur'ān* means "recital")—with its exquisite language, style, rhythm, rhyme, and melody—but it can be appreciated in the form of the written text as well. Unfortunately, that power is clearly lost in the act of translation, or can be lost on the reader who is not familiar with the sort of literary techniques that the Qur'an uses. This short book is an attempt to offer a glimpse of that power to the interested reader, Muslim or non-Muslim, in English.

Throughout the rest of this chapter, we will equip the reader with the necessary background knowledge for the rest of this book, or even for any further studies of Islam or the Qur'an. This chapter will include a basic summary of Islam and the key themes of the Qur'an; the historical context of the Qur'an in pre-Islamic Arabia and in the prophetic career of Muhammad; some points about the Arabic language; and a few of the Qur'an's basic literary features. Unavoidably, this will be the longest and most content-packed chapter of the book. Nevertheless, it will also be extremely rewarding for non-Muslim and even Muslim readers who desire a succinct but comprehensive overview of these topics—*in shā'a 'llāh* (God willing).

A Brief Summary of Islam

The basic principles of Islam are straightforward and easy to grasp, and are repeated throughout the Qur'an. The Qur'an stresses that the path of salvation lies in the combination of "faith and righteous deeds," and the entire scripture is aimed at reforming the beliefs and improving the behavior of its reader or listener. Accordingly, Islam is best understood by looking at both of these aspects: belief and action.

The faith that the Qur'an advocates can be summarized in terms of three main ideas: monotheism (*tawḥīd*), the message (*risāla*), and the afterlife (*ākhira*). These do not represent merely theoretical concepts, but are meant to practically impact a person's behavior. At the same time, the Qur'an places a strong emphasis on reason and contemplation—repeatedly urging its audience to "reason" and "reflect"—and cites evidence from human experience, as well as logical arguments, in order to persuade its audience of the truth of these ideas. Here, we will discuss these ideas one by one, while considering their logical relationships and implications for thought and behavior.

Monotheism

The central theme of the entire Qur'an is what Muslims call *tawḥīd*, meaning the "oneness" or "unity" of God—or roughly, "monotheism." This idea signifies not only the *concept* of God, but also how human beings should *relate* to Him.

The Qur'an is full of descriptions of God and refers to Him with many names and attributes. For example, it describes Him as "the Creator of the heavens and the earth"[4] (2:164, etc.). God is also described as *al-Ḥayy al-Qayyūm* (2:255), the Eternal and Self-Existent Being, who sustains all of existence. He is described as "the All-Powerful", "the All-Knowing", "the Most Merciful" and "the Just", among many other names and qualities. From the same root as the word *tawḥīd*, God is described as *aḥad* (112:1), meaning "One" or "Unique." The principle behind all of God's descriptions in the Qur'an is that "To God is the highest description" (16:60; 30:27) and that "There is nothing comparable to Him" (110:4). The concept of God in the Qur'an is that of a being who is perfect in every respect: eternal, personal, all-powerful, all-knowing, and infinitely good, and to whom nothing else can be compared. Nothing shares in His divinity and He must be worshipped alone. Although God is transcendent, He is also close to His creatures by virtue of His compassion and awareness (2:186; 50:16).

The concept of God's exclusive divinity and unique perfection is summarized in the word for God in Arabic, "Allah." Most scholars of the Arabic language consider this word to be a contraction of *al-Ilāh*, meaning "the God" or "the One worthy of worship." It is a cognate to one of the two main Hebrew words for God in the Bible, *Elohīm* (or its shorter forms *El* and *Elōah*), as well as the name for God in Aramaic, the language spoken by Jesus: *Elaha*. The God of the Qur'an is therefore the same God worshiped in Judaism and Christianity (see 3:54; 29:46), the God of the Biblical patriarch Abraham.

From the Qur'an's perspective, however, it is not enough to simply affirm God's divine perfection in a theoretical or abstract way. Human beings must also relate to God in their daily lives by worshiping and serving Him, and not worshiping anything besides Him. The Qur'an's concept of "worship" (*'ibāda*) and "servitude" or "slavery" (*'ubūdiyya*) to God is comprehensive. It does not only refer to ritual acts of devotion, but also regulates how a person conducts himself throughout the day, including how he or she interacts with other people. A faithful Muslim strives to please God in all actions, and the Qur'an's concept of worship gives every aspect of life—not just the ritual aspect—profound purpose and meaning, encouraging people to reach the heights of their moral and spiritual potential. This is the idea expressed in

---

4 In Semitic languages, this is an expression for the whole of creation.

one of the most comprehensive verses of the Qur'an, in which God announces, "I have not created jinn[5] and mankind except to worship and serve Me" (51:56).

From the Qur'an's perspective, this concept of God is not a novel or alien philosophy, but a truth that is deeply embedded in the human conscience (30:30; 7:172). This spiritual instinct, however, can become weakened, obscured, or distorted as a result of sins and other corrupting influences. To revitalize it, the Qur'an directs the human being to "signs" (*āyas*) of God in nature and human experience, which provide evidence or "remind" (20:44) the individual of His presence, creative power, providence, greatness, wisdom, and purpose, and stimulate in the human conscience the desire to worship Him alone. For example, the Qur'an says:

> In the creation of the heavens and the earth, and the alternation of the night and day, and the ships that sail through the sea with that which benefits people, and what God sends down of water from the sky, giving life thereby to the earth after its lifelessness and dispersing on it all kinds of beasts, and in the changing of the winds and clouds that run their appointed courses between the heavens and earth, there are signs (*āyas*) for people who reason. (2:164)

> In the creation of the heavens and the earth and the alteration of night and day, there are signs (*āyas*) for those of understanding: who remember God while standing or sitting or lying on their sides, and reflect over the creation of the heavens and the earth, saying, "Our Lord, You did not create this aimlessly…" (3:190-191)

The term *āya* is found all over the Qur'an, occurring almost four hundred times. As we will see later in this chapter, the Qur'an uses this term not only in reference to God's natural signs in creation, but also His verbal revelations and miracles given to prophets.

The Message

The other two major tenets of the faith, and key themes of the Qur'an, follow from monotheism. The concept of "the message" is that God has sent prophets or messengers to people throughout history, in order to call them

5 Jinn are a kind of creation the Qur'an mentions who, like humans, are intelligent, have free will, and are morally accountable. They have some supernatural abilities—such as the ability to possess humans, quickly traverse long distances, and sometimes manipulate objects—equivalent to the spirits or demons mentioned in the Bible (e.g., 1 Kings 22:21-23; Matt. 9:36) and found in other cultures and belief systems.

to monotheism and teach them how to live as God expects. These prophets include many famous personalities from the Bible, such as Adam, Enoch, Noah, Abraham, Lot, Isaac, Ishmael, Jacob, Joseph, Moses, Aaron, David, Solomon, Elijah, Elisha, Jonah, Zechariah, John the Baptist, and Jesus. The Qur'an also mentions prophets specifically from Arabian tradition: Hud, sent to the people of 'Ad; Salih, sent to the people of Thamud; and Shu'ayb, sent to the people of Midian. While the Qur'an mentions around two dozen prophets by name, it also insists that God has sent countless prophets throughout the world, to every people. Although each prophet came with miraculous signs demonstrating their truthfulness, their people mostly dismissed and rejected their calls, bringing down on themselves divine punishment (16:36; 23:44; 40:5).

Some of these prophets were given revealed scriptures for their people. Abraham was given the "Scrolls" (53:37; 87:19), Moses the Torah, David the Psalms, and Jesus the Gospel. Although each community was given the task of faithfully preserving these revelations, the Qur'an claims that some of the "People of the Scripture"—a term referring mainly to the Jewish and Christian communities—altered them (2:75; 3:78; etc.). Thus, Muslims generally hold that these revelations no longer remain in their complete, original form.

This made it necessary for there to be a final revelation that would be divinely protected (15:9; 18:27) and that would be universal (6:90; etc.). For this purpose, when human history reached the appropriate stage, God revealed the Qur'an to Muhammad. The Qur'an states that Muhammad is a perfect model of human conduct (33:21; 68:4), is the "seal of the prophets" (33:40), and was sent as "a mercy to all peoples" (21:107). However, he is not the author of the Qur'an (25:5-6), nor does he have the power to guide people (28:56); he is only a reminder (88:21), who gives glad tidings of divine reward and warnings of punishment (7:188). Accordingly, Muslims revere the Qur'an as the very words of God, communicated to Muhammad through the angel Gabriel, and they devotionally memorize, listen to, and recite at least portions of the Qur'an in its original Arabic, with millions alive today having memorized the entire scripture. Thus, while the Qur'an has been recorded in manuscripts since the seventh century, its primary method of transmission was oral, and the same Qur'an is recited throughout the world to this day. In addition to the Qur'an, Muslims also turn to the **hadiths** (*ḥadīth*s, literally "reports" or "accounts"), reports of the sayings and practices of the Prophet, which are needed to demonstrate the practical application of the Qur'an's injunctions.

Of course, it is one thing to claim to be a prophet of God; it is another thing entirely to support that claim with evidence. In order to make clear who the true prophets were, God only appointed men of the most outstanding trustworthiness, moral character, and piety, and additionally provided them with *āyas* —here meaning "miracles" in addition to "signs."[6] Some Muslim scholars have argued that these signs are especially fitted to the cultural context of each people. The ancient Egyptians excelled in performing magical feats, so Moses was given the miracle of transforming his staff into a real, live snake, outdoing the illusion of the magicians (20:65-70). By the time of Jesus, the Mediterranean world had benefited from advances in Greek and Roman medicine. Accordingly, Jesus was given the miracles of healing the blind and the leper and raising the dead to life, outdoing what medicine was capable of at the time. The Qur'an takes care to point out that these miracles were only done in specific instances, with God's permission; the messengers did not have the ability to perform these miracles on their own (3:49; 5:110; 13:38; 14:11; 40:78).

Since the Qur'an is a revelation intended for people of all times and places until the Day of Judgment, a miracle that could only be witnessed and experienced for a single generation would not be sufficient. Instead, the miracle had to be intrinsic to the message itself, so that it could be continually examined and experienced by later generations. Additionally, the pride of the Arabs of the seventh century was not their medicine, architecture, or sciences, but their skills in language and poetry. The Qur'an therefore presented *itself* as the miracle, traditionally understood as (at least in part) a miracle of language, literature, and rhetoric, which even the greatest poets and orators of Arabia could not match, and whose mesmerizing power they could only explain as "clear magic" (10:2; 11:7; etc.). When its staunchest opponents claimed, "If we wished, we could say something like this: it is nothing but mere fables of the ancients" (8:31; cf. 74:24-25), the Qur'an challenged them to come up with something similar to it, or even to a small portion of it, to substantiate their claim: "then produce a sura like it and call your witnesses beside God, if you are truthful. If you do not—and you will not—then guard yourselves against the Fire, whose fuel is men and stones, prepared for the disbelievers" (2:23-24; cf. 10:38; 11:13). From the believer's perspective, the Qur'an's inexhaustible spiritual depth and guidance, the historical transformation it effected, the circumstances of its emergence, its prophecies, and the character, teachings, and life history of its Messenger all serve as signs of its divine origin, in addition to its literary and rhetorical preeminence. It is solely the Qur'an's literary dimensions, however, that form the focus of this book.

---

6 The same concept exists in the Bible. For the signs of God, see Exod. 8:19; Deut. 4:34; Ps. 78:43. For signs given to prophets and apostles, see Exod. 3:12; 1 Sam. 10:7-9; Mark 16:17, 20; John 20:30; Acts 2:22, 19, 43; Rom. 15:19; 2 Cor. 12:12; Heb. 2:4.

The Afterlife

The third and final key theme of the Qur'an is the afterlife. This is closely tied to the Qur'an's monotheism because belief in a merciful and just God means that people must be held accountable for their wrongdoings, rewarded for their good, and compensated for any innocent suffering they have experienced. The afterlife is the realm where God's mercy and justice are fully realized and His purposes for creating the world achieve their complete fulfillment. The Qur'an contains extensive descriptions of the reality of the Resurrection, Judgment, the joys of the Garden of Paradise, and the torments of the Fire of Hell. These alert the Qur'an's readers or listeners to the consequences of their actions before God, deter from wrongdoing, and encourage good deeds.

At the same time, the Qur'an aims at balance. God is not only portrayed as Just: His forgiveness is repeatedly emphasized as well, especially for those who repent and turn towards him. The Qur'an also insists that God punishes no one beyond what he deserves and yet multiplies the value of good deeds (4:40), and that mercy is God's dominant quality (6:54; 7:156; 25:59; 40:7). While the Qur'an offers constant warnings and graphic descriptions of punishment for "the wrongdoers" and "the disbelievers" (the Qur'an's term for those who are intent on rejecting the message or engage in hostilities against the believers on account of their faith), it typically balances them with descriptions of God's pardon for those who seek forgiveness and unlimited reward for "those who have faith and do righteous deeds." The revelations of the Meccan period (see "Meccan vs. Medinan Suras" below) frequently offer "double portraits that balance heaven and hell, the garden and the fire, or the righteous and the damned."[7] Recent scholars have named these contrasting portraits "diptychs," in reference to "the double panels of that name that were commonly used to illustrate heaven and hell in medieval Christian art."[8]

The revelations of the Meccan period are filled with descriptions of the day of judgment and afterlife (such topics are known as **eschatology**). Early revelations offer poetic and startling descriptions of the apocalyptic catastrophes that will take place just before the end of the world—the trembling of the earth, the fracturing of the sky, the falling of the stars, the drifting of the mountains, the eruption of the seas—and the overwhelming fear and dread

7 Carl Ernst, *How to Read the Qur'an: A New Guide, with Select Translations* (Chapel Hill: University of North Carolina Press, 2011), 53; see Neal Robinson, *Discovering the Qur'an: A Contemporary Approach to a Veiled Text*, 2nd ed. (London: SCM Press, 2003), 105-106.

8 Ibid.; see Neal Robinson, *Discovering the Qur'an: A Contemporary Approach to a Veiled Text*, 2nd ed. (London: SCM Press, 2003), 105-106.

that will consume people's hearts and minds. Meccan revelations also emphasize God's ability to raise the dead for judgment, which the polytheistic Arabs questioned. In response to them, the Qur'an demonstrates God's power by pointing to *āyas* or "signs", such as the creation of the universe, the creation of the human being, and the revival of the barren earth and its production of vegetation, as evidence that God is able to revive the dead.

"Faith" and "Disbelief"

Closely tied to these three tenets of the Qur'anic worldview are the themes of *īmān* and *kufr*, which are usually translated as "belief" or "faith" and "disbelief" respectively. The messages that God sends through His messengers have an unavoidably divisive effect. By offering "clear signs" and repeated "warnings" to their audiences, the revelations have the effect of sorting them out into two categories of people: "believers," who acknowledge their responsibility and accountability before God and follow the messengers, and "disbelievers," who cling instead to worldly interests, inherited custom or tradition, or reject the message because of their hard-heartedness or arrogance.

Given the moral implications of these categories, the Qur'anic terms "belief" faith," "believers," "disbelief," and "disbelievers" have much richer fields of meaning than their translations may suggest. In English, these terms signify no more than the intellectual state of being convinced or unconvinced of the truth of revealed scripture. In the Qur'anic sense, to "believe" or "have faith" in God, His messengers, and His revelations means to accept and follow their messages, thus devoting worship to God, and God alone. The opposite term, *kufr*, usually translated as "disbelief," literally refers to the act of "covering" something up, suggesting the deliberate act of rejecting, concealing, or ignoring the truth of one's debt to God. The same word is also used to signify ingratitude towards God, showing that the two ideas are really inseparable. "Disbelief" is an internal condition that takes form in various kinds of actions, such as refusing to acknowledge or worship God, associating others with Him in worship, opposing His messengers, deliberately concealing or distorting His revelations, or giving greater weight to the judgments of religious or political leaders than to His explicit commands. In our study in chapter 13 of the second sura of the Qur'an, it will be evident that when Satan, the Children of Israel, or the idolaters of Mecca are accused of "not believing" or of "disbelief" in God or His messages, it does not mean that they failed to recognize the existence of God or the truth of the divine messages delivered to them (on the contrary, see 2:75, 144, 146), but rather it indicates that they chose to oppose them. While "faith" involves embracing

God, one's supreme moral responsibility, and one's very purpose as a human being, "disbelief" or *kufr* entails voluntarily rejecting them, and for this reason the Qur'an speaks of it as the height of moral wrongdoing. The Qur'an discusses the contrasting spiritual states of faith and disbelief in great depth, analyzing and describing their psychology, associated moral characteristics, and ultimate consequences. In these descriptions, both positive and negative, the reader sees reflections of himself, and is thereby confronted with the choice of self-reform.

Practicing Islam

As should now be clear, the Qur'an not only calls people to believe in God, His revelations, and the afterlife, but to be moved by them to reform their attitudes and behavior. The early revelations urge people to be grateful to God for His countless blessings; to make Him the object of their faith, trust, and devotion; to fear Him; and to strive towards virtue and social justice. They prescribe prayer, remembrance of God, and charity, while also demanding repentance to God, fair and honest business practices, freeing of slaves, and taking care of the poor, the needy, orphans, and widows.

During the Medinan period, the Muslim community established its independence and the Qur'an prescribed more detailed religious and social legislations. It is during this period that the famous "five pillars of Islam" took their complete form. These include the testimony of faith ("There is nothing worthy of worship except God, and Muhammad is His Messenger"), the five daily prayers, the obligatory charity, fasting during the daylight hours throughout the month of Ramadan, and the pilgrimage to Mecca. The Qur'an also contains regulations for trade, marriage and divorce, inheritance, criminal law, and war. All of these legislations focus on spirituality and ethical principles, such as truthfulness, justice, humility, modesty, kindness, forgiveness, and mindfulness of God.

The Historical Background of the Qur'an[9]

The historical audience of the Qur'an consisted of the early Muslims, polytheistic Arabs, Jews, and Christians, in the western Arabian Peninsula and its surroundings. The Qur'an frequently shifts from one audience to another. It teaches, commands, encourages, consoles, and—at times—even admonishes its listeners, specifically the Prophet Muhammad (addressed simply as "you,"

---

9 This and the next section, "The Compilation of the Qur'an," summarize the accounts about the origins of Islam as represented in standard Muslim historiographical sources.

or in later revelations as "Messenger" or "Prophet") and his followers (known as the *ṣaḥāba*, or "Companions" of the Prophet, but typically addressed as "those who believe" or "the believers" in the Qur'an). It debates with, and criticizes, the wealthy leaders of the largest and most powerful tribe in Mecca, the **Quraysh**, who bitterly resisted the Qur'an's call to monotheism and social justice. (They are called the *mushrikūn*, or "those who associate partners" with God.) Later, it reaches out to, and eventually debates with, the "People of the Scripture," who consisted, at the time, of the Jews of Medina as well as various Christian sects. The Qur'an confronts the social problems of Arabia, the troubles of the Prophet, the plight of the early Muslims who were being persecuted for their faith, the arguments of its detractors, and the religio-political problems that arose when the Muslim community established its independence in Medina. It is important to keep this background in mind when reading the Qur'an.

The Prophet Muhammad was born in the city of Mecca around the year 570. Mecca was a city in the Hijaz, the mountainous region on the western edge of the Arabian Peninsula, bordering the Red Sea. The Hijaz included part of northern Arabia and was also geographically and culturally close to central Arabia. Unlike the fertile paradise of Yemen (South Arabia), the landscape of these regions was characterized by arid desert wilderness and rugged mountains. While the Bedouins, or Arab nomads, led pastoral life-styles in the desert, cities formed around the occasional oases of the Hijaz and central Arabia, which made agriculture possible. Mecca, however, was not an agricultural settlement, but the commercial center of the region. This was because of its location on the crossroads of the caravan trade routes, on which merchants carried valuable spices and incense and other goods from Yemen in the south to Jordan and Syria in the north. The commercial success of Mecca also owed to the presence of the **Ka'ba**, a shrine whose foundation was known to date back to the Biblical patriarch Abraham and his son Ishmael, the ancestor of various tribes of northern Arabia and the Hijaz. During the annual Hajj, or "Pilgrimage," initiated by Abraham, the Ishma-elites would gather in Mecca to ritually circle around the Ka'ba. While the Qur'an identifies the Ka'ba as a symbol of the monotheistic faith of Abraham, however, his descendants among the Arabs contaminated it by installing and worshiping idols. The chiefs of the tribe of the Quraysh in Mecca were privileged to be in charge of the Ka'ba and the lucrative trade associated with it, making them extremely wealthy. Yet, their wealth and power only served to marginalize and oppress the lower classes of Mecca—the poor, slaves, orphans, and widows.

While the majority of Arabia's inhabitants at this time were polytheists, there were sizeable groups of Jews and Christians, as well as some individuals who were called *ḥanīfs*—people who believed in the simple and pure monotheism of Abraham. Jews flourished in the city of Yathrib, later renamed Medina under Islam, as well as in Yemen. Christian presence was also significant in Yemen, as well as in northern Arabia, around the Byzantine territories. Modern scholarship has also demonstrated that the influence of Syriac Christianity was especially great because of trade caravans that would travel between Mecca and Syria. All these groups worshiped the God of Abraham, called Allah in Arabic, but the pagan Arabs added to this the variety of gods whom they worshiped in the form of idols. While Allah was considered to be the most powerful deity, and was even acknowledged as the creator of the earth and skies, He was seen as too distant to be called on for day-to-day matters. Instead, the pagan Arabs would normally pray to their local deities and regarded tand regarded these deities as mediators between them and Allah.

Muhammad was born to a prominent family in the Quraysh tribe, but because his father Abdullah died before he was born and his mother Amina

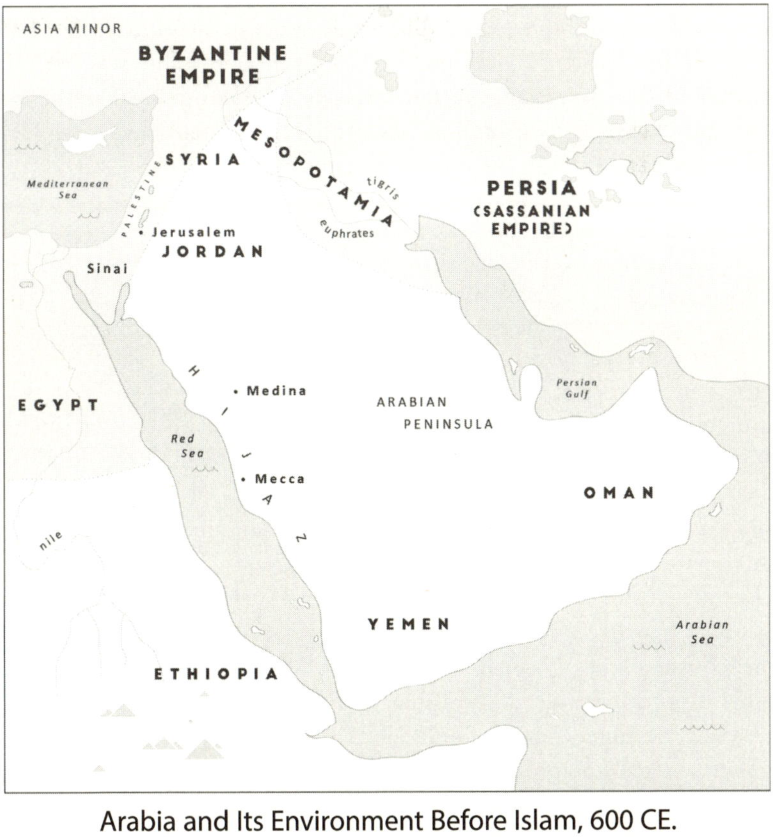

Arabia and Its Environment Before Islam, 600 CE.

died when he was only six years old, he was reduced to the vulnerable status of an orphan. His guardianship passed to his widely-respected paternal grandfather Abd al-Muttalib, son of Hashim, until his death less than two years later. Fortunately, after this, Muhammad was taken care of by his paternal uncle, Abu Talib, who at the same time assumed leadership of the Hashimite clan of the Quraysh. Muhammad accompanied Abu Talib on trade journeys to Syria and, in his early adulthood, became a successful merchant himself. By this time, he had acquired a reputation for his character and honesty. When he was about twenty-five years of age, he accepted a marriage proposal from a wealthy businesswoman and widow named Khadija. Khadija remained Muhammad's only wife and one of his dearest sources of comfort and support until her death over two decades later, and she bore him four daughters.

The first revelation of the Qur'an came to Muhammad in the year 610, when he was forty years old. Muslim tradition holds that he was in one of his customary retreats at the Cave of Hira', outside of Mecca, where he would worship God and contemplate the plight and purpose of humanity. A mysterious figure appeared to him and squeezed him, saying, "Read!" Because Muhammad did not undergo any schooling and was, therefore, unable to read or write, he did not know how to comply. After the figure repeated the demand two more times, with Muhammad answering, "How am I to read?" each time, the figure pronounced:

> Read, in the name of your Lord, who created—
> Created man from a clinging entity.
> Read, and your Lord is most gracious,
> Who taught man by the use of the pen—
> Taught man what he did not know. (96:1-5)

In most pre-modern societies, the activity of reading often included recitation, because it involved a literate individual reading out loud to an audience. The command, "Read" (*iqra'*), therefore, also means, "Recite!" From this root comes the very name of the Qur'an itself, which means "recital."

Greatly worried and distressed, Muhammad rushed home to the comfort of his wife Khadija. Khadija contacted a relative of hers, a Christian monk named Waraqa ibn Nawfal, who assured Muhammad that he was the awaited prophet foretold in the Bible, and that he had been visited by none other than the angel of revelation, Gabriel.

The earliest Qur'anic revelations provided comfort to Muhammad and prepared him for his mission of preaching and activism that would last twenty-three years. At the center of this preaching was the recognition of Allah as the only true god, faith in His prophets and revelations, and accountability before Allah on the Day of Judgment. Initially, Muhammad only preached to his family and close associates. His earliest followers included his wife Khadija; his close friend Abu Bakr; his young cousin Ali, a son of Abu Talib; and Zayd ibn Haritha, a slave whom Muhammad had freed and adopted as his son. While Abu Talib remained a pagan, he nonetheless loyally supported Muhammad with his wealth and protection until his death.

It was only after three years that Muhammad went public with his message. At first, it was met with ridicule by most of the leaders of the Quraysh. The Qur'an records their attempts to discredit the Prophet, claiming that he was crazy or possessed. However, as the Qur'an's call to monotheism and social justice built up a following among the lower class of Mecca, Islam increasingly came to be viewed as a threat to the Quraysh elite. It undermined their source of wealth, since they profited from the pilgrims who came to worship the gods at the Ka'ba. Moreover, the Qur'an's demands for fair economic practices, for spending on orphans and widows, and for freeing slaves disturbed the social status quo that the Quraysh were intent on preserving. Finally, Arabia was a tribal society, and the Arabs cherished nothing more than they did their ancestry. The Qur'an's criticism of idol worship was viewed as a treasonous assault on the ways the Arabs had inherited from their revered ancestors.

The attempts to suppress the Qur'an's message grew increasingly harsher, from initial ridicule and propaganda to the outright physical torture of Muhammad's followers, who had no means of social protection. In the fifth year of his prophetic career, Muhammad sent a large group of his followers to asylum in Ethiopia, where they would be under the protection of its Christian king, free to practice their religion in peace. Yet, the situation in Mecca did not improve. When Abu Talib refused to put a stop to Muhammad's preaching, the pagan leaders of the Quraysh imposed a social and economic boycott on their clan, the clan of Hashim. The ban dissolved after three years, in 619, due to the strength of tribal ties between members of different clans.

That year, however, would be remembered as the Year of Sadness. Muhammad's two dearest and most vital sources of support, his uncle Abu Talib and his wife Khadijah, passed away. Leadership of the Hashimite clan transferred to Abu Lahab, who, despite being the Prophet's uncle, was one of his most ruthless antagonists. When Muhammad traveled south to the city of Ta'if, in hope of gaining sympathetic followers and sanctuary, the inhabitants of the city responded by stoning him. However, Muslim tradition holds that God subsequently rewarded the Prophet with an extraordinary distinction. The angel Gabriel took him on the Night Journey and Ascension, from Mecca to Jerusalem and then to Heaven. Muhammad led various Biblical prophets in prayer, conversed with them, and was physically brought closer to God than any other creature had been permitted before him.

Shortly afterwards, a historical turning point occurred. A group from Yathrib—another city of the Hijaz, though located a two weeks' camel journey north of Mecca—visited Mecca for the Hajj. Fortunately, the Prophet had some family connections with the people of Yathrib. Upon meeting the Prophet and hearing the Qur'an, some of the visitors accepted Islam. Over the next two years, representatives from Yathrib pledged allegiance to him and invited him and his followers to take refuge in their city, hoping that if they made him the city's leader, he could reconcile its two warring tribes. The Prophet's followers in Mecca began emigrating to Yathrib, leaving their houses and possessions behind. In 622, the Prophet escaped a conspiracy by various representatives of the clans of the Quraysh to assassinate him, and took off to Yathrib. This Emigration, or **Hijra**, marks the beginning of the Islamic calendar.

Yathrib was now a city that included several groups: the two native Arab tribes, who were called the "Helpers" (*Anṣār*), and who quickly embraced Islam; the new Muslim "Emigrants" (*Muhājirūn*) from Mecca; and three major Jewish tribes, who largely continued to practice their own faith. The Prophet drew up an agreement between these different groups, establishing solidarity and brotherhood between the Emigrants and the Helpers, based not on traditional Arab tribalism but on a common faith. The Jewish tribes also entered into an agreement, which stated that in the event of an outside attack, the different tribes of Yathrib would defend one another, as members of a single community or *umma*. The Prophet became the city's political and judicial authority, and it was renamed *Madīnat an-Nabī*, "the City of the Prophet," or simply Medina for short.

As Islam established itself in Medina, however, new religious and political problems arose. Many of the tribal leaders of the city resented Muhammad's new power and only converted to Islam in order to maintain their own. While the Muslim community previously consisted of only the most sincere of followers, who were willing to even withstand persecution for their faith, there now existed a segment of insincere Muslim converts, who were intent on undermining Islam. The Qur'an refers to this group as "the hypocrites." Despite their agreement, the majority of the Jewish tribes also had hostile feelings towards the Gentile Prophet. The Qur'an comments extensively on the various political and religious problems these groups posed for the Muslim community.

In 624, the Qur'an, for the first time, permitted the Muslims to defend themselves militarily against their Meccan enemies and to fight for their rights and possessions:

> Permission has been given to those who are being fought, because they have been wronged. God is able to give them victory. Those who have been expelled from their homes without right, only because they say, "Our Lord is God." If God did not repel some people by means of others, then monasteries, churches, synagogues, and places of prostration in which God's name is mentioned would be destroyed. (22:39-40)

The Muslims began raiding Meccan caravans and soon won their first battle, the Battle of Badr, despite being outnumbered threefold. Several of the leading men of the Quraysh were killed and the Muslims were now a force to be reckoned with. A number of important battles occurred in the following years, such as the Battle of Uhud in 625 and the Battle of the Trench in 627, in which the Muslim community in Medina successfully resisted the most formidable attack that had been launched by the Meccans. (Because the topic of fighting comes up occasionally in Qur'anic citations in this book, and given contemporary misconceptions about the topic of jihad in the Qur'an, we have given further attention to the topic in the appendix at the end of this book for interested readers.)

However, what the Qur'an distinguished as the "clear victory" (48:1) came in 628, without any military confrontation. Newly emboldened, the Prophet and a large group of his followers, for the first time, decided to make a minor pilgrimage (*'umra*) to Mecca. The Quraysh were faced with a serious dilemma. Their authority among the Ishmaelite Arabs depended on their status as the custodians of the sanctuary, especially during the sacred months, during which it was especially important that pilgrims to Mecca not be harmed. On the other hand, if this large group of Muslims were publically allowed to make the pilgrimage, it could legitimize their faith and attract more converts from the people. They agreed to a truce, known as the Treaty of Hudaybiyya. Although the treaty placed several strict conditions on the Muslims, such as preventing them from completing the minor pilgrimage that year, it permitted both sides to form whatever alliances they desired, and, in effect, allowed Islam the chance to spread without fear of war. In the next two years, the number of converts to Islam doubled. When the Meccans violated the treaty in 629, the Prophet now had the opportunity to lead an army of over ten thousand against Mecca. The Meccans surrendered and the city was conquered peacefully, except for a small number of war criminals and propagandists who were specifically marked for execution. Mecca was now under Muslim control, and Islam was the most powerful force in Arabia.

While a number of former allies of the Quraysh still existed in Arabia and were hostile to Islam, the religion's increasing size and authority legitimized it in the eyes of observers. By the time of the Qur'an's last revelation and the Prophet's final breath in 632, the previously warring tribes of Arabia had been united under the call of Islam—which hardly more than a decade earlier had been the religion of a small, persecuted minority. Over the course of the Prophet's ministry, many of his most hardened political and religious enemies embraced the faith and joined the ranks of his closest companions.

In the following three decades, Islam continued to grow rapidly under the leadership of what Sunni Muslims call the Four Rightly-Guided Caliphs—the Prophet's Companions Abu Bakr (632-634), Umar (634-644), Uthman (644-656), and Ali (656-661). During the caliphate of Umar, Islam expanded at an extraordinary rate. The Muslims conquered the whole of the Sassanian Persian Empire and all of the **Near Eastern** lands of the Byzantine Roman Empire.[10] By the year 711, Islam had reached all the way to Spain in the West and Sindh in the Indian Subcontinent in the East. For many Muslims, the transformation of Islam from a small, persecuted minority faith into the dominant world power in less than a century is an outstanding sign of God's direction of human history—an extension of the philosophy through which the Biblical prophets and writers interpreted their history, reaching all the way back to the time of Abraham.

The Compilation of the Qur'an

Whenever a new portion of the Qur'an was revealed, the Prophet would recite it to his followers, and explain where the new revelation belonged among the suras and verses of the scripture. They, in turn, would memorize it and some of them would write it down on various scraps of materials or keep their own personal, though incomplete, copies of the Qur'an. The Prophet also had a committee of around twenty personal scribes. However, during his lifetime, there was no need to assemble a complete copy of the entire Qur'an, since it had been memorized in part by almost all the early Muslims, and many memorized it in full. Nor was it feasible to assemble it in that way, due to the fact that the Qur'an's revelation continued progressively until shortly before the Prophet's death.

---

10 The Persian and Roman empires had been the two superpowers of the Near East and beyond for over four hundred years. "Near East" is the term historians use to denote what roughly corresponds to the modern Middle East in ancient times. It includes Egypt, the Arabian Peninsula, the Levant, Asia Minor, Mesopotamia, and Persia.

Shortly afterwards, however, during the Battle of Yamama (633 CE), a significant number of the memorizers of the Qur'an were killed, presenting a risk to its preservation. Despite initial hesitation, the first caliph Abu Bakr ordered that an official copy of the entire Qur'an be compiled, assigning the responsibility to the Prophet's leading scribe, Zayd ibn Thabit. Although Zayd had memorized the entire Qur'an, he consulted other witnesses who had learned the scripture from the Prophet, as well as written manuscripts, to make sure that he transcribed it accurately.

As Islam spread to new territories over the next twelve years, a new problem emerged, as discrepancies started to appear in the recitations of new converts. After consulting with the other disciples of the Prophet, the caliph Uthman assembled a committee (again led by Zayd, and using Abu Bakr's written text) to produce copies of a standardized text of the Qur'an, spelled according to the Quraysh dialect. After the completion of these copies, Uthman sent them to the urban centers of the empire, along with learned reciters, and ordered all other copies to be burned to make sure any errors or confusions in them were not reproduced. Uthman's codex has been accepted by all Muslim sects, throughout the fourteen centuries since its establishment, as the authentic text that was revealed to the Prophet.

Pre-Islamic Arabia and Classical Arabic

The harsh Arabian Desert offered very few resources and even fewer forms of entertainment. This had two important consequences. First, outside powers, such as the Roman and Persian empires, took little interest in the region beyond its trade routes and northern border, so the ancient Arab Bedouins were allowed to develop their language and culture in a greater degree of isolation than other peoples of the Near East. To the Arab city-dwellers, who were less insulated from foreign influences, the language of the Bedouins was seen as the purest version of Arabic, and later sources claim that those who lived in urban areas would send their sons into the desert to learn this version of Arabic from them—a practice that continued even centuries after the birth of Islam.

Second, and more importantly, the Arabs themselves responded to this environmental lack by producing a culture that was highly focused on oral literature. A strong sense of folk tradition emerged, and storytellers shared legends of ancient Arab nations (like the 'Ad and the Thamud mentioned in the Qur'an), told battle stories, and commemorated the acts of honor and heroism of their tribesmen. Placing a great emphasis on lineage, the Arabs would also pass down family histories and memorize lengthy genealogies going back dozens of generations.

Most importantly, for our purposes, they prided themselves in their language and placed great emphasis on refined expression. Consequently, the celebrities of Arab society in the sixth and early seventh centuries were its poets. They were not only its entertainers; they were also its main source for commentary on the themes of life, death, time, fate, love, and war. Poets even carried political influence: they possessed a powerful tool that could be used as propaganda in support of their clients or tribes, or to attack an enemy tribe or person. The eleventh-century literary scholar Ibn Rashiq commented on the status of the poet,

> When there appeared a poet in a family of the Arabs, the other tribes round about would gather together to that family and wish them joy of their good luck. Feasts would be got ready, the women of the tribe would join together in bands, playing upon lutes, as they were wont to do at bridals, and the men and boys would congratulate one another. For a poet was a defence to the honour of them all, a weapon to ward off insult from their good name, and a means of perpetuating their glorious deeds and of establishing their fame for ever.[11]

This clear and refined form of Arabic in which the poets wrote is known as *Classical* Arabic. This was the high, literary language recognized across the north and central Arabian tribes, and is the language in which the Qur'an would be revealed. Classical Arabic is remarkable for the profound richness of its imagery, and the precision and thoroughness of its grammar and vocabulary.

The creativity, subtlety, and focus on imagery that characterize Classical Arabic are partly illustrated by how the Arabs derived new words from old ones. Arabic words are derived from roots made up of three consonants, or sometimes more. Each root has certain basic meanings, and from a single root, dozens or even hundreds of new words may be derived. (To highlight when different words share a root, we will sometimes print the root letters in capitalized form.) For instance, the root of the words Islam (*iSLāM*, "submission") and Muslim (*muSLiM*, "submitter") is *s-l-m*, which is the same root for many other words such as "peace," "safety," and "greetings" (*SaLāM*, *SaLāMa*, and *taSLīM*). As a result, even abstract verbs and nouns tended to derive from an image or scene that was common to the experience of the Arabs. To give just one example, the word *'aqala* means "to reason" or "to understand"—something that cannot easily be captured in tangible or concrete terms. Yet,

11 Hasan ibn Rashiq, *al-'Umda*, vol. 1 (Cairo: Matba'at al-Sa'ada, 1963), 65, qtd. in Robert Hoyland, *Arabia and the Arabs: From the Bronze Age to the Coming of Islam* (London: Routledge, 2002), 212.

the Arabs derived this word from the noun *'iqāl*, which refers to a rope the Arab would wrap around his head and then use to leash his camel when resting on a journey. What is the connection between using one's reason and using a rope to leash an animal? The Arabs viewed the intellect as what holds a person back from doing foolish things, in the same way the rope detains the camel. Hence the word for "reasoning" was creatively derived from a scenario that represented a common experience for the Arab. We will see more examples of this feature of Classical Arabic at play in the Qur'an when we explore the topic of idioms in chapter 6, "Figurative Language and Imagery."

The focus on imagery and the precision of Classical Arabic is also apparent in its vocabulary. Where other languages may have only a single word to refer to an object, or may have one or more words that are interchangeable, Classical Arabic often has a diverse range of words, each with very specific meanings, so that a single word would create a detailed picture of that object and its characteristics. These distinctions and implications are usually lost in translation. For instance, the word *qabr* could refer to any grave or burial site, but the word *marqad* (literally, "place of slumber") is used to refer to the grave of a deceased loved one in his prolonged slumber, while the word *jadath* describes a burial site of which not even a trace remains.[12] A cave that heads downward is called a *ghār*, while one that leads up into an open space is a *kahf*. Prolonged cold is *shitā'*, deathly cold is *ṣirr*, cold felt in the wind is *ṣarṣar*, the pleasant coolness of a breeze is a *nafḥa*, and the cold associated with a particular geographical location—such as the peak of a mountain—is its *zamharīr*.[13] At least ten different words exist for "friend." A *ṣadīq* is a friend whose truthfulness and loyalty is proven over and over again. A *walī* is a friend who never leaves your side, whose closeness can always be felt, and in whose hands you would not hesitate in confiding your personal matters. A *rafīq* is a friend who represents a source of comfort and whom you can lean on in times of difficulty. On the other hand, a *khadhūl* is a friend who abandons you in your hour of need, revealing his true colors at the worst possible moment—and so on.[14] These qualities extend to even abstract concepts, such as "doubt," for which the Arabic language has six different words. Among them, a *shakk* is a doubt that results from two possibilities appearing equally viable, whereas *maraj* is doubt and confusion resulting from two separate issues, each one clear on its own, that become muddled together. *Rayb* is doubt that leads to problems in life or causes a

12 'Abd ar-Raḥmān Kaylānī, *Mutarādifāt al-Qur'ān ma'a al-Furūq al-Lughawiyya* (Lahore: Maktabat as-Salām, 2009), 673.

13 Ibid., 582.

14 Ibid., 698.

person distress, and *mirya* is doubt over something previously taken to be a fundamental truth, as a result of prolonged criticism.[15] These are just a small handful of examples that illustrate the richness of the language's vocabulary.

Finally, the grammatical system of Classical Arabic is also highly sophisticated. Choices of grammatical usage—such as the order in which a person arranges the words of a sentence, what form of the word he uses (e.g., a nominal or verbal form, perfect or imperfect tense, active or passive), and whether a person uses certain words or even letters to add emphasis—all contribute to the art of composing an eloquent expression and the emotional impact it will have on the audience. These are the concerns of rhetoric (in Arabic, *balāgha*), which this book aims to explore in relation to the Qur'an.

The Arabs valued the precision and eloquence of their language so much that the word they used to mean "non-Arab," *'ajam*, originally describes people who speak unclearly. The Qur'an also associates Arabic with clarity, describing itself as "clear Arabic speech" (16:103; cf. 43:2-3). Again, it is important to emphasize that this language was *Classical* Arabic, the language of poetry. But the Qur'an not only matched the Arab poets in the clarity, precision, and eloquence of its language: it *surpassed* them. The Qur'an itself refers to its unmatched beauty and power as a proof of its divine origin, challenging its detractors to produce something comparable to it, or even to a single portion of it, if they claimed it was of human design (10:38; 11:13; 17:88). Islamic tradition has regarded the inability of even the most outstanding literary figures in the Arabic language to meet this challenge as a proof that it could not have been produced by a human being—let alone someone like Muhammad, who grew up and lived amongst them, and was known to have lacked any formal education, reputation as a poet, or even the ability to read and write.

Because of the role of pre-Islamic Arabic poetry in appreciating the language of the Qur'an, when Islam spread beyond the Arabian Peninsula, Muslim scholars and linguists preserved and studied this poetry in order to determine the rules of Arabic grammar, shed light on the meaning of words and expressions in the Qur'an, and grasp the scripture's eloquence. Classical Arabic continued to be the language of scholarship and poetry for centuries after. However, it is important to note that Classical Arabic is no longer used today in speaking and writing. The language used in formal contexts (such as newspapers, television, and most books) across the Arab world today is called Modern Standard Arabic. Modern Standard Arabic is essentially the same as Classical Arabic in its grammar and has inherited most of its vocabulary, but lacks its stylistic and rhetorical nuances, which are of central importance to this

---

15 Ibid., 606.

book. Both are known as *Fuṣḥā* Arabic, literally meaning "correct," "clear," "pure," and "eloquent." They are in contrast to the colloquial, spoken dialects (*'Āmmiyya*), which differ significantly from place to place, often even at the level of individual letter-sounds. In this book, when we refer to "the Arabic language" or "Arabic," we will be referring specifically to Classical Arabic.

The Literary Units of the Qur'an: Suras and *Āyas*

Every book is composed of smaller units of composition, such as chapters, which can further be divided into even smaller units, such as paragraphs or sentences. The way the sections of the book are arranged depends on the genre. A novel or a history will usually be written chronologically, while an academic treatise will be written according to the logic of its argument. A book containing distinct works, such as a book of essays or letters, will likely have a looser arrangement. In this case, the compiler may arrange them chronologically, thematically, or based on other considerations.

The Qur'an consists of 114 compositions of varying sizes, which it refers to by the unique term *sūra*. (Because we will be using this term frequently, from here onward we will print it more simply as "sura.") The sura is often thought of or translated as a "chapter" of the Qur'an, but this can be misleading for a number of reasons:

First, while there is no consensus on the meaning of the word sura (though one explanation will be mentioned below), it is not used to refer to the chapters or sections of any book besides the Qur'an.

Second, each chapter of a book is usually devoted to a specific topic, but this is not the case with the Qur'anic suras. A single sura usually discusses a variety of topics that may not be obviously or inherently related, and the Qur'an will usually address a single topic in more than one sura, albeit from different angles. This is not to say that each sura does not possess its own distinctive themes or coherence, which unites the composition as a whole. As we will see later, the suras of the Qur'an, in fact, possess remarkable literary coherence, even though this has often been overlooked by both traditional Muslim and modern Western scholars, until very recently.

Third, chapters are usually arranged chronologically or topically, but again this is not the case with the Qur'anic suras. Apart from the first sura, *The Opening* (to be discussed in the next chapter), the suras of the Qur'an are arranged very roughly in order of decreasing length. Accordingly, the second sura is the longest sura, while those at the end of the Qur'an tend to be the shortest. As for chronology, the earliest suras tend to be the shortest and are therefore found at the *end* of the Qur'an rather than at its beginning, while the longer suras tend to be later and therefore are placed at the beginning of the Qur'an. All of this prompts the question of why the suras are arranged the way they are. While this subject continues to be researched, what has been discovered so far is awe-inspiring. We will consider this subject more fully in chapter 14, "The Order of the Suras."

Fourth, a chapter is usually given a title that indicates its main topic, but this is not the case with most of the suras. These names typically are merely labels used to distinguish one sura from another, but do not usually communicate their contents. According to Muslim sources, some of the suras were given names by the Prophet Muhammad—and in fact many suras have more than one name—but Muslim tradition does not supply explicit evidence for the origin of all the sura names. Many suras are named according to their first line; this is the case for most of the suras at the end of the Qur'an. Others are named after a specific word, incident, or parable that occurs either uniquely or prominently in the sura. For example, the second sura, called *The Cow* (*al-Baqara*), is not all about a cow; rather, it is named after a story that is mentioned in the sura. Similarly, although suras 14 and 71 are named *Abraham* and *Noah* respectively, they are by no means the only ones that feature these two personalities.

How, then, should we think of the sura? Neal Robinson, in his seminal book, *Discovering the Qur'an: A Contemporary Approach to a Veiled Text*, writes:

> The difference between surahs and chapters was put succinctly by the eighteenth-century Indian theologian Shah Wali-Allah of Delhi, when he wrote that the Qur'an should not be thought of as a book arranged in chapters and dealing with its subject systematically, but rather as a collection of epistles by a king, each written for his subjects according to the requirements of the situation. The comparison of surahs with epistles is a highly suggestive one...We shall see later that it apparently throws light on the order in which the surahs occur. In addition it helps prepare the reader for many of the themes and motifs to be repeated in surah after surah, but with subtle modifications to fit the different circumstances of the recipients of the message.[16]

Another analogy was put forth by the twentieth-century Indian scholar Hamid ad-Din Farahi, whose pioneering work on the coherence and arrangement of the suras will be referred to later. Farahi favored the argument that the word sura means "a wall enclosing a city" (*sūr*).[17] He drew from this several key implications. A wall must enclose a single, distinct city, and

---

16 Robinson, *Discovering the Qur'an*, 257.

17 Mustansir Mir, *Coherence in the Qur'an: A Study of Iṣlāhī 's Concept of Naẓm in Tadabbur-i Qur'ān* (Indianapolis: American Trust Publications, 1986), 37.

therefore each sura must constitute a distinct composition. Moreover, although different cities may have common facilities—such as hospitals, police departments, or grocery stores—each city is nevertheless unique, both in its individual parts (no two grocery stores are exactly the same) and, more significantly, in its distinct arrangement and features. Similarly, although each sura treats a number of common themes in the Qur'an, it treats each of them from a different perspective and also relates them together in distinct ways. We will consider some examples of this in the course of our exploration.

Each sura is further broken down into verses, which the Qur'an calls *āya*s. When citing a passage of the Qur'an, the number of the sura is written first, followed by the number of the *āya*, separated by a colon (for example, 49:2 refers to sura 49, *āya* 2). The shortest sura (Sura 108) consists of only three short verses, while the longest (Sura 2) consists of 286. Just like the length of the suras, the length of individual verses can vary dramatically, from just two letters (20:1; 41:1) to almost an entire page (2:282). The division of the verses is determined by a number of factors, such as rhythm and rhyme, context, the ending sounds of surrounding verses, and so on.[18] The Qur'an often refers to its verses as being "recited"—for example: "When His *āyas* are recited to them, it increases them in faith" (8:2). Previous revelations are also said to consist of *āya*s (28:45), including what is preserved in the Bible of authentic revelation (3:113).

The fact that the Qur'an refers to itself, as well as previous revelations, as a collection of *āya*s is significant, because the word carries a wide range of meanings. As we have seen, the word *āya* means "sign"—that is, an indication or evidence of something beyond itself. When used in the context of Scripture, the word *āya* primarily means "message" or "communication," and sometimes "example" or "lesson" (e.g., 16:11). The fact that the Qur'an uses the same term for a sign of God in creation as it does for a verse of the Qur'an is suggestive. The idea proposed by some Christian theologians, that God's "revelation" includes both "special revelation" (revealed Scripture) as well as a figurative "general revelation" (nature or creation), both guiding to knowledge of God's existence and attributes, is similar to the Qur'anic usage of the word *āya* for both phenomena. The term *āya* can also refer to a "marvel" or "wonder," or even a "miracle," as in the miracles given to prophets as proofs of their truthfulness (e.g., 2:211), or to something valuable, amazing, attention grabbing, or which inspires curiosity. When the Qur'an refers to itself as a collection of *āya*s, it may have all of these meanings in mind.

---

18 Abu Ammar Yasir Qadhi, *An Introduction to the Sciences of the Qur'aan* (Birmingham: Al-Hidayah, 1999), 154.

Meccan vs. Medinan Suras

Muslim scholars have traditionally divided the suras of the Qur'an into two main categories, in accordance with the historical backdrop presented earlier in this chapter. "Meccan" suras are those that were revealed before the Hijra in 622 (hence predominantly in Mecca), while "Medinan" suras are those that were revealed from the Hijra onwards (hence, predominantly in Medina). This division is important because the content, style, and even length of the two types of suras differ greatly. Following the work of the German scholar Theodor Nöldeke (d. 1930), Western scholars have further divided Meccan suras into "Early," "Middle," and "Late Meccan," according to the same sorts of criteria. Here we will briefly consider the differences between the suras of these different phases.

During the Meccan period, the main opposition to Islam was by the pagan elite of the Quraysh. As a result, the Meccan suras share a strong and consistent focus on core themes of the faith: monotheism, as opposed to idolatry; God's vast bounties to humankind, and man's debt and ingratitude to God; the inevitability of the Day of Judgment, and portrayals of the Judgment, Paradise, and Hell; and the truth and divinity of revelation. The Meccan suras are also filled with stories of punishment of previous nations who disbelieved in their messengers; instructions and comforting words for the Messenger; and condemnations of the tendencies of the wealthy and powerful disbelievers, such as unjust business practices, hoarding wealth and even orphans' property, and negligence of the poor and disadvantaged. At this stage, nightly prayer and charity were incumbent on the believers, but the specific rituals or laws of Islam did not yet exist.

The differences between the Early and Middle-to-Late Meccan suras may be summarized as follows. The Early Meccan suras tend to be the shortest in the Qur'an, and therefore appear at the *end* of the scripture. They consist of shorter verses, are more melodious with diverse rhyme scheme, and commonly begin with divine oaths (see chapter 7, "The Divine Oaths"). The Middle-to-Late Meccan suras, on average, are six times longer, have longer verses, and more regular rhyme schemes, and frequently begin with lengthy affirmations of revelation.[19] There is an increased focus on the truth of revelation, criticism of the disbelievers, and inclusion of Jewish and Christian stories adapted to the Qur'an's message and purpose.

In the Medinan period, the Muslim community grew rapidly and established itself as an independent, self-governing body. As a result, there was less need to focus on the basic matters of faith (the Meccan suras continued to be recited and to fulfill this function), and almost all the religious and social

19 Carl Ernst, *How to Read the Qur'an: A New Guide, with Select Translations* (The University of North Carolina Press, 2011), 105.

laws were introduced. In the Medinan suras, there is more engagement and debate with the "People of the Scripture"—Christians and, especially, Jews, who thrived in Medina—as opposed to the polytheists of Mecca, and the narratives focus especially on Israelite history. Some of the Medinan suras also confront the new challenge of "the hypocrites," people who publically claimed to be Muslim but who privately tried to undermine the faith and its community. Permission and regulations for fighting are introduced, and some suras comment on the battles that took place. The Qur'an's ethical focus is extended to societal issues that had become relevant to the new community. The parties frequently addressed in these suras include "the Messenger" or "the Prophet" (who is now addressed more formally), "those who believe" (the Muslims), and "the Children of Israel" (the Jews). The basic subjects of the Meccan suras—such as the afterlife or God's bounties in nature—continue to exist, but no longer form the main subject material of the suras. The Medinan suras also contain lengthier passages, longer verses, and a simplified rhyme scheme. While the aesthetic quality of the Qur'an when recited aloud remains a significant aspect of the scripture, the gradual shift from the forceful and highly poetic style of the Early Meccan suras to the more prose-like style of the Medinan suras reflects an increase in emphasis on the written text (*kitāb*).[20]

The Speaker of the Qur'an

According to orthodox Muslim belief, the Qur'an is the spoken word of God, preserved in a heavenly tablet, and gradually communicated by the angel Gabriel to the Prophet Muhammad. This understanding differs from most of the Bible, which does not present itself as the direct speech of God, and which modern Jews and Christians (barring the position of Orthodox Jews regarding the Torah) tend to view as the divinely inspired words of its human authors—and thus "God's word" in a more limited or indirect sense. Even in the prophetic books of the Old Testament, God's words are presented by a human author, the prophetic writer. In contrast, Muslims do not view Muhammad as the author of the Qur'an in any sense, but only a recipient of the revelation, entrusted with conveying it faithfully. Nonetheless, a few aspects of the Qur'an's narrative point of view can be initially confusing to the reader who is unfamiliar with the Qur'an's style. This subject will be covered in more detail in chapter 4, "Grammatical Shifts," but a few points should be noted here, in order to avoid confusion in the intervening chapters.

---

20 Ibid., 43.

When God (as the implied speaker in the Qur'an) speaks in the first person, He usually does not use the singular ("I/Me/My"), but the plural ("We/Us/Our"). This plural does not signify actual number—the Qur'an repeatedly insists that God is One—but is a rhetorical device used by the speaker to convey His own majesty. This is used even in English, and is called the "royal 'we'" or the "majestic plural." A person in a high office, such as a king, may announce, "*We* decree the following..." while referring only to himself. Similarly, it is common in academic writings for a single author to use the first-person plural in this manner, such as "We will treat this problem in chapter 9."[21]

An author might also refer to himself in the third person, such as "In the opinion of this author," or "this author has an acquaintance..." Likewise, the Qur'an frequently refers to God in the third person, such as in the verse, "It is He who created for you whatever is on the earth" (2:29). This does not entail that the speaker is other than God, but is a device used to produce a rhetorical effect.

The Qur'an therefore shifts from one pronoun to another, in a way that is not common in most written works today. As we will see, however, the Qur'an's pronoun usage is far from inconsistent. The Qur'an utilizes these shifts to achieve different kinds of rhetorical impact on the listener, and with remarkable skill. Moreover, the choice of one pronoun over another (for example, the occasions in which the Qur'an uses "I" instead of the more typical "We" or "He") is determined by very precise considerations of context, such as mood. This is one of the stylistic aspects of the Qur'an we will explore in this book.

The Qur'an and Biblical Narratives

Most Western readers of the Qur'an will quickly notice the abundance of references to Biblical characters and retellings of Biblical stories in its pages. This feature of the Qur'an should not come as too much of a surprise, since it claims to be a revelation in the line of the Biblical prophets. Nonetheless, the way the Qur'an presents these stories differs from the Bible in some significant ways.

Much of the Hebrew Bible, or Old Testament, is a continuous narrative of the sacred history of the people of ancient Israel (Hebrews or Israelites,

---

21 It is important to note that while God often speaks in the first-person plural, He is never designated by the second- ("You/Your") or third-person plural ("They/Them/Their"). In English, "you" and "your" are used for both the singular and the plural, but Arabic has separate pronouns for these.

later called Jews). It includes such famous stories as Adam and Eve in the Garden of Eden, the Flood of Noah, God's friendship and covenant with Abraham, the slavery of the Israelites in Egypt, their Exodus into the Promised Land, God's revelation of the Torah to Moses on Mount Sinai, and the subsequent history of the people of Israel, leading all the way up to the time of Jesus and its aftermath in the New Testament.

The Qur'an also contains these stories, but not in one continuous narrative. As we have already noted, the Qur'an as oral literature is structured very differently from most books. Some stories, such as the stories of Adam or Moses, are retold numerous times throughout the Qur'an, with different emphases and drawing out different lessons. Frequently, parts of a story will be told in one place and other parts will be related in another. Sometimes the Qur'an even refers to a Biblical story or figure without relating the story in detail. Moreover, many of these stories include incidents or episodes not found in the Bible.

All of this is, at least in part, a result of the fact that the Qur'an was revealed in the Near East in the period known as Late Antiquity, where the different Jewish and Christian communities had preserved and developed their own interpretations, elaborations, and expansions of their Biblical heritage. In Arabia, these communities included Jews, who were versed in rabbinic tradition, as well as Ethiopic and (especially) Syriac Christians. The Qur'an communicates to these different groups with reference to their own traditions and interpretations. Accordingly, the Qur'an invokes traditions known not only from the Bible, but also from a range of other sources that were cherished and well known among these communities. These traditions were preserved and communicated in Hebrew, Aramaic, Syriac, and Ethiopic, which are all Semitic languages, thereby allowing the easy transfer of religious vocabulary, motifs, imagery, and even special phrases into Arabic. Similarly, many of the narrative episodes in the Qur'an are not found in the Bible, but in extra-Biblical Jewish and Christian traditions. The Qur'an does not simply reproduce these stories, however. As much recent scholarship has shown, it critiques, omits, and adapts them to its own program of reform, imbuing these stories with new meanings and lessons consistent with its own distinct message.

The Literary Approach to the Qur'an

In this book, we approach the Qur'an from a literary perspective—that is, with a focus on its literary forms and devices through which it communicates its teachings, such as wordplay, metaphor, allegory, rhythm, rhyme, narrative techniques and styles, composition, and much else besides. This way of studying the scripture has several advantages, such as giving Muslims and non-Muslims equal opportunity to appreciate the sophistication, richness, and beauty of the text using the same tools of analysis. The literary study of the Qur'an can also make the scripture more accessible to non-specialists who wish to understand its contents and message, apart from the highly academic treatments found in traditional commentaries and contemporary academic journals. Moreover, while the Qur'an has always been regarded as a masterpiece—and even a miracle—of literature, the theological and legal approaches to the text have tended to overshadow a literary approach, resulting in the neglect of the study of the Qur'an's literary qualities in both traditional and modern institutions of learning. Approaching the Qur'an as literature thus fills an important gap.

In short, the literary approach to the Qur'an makes the scripture accessible both to believers and to those who with no prior theological commitments to it; to people of both religious and secular interests; to non-specialists, university students, and scholars alike; and to people of both east and west.

Before proceeding, one more thing should be noted. As should now be clear, the Qur'an defines itself as the word of God revealed in the Arabic language, and the beauty of its language and sound cannot be reproduced in other languages.[22] As a result, a translation of the Qur'an into another language cannot accurately be called "the Qur'an", nor can a translation of one of its verses be properly considered an *āya*. When we state in this book that "the Qur'an says…" or "the verse says…" this should only be understood as a shorthand way of speaking. The English translation of the Qur'an is not equivalent to the Qur'an itself, but only an inherently limited reflection of its meanings.

* * *

You should now have a good basic understanding of what Islam is about, what the Qur'an is, why it is worth studying from a literary perspective, and a few things about Arabic. You are now prepared to step into the world of the Qur'an, and to taste something of the literary beauty that has been the subject of almost a millennium and a half of devoted study, and which continues to be a source of discovery and fascination to this day.

---

22 However, Michael Sells, *Approaching the Qur'an: The Early Revelations*, 2nd ed. (Ashland, Oregon: White Cloud Press, 2006), 159-223, offers readers of English a beautiful and accessible study of some of the short, hymnic, Early Meccan suras, with a focus on the role of sound in the meaning and experience of the Qur'an. The study is accompanied by audio recordings of recitations of the respective suras.

PART I

Micro Literary Features

In the next seven chapters, we will explore some of the "micro" literary features of the Qur'an, at the level of individual words, sentences, and small passages. We will look at examples of how words are carefully selected (chap. 2) and ordered (chap. 3) in the Qur'an to form patterns or to convey subtleties of meaning; the use of calculated shifts in person, number, and tense in the Qur'an (chap. 4); its masterful use of Arabic grammatical and rhetorical devices (chap. 5); its rich use of figurative language and imagery, including similes, metaphors, idioms, and parables (chap. 6); and the functions of oaths, a common literary device in the Qur'an (chap. 7). This will be concluded with a study of one of the opening verses of the Qur'an (chap. 8), which is roughly translated as "All praise is due to God, the Lord of all peoples," but which is crafted to the highest possible standard of rhetoric in the original Arabic. Through a close study of the word choice and grammatical devices contained in this verse, the chapter will attempt to provide readers of English with a sense of the depth and subtlety of the original Arabic.

CHAPTER 2

Word Choice

In the first chapter, we saw how Classical Arabic offers a remarkable diversity of options for expressing even a single idea. Context, imagery, sound, and meaning will affect whether one chooses to refer to the cold as *shitā'* (prolonged cold), *ṣirr* (deathly cold), *ṣarṣar* (cold felt in the wind), or one of several other words. One's choice of a word for "friend" can have subtle but profound implications on the type, strength, or reason for one's friendship, or what makes that friendship special. To the poets and orators of Arabia, the choice of words used in a poem was an extremely important part of determining its literary quality. A keen and creative use of language would have an immediate impact on the attentive listener or reader, and literary critics would pay very close attention to word choice when scrutinizing a composition. A charming example of the latter may be found in a story about the famous poet Hassān ibn Thabit. In the market town of 'Ukāẓ, a center of poetic readings and competitions, Hassān read out the following verses in praise of the charity and heroism of his own tribe:

La-nā 'l-jafanātu 'l-ghurra yalma'na bi 'ḍ-ḍuḥā
Wa-asyāfu-nā yaqṭurna min najdatin damā.

Ours are the bowls of white twinkling in the forenoon,
And our swords drip with blood on account of our bravery.

These verses employ one of the typical rhyme schemes of Classical Arabic poetry, and use vivid imagery to glorify the tribe, a familiar pre-Islamic Arabic theme. But unimpressed was an-Nabigha, one of the most revered poets of late pre-Islamic times, who found fault with almost each of Hassān's choice of words:

> He said *jafanāt*, but that is only a few bowls; *jifān* would have indicated a multitude of bowls, and the Arabs boast by what is many and not what is few. He said *al-ghurra*, but that is used to refer to a speck of white; *al-bayāḍ* would have signified "whiteness," which is more extensive and total. He said *yalmaʿna*, they "twinkle," but *yashruqna*, they "give off light," would have been more intense in meaning. He said *bi 'ḍ-ḍuḥā*, "in the forenoon," but everything twinkles in the forenoon; it would have been better to say *bi 'd-dujā*, "in the night." He said *asyāf*, but that means only a few swords, whereas *suyūf* would have indicated many swords. He said *yaqṭurna*, they "drip" with blood, but *yajrīna*, they "flow," would have been more impressive. He said *damā*, which indicates less blood, whereas *dimā'* would have been more.

On the other hand, the early accounts show that the Qur'an dazzled layman and critic alike. Muslim tradition records countless stories of its language and melody moving its listeners from the first time they heard it, including even the strongest opponents of its message. As increasing numbers of converts held the Qur'an up as a tangible miracle of Arabic literature, sworn opponents of the faith—despite their every attempt to dismiss it—were unable to meet the scripture's challenge to "produce a sura like it" (2:23).[23]

Closer studies of the Qur'an, carried out by medieval and especially modern scholars of Classical Arabic, have revealed that the Qur'an's selection of words is indeed extraordinary in its precision.[24] Here, we will not consider the elements of sound that make the Qur'an's word choice beautiful—rhythm, rhyme, assonance, phonetic consonance, and other such qualities—which deserve their own study. Instead, we will focus on how suitably words are selected to fit their contexts, and the impressive literary and semantic implications that these choices of words have. Because this book aims to provide examples of literary qualities of the Qur'an in English that can be easily grasped by audiences with no training in Classical Arabic language or

---

23 On the reception of the Qur'an and its rhetorical acclaim in Arabic and Muslim tradition, see Navid Kermani, "The Aesthetic Reception of the Qur'ān as Reflected in Early Muslim History," in Issa J. Boullata (ed.), *Literary Structures of Religious Meaning in the Qur'ān* (Richmond, Surrey: Curzon, 2000), 255-76; and Navid Kermani, *God Is Beautiful: The Aesthetic Experience of the Qur'an* (Cambridge, UK: Polity, 2015).

24 By "precision" we do not mean that the Qur'an never uses ambiguous or open-ended language—e.g., to accommodate multiple meanings, to give a specific historical event or phenomenon timeless relevance, or to provoke study and reflection. We are instead referring to how meticulously the Qur'an selects a word or form of a word to suit its context or to convey subtle meanings and rhetorical implications that would otherwise be absent.

literature, we will focus on just a handful of fairly simple and straightforward examples. Nonetheless, scholars of the language have uncovered thousands of treasures embedded in the Qur'an's word choice, many of which call for being made accessible in future English publications.[25]

Precise Word Choice

We will start off by looking at examples where the Qur'an has carefully chosen a word over near-synonyms, or in which it has broken an expected pattern, in order to precisely suit its context and convey subtleties of meaning that would not otherwise exist.

"Go down to a settlement!"

The Qur'an frequently retells parts of the story of the Biblical Exodus, when God appointed Moses to lead the Israelites out of slavery in Egypt and miraculously saved them from the pursuit of Pharaoh and his army. After that, however, the Bible and the Qur'an both relate that the Israelites showed continuous ingratitude towards God while they were wandering in the desert on their way to the Promised Land. For example, God provided them with miraculous sustenance in the form of manna, quails, and springs of water. Nevertheless, despite this miraculous deliverance *and* provision, some of the Israelites complained of having to eat the same food day after day:

> Remember when you said, "O Moses, we cannot bear only one kind of food. Call upon your Lord to bring forth for us what the earth produces of its green herbs, its cucumbers, its garlic, its lentils, and its onions." He said, "Would you exchange what is better for what is inferior? Go down to a settlement (*miṣran*). Then you will have what you have asked for!" Humiliation and misery struck them, and they drew on themselves God's wrath. (2:61)

The word used for "a settlement" (or "town," "countryside") is *miṣran*. The Arabic language has many words that have similar meanings, such as *baladan*, *qaryatan*, and *arḍan*, but the word used in this verse is striking in

---

25 For modern studies in Arabic, Urdu, and English, see the works of Faḍil Ṣāliḥ as-Sāmarrā'ī, 'Abd ar-Raḥmān Kaylānī, and Mustansir Mir listed in the bibliography. Among classical resources, the Qur'anic commentary of Zamakhsharī (d. 1143) is the most acclaimed and exhaustive study of the Qur'an focusing on its language and rhetoric. Some other prominent commentaries of the Qur'an in this genre are those of Ibn 'Aṭiyya (d. 1147), Abū Ḥayyān al-Gharnāṭī (d. 1344), and Abū 's-Su'ūd (d. 1574).

its resemblance to the word for Egypt, *miṣr*.[26]

The wordplay here is both striking and highly meaningful. The Israelites could only have known of these food items from their experience in Egypt, since they lived their entire lives there. When Moses replies, "Go down to *miṣran*. Then you will have what you asked for!" he is implying, tongue-in-cheek, "Go back to Egypt, where you suffered the bitter life of slavery, if you insist on having those foods again!"

His statement, "Then you will have what you have asked for!" also carries a note of sarcasm. What is it that they were *really* asking for? This is illustrated in the next sentence: "humiliation (*dhilla*) and misery (*maskana*) struck them, and they drew on themselves God's wrath (*ghaḍab*)." This recalls the kinds of misfortune that the Israelites suffered in Egypt. As slaves and forced laborers, they suffered the lowest status possible in a society, and thus humiliation (*dhilla*). The Israelites were also unable to change their situation. This is implied by the word *maskana*, which entails misery that a person is powerless to escape. Finally, they were the special objects of Pharaoh's wrath (*ghaḍab*). In this case, by being ungrateful for the unique blessings God favored them with, they earned God's wrath. The wordplay and irony in this verse drive home a profound lesson about the preciousness of freedom among God's blessings, as well as the seriousness of ingratitude towards such blessings.[27]

"O Children of Israel!"

In the Qur'an's narratives, most messengers are sent to their own people. It is therefore typical for the messengers to address their audiences, "O my people!" or "O my nation!" (*Yā qawmi*). For instance, Moses pleads with the Israelites, "'O my people, why do you hurt me when you know I am the messenger of God to you?'" (61:5). He addresses them the same fashion in 2:54, 5:21, 10:84, and 20:86, as do most other messengers in the Qur'an. It is curious, then, that in the very next verse, when Jesus also speaks to the Israelites, he addresses them differently:

> When Jesus, the son of Mary, said, "*O Children of Israel,* indeed I am the messenger of God to you, confirming what came before me of the Torah and bringing good news of a messenger after me…" (61:6)

---

26 In fact, many translations mistakenly render it as "Egypt." This is incorrect because the word for Egypt is a diptote (*mamnūʿ min aṣ-ṣarf*) and cannot receive nunation (*tanwīn*), while the word *miṣr* in the verse is nunated (*miṣran*). "Egypt" in the accusative is instead *miṣra*.

27 Mustansir Mir, "The Qur'an as Literature," *Religion & Literature* 20.1 (1988): 58.

Similarly, a later verse says:

> They have certainly disbelieved who say, "God is Christ, the son of Mary."[28] But Christ himself said, "*O Children of Israel*, worship God, my Lord and your Lord." (5:72)

Unlike Moses, Jesus does not address the Israelites as "my people," even though he is also an Israelite prophet. There are two likely reasons for this exception.

The first is that these verses define Jesus's mission not as a divine incarnation or universal savior, as in Christian theology, but as a human prophet sent specifically to the Israelites. The Qur'an's view in this respect is similar to the Gospel of Matthew, which portrays Jesus as the Jewish Messiah sent specifically to "the lost sheep of the House of Israel" (Matt. 10:6; 15:24) in order to reinforce the teachings of the Torah (Matt. 5:17). While the missions of other prophets to their respective peoples are clear, from the Qur'an's perspective, the nature and audience of Jesus's mission had become obscured by Christian theology. Accordingly, the Qur'an portrays Jesus as addressing his audience unambiguously as the "Children of Israel" and defining his role as that of a prophet sent to them.

---

28 cf. 5:17. In the past, Western scholars have taken this to be either an example of the Qur'an's "confused understanding" of orthodox Christian doctrine or a reference to the beliefs of some obscure "heretical" Christian sects. The same interpretations were applied to 5:73, where the Qur'an attributes to Christians the view that "God is the third of three," and 5:116, where it attributes to Christians the notion that both Christ and Mary are "gods besides God." However, more recent scholarship has shown that neither of these interpretations is correct; instead, the Qur'an is offering rhetorical arguments against Orthodox and Monophysite Christian beliefs, drawing on the theological disputes that were taking place among Christian sects in the Late Antique Near East. This is summarized by Neal Robinson, who writes,

> Finally, for a plausible explanation of the odd-sounding theological statements anathematised in the Qur'an we need look no further than the intra-Christian disputes between Nestorians and Orthodox. From a Nestorian perspective, by honouring Mary with the title 'Mother of God', the Orthodox laid themselves open to ridicule. For they appeared to have relegated God the Father to third position after Jesus and Mary, to have identified God with Jesus, or to have made Mary and her son into two additional deities. The Qur'an reiterates Nestorian anti-Orthodox polemic but develops it to its logical conclusion, denying that Christ was in any sense divine. (Neal Robinson, "Jesus in the Qur'an, the Historical Jesus, and the Myth of God Incarnate," in *Wilderness: Essays in Honour of Frances Young*, ed. R. S. Sugirtharajah, London: T&T Clark, 2005, 189.)

For further detail, see Claus Schedl, *Muhammad und Jesus: Die christologisch relevanten Texte des Korans* (Vienna: Herder, 1978), 523-527.

Another, more subtle, reason may also be at play. The Qur'an affirms that Jesus, although he was not divine, was miraculously born to the Virgin Mary, and therefore did not have any real lineage on his father's side. Consequently, the Qur'an usually refers to him as "Jesus, the son of Mary." Although in Jewish law a person's status as an ethnic Jew derives from his mother, to the Qur'an's Arab hearers, lineage was strictly patrimonial. From that perspective, Jesus could not have attributed himself genealogically to the Israelites—or, for that matter, to any people. Therefore, the Qur'an also safeguards the virginal conception of Jesus by *not* having him address the Israelites as "my people" in the normal manner of its prophets.

"What will make you know?"

Many of the short Meccan suras found at the end of the Qur'an feature a rhetorical device in which a heavy and mysterious topic is mentioned suddenly using a word or phrase that is both enigmatic and attention grabbing: we will call it (X). More often than not, the topic involves the Day of Judgment. This is immediately followed by the rhetorical question, "*wa-mā adrā-ka mā* (X)?"—"what will make you know what (X) is?" Take the following examples:

> And what will make you know what the Day of Recompense is (***wa-mā adrā-ka mā*** *yawmu 'd-dīn*)? Again, what will make you know what the Day of Recompense is? (82:17-18)

> But he has not attempted the Uphill Path! And what will make you know what the Uphill Path is (***wa-mā adrā-ka mā*** *'l-'aqaba*)? (90:11-12)

This style was effective because during the Early Meccan period, there was formidable resistance to the Qur'an's message, and its opponents were particularly unwilling to listen. Therefore, brief, forceful verses were more likely to get the message across. In a few cases, this formula is used to introduce and define the subject matter of a sura:

> Indeed, We revealed it on the Night of Power. And what will make you know what the Night of Power is (***wa-mā adrā-ka mā*** *laylatu 'l-qadr*)? (97:1-2)

> The Crashing Blow! What is the Crashing Blow? And what will make you know what the Crashing Blow is (***wa-mā adrā-ka mā*** *'l-qāri'a*)? (101:1-3)

Before going further, let us first direct our attention to the verb used in the question, *adrā*. The verb comes the root *d-r-y*, which means "to know," "to perceive," or "to understand." The form *adrā* means "to make [someone] know or perceive; to explain, convey." *Adrā* is in the **perfect tense**, which is used to signify a completed action. This is usually equivalent to the past tense in English, but that is clearly not the case here, since these verses are not speaking about the past. In this case, a better explanation for why the perfect is used would be that the perfect indicates a completed act, and thus represents *only a single event*. For example, "I drove this car" indicates a single, completed event, while "I drive this car" or "I used to drive this car" suggests not a single event but a recurring action.

Similarly, unless one has a particularly poor memory, he can only "come to know" of a given matter once; the act of "coming to know" it is not going to be repeated again and again. If someone first learns, for instance, that a certain team won a sports tournament, he will not afterwards come to know it afresh every time he hears it! The use of the perfect tense in the phrase "*wa-mā adrā-ka mā* (X)?" therefore suggests that once someone is informed of the matter X, he will at once come to know it—or, at least, something about it.

In three cases, however, a variant of this question is posed: "*wa-mā yudrī-ka*?" This is the same question, except that the verb this time occurs in the imperfect tense (to be explained in a moment). In translation, there is no obvious difference from the already established "*wa-mā adrā-ka*":

> People ask you about the Hour. Say, "Knowledge of it is only with God. And what will make you know (***wa-mā yudrī-ka***)? Perhaps the Hour is near…" (33:63)

> And what will make you know (***wa-mā yudrī-ka***)? Perhaps the Hour is near…" (42:17)

> He (Muhammad) frowned and turned away, that a blind man came to him. And what will make you (Muhammad) know (***wa-mā yudrī-ka***) that he might be purified, or be reminded so that the reminder might benefit him? (80:1-4)

Why, then, do these three instances break from the established pattern? While the perfect tense implies a completed act, the **imperfect tense** is used for an action that is not complete. It may be going on at the moment, as with the progressive tense in English ("I am/was driving my car"); it may be recurring, as in the present tense in English ("I drive my car"); or it *may not have happened yet*, as in the future tense in English ("I will drive my car"). It is the last of these that pertains to these three verses. In each of the three cases, quoted above, observe that the questions ("When is the Hour? Will the blind man be purified or benefit from the Reminder?") are not followed up with an answer. This is because the knowledge of these matters *cannot yet occur* to the human being. In two of the three examples, the subject matter is the time of the Hour, i.e., the coming of the Judgment Day. The Qur'an makes clear that the knowledge of this lies only with God (7:187; 33:63; 41:47). Similarly, the third example involves someone (the blind man) "being purified" or "benefiting from the Reminder" (the Qur'an)—a matter of guidance. Again, the Qur'an states that guidance is exclusively in God's hands and that it is not the Prophet's decision who will be guided, as his duty and ability is only to share the Reminder (28:56; 88:21; etc.). Therefore, whether any given person will be guided is also a matter only known in advance by God. For this reason, in these three examples, the questions are not answered: When is the Hour? Will the blind man be purified or benefit from the Reminder? These are matters that a human being cannot have access to, not even the Prophet. Accordingly, the imperfect tense is used in these three cases to highlight that the act of "making (someone) know" these matters may yet be accomplished. Knowledge of them lies only in the future; they cannot be known ahead of time.

Now let us return to the earlier examples, in which the perfect tense (*wa mā adrā-ka*) was used. Recall that the perfect tense is used in these verses to suggest that once someone is informed of the matter X, he will at once come to know about it. It is striking, then, that in every single case where the question was asked in the perfect tense, an answer immediately followed. To complete the examples already introduced:

> Then what will make you know what the Day of Recompense is? A day no soul will possess power to do anything for another soul. And the matter, that day, is wholly God's. (82:18-19)

> And what will make you know what the Uphill Path is? To free a slave; or to feed on a day of severe hunger, an orphan near of kin or a poor person in distress; and to be of those who believe, and urge one another to patience, and urge one another to mercy. (90:12-17)

> And what will make you know what the Night of Power is? The Night of Power is better than a thousand months. The angels and the Spirit descend in it again and again by their Lord's permission on every task. It is peace until the break of dawn. (97:2-5)

> The Crashing Blow! What is the Crashing Blow? And what will make you know what the Crashing Blow is? On a day when people will be like scattered moths and the mountains like tufts of wool, the one whose good deeds

> are heavy on the scales will have a pleasant life, but the one whose good deeds are light will have the Bottomless Pit for his home. What will explain to you what that is? A blazing fire. (101:1-11)

Other such examples start at 69:1; 74:26; 77:13; 83:7, 18; and 86:1. This rule is consistent in every case in which *wa-mā adrā-ka* is used.

The consistency with which *mā adrā-ka* and *mā yudrī-ka* are distinguished and follow specified patterns provides another example of the consistency and sensitivity to context that is exhibited by the Qur'an's word choice, despite the diverse and occasional nature of its revelations.

Verb vs. Noun Word Forms

In Arabic, a speaker can express the meaning of a verb in the form of a noun. For example, the word *kātibun* is a noun meaning "writer," but in the phrase *huwa kātibun* ("he is a writer") it can also function the way a verb ending in *-ing* does in English, giving the meaning "he is writing." In modern Arabic, it makes no difference whether one conveys the idea "he is writing" by simply using a normal verb (*yaktubu*) or by using a noun in its place ([*huwa*] *kātibun*). In Classical Arabic, however, it does make a subtle but meaningful rhetorical difference. *Verbs are considered temporary and changing, while nouns are considered more permanent and stable.* In consideration of this principle, the Qur'an is exceptionally particular in whether it uses a verb or a noun to express an action. The Qur'an's choice of the verb or the noun form is profoundly sensitive to context and has meaningful implications. Since either form will simply be translated as a verb in English, this distinction is lost in translation.

"We are only mocking"

The beginning of the second sura describes three different types of people with respect to how they receive and respond to revealed guidance: the believers, the disbelievers, and a third group who claim to be believers, but whose words, character, and actions betray that they are actually disbelievers. Among the descriptions of this third group is the following:

> When they meet those who believe, they say, "We believe (*āmannā*)," but when they are alone with their devils, they say, "We are only mocking (*mustahzi'ūn*)." (2:14)

Here, "we believe" appears as a verb rather than as a noun, and is therefore more temporary. However, "mocking" in "We were only mocking" appears in the form of a noun—a more permanent description. Although this group of people attempted to show loyalties on both sides, the subtle shift to the noun form highlights that their long-term allegiances are actually to "their devils".

"Those who exalt God"

The Qur'an makes frequent reference to making *tasbīḥ* of God. *Tasbīḥ* is commonly translated as "glorification", but more precisely it means to declare that God is above any imperfection. Because human worshipers cannot be in a perpetual state of declaring God's perfection, the normal verb form is the rule throughout the Qur'an. However, there are two exceptions where the noun form is used. The first is used for the Biblical prophet Jonah, when he was in the belly of the whale. The Qur'an says,

> Had he not been among those who exalt [God] (*al-musabbiḥīn*), he would have remained in its belly until the day they are resurrected. (37:143-144)

Since the noun form is used, it suggests that Jonah was among those who *constantly* exalt God, without pause. This fits the context well because in the belly of the whale, Jonah had nothing to do but declare God's perfection. This would not be possible for other human beings, who must tend to daily life and take breaks from ritual worship. But this raises the question: Who, then, are the other beings "who constantly exalt God"? The answer comes later in the same sura:

> "'And indeed we surely exalt God (*naḥnu musabbiḥūn*).'" (37:166)

The speakers here are the angels. The use of the noun form here makes perfect sense, since the Qur'an says that the angels "exalt Him by night and by day, and they do not tire" (41:38). These are the only two instances in which the noun form is used, and in both cases the use of the noun form highlights something unusual about their given contexts.

"He would not be one to punish them..."

As a final example, the Qur'an says:

> God would not be one to punish them (*mā kāna 'llāhu li-**yu'adhdhiba**-hum*) while you (Muhammad) are among them. And He would not be one to punish them (*mā kāna 'llāhu **mu'adhdhiba-hum***) while they are asking for forgiveness (*yastaghfirūn*). (8:33)

In the first sentence, when God says He would not punish the people of Mecca as long as the Prophet is among them, the verb form of "to punish" (*yu'adhdhibu*) is used, which is more time-bound. This is fitting because the Prophet's "being among" the Meccans is necessarily a temporary condition, and can therefore only hold off God's punishment temporarily. On the other hand, in the second sentence, God says that He would not punish them so long as they ask for forgiveness. Asking for forgiveness is something more open-ended and can continue for generations, instead of being limited to one man's lifespan, so the more permanent *noun* form of "to punish" (*mu'adhdhib*, literally "punishing" or "punisher") is used, indicating that this would be a reason for God to *never* punish them.

Additionally, when "asking for forgiveness" is mentioned, the sentence reverts back to the verb form (*yastaghfirūn*). This implies that the Meccans do not have to be constantly asking for forgiveness to be saved from God's punishment (in which case the noun form would be more appropriate), but only once in a while. So long as they continue to ask for God's forgiveness every so often, God's forgiveness will remain permanently. These specific uses of the verb and noun forms of words therefore capture beautiful and important lessons, which are lost in translation or even in a casual reading of the Arabic text of the Qur'an.

Word Distinctions Unique to the Qur'an

In all the above cases, the Qur'an shows an extraordinary sensitivity and consistency in fitting the best possible words in Classical Arabic to various contexts. In some cases, however, the Qur'an actually distinguishes words in its usage that do not have any distinction in Classical Arabic, and this can be seen as the Qur'an's own literary signature.

"He has enjoined upon me..."

The Qur'an uses several different words for the meaning of "to counsel, instruct, or enjoin." Two of them are *waṣṣā* and *awṣā*. These two words derive from the same root but have two different verb forms.[29] *Waṣṣā* is constructed on the Arabic verbal form II (*fa''ala*), which tends to be continuous, gradual, or repetitive. On the other hand, *awṣā* is constructed on the verbal form IV (*af'ala*), which tends to refer to a single action. However, the "tendencies" of

29 In Arabic, a single root can be "plugged in" to several of fifteen different preset patterns or "forms," so that from the same root, many different verbs and nouns can be derived. For example, the root *n-z-l* can be plugged into forms I, II, and X, yielding the verbs *NaZaLa* ("to come down"), *NaZZaLa* ("to send down"), and *istaNZaLa* ("to ask to step down") respectively.

these Arabic verbal forms are not hard and fast rules, and the Arabs used *waṣṣā* and *awṣā* interchangeably even though they have two different forms. The Qur'an is exceptional in distinguishing between these two verbs, showing a unique sensitivity to the contexts in which it uses each one.

The Qur'an uses *awṣā* when God provides instructions for dividing inheritance or when a person leaves a will (4:11-12). This is especially appropriate given the form of this verb, because these are matters that only need to be stipulated a single time. In contrast, *waṣṣā* is used in cases of moral, spiritual, or religious instruction (2:132; 4:131; 6:144; 6:151; 29:8; 31:14; 42:13; 46:15). The usage is again highly suitable in light of the form of the verb, because these kinds of counsel require frequent reiteration. There is only one exception to this. In the Qur'anic story of Jesus's nativity, the newborn Jesus miraculously speaks from the cradle, authenticating his mother Mary's incredible claim to have conceived him as a virgin. In his speech, the infant Jesus says about God:

> He has made me blessed wherever I am and He has enjoined upon me (*awṣā-nī*) prayer and almsgiving as long as I live. (19:31)

This is the only instance in which the verb awṣā is used referring to religious counsel, instead of *waṣṣā*. Yet it is wholly appropriate here, since Jesus was hardly a day old when he was inspired with this commandment, and could not yet been given the instruction repeatedly, over a length of time.[30]

"A terrible rain"

The Qur'an uses several different Arabic words to refer to rain. We will look at just the three most common of these, to see how the Qur'an gives each one its own unique meaning and subsequently uses each in fitting contexts.

Most frequently, such as in descriptions of God's signs and blessings in nature, the Qur'an uses the generic word "water" (*mā'*) or the phrase "water from the sky," as in the following verses:

> It is He who sends down water from the sky for you: from it is drink and from it is vegetation in which you pasture your animals. (16:10)

> Do you not see that God sends down water from the sky, and We produce thereby fruits of varying colors? (35:27)

> And We send down from the rain clouds water pouring abundantly. (78:14)

30 Fāḍil Ṣāliḥ as-Sāmarrā'ī, *at-Ta'bīr al-Qur'ānī*, 4th ed. (Amman: Dar al-'Ammār, 2006), 15-16.

In all of these contexts, water, in the form of rain, is highlighted as a divine mercy, to the extent that even revelation itself is compared to it: like water, God "sends down [revelation] from the sky," and He gives life to dead hearts through it the way He gives life to the dead earth through rain. By describing rain as "water" that is "sent down from the sky," the Qur'an reminds its audience of divine mercy and draws a parallel between the natural gift of rain and the spiritual gift of revelation.

Though less frequently, the Qur'an also uses the two most common Arabic words for rain numerous times: *ghayth* and *maṭar*. Even though both were common words for rain in Classical Arabic and were used interchangeably, the Qur'an assigns each word its own unique type of situation.[31]

Since rain could be a matter of life or death in the Arabian Desert, the Arabs derived the word *ghayth* from *ghawth*, meaning "help" or "aid," highlighting the fact that for the Arab, the coming of rain is always positive and life-giving. This word is also used to refer to the pasture or vegetation that is produced by the rain. From this point of view, it is logical that the Qur'an uses *ghayth* only in positive contexts:

> [Joseph said:] Then a year will come after that in which people will be given rain (*yuGHāTHu*), and in it they will press [grapes and olives]. (12:49)

> Indeed, God has knowledge of the Hour and sends down rain (*GHayTH*) and knows what is in the wombs. (31:34)

> It is He who sends down the rain (*GHayTH*) after they had despaired, and spreads out His mercy. (42:28)

> Like the example of rain (*GHayTH*): the vegetation it yields delights the sowers. (57:20)

Nonetheless, the Qur'an highlights that even agents of mercy—such as the winds, clouds, and rain—can become agents of harm or divine punishment if God wills. Accordingly, numerous passages of the Qur'an also highlight rain's capacity to harm or punish. To emphasize this potential, the Qur'an gives the other common word for "rain" in Arabic, *maṭar*, an ominous quality, using it only in negative contexts:

> There is no blame on you, if you are troubled by rain (*MaṬaR*) or sickness... (4:102)

---

31 as-Sāmarrā'i, *al-Ta'bīr al-Qur'ānī*, 15.

> When they said, "O God! If this is really the truth from You, then rain (*aMṬiR*) stones on us or bring us a painful punishment!" (8:32)

> They have already come upon a town that was rained on (*uMṬiRat*) with a terrible rain (*MaṬaR*). Did they not see it? Yet they do not expect to be raised from the dead. (25:40)

> When they saw it as a cloud approaching their valleys, they said, "It is a cloud bringing us rain (*muMṬiRu-nā*)!" Rather, it is what you sought to hasten, a wind containing a painful punishment. (46:24)

Hence, although *mā'*, *ghayth*, and *maṭar* were used without distinction in Classical Arabic, the Qur'an imbues each of them with a unique shade of meaning through the particular manner and context in which it is used.

"Eyes" vs. "Springs"

The word *'ayn* primarily means "eye," but the ancient Arabs applied the word to dozens of things that they found pleasing to their eyes. As a result, another common meaning of *'ayn* is a "spring of water"—a very pleasant thing to lay one's eyes upon in the desert. The words *a'yun* and *'uyūn* are plurals of *'ayn*, and both are used in Classical and Modern Arabic with either meaning: "eyes" or "springs of water." However, the Qur'an consistently distinguishes between these two plurals, giving them unique patterns. While *a'yun* occurs 21 times in the Qur'an and *'uyūn* occurs ten times, in each instance the former refers to "eyes" and the latter to "springs of water."[32]

* * *

The Qur'an alludes to its own extraordinary consistency, even offering it as a sign of its divine origin: "Then do they not reflect on the Qur'an? If it had been from anyone other than God, they would have found in it much inconsistency" (4:82). In this chapter, we acquired a small taste of the precision, significance, and beauty that the Qur'an's word choice exhibits. The consistency of these patterns is even more striking when one considers the fact that the scripture was revealed piece by piece, in response to a variety of different occasions, over a period of twenty-three years. As we will see in

32 Ibid. *A'yun* occurs in 5:83; 7:116, 179, 195; 8:44; 9:92; 11:31, 37; 18:101; 21:61; 23:27; 25:74; 32:17; 33:19; 33:51; 36:66; 40:19; 43:71; 52:48; 54:14; and 54:37. *'Uyūn* occurs in 15:45; 26:57, 134, 147; 36:34; 44:25, 52; 51:15, 54:12; and 77:41.

some of the following chapters, this consistency is not limited to the Qur'an's word choice, but extends to other features of its language and style as well.

For further exploration:

For more examples of beauty and subtlety in the Qur'an's word choice, see Nouman Ali Khan's "Amazed by the Qur'an" series on the Bayyinah Institute YouTube channel (www.youtube.com/BayyinahInstitute).

CHAPTER 3

Word Order

Typically, when a speaker is in the middle of a speech or conversation and he mentions two or more items together, the listener does not attach any significance to the order in which the items are presented. For example, imagine that a teacher describes one of her students to you as "intelligent, inquisitive, and hard-working." On the grounds that intelligence was mentioned first, you might speculate that it is the foremost quality of the student in the teacher's mind. However, you will probably not attach much weight to this thought, and you are likely not to even give thought to it in the first place. If you later hear her praise the same student as "hard-working, intelligent, and inquisitive," you will probably not assume that the teacher has deliberately adapted her description to a new context. Virtually any listener would take these two statements as equivalent, and would not attribute any design or special meaning to the difference in order. Speakers and listeners do not tend to give thought or attach meaning to the sequence in which items are mentioned, unless an obvious order of chronology, rank, or some similar consideration applies.

In this regard, the Qur'an is a unique case. The subtlety and precision that we observed in the Qur'an's choice of words also extends to the order in which it presents them. It is often necessary to compare different passages that employ the same words, but in different or unexpected sequences, to appreciate how the Qur'an adjusts its word order to context. In this chapter, we will study a selection of examples of meaningful word order in the Qur'an that have been highlighted in scholarly literature.

"And He is the Merciful, the Forgiving"

When first reading the Qur'an, a person is likely to notice that it frequently concludes statements with an affirmation of (usually two) divine names or qualities. The most common combination involves the divine attributes "Forgiving" (*Ghafūr*) and "Merciful" (*Raḥīm*), appearing together almost sixty times in the Qur'an. This occurs with some slight variations, such as "Indeed, God is Forgiving, Merciful" (*inna 'llāha kāna ghafūran raḥīman*), or "Your Lord is the Forgiving, the Possessor of Mercy" (*wa rabbuka 'l-ghafūru dhū 'r-raḥma*), but in almost every instance, the same sequence is maintained: God's quality of forgiveness is mentioned before His quality of mercy. This is logical because, as an Islamic legal principle says, "Averting harm comes before securing benefit." A person must be spared from the threat of punishment before he can enjoy, or even think about, any favor and reward.

However, there is a single instance in the Qur'an in which the order of these two divine qualities is reversed:

> He knows what goes into the earth and what emerges from it, and what descends from the sky and what ascends into it, and He is the Merciful, the Forgiving. (34:2)

This verse presents an agricultural image, which is a common expression of God's mercy in the Qur'an. A seed enters the earth and a plant sprouts from it. Rain pours from the sky and vapor rises to it. Yet, the mention here of God as not only merciful but also *forgiving* prompts second consideration. What does the cycle of rain and vegetation have to do with forgiveness? Every other instance in which these two divine attributes are mentioned occurs in a context that involves people, since naturally it is people who are in need of forgiveness and mercy. But human beings are not referred to here.

Or are they? On further consideration, the reader realizes that the human being also goes into the earth when he dies, and according to the Qur'an he will be raised up after death (30:50; etc.). Divine revelation and sustenance in the form of rain descend from the sky for human benefit (2:4; 2:22; etc.), and the deeds of the living and souls of the dead ascend to God (32:5; 35:10; 39:42).

The mention of God's mercy before his forgiveness, departing from the normal sequence in the Qur'an, reflects these considerations. When a human being is experiencing the anguish of death, he is in need of God's mercy, in order to bring relief to his suffering. On the other hand, when he is later resurrected and the record of his deeds is presented before him, his immediate need is God's forgiveness of his past wrongs. This exception to the normal order in which these divine qualities are mentioned is not an accident, but a literary device that reinforces the themes of the verse by echoing their logical and sequential order.

"Do not kill your children!"

The Arabian Desert was scarce in resources, and the twin threats of poverty and hunger were constant concerns. Though it was the most extreme measure for tackling such scarcity, child murder was sufficiently common that the Qur'an had to decisively abolish it—*twice*:

> ...and do not kill your children out of poverty. We will provide for you and for them. (6:151)

> Do not kill your children out of fear of poverty. We will provide for them and for you. Truly, killing them is an enormous wrong. (17:31)

Notice the shift in word order. The first of these verses says, "We will provide for you and for them," while the second says, "We will provide for them and for you." There is also another difference: The first says "do not kill your children out of poverty" while the second says "out of *fear* of poverty." These seemingly inconsequential differences are in fact meaningful. For example, if a person steals *out* of poverty, this entails that he is already poor; but if he steals out of *fear* of poverty, it entails that he has not experienced poverty yet, but is expecting it.

The two verses actually address two different categories of parents. The parents in the first scenario are told not to kill their children "out of poverty." This alludes to the situation of parents who are already suffering poverty and hunger, and are considering killing their children because they feel that they are unable to feed themselves. The promise of provision is directed first to them, because the immediate concern is their own suffering: "We will provide for *you* and for them."

The parents in the second scenario are told not to kill their children "out of *fear* of poverty." They have yet to actually experience poverty, but anticipate that if they have to provide for a child, it will lead to a state of bankruptcy. God assures them, "We will provide for *them* and for you." Since the parents' fear is directly associated with providing for an expected child, the promise of provision for the child *first* assures them that he or she will not be their responsibility, but God's.

"Trade and entertainment"33

In Sura 62, *The Day of Congregation* (*al-Jumu'a*), the Qur'an mandates attending the Friday congregational sermon and prayer as an obligation upon men. At the end of the sura, God reprimands members of the congregation who deserted the Prophet while he was administering the sermon:

> When they saw trade (*tijāra*) or entertainment (*lahw*), they rushed to it and left you standing. Say, "What is with God is better than entertainment (*lahw*) and trade (*tijāra*), and God is the best of providers." (62:11)

Notice that in the first sentence, trade is mentioned as the first reason they left the sermon, while entertainment is mentioned as the second reason. In the second sentence, however, this sequence is reversed; trade and entertainment are mentioned in the opposite order. Each of these two sequences is, in fact, subtly tailored to its context.

The verse alludes to an incident in which a trade caravan arrived in Medina while the Prophet was delivering a Friday sermon. Some of his followers arose during the sermon and left him in order to engage in business. While business was the main purpose, there was a secondary attraction as well: since business was such a big matter, such trade fairs would always be highly embellished and festive. This provided a secondary incentive, drawing even people who were not involved in trade. The mention of trade before entertainment in the first sentence is logical because it refers to a specific incident, and in that incident trade was the main priority.

In contrast, the following sentence refers not merely to that specific event, but offers a more universal maxim: "'What is with God is better than entertainment (*lahw*) and than trade, and God is the best of providers.'" The mention of entertainment before trade in this case is more suitable, given that the context has shifted to the statement of a universal principle. Interest in entertainment is more universal, shared by the majority of people, while only a minority of people engages in business.

"God has sealed their hearts and their hearing"

In three places, the Qur'an mentions God's "sealing" of certain people's hearts and hearing. In two of these instances, the sealing of the heart is mentioned first, but in one instance, the sealing of hearing is mentioned first. In each of

---

33 Fāḍil Sāliḥ as-Sāmarrā'i, *Lamasāt Bayyāniyya fi Nuṣūṣ min at-Tanzīl*, 3rd ed. (Amman: Dar al-'Ammār, 2003), 175.

these cases, what is given priority by being given first mention is tailored to the surrounding context.

The first instance occurs in the beginning of the second sura, which contrasts the receptiveness of three kinds of people with respect to the Qur'an's guidance: "the God-conscious" or "those who believe," "those who disbelieve," and a third group who claim to believe but who actually disbelieve. The category of "those who disbelieve" describes people who are completely intent on rejecting the scripture's guidance. The Qur'an says about them:

> **God has sealed** their **hearts** and their **hearing**, and over their vision is a veil. (2:7)

In this case, the sealing of hearts is mentioned before that of hearing. Zooming out, one sees that the verse is embedded in a discussion that largely characterizes people's psychological states:

> This is the Book concerning which there is no **doubt**, a guidance for the **God-conscious**: who **believe** in the Unseen…who **believe** in what was revealed to you and what was revealed before you, and in the Hereafter are **certain**. (2:2-3)

> **Those who disbelieve**, it is the same whether you warn them or you warn them not. They will not **believe**. God has sealed their hearts and their hearing, and over their vision is a veil. (2:6-7)

> And among the people are those who say, "We **believe** in God and the Last Day," but they are **not believers**…**In their hearts is a disease**, so God has increased their disease. (2:8, 10)

The qualities with which the different groups are described—doubt, God-consciousness, faith, certainty, disbelief, and spiritual sickness—are almost entirely focused on the spiritual heart. Hence, mention of the sealing of the heart before other faculties of perception corresponds with this emphasis.

The second place in which the sealing of hearts and hearing occurs is 16:108:

> Those are the ones whose **hearts**, **hearing**, and vision **God has sealed**, and it is they who are the heedless.

As in the previous example, the sealing of the hearts is mentioned before the sealing of hearing. The preceding context of the verse shows why:

> Whoever disbelieves in God after his faith—except the one who is forced while his **heart is content with faith**. But whoever **opens his chest to disbelief**, God's wrath is upon them and they will have a tremendous punishment. That is because they gave preference to the worldly life over the afterlife, and God does not guide the disbelieving people. (16:106-107)

The context is that of the faith or disbelief that is in a person's heart, so the sealing of the disbeliever's heart is mentioned first.

In contrast to the previous examples, in the final example, God's sealing of a person's *hearing* is mentioned first, before that of his heart:

> Have you seen the one who has taken his own desire as a god, whom God allows to stray in the face of knowledge, and **He has sealed his hearing** (*SaM*ʿ) and **his heart**, and has placed a veil over his eyes...? (45:23)

The preceding context of this verse contains some of the same themes: revelation, faith, guidance, and persistent disbelief. In this case, however, the sealing of the disbeliever's "hearing" (*SaM*ʿ) recalls a statement that occurred fifteen verses earlier:

> Woe to every sinful liar, who **hears** (*yaSMaʿu*) God's verses recited to him, yet persists in arrogance as if he had not **heard** (*yaSMa*ʿ) them. (45:8)

According to this verse, the disbeliever repeatedly pretended not to have heard the revelations. For this reason, it is appropriate that later, in v. 23, priority is given to God's sealing of his hearing over that of his heart, with his hearing being mentioned first.

In all three of the above cases, the order in which the sealing of hearts and hearing is mentioned is carefully tailored to the particular context of each statement.

"We have seen and heard"

"Hearing" and "seeing" are recurrent themes in the Qur'an, and they are mentioned together frequently. God is described as "Hearing" (*Samī*ʿ) and "Seeing" (*Baṣīr*) dozens of times in the Qur'an, often in conjunction, and hearing and seeing are constantly alluded to as senses that enable the human being to discern God's *āya*s, or signs, in verbal revelation and in nature. It is also remarkable that, in nearly all these references, hearing is mentioned *before* seeing. For example:

> Indeed, We created man from a sperm-drop mixture so that We may try him; and We made him hearing and seeing. (76:2)

Hearing also plays the more vital role of the two because it is the primary mechanism for receiving divine communications: God calls on people to listen to His commandments (2:75, 93, 186, etc.); believers respond, "We hear and we obey" (2:285; 24:51); and the miracle of the Prophet Muhammad is audial-oral, rather than visual.

The sequential priority of hearing over seeing is only reversed in two instances. One of them is in Sura 18, *The Cave* (*al-Kahf*):

> Say: God knows best how long they remained [sleeping]. He has knowledge of the unseen of the heavens and the earth. How well He sees and how well He hears! (18:26)

The context is the story of the Sleepers of Ephesus, a group of youth who clung to their faith in one God in the face of persecution, and, after fleeing and praying to God, took refuge in a cave. To honor their outstanding faithfulness, God lulled them into a deep sleep in the cave for a miraculously prolonged period of time, causing them to wake up in a different era, in which they would not be persecuted for their faith. During their sleep, however, the cave protected them from being found, and the light of the sun was even miraculously steered away from them (18:17). God's seeing is mentioned before His hearing, highlighting that even in a situation in which no one else could discover the youth, God's vision was still watchful over them.

The other instance in which seeing is mentioned before hearing occurs in a scene of the Day of Judgment:

> If you could only see when the criminals hang their heads before their Lord, saying, "Our Lord, we have seen and heard, so return us so that we may do righteous deeds. Now we are certain." (32:12)

The priority given to seeing in this quotation is fitted to the disbelievers' insistence in this world that they would not believe until they could *see* a miracle from God, rather than accepting the audial-oral signs of revelation. Elsewhere, the Qur'an responds to this claim, stating that even a visual sign would not satisfy them until death arrives to them (2:55; 6:25; 7:146; 10:88; 26:201). Only after death do the disbelievers express willingness to perform righteous deeds, having received not only the visual proof they demanded, but now facing the inescapable prospect of divine retribution. The mention of seeing before hearing underscores that the disbelievers *will* receive all the visual proof they demand, but then it will be too late since the Judgment will have already begun.

"Purify My House"

In Sura 2, *The Cow* (*al-Baqara*), the Qur'an tells the story of the construction of the Ka'ba by Abraham and his son Ishmael. After Abraham demonstrates his superior obedience and trust in God, God privileges him as "a leader for the people." God then entrusts Abraham and his son Ishmael with the construction of the Ka'ba:

> We commanded Abraham and Ishmael, "Purify My House for those who circle around it, those who seclude themselves for worship, those who bow, and those who prostrate" (2:125).[34]

These four acts of worship are listed in the ascending order of their frequency of performance in Islam. The first of them, circling the Ka'ba in devotion to God, is a ritual that can only occur in a specific location, and is therefore the act of worship that is most limited in frequency. The mention of this ritual first is also appropriate because it has the most exclusive association with the Ka'ba. The second ritual, secluding oneself for worship, is more common, because it does not require pilgrimage to a particular location, but is still fairly occasional and is particularly associated with special times of the year. The third ritual, bowing, is far more common, as it is performed once in each unit of the ritual prayers. However, the final ritual mentioned in this list, prostration, is the most frequent act of worship, as it is performed twice in each unit of the prayers, in addition to other situations.

"The King, the Holy, the Almighty, the Wise"

For this last example, we will consider a word order of a different type, where two lists of items are presented in a sequence that links them both closely together.

The Suras of the Qur'an from the Middle Meccan period onward typically begin with praise of God (a statement of monotheism) or an affirmation of the truth of the Qur'anic revelation (a statement about the message). Sura 62, *The Day of Congregation*, opens with the following statement of divine praise:

> Whatever is in the heavens and whatever is on the earth exalts God—the King, the Holy, the Mighty, the Wise. (62:1)

---

34 In the Qur'an, the designation of the Ka'ba as the "House of God" does not imply that God physically dwells in it, but that it is a sacred building especially designated for worshiping God. In the Bible, the same term is frequently used in reference to the Temple of Jerusalem, and also occurs in reference to Jacob's shrine at Bethel, which literally means "House of God" (Gen. 28:17, 22).

The next verse is a comprehensive statement about the message:

> It is He who has sent among the unlettered folk a messenger from them, reciting to them His verses/signs (*āyas*), purifying them, teaching them the Book and wisdom, even if before that they were in clear error. (62:2)

The duties of the Messenger listed in the second verse are closely related, in the same sequence, to the four divine names mentioned at the end of the first:

1. The first of these divine titles is "the King" (*al-Malik*). One task of a king is that, when he wishes to convey a message, he will dispatch a messenger to his desired audience with the job of delivering that message. The audience, in turn, will recognize the status of the messenger because he will bear emblems or signs (*āyas*) of the king, such as on his uniform. This corresponds with the first part of v. 2, "It is He who has sent among the unlettered folk a messenger from them, reciting to them His signs (*āyas*)."
2. The second divine name is "the Holy" or "the Sacred" (*al-Quddūs*). This word in Arabic also has the connotation of "the Pure." This corresponds to the second task of the Messenger in v. 2, that "he purifies them" (*yuzakkī-him*).
3. The third divine name requires some explanation, because it is difficult to capture in translation. Thus, *al-'Azīz* (frequently translated as "the Mighty") signifies not only one who is powerful, but one who has authority that is respected. The word "Book" (*kitāb*) in Classical Arabic and in the Qur'an has the connotation of "Law." Even in English, when a judge is said to "throw the book at someone," it indicates that he is going to hold him fully accountable to the law. A law is, naturally, only effective if it comes from a respected authority. The Messenger's task of teaching "the Book" is therefore closely tied with God's authority to issue laws and commands.
4. The Messenger's task of teaching "wisdom" (*al-ḥikma*, usually understood as the Prophet's divinely-inspired teaching and example that supplements the Qur'an) is tied to God's attribute of being "the Wise" (*al-Ḥakīm*).

Thus, the functions of the Messenger are listed in a sequence that draws precise thematic connections with the preceding context, tying them directly to God's names and attributes in four distinct, but related, ways.

CHAPTER 4

Grammatical Shifts

In modern prose, consistency in the use of person and tense is a basic requirement of good composition. For example, when telling a story, the author is expected to restrict himself to either the past or the present tense. If the author must refer to himself, he may either say "this author" (third-person), "I" (first-person singular), or "we" (first-person plural), but once one of these narrative perspectives is adopted, it must be used consistently throughout the work.

Modern readers, accustomed to this supposedly fundamental rule of composition, are often thrown off by the Qur'an's disregard for it and its seeming lack of consistency of its narrative voice. The Qur'an contains rather frequent shifts in person, number, tense, voice, mood, and subject matter, to the extent that there may be multiple shifts in as little as a single sentence. The divine speaker of the Qur'an will allude to Himself various times as "We," "I," or even in the third person as "Allah," "Your Lord," or "He/Him." The tense may shift from perfect to imperfect tense, or vice versa. Sometimes events in the future are described in the perfect tense, which is typically associated with the past. The Qur'an may also shift in addressing one audience to another. Finally, it routinely changes from one topic to another, without preparing the reader, and oftentimes without an immediately obvious connection between the two topics. This style is often disenchanting to the modern reader, who sees it as random, disorderly, and poorly composed.

As the reader may have come to expect by now, beneath this apparent randomness in fact lies a stunning degree of order, consistency, and design. These shifts in narrative perspective and subject matter are an intended part of the Qur'an's rhetoric, and when properly understood, can have a powerful impact on the audience and deepen one's understanding of the Qur'an's meanings. These shifts, in fact, occur according to consistent patterns, which, upon careful study, reveal a great deal of foresight and sophistication on the part of the Qur'an's speaker.

In this chapter, we will tackle the subject of grammatical shifts—shifts in person, number, tense, and other grammatical aspects—which may occur within a single verse or a small group of verses. While modern readers of the Qur'an tend to find this aspect of the scripture strange and perplexing, medieval Arab linguists and literary critics judged it to be one of the Qur'an's exquisite literary features. They gradually came to refer to this phenomenon as *iltifāt*, meaning "to turn (one's face)" from one audience to another, defining it as:

> the change of speech from one mode to another, for the sake of freshness and variety for the listener, to renew his interest, and to keep his mind from boredom and frustration, through having the one mode continuously at his ear.[35]

These specialists observed that, despite their frequency, these shifts do not occur in the Qur'an except to produce calculated and discernible rhetorical effects on the audience. The Qur'an thereby conforms to a principle of Arabic rhetoric that maintains that the normally expected usage may not be departed from, except to bring out a subtlety that would not appear otherwise. Every departure from the norm therefore carries a risk, and can potentially enhance or blemish the composition. For this reason, Arab literary critics regarded *iltifāt* as an aspect of what they called *shajāʿāt al-ʿarabiyya*, "the boldness of the Arabic language." They observed that although this phenomenon finds occasional expression in pre-Islamic Arabic poetry,[36] it is is used in far more bold, extensive, and innovative ways in the Qur'an. For this reason, the Arab specialists considered it to be an aspect of the Qur'an's miraculous and inimitable nature.

As always, it must be kept in mind that the Qur'an is primarily an oral composition, intended to be recited and even performed before its audience(s). Much of its rhetorical impact therefore comes from the sensa-

---

35 Badr ad-Dīn az-Zarkashī, *al-Burhān fī ʿUlūmi 'l-Qur'ān*, vol. 3 (Cairo: 1958), 314-315, quoted in M.A.S Abdel Haleem, "Grammatical Shift for Rhetorical Purposes: *Iltifāt* and Related Features in the Qur'ān," *Bulletin of the School of Oriental and African Studies* 55 (1992): 407-432.

36 In fact, this rhetorical device is not unique to Classical Arabic literature, but also occasionally finds expression in various books of the Hebrew Bible. See David Bokovoy, "From Distance to Proximity: A Poetic Function of Enallage in the Hebrew Bible and the Book of Mormon," *Journal of Book of Mormon Studies* 9.1 (200): 60-63—accessible online. Scholars who have observed this phenomenon in the Hebrew Bible have described it with the Greek term "enallage," meaning "interchange." Nonetheless, it stands out as a far more salient, pervasive, and consistent feature in the Qur'an.

tions produced by these narrative shifts. This chapter will focus specifically on grammatical shifts, surveying several kinds that appear in the Qur'an.[37] The topic of shifts in subject matter will be reserved for chapter 11, "The Coherence and Structure of the Sura."

1. Shifts in Person: The Speaker

While the Qur'an presents itself as a direct communication from God to humankind, God does not always refer to Himself in the first-person singular ("I/Me/My"). More commonly, He uses the first-person *plural* ("We/Us/Our") or even the third-person ("He/Him/His"). In this section, we will briefly note some of the patterns behind each of these usages before looking at specific examples of shifts from one to another.

The Divine Speaker as "We"

Most commonly, the Divine Speaker of the Qur'an refers to Himself in the first-person plural. As stated already in chapter 1, this is not a plural of actual number, but a rhetorical device that the speaker uses to communicate something in a way that emphasizes his authority or majesty. This technique is known as the "royal 'we'" or the "majestic plural" in English. Once this is understood, it is not so surprising that the majestic plural is the most common mode of divine communication in the Qur'an.

Fittingly, God uses the majestic plural especially in contexts that highlight His *grandness*, *power*, or *providence*, such as in the following thematically typical examples:

> From it (the earth) **We** created you, to it **We** will return you, and from it **We** will bring you forth another time. (20:55)

> **We** have certainly revealed to you verses that are clear proofs… (5:44)

> And those cities—**We** destroyed them when they wronged, and **We** made for their destruction an appointed time. (18:59)

37 For the sake of brevity, some types of grammatical shifts have been left out of this chapter, namely shifts from indicative to imperative, shifts in case ending, and the use of a noun where a pronoun is expected. For examples of these, see Abdel Haleem, "Grammatical Shift," cited in the first footnote of this chapter. Abdel Haleem's seminal essay is the primary source of this chapter and can be easily found and accessed online. For a deeper and more thorough treatment of the Qur'an's narrative perspective in general, including a discussion of grammatical shifts, see Robinson, *Discovering the Qur'an*, 224-255.

In each of these cases, the first-person plural is used to suit the tone of divine majesty and grandeur that is evoked by the subject matter—in these examples, creation, revelation, and retribution. Additionally, the use of the first person rather than the third person emphasizes the connection between the Divine Speaker and the events being referred to, which illustrates His involvement with the world and mankind. Such considerations underlie all instances of the Speaker's uses of the majestic plural in the Qur'an.

The Divine Speaker as "He"

While the majestic plural is used when God wishes to express Himself directly to His audience, the third-person ("He/Him/His") is used of God in contexts where the primary aim is the delivery of the Qur'ān's central message—monotheism.[38] In these cases, the audience is influenced to think of God's attributes or actions as an objective reality, independent of the communication of the Speaker.[39] For example:

> It is **He** who created for you all of that which is on the earth. Moreover, **He** directed Himself to the heaven, and made them seven heavens—and **He** is Knowing of all things. (2:29)

Here, the primary intent is not for the Divine Speaker to communicate to the audience from His own standpoint, but to convey as an objective reality that God is the maker of the earth, the heavens, and all of mankind's provisions.

Frequently, the use of the third person for God gives rise to a universal expression that believers can quote in relevant contexts when delivering or reinforcing the message:

> Truly, **God** is but One God. Exalted is **He** above having a son. To **Him** belongs whatever is in the heavens and the earth, and **God** is sufficient as a trustee. (4:171)

> **God**, there is no deity but **Him**, the Living, the Maintainer of Existence. Sleep and drowsiness do not overtake **Him**. To **Him** belongs whatever is in the heavens and whatever is in the earth … (2:255)

> Say: "**He** is **God**, the **One**. **God**, the **Eternal Source of Refuge**. **He** does not beget, nor is **He** begotten. And there is none comparable to **Him**." (112:1-4)

---

38 Abdel Haleem, "Grammatical Shifts," 416.
39 Robinson, *Discovering the Qur'an*, 229.

The use of the third-person therefore serves, in Robinson's words, "the task of conveying to humankind a universal message in language which they themselves can re-use in speaking about God and in addressing Him."[40]

Shift from "We" to "He"

Now that we understand the Qur'an's usage of the first-person plural and third person, we can see the effects of the shift from one to the other in the following example:

> **We** are sufficient for you against the mockers who make gods alongside God (Allah). They will soon know. **We** already know that your chest is constricted by what they say. So exalt **your Lord** with praise and be among the prostrators and worship **your Lord** until the certainty [death] comes to you. (15:98)

As is the norm in the Qur'an, God comforts His messenger directly in the first person, appropriately using the majestic plural to highlight His grandness and bounty. When the mockers are depicted as worshiping other deities besides God, God is referred to in the third person by His name Allah, which literally means "the God," stressing His exclusive divinity. Finally, when the Prophet is given instructions to worship, God is mentioned as "your Lord" to emphasize His relationship to the Prophet as his master.[41]

Take also the following verse:

> It is **He** who sends down water from the sky. With it **We** produce the shoots of each plant, then bring greenery from it, and from that **We** bring out grains, one riding on the other in close-packed rows. From the date palm come clusters of low-hanging dates, and there are gardens of vines, olives, and pomegranates, alike yet different. Watch their fruits as they grow and ripen! In all this there are signs for those who would believe. (6:99)

In the first sentence, God is represented as distant and elevated, sending water down from the sky, so the third person is used. In the rest of the verse, God speaks about His production of vegetation on the earth. This is a closer vantage point to the human audience to whom the speech is being delivered, so the first person is used.

---

40 Ibid., 253.

41 Abdel Haleem, "Grammatical Shifts," 417.

The Divine Speaker as "I"42

Finally, the first-person singular ("I/Me/My") is used more sparingly than both the majestic plural and the third person, but it is the most frequent and appropriate usage in certain types of situation:

(1) Quotations from the creation story, in which God speaks to the angels, Satan, Adam, and the prospective human race directly, without any intermediary:

> When your Lord said to the angels, '**I** am going to create a vicegerent on the earth." They said, "Will you make on it one who will cause corruption and shed blood, while we exalt you with praise and sanctify you?" He said, "Indeed, **I** know what you do not know." (2:30)

> We said [to Adam and his descendants], "Go down from it, altogether. Then if guidance comes to you from **Me**—then whoever follows **My** guidance, there will be no fear on them, nor will they grieve." (2:38)

> [God said to Satan] "**I** will surely fill Hell with you and any of them who follow you, altogether." (38:85)

> When your Lord took from the Children of Adam their offspring from their loins and made them testify against themselves, "Am **I** not your Lord?" They said, "Yes, we testify!" (7:172)

(2) Quotations in scenes of Judgment Day, in which God is likewise depicted as speaking directly to humanity without a human or angelic messenger. Typically, these addresses are threatening. God will address the disbelievers, "did there not come to you messengers from among you, narrating to you **My** verses and warning you…?" (6:130; cf. 23:105; 27:84, 39:59; 45:31; 50:28). He will challenge them, "'Where are **My** "partners" that you used to deem?'" (28:62, 74; cf. 16:27; 18:52; 41:47). Likewise He will say to them,

> "'Go into it despised, and do not speak to **Me**. There was a party among **My** slaves who said, 'Our Lord, we believe, so forgive us and have mercy on us. You are the best of the merciful.' But you took them in mockery until it made you forget **My** remembrance, and you used to laugh at them.'" (23:108-111).

(3) Divine promises and threats in the stories of past messengers and their people. The use of the first-person singular in these contexts gives the

---

42 These observations are summarized from Robinson, *Discovering the Qur'an*, 230-234.

promises and warnings a very personal and direct quality. For example, Noah is urged, "'Do not address **Me** concerning those who have done wrong. Indeed they will be drowned'" (11:37). The people of Lot are told, "Taste **My** punishments and **My** warnings!" (5:37; 39). The Children of Israel are promised, "'**My** punishment, **I** afflict with it whom **I** will, but **My** mercy encompasses all things, and **I** will decree it for the God-conscious...'" (7:156)

(4) Key moments in salvation history, such as when God makes His covenant with Abraham:

> When Abraham was tried by his Lord with commands and he fulfilled them. [God] said, "**I** am going to make you a leader for mankind." [Abraham] said, "And my offspring?" [God] said, "**My** covenant does not include the wrongdoers." (2:124)

Another example is when God honors Moses by calling out to him and speaking directly to him in the sacred valley:

> "Indeed, **I** am your Lord. So remove your sandals: you are in the sacred valley of Tuwa. **I** have chosen you, so listen to what is revealed: Indeed, **I** am Allah; there is no god but **Me**. So worship **Me** and establish prayer for **My** remembrance." (20:12-14; cf. 7:143; 27:9-11; 28:30)

Other examples include when God instructs Abraham to purify the Ka'ba (22:26), when He makes His covenant with the Israelites (5:12; 17:2), when He tells Jesus that He is going to cause him to ascend to heaven (3:55), and when God reinforces the believers with angels at the Battle of Badr (8:9)

(5) Contexts in which God's oneness is emphasized or needs to be safeguarded. The covenant with mankind in which God asked rhetorically, "'Am **I** not your Lord'" and His call to Moses in the verse just quoted above also provide examples of this. Likewise, in His instruction to Abraham, God said, "Do not associate anything with **Me** [in worship]" (22:26), and God declares, "'**I** did not create jinn and mankind except to worship **Me**" (51:56). Robinson also notes the following examples:

> 'dread Me' (2.150); 'remember Me"(2.152); 'be grateful to Me' (2.152); 'fear Me' (2.197); 'revere Me' (3.175, 5.44); 'worship Me' (21.92; 29.56; cf. 43.61); 'follow Me' (51.56); 'seeking to please Me' (60.1). Note that equivalent expressions are never found with the object in the first person plural: 'dread Us', 'remember Us', 'be grateful to Us', and so forth.[43]

43 Robinson, *Discovering the Qur'an*, 234.

In all these contexts, the use of the majestic plural would detract from the emphasis on God's oneness.

(6) Intimate communication to the Messenger or the believers. For instance:

> When **My** slaves ask you (Muhammad) about **Me**, then indeed **I** am near. **I** respond to the prayer of the supplicant when he calls on **Me**. So let them respond to **Me** and believe in **Me** so that they may be rightly guided. (2:186)

> **I** will accept their repentance. **I** am the Oft-Returner, the All-Merciful. (2:160)

> This day **I** have perfected for you your religion and completed **My** favor upon you, and **I** have approved for you Islam as a religion. (5:3)

Shift from 'I' to 'We'

An example of the shift from "I" to "We" occurs in the seventy-fifth sura:

> No! **I** swear by the self-reproaching soul! Does man think that **We** will not gather his bones? Yes indeed: **We** are able to shape again the tips of his fingers. (75:1-4)

As in other verses (56:75; 69:38; 70:40; 75:1; 81:15; 84:16; 90:1), God swears an oath in the singular, and thus in a direct and personal manner. The shift to the majestic plural draws attention to God's power to raise the dead, which was doubted by polytheistic Arabs.[44]

Shift from "I" to "He"

The following verse stands out for its ability to console. Its emotional impact is enhanced by the grammatical shifts:

> "'O **My** slaves who have transgressed against themselves, do not despair of **God's** mercy. Indeed, **God** forgives all sins. Indeed **He** is the Forgiving, the Merciful.'" (39:53)

God's reassurance begins in the first-person singular, "My slaves." This has at least two functions. First, whenever God attributes His slaves to Himself, He always uses the first-person singular in order to safeguard His

---

44 Abdel Haleem, "Grammatical Shifts," 420.

monotheism. (The word "slaves," it should be kept in mind, comes from the same root as the word "worship" in Arabic.) Second, the first-person singular gives a very personal, loving, and reassuring quality to God's designation of His slaves, thus setting the tone for the rest of the verse.

The shift to the third-person in the subsequent statements gives them a proverbial quality: "do not despair of God's mercy," "God forgives all sins," "He is the Forgiving, the Merciful." These are presented as reassuring facts that the believer can remember in times of intense regret and penitence.

Shift from "He" to "I"

After describing the punishment of evildoers on Judgment Day, Sura 89, *The Dawn* (*al-Fajr*), arrives at a calming conclusion, a scene of the righteous soul being lovingly welcomed by God into His eternal Garden:

> "'O soul at peace. Return to **your Lord**, pleased [with Him] and pleasing [to Him]. And enter among **My** slaves, and enter **My** Garden.'" (89:27-30)

God first mentions Himself in the third-person, from the perspective of the soul He is addressing: "Return to your Lord." The phrase "your Lord" has a very comforting sense, setting a tone of love and intimacy between the soul and its Master.

The shift to the first-person singular in "My slaves" maintains the focus on this relationship. Yet, by attributing the slaves to Himself in this way, God particularly highlights His own special and intimate love for them, the way a father might lovingly call his child over by saying, "Come here, my son." The use of the first-person singular in "My slaves" also safeguards God's monotheism, as in the previous example.

The continuation of the first-person singular in "My Garden" highlights the soul's entry into the Garden that God has personally and specially prepared. These usages are also consistent with the fact that these are descriptions of Judgment Day, when God addresses His slaves without an intermediary.

2. Shifts in Person: The Audience

Second to Third Person

The Qur'an not only exhibits grammatical shifts from its narrative perspective, but also in its address to its audience(s). By using these shifts, the Divine Speaker manages to address more than one audience within one passage, and also display the relationships between these audiences. We will start by looking at some examples of shifts in person in the Qur'an. Take the following example, which talks about the manna and quails God provided the Israelites in the desert:

> We shaded **you** with clouds and sent down on **you** manna and quails. "**Eat** of the good things We have provided **you**!" And **they** did not wrong us, but rather **they** were wronging themselves. (2:57)

The first two sentences are addressed to the Israelites entirely in the second person (plural): *you*. God reminds them of some of the favors He specially gave to them, while they in turn persisted in rebellion. In the third sentence, however, the Israelites no longer constitute the intended audience, and instead are the subjects, addressed in the third person: *they*. This gives the impression that after addressing the Israelites, God turns away from them in displeasure towards a new audience (such as the early Muslim community) to teach them that they had better not act with the same ingratitude. By using the first audience as an example, the danger of falling into the same condemnation is made to appear more real to the second audience. Not only should the first audience feel the impact of the disappointment, but the second will be on their toes—careful not to bring on themselves the same scolding. This sensation becomes more apparent when one thinks of the Qur'an as a live speech, being recited to the ears of its various audiences.

Another interesting example is 10:22-23:

> It is He who conveys **you** by land and sea until, when **you** are in ships and they sail with **them** rejoicing in a favoring wind, a stormy wind overtakes **them** and waves come upon **them** from every side, and **they** think **they** will be encompassed by them, **they** call upon God sincerely to Him, "Truly, if you save us from this, then we will be among the grateful!" But when He saves **them**, **they** rebel on the earth wrongfully. **O people**, **your** insolence is only against **your** own selves.

As Abdel Haleem comments,

> Here, the shift to 3rd person adds another dimension, making the sea travellers seem truly helpless, far away, cut off from anyone to aid them except the Lord they feel they have to turn to. This would have been lost if the verse continued in the initial second person. Moreover, had the verse continued to address them in the 2nd person, then listeners to the Qur'ān who sit in the security of their homes, some never going to sea, would have been less convinced and less affected. He shifted to addressing them again only when the travellers had landed and began, in safety, 'to rebel wrongfully'. Moreover...when He spoke of the travellers in the 3rd person, He made others

witness how they behaved in their helplessness compared to their subsequent behaviour in safety.[45]

Other examples of this phenomenon, which scholars have called "distancing for humiliation," are also found in 16:72, 30:38, 47:23.[46]

Third- to Second-Person

There are also plenty of examples of the opposite shift. This can convey very different effects, depending on the mood of the passage. In some cases, the shift from the third to second person occurs to honor the addressee, as in the following examples:

> Indeed, **the God-conscious** will be in gardens and bliss, enjoying what **their** Lord has given them, and **their** Lord protected **them** from the punishment of Hellfire. "**Eat** and **drink** in satisfaction for what **you** used to do!" (52:17-19)

> Upon **them** will be green garments of fine silk and gold embroidery. **They** will be adorned with bracelets of silver, and **their** Lord will give them a pure drink. "Indeed, this for **you** a reward, and **your** effort has been appreciated." (76:21-22)

Both passages describe the righteous enjoying their heavenly rewards in the third person, but suddenly shift to a direct personal address from God. There also exist opposite examples, such as the following verse:

> **They** say, "The All-Merciful has taken to Himself a son." **You** have put forward an atrocious thing!" (19:88-89)[47]

As Abdel Haleem observes, "The effect of *iltifāt* in such examples is that it makes God Himself appear in the midst of a situation to address a particular group at a crucial point."[48]

Second-Person Singular to Plural

Another type of shift in audience involves addressing a single individual, usually the Messenger, and then switching to a plural audience, such as the believers. For example:

---

45 Ibid., 419-420.
46 Ibid., 419.
47 These examples are each taken from ibid., 418.
48 Ibid.

> Turn **your (singular)** face towards the Sacred Mosque. And wherever **you (plural)** are, turn your faces towards it. (2:144)

While the command to face the Sacred Mosque in prayer is at first specifically addressed to the Prophet, the shift to the plural indicates that the command applies to all his followers as well, wherever they may be.[49]

A similar example is in *Sura* 65, *Divorce (aṭ-Ṭalāq)*, which begins with regulations for divorce:

> O **Prophet**, when you (plural) divorce your wives…

What follows is a series of commands, all in the second-person plural. The shift from addressing the Prophet in the singular to giving the commands in the plural indicates, in Mir's words, "that the prophet is being addressed as a representative of the Muslim community and that the injunction applies not only to him but to all of his followers as well. A simple shift of number thus widens the scope of application of the injunction."[50] It also suggests that the Prophet himself has to intervene in the matter of divorce, to ensure that his followers only issue it with the proper conditions and do not misuse it.

A final example of this shift occurs in 17:63. This time, God speaks to Satan:

> **Go (singular)**! Whoever follows **you (singular)** among them, then Hell will be **your (plural)** recompense.

In this case, God adds to His condemnation of Satan and promise of punishment all of Satan's followers among the future generations of the human race. Abdel Haleem notes, "The shift has a powerful effect: anyone that follows Satan at any time or place is thus addressed directly by God with this strong warning, rather than merely being informed that any one of 'them' will meet with such a reward."[51] Put another way, it is as if God is seeing across time and addressing people of all generations in a single instant.

3. Shifts in Tense

Perfect to Imperfect Tense

The final kind of grammatical shift that we will look at in the Qur'an is between the perfect and imperfect tenses. The perfect tense indicates a completed action, usually associated with the past (e.g., "he wrote," "it was

---

49 Ibid., 421.

50 Mustansir Mir, "Language," in Andrew Rippin (ed.), *The Blackwell Companion to the Qur'ān* (Malden, MA: Blackwell, 2006), 94-95.

51 Abdel Haleem, "Grammatical Shifts," 421.

written," "he had written"). The imperfect tense indicates an action that is not complete, and most often has the meaning of the present tense ("he runs" or "he is running").[52] The following example describes God's provision of natural sustenance:

> Do you not see that God **sent** down water from the sky, and then the earth **becomes** green? Indeed God is the Subtle, the Aware. (22:63)

The sending down of rain is described in the perfect tense ("sent"), as a completed action in the past. However, the process of vegetation following the rain is current and ongoing, so the imperfect tense is used ("becomes"). A similar example occurs in the following verse:

> God **subjected** for you whatever is in the earth, and the ships **run** upon the sea by His command. (22:65)

The earth was prepared for human beings prior to their existence, so the perfect tense is used ("subjected"). The sailing of ships on the sea continues to happen, however, so a shift to the imperfect occurs ("run").[53]

Another example concerns the plight of believers, who are persecuted on account of their faith:

> Or do you think that you will enter the Garden while a trial has not yet come to you the like of those who have passed before you? They **were touched** with distress and hardship, and **were shaken** until their messenger and those who believed **say**, "When will the help of God come?" Indeed, God's help is near! (2:214)

The description concerning the believers of the past is, naturally, in the perfect tense: "were touched," "were shaken." Yet, it then blends into the present with the imperfect tense: "their messenger and those who believe *say*." As Mir observes,

> The strategic use of the imperfect links up the past ages with the present: it establishes an identity between the struggles of the previous prophets and their followers on the one hand and that of Muhammad and his followers on the other. The net effect of the identification is to console Muhammad and his companions, who are being assured that God will help them just as he helped earlier prophets in similar situations.[54]

---

52 However, it also includes the past progressive ("he was running") and the future ("he will run"), as well as some other less common tenses and/or aspects in English.

53 Ibid., 422.

54 Mir, "Language," 95.

Imperfect to Perfect Tense

The opposite transition also occurs. The shift from imperfect to perfect makes an action appear as if it has already been completed. This shift occurs especially in descriptions of the afterlife, signifying their inevitability and rhetorically suggesting the fluid nature of time, as if the events of the future are close to melding into the past:

> On the day when We **will set** the mountains in motion, you **will see** the earth leveled. And We **gathered** them, and We **did not leave** anyone behind. (18:47)

When the scene describes the upheavals of nature, the imperfect tense is used in this case indicating the future: "when We *will set* the mountains in motion, you *will see* the earth leveled." But when the scene moves on to describe the gathering of humanity for Judgment, it shifts to the perfect tense: "We *gathered* them, and We *did not leave* anyone behind." Not only does this shift to the perfect tense draw the audience's attention in, making them visualize their own gathering on Judgment Day, but it also makes the gathering of the human race seem even more certain and concrete than the descriptions of natural disaster. Moreover, the scene leaves the audience with the impression that time is almost an illusion, as if past, present, and future are jammed together: what will happen on Judgment Day is just as inevitable as what has already passed.

* * *

In this chapter, we have seen that far from being chaotic or random, the grammatical shifts in the Qur'an are masterfully calculated for rhetorical impact. These shifts conform to consistent rules and patterns, but allow for an impressive diversity of effects according to mood and context, thereby enriching the meaning of the Qur'an's verses in subtle but powerful ways. Indeed, one may go as far as to say that they represent a feature of the Qur'an that is without parallel in any other work of literature.

CHAPTER 5

Other Subtleties of Style and Grammar

In Classical Arabic, grammar and rhetoric are intimately connected. A skilled author or speaker can manipulate the structure of sentences and the forms of words (the concerns of grammar), altering them from the normally expected usage, in order to convey additional shades of meaning, strengthen a point, or produce a certain effect on the audience (concerns of rhetoric). In other words, the grammar of Arabic provides the speaker with a variety of tools or devices that he can use to customize his language, making it appealing to his audience and appropriate to his message. Some of these grammatical devices exist solely for purposes of style and embellishment, while others serve to communicate subtle shades of meaning. In this chapter, we will explore a sample of these devices and see how the Qur'an uses them to enhance the beauty, power, and meaning of its verses.

Styles of Emphasis and De-Emphasis

One subject of Arabic rhetoric is the skilled use of techniques for emphasis, or even de-emphasis, when the situation calls for it. The Arabic language provides many tools that can be used to highlight particular words or entire clauses.

Consider verb usage, starting with tense. The statement "Sam cooked" conveys more certainty than "Sam will cook", because the first tells you that it has already happened, while the second still might not. For this reason, the perfect tense, as in "Sam cooked," though usually associated with the past, is sometimes used for the future in Arabic and in the Qur'an to indicate that something is guaranteed to happen, as if it is as good as done.

The speaker can also use different adverbs or conjunctions to strengthen or weaken the statement. For example, he can also remove doubt about whether Sam will really cook by adding certain words for reinforcement:

"Sam will *definitely* cook" or "Sam will *indeed* cook." He can also weaken a statement by making it uncertain or conditional—"Sam *might* cook," "*If* he is home, Sam will cook," or "*When* he is home, Sam cooks"—or by adding other kinds of qualifiers: "Sam *sometimes* cooks" or "Sam *occasionally* cooks."

Nouns are considered stronger and more stable than verbs, which are time-located and subject to change. Compare the statement "Sam is a cook" to the previous statements "Sam cooked," "Sam cooks," "Sam is cooking," and "Sam will cook." By describing Sam with a noun ("a cook"), the first statement is stronger, as it makes cooking a part of his identity, a permanent characteristic, while the statements employing verbs only indicate Sam's cooking at a certain time ("cooked/cooking/will cook") or times ("cooks").

A speaker can also modify the noun in other ways to lend emphasis. He may use a noun that is similar in meaning, but stronger: "Sam is a *chef*." He may strengthen the statement by use of the definite article, "Sam is *the* chef," as opposed to the indefinite article, "Sam is *a* chef." He may use an adjective to strengthen the statement ("Sam is a *great* chef") or to weaken it ("Sam is an *okay* chef"). He can make the statement even stronger by using the definite article along with a superlative adjective: "Sam is *the greatest* chef." Finally, he may again use certain words for emphasis, such as "*Indeed*, Sam is the greatest chef" or "Sam is *certainly* the greatest chef."

Classical Arabic assigns considerable value to the skillful and appropriate use of such techniques, and the Arabic language offers other devices for emphasis that do not have direct parallels in English. Among these are letters that can be used as prefixes or suffixes of a word, simply to emphasize it, such as *l(a)-* at the beginning of a word, *-n* or *-nn(a)* at the end of a verb, or sometimes the "bound *tā*" (*tā' marbūṭa*) at the end of a noun. A speaker can also add emphasis by changing the normal sentence order—in Arabic, verb, then subject, then object:[55] by placing the subject or even the object earlier, the speaker can bring it to the fore and distinguish it with further emphasis. Furthermore, a class of word forms in Arabic (called *ism mubālagha*) even exists solely to strengthen the meaning of a noun.[56] For example, *ghāfir* simply means "forgiving," but *ghafūr* means "extremely forgiving" and *ghaffār* means "repeatedly forgiving." In sum, Arabic allows for an extremely wide variety of styles of emphasis.

---

55 There is an exception if the subject and/or object is a pronoun. This is because in Arabic, if the subject is a pronoun, it will be implicit in the form of the verb, while if the object is a pronoun, it will be attached as suffix to the verb or to a preposition associated with the verb.

56 This type of word is called an *ism mubālagha*, or "intensified noun."

"A breeze from the punishment of your Lord"

Almost every verse of the Qur'an contains examples of the skillful use of techniques for emphasis and de-emphasis. These may be explicit and direct, or subtle. However, the Qur'an uses these styles appropriately and with variety, so the emphasis does not become repetitive or meaningless. Here, we will explore one example in detail: 21:46. This verse alerts the audience to the gravity of the danger of Hell, painting a hypothetical scenario of what the *smallest* possible punishment of Hell would be like for the *ẓālimūn*, meaning the "wrongdoers," "oppressors," or "those who commit injustice." Let us start by considering only the first part of the verse:

> *Wa-la-in massat-hum nafḥatun min 'adhābi rabbika*
> And even if a breeze from the punishment of your Lord touched them…

This clause employs a range of styles used for *de*-emphasis. These all serve to underscore that the image here is only a hypothetical scenario of what the lightest possible touch of the punishment of Hell would be like, let alone the actual intensity of the punishment that will be experienced:

1. First and foremost, it is worth noting that the clause lacks any usages that would create positive emphasis. The verb "touched" (*massat*), though appearing after the subject ("a breeze," *nafḥa*) in English, appears before it in the Arabic, conforming to the normal sentence order. If instead the subject had come first, making the sentence a nominal (noun-based) one, it would have given the "breeze" emphasis. This would be undesirable, because the point of the clause is to diminish the weight of the description, to show what even the lightest possible smattering from the punishment of Hell would be like. Similarly, the word *nafḥa* is in the indefinite (*nafḥa**tun***, "*a* breeze"), while the definite form (*an-nafḥa*, "*the* breeze") would have also added misplaced emphasis.
2. The choice of the word *massat* is significant. Arabic contains numerous verbs that mean "to touch," but *massat* is the weakest of these, signifying the least degree of contact possible—i.e., the breeze *barely* touched them.
3. Furthermore, the verb is in the perfect tense ("touch*ed*"), used to indicate a completed action, as opposed to the imperfect ("touch*es*"), which may suggest continuity or repetition. The perfect tense, as opposed to the imperfect, indicates that the breeze touched them only a single time, and for an instant.
4. The entire sentence is qualified with the word "if" (*in*), entailing that it is only depicting the hypothetical scenario of what the slightest possible touch from the heat of Hell would be like to experience, and is far from depicting the magnitude and duration of the *actual* punishment.

5. Even the "if" is qualified, as the verse says "*even* if" (***la**-in*). If you said, "*Even* if I worked twenty hours a day, I would still not make as much money as he," this would imply that not only do you *not* work twenty hours a day, you do not plan to—it is not expected to happen. This further underscores that the punishment of the wrongdoers will not be limited to this "breeze."
6. The word *nafḥa* ("breeze") refers to a small, pleasant breeze. For instance, *nafḥa* can refer to the soft gust of air that pushes towards you from inside a room as you are exiting it and closing its door. It contrasts with the word *lafḥa*, which refers to the scorching heat of a fire. Since it is the Hellfire that is being described, *lafḥa* would be the more expected word. The use of the word *nafḥa* in the verse clarifies that this is but a "soft breeze" compared to the actual heat of the fire. It suggests the image of the wrongdoers standing outside of Hell, being momentarily grazed by a small draft of its mildest air. The intensity of the actual flames inside is not even given a description, as though it is beyond the ability of words to convey.
7. The Qur'an distinguishes Hell with a variety of names, most commonly "Hell" or "Gehenna" (*Jahannam*), "the Blaze" (*al-Jaḥīm*), and "the Fire" (*an-Nār*). Despite this, the place of punishment is not mentioned here by any of its explicit titles: the generic term "punishment" (*'adhāb*) is used, lacking any of the fiery imagery that the names of Hell call to mind. The reference is free of any of the graphic associations of burning and fire that are conveyed in other Qur'anic descriptions of Hell.
8. The "breeze" is not described as "a breeze of the punishment" (*nafḥatu 'adhāb…*), but "a breeze *from* the punishment" (*nafḥatun **min** 'adhāb…*). The difference is clearer in Arabic, because the word "of" does not exist as an independent preposition but is implied by the grammatical construction. As a result, "a breeze *of* the punishment" involves a closer and more direct association between the "breeze" and the "punishment," whereas "a breeze *from* the punishment" involves the addition of an extra preposition (*min*, "from") between the two words, creating distance between them. The result is that the "breeze" represents only a trifle of the punishment, in contrast to the actual proportions of the punishment itself.
9. The punishment is also described as "the punishment of your Lord" (*'adhābi rabbi-ka*). The phrase "your Lord" is (as a general rule) addressed to the Prophet Muhammad, and therefore tends to carry a personal and comforting tone. Its placement here further lightens the impression that the description makes on the reader or listener.

Now, we may turn to the main clause of the sentence, which portrays the reaction of the wrongdoers to even this slightest of punishments. Despite every indication that the "wrongdoers'" have experienced only the lightest, smallest, and briefest possible contact with the punishment of Hell, their reaction, while still outside of its fringes, is an expression of the most extreme anguish and of profound admission to their crimes:

> *la-yaqūlunna yā-wayla-nā innā kunnā ẓālimīn*
> …they would surely say, "Woe to us (*yā-wayla-nā*)! Indeed we have been wrongdoers!

To give an analogy, imagine that a confirmed criminal is subjected to forced interrogation. Even after suffering a round of bruising and battering, the determined criminal may still refuse to disclose where he put the money. If the interrogator resorts to increasingly intense, thorough, and longer-lasting methods of torture, however, the criminal will eventually break and confess the details of his crimes. In this verse, the wrongdoers were exposed to only a momentary ounce of punishment, but it was painful enough for them to fully confess their wrongs. A number of devices are used here to underscore the anguish of the wrongdoers and the heaviness of their confession:

1. The verb *yaqūlunna* means "they say." It is not in the perfect tense, as was the verb in the first clause ("the breeze *touched* them"), but in the imperfect tense. This means that their confession may be continuous, unlike the sample of the punishment itself, which only happened for a single instant.
2. *Yaqūlunna* is given the prefix *la-*, which, when attached to the verb, serves exclusively to add emphasis.
3. *Yaqūlunna* also contains the suffix *-nna*, which gives it another two degrees of emphasis.[57]
4. The word *wayl* ("woe," here *yā-wayla-nā*, "woe to us!") expresses the deepest misery, despair, or agony that a person can express in words.
5. The wrongdoers begin their confession with *innā* ("indeed," "truly"), which is again used solely for emphasis.
6. Finally, they do not confess to their crimes with a perfect tense verb ("we committed wrong") or even the stronger past progressive tense ("we had been committing wrong"). They use a noun, branding themselves as having been wrongdoers ("we were wrongdoers!" *kunnā ẓālimīn*), indicating that wrongdoing had been a constant tendency and had become part of their character. This adds a concluding layer of force to their admission.

Thus, every element of the sentence is carefully chosen and stylized in order to convey the sternness of the message to the audience. Yet, if the description

57 The normal form is *yaqūlūna*. One degree of emphasis would be represented by *yaqūlun*.

seems too intense, the very next verse balances it with an assurance that no injustice will be done to anyone on the Day of Judgment. The only punishments to be dealt out will be those that (at most) are in just proportion to the crimes: "And We set up the scales of justice for the Day of Resurrection, so that no soul will be wronged at all" (21:47).

"This is a strange thing!"

The Qur'an thoroughly engages with the different audiences of its environment, while teaching far-reaching lessons through its exchanges. One interesting feature of the Qur'an's discourse is that it frequently records the doubts and criticisms of its detractors. The following two very similarly worded passages are examples:

> But they wondered that a warner from among them has come to them. The disbelievers said, "This is a strange thing (*hādha shay'un 'ajīb*)!" (50:2)

> And they wondered that a warner from among them has come to them. The disbelievers said, "This is a magician, a repetitive liar. Has he made the gods into a single god? Indeed this is a strange thing (*inna hādha la-shay'un 'ujāb*)!" (38:4-5)

These two passages have much in common. The disbelievers expressed surprise at the idea that a "warner" had appeared in their own midst, because from their perspective a warner is someone who comes from the outside to warn of an impending threat from a foreign power. How could Muhammad, who lived his entire life within their own community, warn them of something they did not already know?

Almost the same exact wording is used in both these passages, except for two striking differences. The first difference is only apparent in the Arabic. In 50:2, the disbelievers simply exclaim "This is a strange thing!" but in 38:5 their statement is surrounded with several degrees of emphasis. We will return to this difference shortly. The second, much more obvious difference, seen in translation, is that 38:4-5 records three new objections against the Prophet by the disbelievers not found in 50:2: "This is a magician, a repetitive liar. Has he made the gods into a single god?" It is worth pausing to consider the significance of these accusations.

The first accusation was to attribute the phenomenon of the Qur'an to "magic." While this falls short of being an admission of its divine origin, it is an indirect confession that they found the rhetorical power of the Qur'an to be beyond typical explanation: one only calls something "magic" if he is unable to explain it. The second accusation was to label the Prophet a "repetitive liar" (*kadhdhāb*). This implies that he was consistent and resolute in his call, despite their every effort to deter him. While they refused to give credence to his prophetic claim, what they found "strange" was that he was not changing his story, was continuing to preach to the same audience, and was not being dissuaded by their attempts to silence him. These are very peculiar traits for a liar. Finally, they could not fathom why he was trying to do away with their gods and reduce their pantheon to a single God, who is eternal, all-powerful, and created and sustains the world. What purpose or advantage would this radical measure achieve? The objections that the Qur'an preserves in fact look to impartial observers like evidence in favor of the Prophet's truthfulness.

Let us return now to the additional layers of emphasis that are found in 38:5 (*inna hādha la-shay'un 'ujāb*)—to use a typical translation, "Indeed this is a strange thing!"—but which are absent in the earlier and plainer 50:2. First, the statement is prefaced with inna, "indeed," which exists for emphasis. Second, the phrase "strange thing" (*shay'un 'ujāb*) is prefixed with the letter *l(a)-*, which also serves simply to add emphasis. Finally, the word "strange" in 38:5, *'ujāb*, actually differs from the word "strange" in 50:2 in that it is an intensified form. To capture this, it would be better to translate it with a stronger word, such as "most peculiar" or "bizarre." A translation of the phrase that preserves the additional emphases of the Arabic would then be something like, "Indeed, this is surely a most peculiar thing!"

The three additional layers of emphasis in the statement "Indeed, this is surely a most peculiar thing!" in 38:5 corresponds to the fact that the Prophet's critics expressed disbelief over three aspects of his message not mentioned in 50:2. It thereby becomes clear that these additional layers of emphasis in 38:5 are not random or accidental, but precisely complement the added context that was not present in 50:2.

Sentence Structure

Another interesting aspect of the Qur'an related to grammar and rhetoric is how the parts of a sentence are ordered and placed in relation to one another. This is of special interest in cases where the parts of a sentence are ordered differently from the normal sentence order in Arabic. This is a commonly used device in the Qur'an for conveying subtle shades of meaning, as we will see under "If you only worship Him" below. However, first we will look at another kind of meaningful change in sentence structure in the two prayers of Abraham at the site of the Ka'ba.

"A secure city"

Even in pre-Islamic times, Mecca was viewed as a holy city and the Ka'ba recognized as a sacred shrine built by Abraham. However, the polytheists among his Arab descendants made it a center not only for the worship of the Abrahamic God, but also for the veneration of idols. The Qur'an reports two prayers that Abraham had made at the site of the Ka'ba, in which he affirms his monotheism and asks God to carry out that legacy of monotheism among his descendants. He also prays that the sanctuary itself prospers as a place of both physical and spiritual security for his offspring.

Although these two prayers revolve around the same themes, they also have some important differences. Here, we will consider just one of these differences, which is expressed through a slight variation in sentence structure. In the first prayer, Abraham says,

> My Lord, make this a secure city (*rabbi 'j'al hādha baladan āminan*). (2:126)

In the second prayer, he says,

> My Lord, make this city secure (*rabbi 'j'al hādha 'l-balada āminan*). (14:35)

Both of these requests use the same words, and may even appear to have no real difference in meaning. In fact, however, the slight change in sentence structure has important historical and religious significance.

In the first case, Abraham and his son Ishmael had just laid the foundations of the Ka'ba, but the location was still a patch of barren desert land without any habitation. Abraham therefore prays not just for the location to be safe, but for the very establishment of the city there: "make this *a secure city*." In the second case, however, Abraham declares, "I have settled some of my progeny in an uncultivated valley near Your Sacred House" (14:37), indicating that this prayer was taking place years later, when his descendants had settled in the land. The city, therefore, had already become established, and it was only necessary to pray for the city's peace: "make this city *secure*."

Thus, not only the Ka'ba, but even the city of Mecca itself was established by Abraham as a holy site dedicated exclusively to the one God. This idea, which pre-dated Islam, provides the historical background for Islam's claim to be the restoration of the monotheism of Abraham. It also sets the stage for the conflicts that would later take place between the Muslims and the powerful, disbelieving chiefs of the Quraysh tribe in Mecca, who held custody of the Ka'ba.

"If you only worship Him"

As mentioned earlier in this chapter, sentences in Classical Arabic have a typical sequence. The verb comes first, followed by the subject, and then the object:[58]

---

58 Barring the case of pronouns; see the first footnote of this chapter.

The Normal Sentence Order in Arabic		
Verb (e.g., *hit*)	**Subject** (e.g., *Sam*)	**Object** (e.g., the *ball*)

When this pattern is altered, such as by placing the object *before* the verb, it has at least one of four rhetorical effects. These can also occur to a certain extent in English, though it usually requires additional clues from the intonation of a person's voice or, in written text, punctuation marks or other stylistic devices, such as the use of italics. For example, "Sam hit the ball" is a normal statement, but in special situations a speaker might reverse the order of the sentence and place the object first: "The ball, Sam hit [it]." The speaker might do this to emphasize the ball ("The *ball*, Sam hit it!"), to single it out ("The *ball*, Sam hit it!" e.g., as opposed to accidentally hitting the catcher behind him), to create suspense ("The ball…Sam hit it!"), or in a state of hurry ("The ball—Sam hit it!"). In Classical Arabic, the mere reversal of sentence order gives rise to one of these effects, as determined by the context.

In the Qur'an, this device is used when speaking about God to single Him out, and therefore has a very important theological function. For instance, take the first half of 39:66:

Bali 'llāha f-a'bud…
Rather, *God* worship…

Object (*God*)	Subject (*you*, implicit)	Verb (*worship*)

While it sounds awkward in English, the sentence has been translated literally here in the order that it is constructed in the Arabic. Because "God," the object, is placed before "worship," the verb, in contrast with the normal sentence order, God is made the *exclusive* object of the verb: i.e., "Rather, *only* worship God." This brief statement, only three words in Arabic, epitomizes the monotheism so central to the Qur'an.

The second half of the verse, however, returns to the normal sentence sequence, with the verb ("be") coming before the object ("among the grateful"):

…wa-kun min ash-shākirīn
…and be among the grateful.

Verb (*Be*)	Subject (*you*, implicit)	Object (*the grateful*)

As a result, the object ("among the grateful") does not carry the note of exclusivity that we found in the first part of the sentence with "God." This is logical, since the audience is not encouraged to *only* be "among the grateful," but also to be among the truthful, the patient, the forgiving, and so on.

A similar example is 2:172:

w-ashkurū li-'llāhi in kuntum iyyā-hu ta'budūn
Be grateful to God, if *Him* you worship (i.e., "if you only worship Him").

Object (*Him*)	Subject (*you*, implicit)	Verb (*worship*)

Again, when worship of God is commanded, the object ("Him," i.e., God) is mentioned first, implying "only worship Him." But when gratitude is mentioned, the regular sentence order is used, so there is no suggestion that gratitude should be *only* for God. The Qur'an expects its audience to also be grateful to their parents, to their teachers, to the prophets and righteous predecessors, and to anyone who does an act of good for them. As a famous hadith of the Prophet states, "Whoever does not show gratitude towards people does not show gratitude towards God."[59]

A final example is 67:29:

Qul huwa 'r-rahmān amannā bi-hi wa-'alayhi tawakalnā
Say, "He is the All-Merciful. We believe in Him and on Him we rely."

The statement "We believe in Him" conforms to the regular sentence order, and therefore does not imply exclusivity. This is consistent with the fact that people are commanded not only to believe in God, but also in "the Last Day, the angels, the Scripture, and the prophets" (2:177). In contrast, the declaration "on Him we rely" places God before the verb "rely," making Him the sole object: "and we *only* rely on Him." This is again consistent with other parts of the Qur'an (1:5, 3:160, 5:23, etc.).[60]

Case Endings

One feature of Classical Arabic that has no parallel in English, or in modern dialects of Arabic, is the existence of case markers. These are vowel markers or suffixes at the ends of nouns that indicate their grammatical role in a sentence. For the examples in this section, all that one needs to know is that the ending *-un* indicates that a noun is the subject of a sentence, while the

59 Bukhārī, *al-Adab al-Mufrad*, no. 218, authenticated by Nāṣir ad-Dīn al-Albānī; *Sunan at-Tirmidhī*, no. 1955.

60 It is also worth noting that reliance is not always made exclusive on God through this technique, but it is used consistently in the appropriate contexts, e.g., when monotheism is being emphasized, or when the party involved fears a negative outcome.

ending *-an* indicates that it is the object of a verb.[61] For example, in the sentence "Zayd wrote a book," (*Kataba Zayd**un** kitāb**an***), the subject "Zayd" is given the case ending *-un* and the object "book" (*kitāb*) is given the case ending *-an*. (*Kataba* is the verb, "wrote.")

	Verb	Subject	Object
Case ending	—	***-un***	***-an***
Example	*Kataba* ("wrote")	*Zayd**un*** ("Zayd")	*kitab**an*** ("a book")

We will look here at a few examples in which the Qur'an manipulates the case endings of nouns for subtle literary purposes.

"Peace!"

In several places, the Qur'an retells the Biblical story of Abraham's visit by mysterious guests, who are angelic messengers in human disguise (cf. Genesis 18). Abraham's manners in receiving his visitors showcase his iconic hospitality:

> Our messengers came to Abraham with glad tidings. They said, "Peace (*salām**an***)!" He said, "Peace (*salām**un***)!" and did not hesitate to bring them a roasted calf. (11:69)

> When they entered upon him and said, "Peace (*salām**an***)!" He said, "Peace (*salām**un***)..." (51:25)

In translation, Abraham's greeting of peace appears no different from that of the angels. However, the difference in the case endings in the Arabic conveys a subtle but very profound difference. The "peace" conveyed by the angels had the case ending *-an* (*salām**an***), which indicates that it is the object of a (hidden) verb. As we have noted in previous examples, a verb is bound by both subject and time. In this case, one can infer that the hidden verb would be something like "convey"; the subject would be the angelic speakers themselves, "we"; and the time would probably be the present. "*Salāman*" ("peace" with the case ending *-an*) would therefore be short for "We convey peace (to you)."

Abraham's response on the other hand was "peace" with the case ending *-un* (*salām**un***), which indicates that it is *not* the object of a verb, bound by either a prior subject or by time (it is rather the subject itself). Abraham's greeting does not mean "*I convey* peace (to you)," restricting the "peace" to a specific subject (Abraham) or time (such as the present). Rather, it expresses the wish that they

61 That is assuming, as in our examples, that the subject and object are not pronouns and are both singular and indefinite.

be immersed in peace in every phase of time and from every possible source, whether that source is himself, his family, the outside world, the legions of angels in heaven and earth, or God Himself. With the mere change of a case ending, Abraham communicated so much more than the angels did. His response to their greeting is a beautiful illustration of the Qur'an's order, "When you are greeted with a greeting, then greet with a better one than it or at least reciprocate it equally. God keeps count of all things" (4:86).

In may be added that Abraham's invocation of peace might not only have been intended for the angels, but for himself as well, for we are immediately told of Abraham's feelings of suspicion and unease about these strange guests:

> He said, "Peace (*salāmun*)!" and did not hesitate to bring them a roasted calf. But when he saw their hands not reaching for it, he mistrusted them and conceived a fear of them. (11:69-70)

> He said, "Peace (*salāmun*)...An unknown people." Then he went to his family and came back with a roasted calf and placed it before them. He said, "Will you not eat?" and so he conceived a fear of them. (51:25-28)

The guests then assure Abraham, revealing themselves to be angels, bringing him the good news that he will have a son named Isaac, but also telling of the punishment coming to the town of Sodom.

"Beautiful patience"

Now we will consider a similar example, but this time one that is divided between separate verses that are far apart from each other. Two of these verses occur in the story of Joseph. Joseph's brothers, envious of their father Jacob's special love for him, cast him into a well.[62] They came to Jacob with Joseph's torn shirt, stained with "deceiving blood," claiming that he was devoured by a wolf. Jacob reacts with suspicion, but realizes that he will not presently be able to get Joseph back. He therefore counsels himself:

> "So beautiful patience (*fa-ṣabr**un** jamīl**un***)." (12:18)

Jacob must exhibit a quality of patience that is unrestricted and constant, because he does not know when his grief for Joseph will come to an end. This is captured by the fact that he gives the "beautiful patience" the case

62 Jacob is Abraham's grandson through his son Isaac. Also known as "Israel," Jacob is the father of the Israelite people, his twelve sons being the ancestors of Israel's twelve tribes. The biblical story of Joseph and his brothers is found in Genesis 37-50. The Qur'anic story is in Sura 12, *Joseph* (*Yūsuf*).

ending *-un*, which indicates that it is not dependent on a verb and thus restricted by time or change. Later, when his youngest son Benjamin is detained in Egypt, Jacob repeats the same phrase (12:83).

The other instance of "beautiful patience" occurs not in the dialogue of a story, but in God's direct address while comforting the Prophet:

> "So endure with beautiful patience (*ṣabr**an** jamīl**an***). They see it as distant, but We see it as near." (70:5)

In this instance, the case ending of "beautiful patience" is *-an*, indicating that it is the object of a verb and is therefore time-bound. This is appropriate, since the very next sentence is a divine assurance that says:

> They see it as distant, but We see it as near. (70:6-7)

General vs. Absolute Negations

This final group of examples involves an entirely different usage of case endings. It is fairly common in ordinary conversation that a speaker might say "no" (as in, "No talking!" or "No food!"), but may not mean "*Absolutely* no". For instance, a teacher may tell her students, "no talking during the exam," but it might be understood that asking one's neighbor for a pencil or asking the teacher a question is permitted. Similarly, she might tell her students, "No food during class," but may sometimes hand out candy as a reward for answering questions. In Arabic, the distinction between these two kinds of "no"—"generally no" versus "absolutely no"—is expressed grammatically, in the case ending of the noun. It plays an important role in the language and sentence structure of many passages in the Qur'an that is not usually evident in translation.

For example, take the following verses. Verse 2:254 refers to the Day of Judgment as "a day in which there is no bargaining, no friendship, and no intercession"—that is, a day when nothing will aid a person except his good deeds. "Intercession" means to plead on someone else's behalf, such as before a judge in court. Yet, the very next verse allows the possibility of intercession in certain, limited cases: "Who is it that may intercede with Him, except by His permission?" (2:255).[63] The two verses may seem to contradict each other in English translation. But in the Arabic, the word "intercession" (*shafā'a*) has the case ending *-un* (*shafā'at**un***), which indicates that this is not

---

63 Muslim tradition recognizes that the Prophet Muhammad will be permitted to intercede before God on Judgment Day for his followers, as well as some other cases of intercession outlined in the hadith.

an absolute negation, but a general one that can permit exceptions. In contrast, had it been given the alternative case ending *-a* (*shafāʿat**a***), this would imply a total negation. In summary:

> *Lā ṭaʿām**un*** = "No food" as a general negation, which may permit exceptions

> *Lā taʿām**a*** = "No food" as an absolute negation, which permits no exceptions

Likewise, the phrases "no bargaining" and "no friendship" (*lā bayʿ**un*** and *lā khullat**un***) in the same sentence are also general negations, which allows some exceptions. For example, the Qur'an says, "God has purchased from the believers their lives and their property, and because of that Paradise will be theirs…So rejoice in the bargain that you have made. That is the supreme success" (9:111). This bargain, which will be completed on Judgment Day, is an exception to the general rule. This type of negation is equivalent to saying "no…for the most part."

On the other hand, there are also cases of absolute negation in the Qur'an. The most important example of this absolute negation is in the Muslim declaration of faith, which says, *lā ilāh**a** illā 'llāh*, "There is *absolutely* nothing worthy of worship but God." Another crucial example is *lā ikrāh**a** fī 'd-dīn*, "There is *absolutely* no compulsion in religion" (2:256), a verse that strictly prohibits forced conversion under any circumstances. Some other examples of absolute negation include:

> *Lā rayb**a** fī-hi* = "There is (absolutely) no doubt about it (the Qur'an)" (2:2, etc.)

> *Lā khalāq**a** la-hum fī 'l-ākhirah* = "There is (absolutely) no share for them in the afterlife" (3:77)

Thus, even something as small as the ending sound of a word can have subtle but profound effects on the meaning of a verse. This is another subtlety of the Qur'an that only becomes evident on a close study of the Arabic text.

For further exploration:

For more examples of grammatical nuances in the Qur'an, see Nouman Ali Khan's "Amazed by the Qur'an" series on the Bayyinah Institute YouTube channel (https://www.youtube.com/user/BayyinahInstitute).

CHAPTER 6

Figurative Language and Imagery

The Qur'an employs a surprisingly small range of vocabulary, which allows for easy memorization. At the same time, this limited set of words gives rise to a rich and complex spectrum of meaning.[64] One way it does this is by employing different figures of speech, such as similes, metaphors, and idioms, as well as extended metaphors in the form of parables or allegories. As an oral literary composition, the Qur'an moves its reader through a combination not only of meaning and sound, but also of visual imagery. This combination of figurative language and imagery also allows the scripture to convey complex or abstract ideas and lessons in terms that are concise, relatable, and memorable. In this chapter, we will aim to capture a glimpse of this aspect of Qur'anic rhetoric, from the perspectives of both its literary beauty and semantic power. While beyond the scope of this book, the reader should (as always) keep in mind that aspects of sound form another crucial dimension of the Qur'an's beauty, which can only be appreciated with the recitation of the Arabic text.

Basic Similes and Metaphors

The Qur'an's use of similes and metaphors varies in scale and complexity. We will first sample some brief, straightforward examples that require little explanation. Then, in the following sections, we will increase in the complexity of the examples we look at, spending more time considering idioms, and finally parables or allegories, in the Qur'an. The following examples of simile

64 See Mustansir Mir, *Verbal Idioms of the Qur'ān* (Ann Arbor: University of Michigan, 1989), 1-2.

and metaphor in the Qur'an have been collected from diverse parts of the text and are grouped together thematically.

"Like the passing of clouds"

One of the most prominent uses for simile in the Qur'an is to depict the realities of the Day of Judgment with familiar imagery that can easily be appreciated by its audience. When the Judgment is at hand, the Qur'an says, the sky will "split open and become rose-colored, like red hide" (55:37). The mountains—which the Arabs referred to as "the eternal ones" (*al-khawālid*) on account of their stability and permanence—will in fact "be like carded wool" (101:5) and will "pass away like the passing of clouds" (27:88). In the meantime, people will be brought out of their graves "quickly, as if they were racing towards a goal post" (70:43). They will then spread out "like scattering locusts" (54:7) or "like scattered moths" (101:4). Among their rewards, the men of Paradise will find maidens exclusively reserved for them "like well-protected eggs" (37:49), alluding to the care with which the mother ostrich guards her egg and to the beauty, purity, and preciousness the Arabs associated with it. However, the disbelievers will receive no rewards, as their deeds will be "like ashes that the wind blows on a stormy day" (14:18).[65]

"A goodly loan"

As with most of the world, trade and agriculture were two of the primary sources of economic prosperity in ancient Arabia. It is hardly surprising then that the Qur'an frequently uses metaphors related to these two themes. Since we will consider a parable using agricultural imagery near the end of the chapter, we will look at some of the commercial metaphors here.

The Qur'an describes human deeds and their returns on the Day of Judgment using an analogy of a business transaction. While this occurs in various places throughout the scripture, it is especially prominent in the second sura. Those who claimed to believe while in fact disbelieving are said to "have purchased error in exchange for guidance, but their transaction has brought no profit" (2:16). Likewise, the Children of Israel are warned, "Do not exchange My signs for a small price" (2:41; 3:77, 187, 199). Those who broke their covenant with God "purchased the life of this world in exchange for the afterlife" (2:86) and "sold themselves" (2:90). Some of the Israelites participated in sorcery, despite knowing that "whoever purchased it would not have any

65 Mustansir Mir, "The Qur'an as Literature," *Religion & Literature* 20.1 (1988): 49-64; Mustansir Mir, "Language," in Andrew Rippin (ed.), *The Blackwell Companions to the Qur'ān* (Malden, MA: Blackwell, 2006), 102-103.

share of the afterlife" (2:102). The one who "purchases disbelief in exchange for faith" has clearly gone astray (2:108; cf. 3:177). Again, those who conceal the revelation "exchange it for a small price" (2:174) and have "exchanged guidance for error, and forgiveness for punishment" (2:175). On the other hand, fighting in the path of God is described as "a goodly loan," which God will "multiply many times over" (2:245; cf. 57:11). While there will be "no bargaining" on the Day of Judgment (2:254), the grammatical form of this negation permits some exceptions. One exception is provided elsewhere, in 9:111, which states, "God has purchased from the believers their lives and their property, and because of that Paradise will be theirs...So rejoice in the bargain that you have made. That is the supreme success." Elsewhere, this "supreme success" is described in more detail according to the same analogy. Those who recite the scripture, establish the prayer, and give in charity may look forward to "a profit that will never fade" (35:29). This theme culminates in 61:10-12, which says:

> O you who have believed, shall I tell you of a transaction that will deliver you from a painful punishment: That you believe in God and His messenger, and fight in the way of God with your wealth and your souls. This is better for you if you knew; and He will forgive you your sins, and make you enter gardens underneath which rivers flow and good dwellings in gardens of eternity. This is the supreme success![66]

"We come submissively"

In addition to similes and metaphors, the Qur'an makes use of personification, the figure of speech in which nonhuman objects are given human qualities. In a variety of cases, personification is used to underscore the message that all of creation engages in *islām*, submission to God's will, and that human beings therefore should as well. The following are representative examples of this image in the Qur'an:

- When the cosmos was in the form of "smoke," God commanded the heaven and earth, "Come, submissively or grudgingly," and they both replied, "We come submissively" (41:11).
- All of creation is said to be engaged in a chorus of divine glorification: "The seven heavens and the earth and everyone in them exalt Him; there is not a thing that does not exalt Him with praise, though you do not understand their praise" (17:44).
- The cosmos is even presented as a spectator of the moral drama of human history, taking the side of good over evil. When Pharaoh and his

---

66 Translation qtd. in Mir, "Language," 104, with slight modifications.

army were drowned, the Qur'an says, "Neither the heaven nor the earth wept for them" (44:29).

- The hearts of those who do not take heed of the revelation are harder than mountains, for God declares, "If We had sent down this Qur'an upon a mountain, you would have seen it humbled, splitting out of fear of God" (59:21).
- Prior to man's creation, the heavens, earth, and mountains were each offered "the Trust," a covenant according to which they would be charged the task of being God's *khalīfa*, or representative.[67] This meant that they would be given certain powers and freedoms, including the freedom to make moral choices, but that in exchange, God would hold them accountable for those choices. Their response was unanimous: "they shrank from bearing it and feared it." However, man, being "ever wrongful and foolish," chose to take up the covenant and to bear the burden of moral and religious accountability (33:72).[68]

Just as with other figures of speech, and in line with the above picture of the cosmos, personification is also one of the techniques the Qur'an uses to portray the realities of Judgment Day. For example, it says that the Final Hour is so close and inevitable that "the heavens and the earth have become heavy with it" (7:187), that is, like a pregnant woman who is about to give birth.[69] Similarly, Sura 99, *The Quaking* (*az-Zalzala*), describes the condition of the earth—which is of feminine gender in Arabic—on Judgment Day in terms reminiscent of "a pregnant woman in crisis":[70]

> When the earth is shaken, quaking
> When the earth bears forth her burdens
> And someone says "What is with her?"
> At that time she will tell her news
> As her lord revealed to her. (99:1-5)[71]

On that Day, the heavens will split apart and the earth will cast out its contents, each of them "obeying [literally, 'listening to'] its Lord as it must" (84:1-5). When the wicked stand in Judgment but are too fearful to confess their crimes, "their tongues, hands, and feet will bear witness against them" (24:24; cf. 36:65). Even Hell is depicted as an animate being, which actively pursues the

67 This will be discussed in chapter 10, "Storytelling in the Qur'an II."
68 Mir, "Some Figures of Speech," *Religion & Literature* 40:3 (2008): 38-40.
69 Ibid., 39-40.
70 Sells, 215.
71 This is the translation offered by Sells, 108.

wicked, like a ravenous predator in pursuit of its prey. It "lies in wait" for the rebellious (78:21) and "calls" those who turn away and hoard wealth (70:17-18). When, on Judgment Day, it finally "sees" its prey, they will "hear it raging and roaring" (25:12). Once the first batch of evildoers is thrown into Hell, God will ask it, "Are you full?" Still hungry, it will ask in its turn, "Are there more?"

Idioms

A more complex mode of expression in the Qur'an is found in its use of idioms. An idiom is an expression whose meaning cannot be known from its individual words, such as, in English, "It's raining cats and dogs" (i.e., it is raining heavily) or "He kicked the bucket" (i.e., he died). The Qur'an is filled with idioms. Many are as simple as the use of a preposition with a verb that gives the verb an entirely different meaning. Others, however, provide rich images and metaphors, whose meanings might be lost outside the context of Classical Arabic.

While some of these idioms already existed in the Arabic language, many of them have a distinctly Qur'anic flavor. One feature of the Qur'an's expression is that it takes words and phrases that had common meanings in Arabic and infuses them with new religious meanings. In effect, the Qur'an not only adopted the Arabic language but refashioned it to its own ends. For example, the word *muslim* simply meant "submitter," whereas the Qur'an assigned it the new meaning of one who submits faithfully to God. The word *zakāh* signifies "purification," but the Qur'an uses it in reference to the annual charity obligatory upon believers, with the implication that it "purifies" the giver from greed.[72] In this section, we will examine this phenomenon on the level of figures of speech, looking at Qur'anic idioms in which the scripture takes an old usage of a word or phrase and, to quote Mir, "by subtly modifying it or using it in a new context, raises it to a higher plane of meaning."

"Lower your wing"

When a bird lifts its wings, it shows off its ability to take flight and soar through the sky, and it raises itself above others. According to this logic, in Classical Arabic, when someone acted with haughtiness and arrogance, he would be said to have "raised his wing" (*rafa'a janāḥa-hu*). In contrast, a bird that descends and grounds itself puts itself on the same level as everything and everyone else, even though it has the ability to fly. Someone who does this, exhibiting humility, compassion, and gentleness, was said to have "lowered his wing" (*khafaḍa janāḥa-hu*).

72 Mir, "Language," 90-91, lists about three dozen examples of this phenomenon in the Qur'an, and many more could be added.

The expression also suggests another image. When a predator, such as a snake, approaches the nest of a mother bird and her chicks, the mother bird will lower her wings over them to shield them from attack. The expression evokes the image of a parent protecting and taking care of a child. (There is some resemblance with the English expression "to take someone under one's wing.") In this spirit, the Qur'an counsels the Prophet to "lower [his] wings" to the believers (15:88; 26:215).

In another place, however, the Qur'an adds to this expression, giving it additional dimensions of meaning. When someone's parents grow old and feeble, the Qur'an urges him, "Lower for both of them the wing of humility out of mercy" (*w-akhfiḍ la-humā janā-ḥa 'dh-dhulli mina 'r-raḥma*, 17:24). The use of this idiom in the particular context of taking care of one's parents gives it special significance. While the idiom on its own brings to mind the image of a parent taking care of the child, in this context the roles are flipped, demanding that the child take care of his parents when they grow to a state of weakness. It is as if the Qur'an is suggesting: just as your parents cared for and protected you while you were grounded and helpless, you must return the favor by taking care of them when you become capable and they become weak.

The Qur'an also adds words to the expression. It characterizes the "wing" as "the wing of *humility* (*dhull*)," emphasizing that the individual must take care of his parents humbly and with a sense of dutifulness towards them, not with the attitude that he is doing them a favor. He must lower his wing for them to the extent that he does not appear to have any other side to him, like a bird that is incapable of flying. The final addition, "out of mercy" (*mina 'r-raḥma*), indicates that one must take care of his parents out of a spirit of compassion and caring. The Arabic word for "mercy," *raḥma*, comes from the word *raḥim*, "womb," calling to mind—once again—the unique and selfless love with which a mother cares for her child. The expression "out of mercy" therefore reminds the individual of how his own parents, and especially his mother, cared for and nurtured him, stirring him to act towards them in the same way. These additions enhance the idiom with additional layers of meaning and emphasis, and give it a Qur'anic signature.

"They venture into every valley"

The verb *hāma* (imperfect tense, *yahīmu*) was used for a camel that roams about in search of pasture, without any clear aim or direction. The Qur'an, however, applies this verb to the poets of ancient Arabia, thereby comparing them figuratively to lost, wandering camels: "Do you not see that they wander about in every valley (*fī kulli wādin yahīmūn*)?" (26:225).

The poets were the performers, entertainers, and celebrities of pre-Islamic Arabia, and success as a poet was directly associated with fame and glory. In this sense, the poets were akin to today's actors and music artists, and we might understand the Qur'anic phrase by relating it to a modern analogy. Take the example of a new, young music artist, who releases a song or music video that goes platinum. Every radio station is playing it, every music fan is viewing and downloading it, and he becomes a household name. After some time, however, his popularity begins to wane and he witnesses a decline in sales. He has to continually come up with the next big hit, but each time it has to be something a little more attention grabbing. Over time, he becomes increasingly desperate to maintain attention, and begins to say and do increasingly controversial things in his songs, music videos, and public life. Like the camel wandering from one valley to another, the entertainer drifts from one exploit to the next, in desperate pursuit of public attention, without any consideration of his moral impact.

The poet of ancient Arabia additionally played the role of the philosopher or intellectual, offering commentary on perennial matters such as life and death, good and evil, and love and hate. The Qur'anic idiom serves also to criticize the tendency among some of these individuals to posture as wise men, when, in fact, they lived hedonistic lifestyles and merely drifted from one subject to another to draw in people's attention, without possessing any genuine principles or direction.

The Qur'an gave an old expression new meaning, making it a timeless warning to those who seek fame and attention, are placed in the spotlight, or drift from one pursuit to another without aim or purpose. It also provides a warning for those who, like idle sheep, risk following them into "every valley."

"Enter the houses through their doors"

According to Muslim sources, the pre-Islamic Arabs had a superstition that it was bad luck to enter one's house from the front door upon returning from the Hajj. The Qur'an not only dispels this notion, but it uses the occasion to teach a far more general lesson:

> Righteousness is not that you enter your houses from their backs, but righteousness is in whoever is mindful of God. Enter the houses through their doors (*w-a'tū 'l-buyūta min abwābi-hā*) and be mindful of God so that you may prosper. (2:189)

In Classical Arabic, the expression "he came to something from its door" (*atā 'sh-shay'a min bābi-hi*) meant "to go about something in the right way."

When the Arabs asked about their custom, the Qur'an responded by employing this expression with a double meaning. The literal meaning ("enter from their doors") addressed the specific problem, while the figurative meaning conveyed a universal rule of conduct: when you undertake any task, do it the right way.

"It was turned over on its roofs"

One of the major themes of the Qur'an is divine justice and human moral accountability. Stories of God's destruction of wicked towns, cities, and nations are retold and referred to as illustrations of that theme. This is conveyed three times in the Qur'an by the expression, "it was turned over on its roofs" (*hiya khāwiyatun 'alā 'urūshi-hā*):

> Or like the one who passed by a town while it had fallen upon its roofs. (2:259)

> And how many a town did We destroy while it persisted in wrongdoing, so it had fallen upon its roofs, and how many an abandoned well and a lofty castle? (22:45)

The verb *khawā* means "to be plucked or uprooted" (e.g., of a plant) and also "to be desolate, bare, or empty" (e.g., of a house). The Qur'an appears to intend both meanings of the verb to produce an image of both complete demolition and lasting desolation.

By adding the clause "upon its roofs," the Qur'an goes further, sketching out these themes even more vividly. This phrase suggests a scene in which the roof of the building has collapsed under the forces of the weather. In this case, there are no inhabitants left to repair the damage. Once the roofs of a building collapse, the walls (which they had helped to keep in place) naturally begin to deteriorate. Eventually, strong winds cause the walls to fall in on the collapsed roofs. What is left is the somber image of a city in ruins, which has remained uninhabited despite a long stretch of time.

The expression also occurs in another place in the Qur'an, with a small variation. In Sura 18, *The Cave* (*al-Kahf*), the Qur'an gives the parable of a man whom God had blessed with lush gardens, which are described in elaborate detail. The gardens contained luscious crops and were encircled by palm trees, which protected the delicate crops from strong winds. However, having this blessing only made the man become more arrogant and heedless of God, and so God sent a disaster upon it. Here (18:42), the same phrase (*wa-hiya khāwiyatun 'alā 'urūshi-hā*) is used, but with a slightly different meaning: "and it [the garden] fell upon its trellises." In a garden, trellises function to support the growing, especially, of delicate plants and fruit trees. In this case, the natural disaster was so strong that it caused the palm trees to fall upon the trellises, destroying the very crops that they were set up to protect. Here, the image serves to emphasize God's control over people's fortunes and especially His ability to revoke His blessings.

In all three of these instances, this Qur'anic idiom virtually tells a story and conveys a solemn lesson in only a few words.

Parables

As with similes and metaphors, the Qur'an uses parables to convey abstract ideas through images that are familiar and memorable to its audience. However, the parables are longer and thus more capable of presenting complex ideas than short figurative, expressions. At the same time, they tend to be extremely concise, condensing a great deal of meaning and profundity into usually no more than a few sentences. The flip side of this is that much of the meaning lies between the lines, and the more complex examples require careful thought and consideration of the overall background of the Qur'an's message to fully grasp their meanings. In all these respects, the Qur'anic parables are much like the famous parables of Jesus in the Gospels.

"As for what benefits man, it remains on the earth"

Sura 13, *The Thunder* (*ar-Ra'd*), presents the following twin parables, both depicting truth and falsehood:

> He sent down water from the sky, so then valleys filled up to their capacity, and the floodwaters carried to their surface a swelling layer of froth. And, from what they heat in the fire to make ornaments and utensils, there is a froth like it. That is how God depicts truth and falsehood. As for the froth, it goes away as waste. As for what benefits man, it remains on the earth. That is how God sets forth a parable. (13:17)

Beginning with the first parable, it should first be noted that water appears in the Qur'an as a symbol for divine revelation, which here and elsewhere is described as "truth." In the Qur'an, both water and revelation are "sent down" by God, are frequently referred to as "mercy" (*raḥma*), are said to "purify," and give life—one physically and one spiritually. While falsehood, like a thick, swelling froth, may at first appear to cover and prevail over the truth, the truth in fact, like a powerful torrent, washes it away into oblivion: "it goes away as waste." When the water sinks into the earth, it produces all sorts of fruits and vegetation (2:22; 6:99; etc.), so that "as for what benefits man, it remains on the earth." Likewise, when the guidance of revelation is absorbed by hearts, it produces people who bring about profound benefit and change in society. The second parable teaches a similar lesson: just as fire removes the impurity (the "froth") from the metal ore, producing beneficial ornaments and utensils, revelation removes falsehood and produces that which is beneficial.

Still, this does not explain why seemingly opposite images are used: in the first, the calm, cool image of water washing away froth and waste; in the second, the fierce heat of fire. This contrast is explained when one considers the differences between the Prophet's career first in Mecca and then in Medina. In the former, the "water" of revelation spread throughout the valley of Mecca and filled it. It was absorbed by the hearts of some people, transforming them. Yet, it caused others to swell and rise to the surface as scum and waste. An example of this would be Abu Jahl, one of the most wealthy and powerful men of the Quraysh. He was known for his wisdom and sophistication, yet his hostility to Islam was such that he physically tortured some of the Prophet's companions, many of them defenseless slaves. Yet, despite the best efforts of the powerful Quraysh elite to mask the truth of revelation, it would eventually sweep them away like a powerful torrent.

In Medina, the situation was different. The opponents of Islam were not clearly distinguished from the believers: instead, they presented themselves as believers in order to undermine Islam from within. In this case, the waste was not separated like the froth upon the surface of the water, but was embedded deep inside, like the unwanted elements within a metal ore. They only became separated from the true believers as a result of the community being subjected to the heat of various trials, such as the battles of Badr, Uḥud, and the Trench. In this connection, it is worth noting that the verb *FaTaNa*, from which the word for "test" or "trial" in Arabic (*FiTNa*) derives, refers to the smelting of ores to separate out the useful and valuable metals from the unwanted ones. As the Qur'an says in another place, "Do the people think that they will be left to say, 'We believe' and they will not be tested (*lā yuFTaNūn*)?" (29:2).

"The enjoyment of delusion"

In a way that should be familiar to readers of the Gospels, the Qur'an uses a variety of metaphors and parables involving agricultural imagery. One of them, a parable about the present life, begins with the following introduction:

> Know that the worldly life is but play, entertainment, beautification, boasting among you, and competition to increase in wealth and children. (57:20)

This introduction portrays the different stages of the life of a human being, according to what he loves and pursues most. When he is a small child, his only desire is play. When he becomes a little older, he additionally takes interest in various forms of entertainment. In adolescence, he develops a concern for his physical appearance. In early adulthood, he seeks to show off his accomplishments to others: his education, his career, and so on. As he continues to grow older, however, those things which were previously of central importance to him (play, entertainment, and beautification) are overshadowed by two concerns: money and children (eventually, grandchildren). This brief overview of life sets the scene for the following parable:

> Like the example of rain: the growth (*nabāt*) it yields delights the sowers (*kuffār*, singular *kāfir*). Then it dries and you see it turn yellow, and then it becomes crushed debris. And in the afterlife there is a severe punishment, and forgiveness from God and good pleasure. And the worldly life is nothing but the enjoyment (*matāʿ*) of delusion. (57:20)

The farmer's entire livelihood is a product of the rain. In past times, without the help of modern technology, the farmer had to plant his entire field by manually sowing one seed into the ground after another. Even then, he would not see the fruits of his labor until the harvest season occurred—and only if it rained. Once he saw the rain and the first sprouts budding from the ground, it brought him relief: he knew it would be a successful year.

The use of the word *kāfir* here for "sower, tiller, farmer" is significant. There are many words that describe this line of work in the Arabic language, but this particular word happens to be the same one used throughout the Qur'an to refer to a "disbeliever" or "ingrate." At the most basic level, the word *kāfir* means "one who conceals, covers, or buries." Just as the farmer buries his seed in the earth, the disbeliever "buries" the truth and conceals his debt to God. The word *kāfir* in this verse draws on the analogy between the farmer in the parable and the disbeliever or ingrate in real life.

The rest of the analogy follows from this. The metaphor of vegetation is used to signify the "enjoyment" (*matāʿ*) that the human being expects his efforts to yield, which have already been listed as play, entertainment, self-beautification, the showing off of his accomplishments, and wealth and children.[73] The word for "growth" (*NaBāT*) comes from the root *NaBaTa*, "to grow," underscoring the sustained effort and time that is required in order for the crop—and accordingly, the enjoyment of the worldly life—to

73 It should be borne in mind that in pre-Islamic Arabian society, one's (male) children were an immense source of pride and status, since it was they who would carry on his lineage—one of the most cherished assets in Arab tribal society.

emerge and ripen. Just like the sower of seeds, the disbelieving or ungrateful person in the various stages of his life invests most of his time and labor in the hope of attaining delight and enjoyment. However, he fails to acknowledge his Creator for these blessings when they appear.

The "delight" that the farmer achieves from seeing his crops ripen will only be short-lived and will not profit him in the long run if he does not reap and sell what he worked so hard to sow. Instead, his crop will "turn yellow" right in front of his eyes and, in the end, decompose into "crushed debris." Similarly, the disbeliever will achieve nothing but short-lived pleasure, since he fails to be grateful to God and use these blessings as they were intended to be used. Not only will the fruits of his labors very quickly "turn yellow" for him in this world, but they will ultimately become as worthless as "crushed debris," as he passes into the next. (The Qur'an elsewhere tells us, "The example of those who disbelieve is that their deeds are like ashes that the wind blows on a stormy day", 14:18.) All he gained through his efforts was the momentary "enjoyment of delusion," whereas in the next life he will be requited with "a severe punishment."

The Qur'an elsewhere reinforces this point with a similar parable:

> Present for them the example of the worldly life—like water We sent down from the sky. The earth's vegetation absorbed it, and then [the vegetation] became crushed debris scattered about by the wind. God is over all things powerful. (18:45)

However, it adds:

> Wealth and children are attractions of the worldly life, *but lasting righteous deeds are better with your Lord in reward and are better grounds for hope.* (18:46)

Both the believer and the disbeliever (or ingrate) strive to acquire "wealth and children" and pass through the various stages of life, but the difference is that the believer expresses gratitude towards his Provider and turns these assets into investments with Him. (Recall the transaction metaphor at the beginning of the chapter.) As a result, they produce continuous good in this world and earn him everlasting good in the next, and he will acquire "forgiveness from God and good pleasure" (57:20). In contrast to the one who remains ungrateful, whose efforts will result ultimately in nothing but "crushed debris scattered about by the wind," God promises, "'If you are grateful, I will surely increase you'" (14:7). God will put lasting blessings in such a person's works and provisions in both worlds.

Finally, it is worth noting that the Qur'an uses the term *mufliḥūn* to describe those who believe, give thanks to God by establishing the prayer, and spend of what God has provided for them on good causes (2:3-5). The term *muFLiḤūn* means "successful" or "prosperous," and it comes from the same root as another word for farmer, *FaLLāḤ*. This refers to a farmer who not only put in the work of sowing his seeds, but attained success and profit at the end of his prolonged efforts. People in this category are "successful" because they expended their time and efforts in the worldly life sowing seeds—that is, good deeds—whose fruits will give them delight in this world and everlasting profit in the next.

"Light upon light"

To conclude this chapter, we will turn to the most famous parable in the Qur'an, the "Verse of Light":

> God is the light of the heavens and the earth. The example of His light is like a niche in which there is a lamp, the lamp in a glass, and the glass as if it were a brilliant star. [The lamp] is lit from a blessed olive tree neither of the east nor of the west. Its oil almost radiates even though a fire had not touched it. Light upon light. God guides to His light whomever He wills. God presents examples for people, and God knows all things. (24:35)

The parable depicts a glowing oil lamp that is placed in the niche of a wall to light up a room at night. A niche functions not only for the placement of the lamp: its arched shape also curves the light of the lamp outward so that it spreads throughout the room. The lamp is placed in a shining glass vessel, to protect the flame of the candle from flickering. The glass itself twinkles like a brilliant star at night. The oil of the lamp is derived from "a blessed olive tree," the word "blessed" in Arabic signifying an increase in good above and beyond what is expected. Just as the glass glistens brightly on its own, the oil is so pure that it virtually glows—"even though a fire had not touched it." Therefore, when the radiant flame does come into contact with the brilliant lamp, it produces "light upon light."

But what does all of this mean? Light is a consistent symbol of divine guidance in the Qur'an. The parable describes "His light" as a lamp that shines from within a sparkling glass. The most plausible view, and the one generally adopted by commentators, is that it refers to an innate goodness or "inner light" that God places in the heart of the human being. For the light to shine through, the "glass" in which it is placed—i.e., the heart—must be carefully protected and kept clean. The heart, in turn, is placed in its own "niche," which may be interpreted as the chest or rib cage, which incidentally is also shaped like an arch.

For the lamp to give off light, it must be supplied with oil. Just as the oil derives from "a blessed olive tree" that is planted in a garden outside the walls of the house, the human spirit originates from a heavenly Garden that is located outside of the material universe. That this source is "neither of the east nor of the west" reinforces this, while also alluding to the quality of the oil it produces: for the tree that yields the purest oil is that which is located in neither the extreme east nor west, but in a central place, so that it is nourished by the light of the sun from morning until evening. In fact, this oil is so pure that it "almost radiates" even before it is lit by fire.

Similarly, the person who keeps his "oil" pure and his "glass" clean—i.e., his spirit and heart, respectively—shines on his own, "like a brilliant star." Thus, when the spirit of such a person does come into contact with divine revelation (the "fire"), the effect is "light upon light." This light is not confined to itself, but is so brilliant that it illuminates whatever is around it, thereby lighting the way for whoever is within its range and helping them to see. It may be added that just as a lamp or a star shines brightest at night, it is in the darkest times and places that the pure soul, lit by divine revelation, shines most brilliantly.

CHAPTER 7

Divine Oaths

A person may swear an oath for a variety of reasons and in a variety of circumstances.[74] On the most basic, but serious, level, an oath is a guarantee that one is speaking the truth. Only the worst kind of person would consciously break the sanctity of an oath, and to do so would be to commit a grave moral, social, and legal offense. To take an oath is therefore to stake one's life or reputation on the truth of one's claim.[75] Thus, an oath is a way of securing the trust of others. As a result, a person may swear an oath when he is not being believed (e.g., "I swear, I really did go there!"). Oaths have also had important functions in legal contexts for millennia, from the ratification of treaties in the ancient Near East, to oaths of political allegiance, to testimony in modern courts. In the ancient Near East, such oaths were usually taken in the presence of witnesses, whether they were people, deities, or even inanimate objects. Finally, an oath is also a way of securing a person's attention and emphasizing the importance of the claim one is making, since one would not make a serious oath under merely casual circumstances.

There are also different ways to swear an oath. Commonly, a person will swear "by" or "on" a sacred object or concept, such as when a person swears on the Bible, or declares something like "I swear on my mother's life!" The oath could be abbreviated, as when one says, "By God"—short for, "I swear by God." It should be added that in pre-Islamic Arabic culture and poetry, the speaker would swear by something of significant value to

74 In this chapter, by "oath" we are not referring to a *promise* to do something (known more specifically as a "vow"), but rather to swear to the truth of a claim.

75 M. Zakyi Ibrahim, "Oaths in the Qur'ān: Bint Al-Shāṭi''s Literary Contribution," *Islamic Studies* 48:4 (2009): 475-98.

himself or others, and/or which would grab people's attention, such as his horse, his sword, the dawn, and so on. The object that the speaker swears by is called the **object of the oath**. Note that there can be multiple objects in a single oath.

The Qur'an contains many oaths stated directly by God, mostly in Meccan suras. They often occur at the opening of the Early Meccan suras that are placed towards the end of the Qur'an, or at the beginning of sections within them. These oaths can be classified into various types, according to the objects that God swears by. In some, He swears by cosmic phenomena, such as the sky, the earth, the sun, the moon, or the stars. In others, He swears by certain phases of the day, such as the dawn, morning, forenoon, late afternoon, or night. The significance of the objects of the oath frequently relates to how they are placed in opposition to each other, such as sun and moon, night and day, or sky and earth. Another type of oath, which Neal Robinson has called "rider oaths", depicts natural or personal forces moving in (usually swift) succession.[76] The sound pattern of these oaths, *al-fā'ilāti fa'lā*, echoes the rhythmic motions of these forces, which are variously identified by commentators as angels, horses, stars or planets, or winds and clouds. God also swears by Himself, by the Day of Judgment, by sacred places connected with revelation, by revelation itself, by elements of human history or experience, and by a variety of other things. The claim that the speaker swears is called the **complement of the oath**, because it completes the oath.[77] For example, in the Qur'anic oath, "No, I swear by this city...and by the begetter and the begotten: We have certainly created man in toil" (90:1-4), "this city" and "the begetter and the begotten" form the objects of the oath, and the statement "We have certainly created man in toil" forms the complement.

The Components of an Oath					
	Oath	=	**Object of the Oath** (i.e., the object sworn by)	+	**Complement of the Oath** (i.e., the claim that is sworn)
Example	"No, I swear by this city... And by the begetter and the begotten: We have certainly created man in toil." (90:1-4)		"This city" and "the begetter and the begotten"		"We have certainly created man in toil."

76 Robinson, *Discovering the Qur'an*, 102-103.
77 Mustansir Mir, "The Qur'ān's Oaths: Farāhī's Interpretation," *Islamic Studies* 29 (1990): 6.

God might swear any of the various kinds of oaths for any combination of the reasons mentioned above—to grab attention, elicit belief, emphasize the importance of something, or to summon testimony—and as such, it can be said that each oath has a unique flavor and significance in its context. Some modern studies have contributed important insights into the methods and purposes of the Qur'anic oaths. Citing the evidence from the ancient Near East, the Indian scholar Hamid ad-Din Farahi (d. 1930) has argued that in the Qur'anic oaths, when God swears by a certain object or objects, He is highlighting them as evidence for His claim.[78] In Qur'anic terms, it might be said that, in effect, the object of the oath acts as a sign (*āya*) pointing to its complement. The Egyptian scholar Bint ash-Shati' (d. 1998) has also argued that when God swears by a certain object, He is using it as a visual symbol to represent a more abstract reality—much like in the parables we saw in the previous chapter.[79] To tie all of these explanations together, one might say that in the Qur'an, God swears an oath to mentally prepare the audience for an important statement He is about to make.

In this chapter, we will see what kind of meaningful connections exist between the object of the oath and its complement, and we will attempt to get a taste of the power of these oaths. Here we will briefly examine five oaths in the Qur'an: one by cosmic objects, one by the phases of the day, one by sacred places, one rider oath, and one by history itself.

"By the sun and its morning brightness"

We will start with an example of an oath that God takes by cosmic phenomena, exploring the connection between the objects of the oath and its complement. Sura 91, *The Sun* (*ash-Shams*), begins with an oath cluster that depicts a series of oppositions showing the duality and balance that exists in God's creation:

> By the sun and its morning brightness, (*ḍuḥā-hā*)[80]
> By the moon when it follows it, (*talā-hā*)
> By the day when it displays it, (*jallā-hā*)
> By the night when it veils it, (*yaghshā-hā*)

---

78 Thus, the objects of the oath play the role of "witnesses" that attest to the truth of the complement, similar, in a certain sense, to how oaths in the ancient Near East involved summoning human or non-human witnesses. 'Abd al-Ḥamīd al-Farāhī, *Im'ān fī Aqsām al-Qur'ān* (Cairo: al-Maṭba'at as-Salafiyya), 1349 AH; Mir, "The Qur'ān's Oaths."

79 Ibid., 488. See 'Ā'isha 'Abd ar-Raḥmān Bint ash-Shāṭi', *at-Tafsīr al-Bayāni li 'l-Qur'ān al-Karīm* (Cairo: Dār al-Ma'ārif, 1962).

80 Throughout this chapter, the final word of each verse has been printed so that the reader may see, on the aesthetic level, the rhyme scheme that runs throughout each sura.

By the sky and how He built it, (*banā-hā*)
By the earth and how He spread it out (*ṭaḥā-hā*) (91:1-6)

Rather than being in a state of conflict, the oppositions are in harmony because each object in the opposition (the sun/moon, night/day, sky/earth) stays within its own divinely prescribed course and does not transgress its bounds to overtake the other.

The oath cluster then terminates with the mention of the human soul:

By the soul and how He proportioned it, (*sawwā-hā*)
And then He inspired it to recognize its vice (*fujūru-hā*)
and its God-consciousness. (*taqwā-hā*) (91:7-8)

After this, the complement of the oath, which forms the main idea of this sura, is stated:

The one who has purified it has succeeded, (*zakkā-hā*)
And the one who has corrupted it has lost. (*dassā-hā*) (91:9-10)

What is the connection between the objects in the oath cluster and this statement, the complement of the oath? Like the other creations described above, the soul was formed with a certain balance or measure appropriate to it, and which it must maintain: for example, between overindulgence and extreme self-restraint, between overzealousness and negligence, between being overly strict and overly compromising, between neglecting one's own needs and taking away from others, and so on. "Vice" (*fujūr*) involves violating that balance, whereas God-consciousness (*taqwā*) involves cautiously maintaining it. The soul must choose the course prescribed for it—God-consciousness—and not transgress it; otherwise, there will be disorder and chaos.

Following this passage is an illustration of this theme in a recap of the story of the rebellion and destruction of the ancient Arabian tribe of Thamud (91:11-15). The Thamud persisted in sin despite receiving clear signs and repeated warnings from their messenger, Salih, so God destroyed them. The lesson for the Meccans was that when a people continue to cross the limits divinely prescribed for them, even after God has sent a messenger with clear signs and warnings, God destroys them in order to prevent complete disorder on the earth.

It is also interesting to note that the rhyme scheme of the initial oath (*-ā-hā*) continues to the very last verse of the sura, and that the two sections of the sura—the oath complex and the narrative of the Thamud—are equally balanced, both consisting of 71 syllables.[81]

81 Robinson, *Discovering the Qur'an*, 131.

"By the forenoon"

Sura 93, *The Forenoon* (*aḍ-Ḍuḥā*), was revealed in the early Meccan period, on an occasion when the Prophet had not received revelation for an extended period of time. This became an opportunity for his opponents to ridicule him, and he himself feared that God had withdrawn from him out of displeasure. The first five verses are as follows:

> By the forenoon (*ḍuḥā*)
> And by the night when it is still, (*sajā*)
> Your Lord has not forsaken you nor is He displeased; (*qalā*)
> The hereafter is better for you than the present; (*ūlā*)
> Soon your Lord will give to you and you will be pleased. (*tarḍā*) (93:1-5)

In the first two lines, God swears by two very opposite phases of the day. The forenoon (*aḍ-ḍuḥā*) is the period of the day in the late morning when the sun is its brightest, and is associated with a lot of activity. In direct contrast is the night, which is associated with darkness, silence, and stillness. The image of the alternation of the brightness of day and the stillness of night symbolically depicts how revelation has its occurrences and its pauses. Just as the stillness of night does not cause us to expect that the daylight will not follow it, a temporary break in the descent of revelation should not be taken as a sign of its permanent end. Similarly, just as the light and activity of the day and the darkness and stillness of the night both play necessary and complementary roles in the scheme of God's creation, both ease and hardship are necessary parts of God's plan for every human being.[82]

"By the fig and the olive"

The Qur'an has a distinctive view of human nature, which differs from the traditional Christian doctrine of original sin and from some modern theories about human nature in philosophy and psychology. It maintains that the human being is not born inherently sinful, corrupt, or broken, but in fact is born pure and upright. It even proclaims that God favored the human being above other creatures (17:70), to the point that the angels were commanded to prostrate to him out of respect when he was first created (2:34; 7:11; 17:61; etc.). Although the human being has animal instincts necessary for his survival, he was also given a spiritual inclination to worship God and a moral compass which drives him to act virtuously. He only becomes corrupted

82 Mustansir Mir, *Understanding the Islamic Scripture: A Study of Passages from the Qur'ān* (New York: Pearson Longman, 2008), 196-197.

gradually, through repeated exposure to negative influences and the accumulation of bad choices. On the other hand, those who place their faith in God and perform good works are not going against their inherent nature, but are instead acting in conformity to the moral nature with which they were created. This thesis is forcefully summarized in Sura 96, *The Fig* (*aṭ-Ṭīn*):

> We had certainly created the human being in the best mold,
> Then We reduced him to the lowest of the low,
> Except those who do believe and do righteous deeds.
> They will have a reward without end. (95:4-6)

The assertion that the human being was created with the best nature, made to do wonderful things and to surpass even the angels in virtue and merit, may seem to fly in the face of much of human history and experience. The Qur'an quotes the angels themselves as asking God, "Will you make upon [the earth] one who will spread corruption on it and shed blood, while we exalt your praise and sanctify you?" (2:30). However, the claim of this sura is prefaced with a divine oath, which gives it context and support:

> By the fig and the olive,
> And by Mount Sinai,
> And by this secure city (95:1-3)

Despite its apparent simplicity, this oath offers a profound overview of human salvation history. Each term in it alludes to a sacred locality that holds special importance in the history of God's revelation to humankind, and is associated with a prophet who exemplified what the human being was designed to achieve. We will look at each term of the oath in reverse order.

"This secure city" refers to Mecca, which God directed Abraham to found as a place for His worship and as a sanctuary for people (2:125-126; cf. 14:35ff). It is also where Abraham asked God to raise a prophet among his descendants, who would call them back to his monotheistic way (2:128). The city of Mecca—founded by Abraham as a center of monotheistic worship and restored as such by Muhammad—offers proof of the claim of this sura in the lives of these two men.

"Mount Sinai" is the location where God spoke to Moses and revealed the Torah to him, as a covenant establishing His sovereignty and right to exclusive obedience and worship among the Children of Israel.

Following both well-known Biblical imagery and the Arab custom of naming a place after its major produce, "the olive" alludes to Palestine, the Holy Land, to which Moses led the Israelites and where the prophets of

Israel preached the exclusive worship God and adherence to the precepts of Torah. It might also refer, more specifically, to Jerusalem, where David installed the Ark of the Covenant and where Solomon built the Temple. From the Qur'an's perspective, the long line of Israelite prophets after Moses culminated in Jesus, who, at the end of his ministry, preached to his disciples on the Mount of Olives, just outside the city of Jerusalem.

Commentators identify "the fig" as either referring jointly with "the olive," to Palestine, or alternatively identify it with the region of Mount Judi, where the ark of Noah rested (11:44). On the latter interpretation, it completes the list of the five most highly esteemed messengers in Islamic tradition: Noah, Abraham, Moses, Jesus, and Muhammad.

In sum, the oath points to the history of God's revelation, the prophetic role models He sent to humanity, and those who followed their examples as evidence of the lofty potential that the human being is capable of if he follows the moral and spiritual disposition with which he was created.[83]

"By the chargers, panting"

Sura 100, *The Chargers* (*al-ʿĀdiyāt*) opens with the following rider oath, an intense and attention-grabbing sequence depicting charging horses, comparable in today's terms to the trailer of an action movie:

> By the chargers, panting, (*wa-'l-ʿādiyāti ḍabḥā*)
> Then igniting sparks as they strike, (*fa-'l-mūriyāti qadḥā*)
> And then raiding at morning, (*fa-'l-mughīrāti ṣubḥā*)
> And then stirring up clouds of dust thereby, (*fa-ʿatharna bi-hi naqʿā*)
> And then penetrating into the midst collectively (100:1-5) (*fa-wasaṭna bi-hi jamʿa*)

Depicted here is a vivid and, to the Arabs, familiar scene of a raid by powerful horsemen, made all the more powerful by the rhythm and rhyme that characterize the rider oaths in Arabic. It immediately provokes the attention of the audience, especially those of the Arabian Desert, who cherished their riding horses and the thrill of battle. However, immediately before the scene reaches its climax, it is abruptly cut off to deliver a profound message, in a short passage with a distinct rhyming pattern:

> Man is truly ungrateful to His Lord, (*-ūd*)
> And to that he is a witness, (*-īd*)
> And he is, in his love of wealth, intense. (*-īd*) (100:6-8)

---

83 For more on this oath, see Mir, "The Qur'ān's Oaths."

At first sight, the interrupting passage may appear to have little to do with the preceding oath, but further reflection reveals otherwise. The oath highlights the devotion, obedience, and loyalty that the horses demonstrate to their masters, to the extent that they are willing to plunge at maximum speed into potential death to fulfill their masters' objective. No other beast displays such loyalty that it is willing to subject its strongest animal instinct, the instinct to survive, in the service of its master. The contrast between the devotion of these animals and the indifference of man towards God, who subjected his mount to him and enabled him to prosper in the first place, is a strong proof indicting man—and one to which he himself is a witness. Similarly, his inclination to attack and plunder in order to increase his material gains bears witness to the intensity of his love for wealth.

Once this point is driven home, the sura transitions to a close, returning to the scene in the original oath. However, there is an unexpected twist:

> Does he not know that when what is in the graves is overturned (*buʿthira mā fī-'l-qubūr*)
>
> And when what is in the hearts is acquired (*ḥuṣṣila mā fī-'ṣ-ṣudūr*)?—(100:9-10)

The audience is struck by the realization that the initial oath did not merely depict a raid of greedy and powerful cavalrymen on some unsuspecting people in the early morning. Rather, it also points forward to the dawn of the Day of Resurrection and Judgment, when the angels will similarly raid the graves of the unsuspecting, rushing to empty their contents and draw out the most precious treasures of the hearts—the secrets that they hold.[84] Finally, the sura draws to a conclusion:

> Indeed His Lord will be, on that Day, fully aware. (*-īr*) (100:11)

Just as the victims of an attack by powerful cavalrymen have no way to protect their valuables and treasures from the raiders, the disbeliever will be unable to keep any secrets on that Day from God and His angels. Everything will be laid out in the open, in preparation for judgment by God.

---

84 Angelika Neuwirth, "Images and Metaphors in the Introductory Sections of the Meccan Suras," in Abdul-Kader A. Shareef and G.R. Hawting (eds.), *Approaches to the Qur'ān* (London: Routledge, 1993), 6.

"By the passing time"

Sura 103, *The Passing Time* (*al-'Aṣr*), is one of the briefest suras of the Qur'an and one of the first that children and new Muslims usually learn. It also contains the last divine oath in the arranged sequence of the Qur'an. It states:

> By the passing time (*al-'aṣr*)!
> Truly man is in a state of loss (*khusr*)
> Except for those who believe, and do righteous deeds, and exhort one another to truth, and exhort one another to patience. (*ṣabr*) (103:1-3)

In the first verse, God swears an oath by "*al-'aṣr*." This word is frequently translated as "time," but it more precisely refers to time that is passing or has passed. It comes from the root *'aṣara*, "to squeeze" or "to press," which is used to describe the squeezing out of the juice (*'aṣīr*) from a fruit. The image this conveys is that time is of limited supply, and once it has been fully "squeezed out," it is no longer possible to obtain more. The word also refers to the late afternoon, when the sun is declining and the daytime is coming to a close. This oath gives the entire sura a strong sense of urgency: each and every human being is in a state of loss, and his time for fixing his situation is running out (103:2). The sura closes with a list of four conditions that one must fulfill before his time is up in order to save himself from that state of loss.

By swearing by past time, God is also invoking it as a witness to this claim. Throughout history, individuals, generations, and nations, one after the other, have spent their lifetimes striving to secure success—by finding the best career and mate, amassing wealth and luxury, seeking social status and prestige, acquiring high positions of power, and so on. But once the human being passes into the next life and Judgment, it becomes apparent that these efforts were wasted and no true success was attained. The exception is "those who believe, and do righteous deeds, and encourage one another to truth, and encourage one another to patience." Whether looked at from the perspective of a single day (reinforced by the alternative meaning of *'aṣr* as the "late afternoon"), the lifetime of an individual or generation, the rise and fall of nations, or the universe itself heading rapidly towards the final Hour, history itself attests to the tragedy and plight of humanity. From an intertextual point of view, "The word *'aṣr* serves as a reference to all those momentous events of history which the Qur'ān elsewhere narrates in detail in order to vindicate [the] moral laws" that govern the rise and fall of nations.[85]

---

85 Mir, "The Qur'ān's Oaths," 13-14.

Finally, from a literary perspective, it is striking that the very root letters that spell *'aṣr*, *'-ṣ-r*, are repeated throughout the last verse (103:3) in the same order:

> Except for those who believe, and do righteous deeds, and encourage one another to truth, and encourage one another to patience.
>
> *Illa 'lladhīna āmanū wa-'amilū 'ṣ-ṣāliḥāti wa-tawāṣaw bi-'l-ḥaqqi wa-tawāṣaw bi-'ṣ-ṣabr.*
>
> *...'..........ṣ-ṣ........................ṣ.......................*
>
> *............ṣ.........ṣ-ṣ...r.*

The effect is that the passage of time itself spells out these four conditions of salvation—or, alternatively: that they are being "squeezed" (*'aṣara*) out of the beginning oath.[86]

For further exploration:

- Mir, Mustansir. "The Qur'an Oaths: Farahi's Interpretation." *Islamic-Awareness.org*. Originally published as: "The Qur'ān's Oaths: Farāhī's Interpretation," *Islamic Studies* 29 no. 1 (1990): 5-27.
- Neuwirth, Angelika. "Images and Metaphors in the Introductory Sections of the Meccan Suras." Ed. G. R. Hawting and Abdul-Kader A. Shareef. *Approaches to the Qur'an*. London: Routledge, 1993. 3-36.
- Ibrahim, M. Zakyi. "Oaths in the Qur'ān: Bint Al-Shāṭi''s Literary Contribution," *Islamic Studies* 48 no. 4 (2009): 475-98.

86 Robinson, *Discovering the Qur'an*, 163.

CHAPTER 8

"All praise is due to God, the Lord of all peoples"

If you open a copy or translation of the Qur'an from the beginning, the very first sura you will find will be the **Fatiha** (*al-Fātiḥa*), which literally means "the Opening." Every practicing Muslim knows this sura by heart because it is the most important part of each of the five daily prayers. While the other 113 suras of the Qur'an are arranged roughly according to length, so that the suras towards the beginning of the Qur'an are the longest and the suras towards its end are the shortest, the Fatiha is the most obvious exception to this rule. It is one of the shortest suras, but it is placed at the very beginning of the Qur'an, like a preface. The Prophet Muhammad also called this sura "*umm al-kitāb*," literally, "the mother of the Scripture." In Arabic, the word *umm* or "mother" can be used metaphorically to mean the summary or essence of something. *Umm al-kitāb* therefore translates to "the summary of the Scripture" or "the essence of the Scripture," pointing to how the Fatiha concisely captures the main themes of the Qur'an. In a way, the rest of the Qur'an is simply an elaboration of the Fatiha. A basic translation of the sura goes as follows:

> In the name of God, the All-Merciful, the Ever-Merciful:[87]
> 1. All praise is due to God, the Lord of all peoples,

87 Every sura of the Qur'an begins with this formula, except for sura 9. However, there is a difference of opinion within Muslim scholarly tradition over whether it is to be counted as a verse of the suras. Most English translations of the Qur'an follow the view that it counts as the first verse of Sura 1, but not of the subsequent suras. However, we take the view that it is not a verse of the Fatiha or of the other suras, but only signals when a new sura begins, so we will be excluding it from the verse count. As a result, the way in which we number the verses of the Fatiha will differ from the numbering that appears in most English translations of the Qur'an.

2. The All-Merciful, the Ever-Merciful,
3. Owner of the Day of Recompense.
4. You alone we worship, and You alone we ask for help.
5. Guide us along the Straight Path,
6. The Path of those whom You have favored,
7. Not of those who have earned wrath, nor of the astray.

In this chapter, as a conclusion to the first half of the book, we will closely examine the first verse of this sura—"All praise is due to God, the Lord of all peoples"—considering its word choice, choice of grammar, and sentence structure.[88]

"All praise is due to God"

Transliteration: al-ḥamdu li-'llāh

The vocabulary of the first part of the verse may be roughly translated as follows, though we will explore the nuances of each word more fully below.

al-ḥamd: "praise," but also "thanks"
li-: "to," "for," "due to"
'llāh: "Allah," shortened for reasons of pronunciation

Word Choice

al-Ḥamd ("Praise")

In Arabic, the first word of this verse is *ḥamd*. (The prefix *al-* is simply an article in Arabic like the word "the". We will see the function this plays in the verse shortly.) Most often, *ḥamd* is simply translated as "praise." However, the Arabic language has two other words that also mean "praise": *madḥ* and *thanā'*. Yet, each of these words has subtle distinctions:

1. The word *madḥ* can be used for non-living beings, unlike *ḥamd*. For example, if you praise a car or a beautiful sunset, that is *madḥ* but not *ḥamd*, because *ḥamd* can only be used for personal (that is, living and rational) beings.
2. Even in the case of personal beings, *madḥ* can include praise for a quality that is only accidental, such as a person's height or eye color. On the other hand, *ḥamd* is only used when the person himself is deserving of credit.

---

88 This chapter owes to as-Sāmarrā'i, *Lamasāt Bayyāniyya*, 11-33.

3. *Madḥ* can also be given insincerely, by way of flattery. In contrast, *ḥamd* expresses sincere, heartfelt admiration.

Thanā' is similar to *madḥ*, but is more magnified. In contrast to both these words, *ḥamd* is very specific. As a result, in using the word *ḥamd*, the person reciting the Fatiha (1) acknowledges God as a living and rational being, rather than as an abstract entity or power, (2) affirms that all of God's attributes and actions are virtuous and worthy of praise, and (3) does this out of a sincere, heartfelt admiration of God. None of these meanings would be guaranteed with the words *madḥ* or *thanā'*.

The word *ḥamd* carries more meanings than just "praise", however: it also conveys thankfulness. In the Arabic language, thanks or gratitude is usually signified by the word *shukr*. The difference with *ḥamd*, however, is that *shukr* can only express appreciation for a favor that someone has personally done for *you*. If someone gives generously to the poor and the needy, but you are wealthy, you would not express *shukr* towards that person's generosity, though you should certainly praise him. In contrast, *ḥamd* can express appreciation to someone for something he has done for you, but it can also express admiration for someone even outside of how he has benefited you personally. In these ways, the use of the phrase *al-ḥamdu li-'llāh* can be compared to the way English speakers use the word "hallelujah," which in Hebrew carries the more general meaning of "praise the Lord," but is also used to show appreciation to God for a blessing that has caused one to rejoice (though Muslims use *al-ḥamdu li-'llāh* in more casual contexts as well). For the sake of concision, we have left this additional meaning of "thanks" out of our translation of the word *ḥamd*; however, the reader should still keep it in mind.

To summarize, *madḥ* and *thanā'*, two other words for "praise" in Arabic, are too broad in scope, so using either of them would not be sufficiently precise, while *shukr*, meaning "thanks," is too narrow in scope and using it would not be sufficiently comprehensive. The choice of the word *ḥamd* conveys very specific implications which would not be captured by using any of its near-synonyms.

There is still one more aspect worth noting here about the usage of the word *ḥamd* in this verse. As in other languages, most nouns in Arabic may either be definite or indefinite. A noun that is definite points to a specific, known entity: e.g., "*the* car." In Arabic, this is typically expressed by adding "*al-*" to the beginning of the noun. On the other hand, if a noun is indefinite—e.g., "*a* car"—the meaning is not restricted to any particular example of that noun. This is usually expressed in Arabic by adding an "*n*" sound to the end of the noun: *ḥamdun*.[89] An indefinite noun cannot have the "*al-*" prefix, and a definite noun cannot have the "*n*" suffix; it can only be one or the other. So the word *ḥamd* here could be used as either *ḥamdun* or *al-ḥamdu*. Both forms in Arabic may be used in a variety of situations for different purposes. In this case, the use of the definite—*al-ḥamdu*—signifies totality: *all* praise and thanks are due to God. This level of completeness would not be achieved by the use of the indefinite, *ḥamdun*.

The Word "Allah" in al-Ḥamdu li-'llāh

So far, we have seen why the specific choice of the word *ḥamd* is significant and why the form *al-ḥamd* is appropriate. Yet, we have not considered the name of the object to whom the *ḥamd* is being directed. Of course, that object is God. But there are many names for God in the Qur'an, such as "the Creator" (*al-Khāliq*), "the All-Powerful" (*al-Qādir*), and "the All-Knowing" (*al-'Alīm*). In fact, other names of God are used in the subsequent verses of the Fatiha. So why is the name "Allah" specifically used here?

Each of the different names of God in the Qur'an signifies one of His particular attributes, or in some cases several of them. For example, the name *al-Qādir* refers to God's limitless power, but it does not by itself point to His mercy or wisdom, while the name *al-'Alīm* refers to God's infinite knowledge, but not to His power or mercy. Each of these names specifies an individual quality of God. The one exception to this rule is the name "Allah," which encompasses all the different attributes that are individually conveyed by the other divine names. (As noted in the introductory chapter, the word "Allah" is a contraction of the phrase *al-Ilāh*, "the God" or "the One worthy of worship," implying that God is uniquely and divinely perfect in every respect.) Had *al-ḥamdu* been tied to His name *al-Qādir*, the praise would only be associated with His power. Similarly, had *al-ḥamdu* been tied to His name *al-'Alīm*, the praise would only be associated with His knowledge. By tying *al-ḥamdu* to the name "Allah," all of God's attributes are included in the praise without distinction. The most basic principle about understanding God is affirmed in the very

---

89 Although it does not matter for our discussion, the reader might wonder why a vowel, *u*, has been added to the end of the word *ḥamd* in "*al-ḥamdu*," and the indefinite form "*ḥamdun*." We saw in chapter 5, "Other Subtleties of Style and Grammar," that in Arabic, the vowel at the end of a noun—*u*, *a*, or *i* (e.g., *ḥamdun or al-ḥamdu, ḥamdan or al-ḥamda, ḥamdin or al-ḥamdi*)—is determined by its grammatical case, i.e., its role in the arrangement of a sentence. In general, *u* is used in the case of the subject or predicate, *a* is used in the case of an object or following certain particles (like *inna*, "indeed" or "truly"), and *i* is used following a preposition or an implied "of." These inflections are usually dropped at the end of a sentence. Once again, however, this does not matter for the purposes of this chapter.

first verse of the Fatiha, and in fact, in the first verse of the whole Qur'an: God is, by definition, perfect in every respect, worthy of the highest praise.

Grammatical Devices & Sentence Structure

al-Ḥamdu li-'llāh vs. Inna 'l-ḥamda li-'llāh

The phrase *inna 'l-ḥamda li-'llāh* occurs in certain Islamic contexts, such as in the opening of a sermon. The wording of this phrase differs from the wording found in the Fatiha because it contains the addition of the word *inna* at the beginning. This word is a stylistic device used at the beginning of a statement or clause for emphasis. It may be used to begin the statement in a forceful or attention-grabbing way, or to remove doubt. It is often left untranslated, but when written, it is roughly equivalent to "indeed," "certainly," "truly," "without doubt," or in older English, "verily."[90] The phrase *inna 'l-ḥamda li-'llāh* is therefore more powerful than just *al-ḥamdu li-'llāh*. So why is it not used here?

Although *inna* makes a statement more powerful, it should only be used in appropriate contexts. If someone asked you what you ate for breakfast, you would not reply, "Behold! I had a bowl of cereal!" or, "Without doubt! I ate a bagel with cream cheese!" (unless, perhaps, you lived in a place where those were particularly rare or exotic foods). Adding this kind of extra emphasis in a situation that does not call for it can be rhetorically awkward.

In this situation, *inna* would also take away from the pragmatic functions of the phrase. *Al-ḥamdu li-'llāh* can serve as both an objective statement about God, as well as an expression for one's own gratitude to God, the way phrases like "Thank God!" or "Hallelujah!" are used in English. On the other hand, *inna* is used only for what are known in the Arabic language as "informational sentences," sentences that can be judged true or false.[91] It cannot be used in other kinds of sentences, such as commands ("Go to sleep!"), questions ("What time is it?"), or interjections ("Excuse me!" or "Thank God!"). The omission of *inna* allows the reciter of the Fatiha not only to convey a piece of information about God, but to express his heartfelt love, appreciation, and amazement towards Him.

Different Ways to Praise God

We saw why the choice of the specific word *ḥamd* in this verse is powerful, especially in comparison to its near-synonyms. Even while using this word,

---

90 As mentioned in the previous footnote, *inna* causes the noun that follows it to end in an *a*, rather than a *u*, sound (in this case *al-ḥamda*), as an effect of lending emphasis.

91 These are known in English as declaratives.

however, there is more than one way someone can verbally express *ḥamd.* Consider the following examples:

a) "I praise and thank God" (*aḥmadu 'llāh*)
b) "We praise and thank God" (*naḥmadu 'llāh*).
c) "Praise and thank God!" (*iḥmadū 'llāh*).

Just like *al-ḥamdu li 'llāh*, each of these are phrases that a worshiper could choose to express *ḥamd* to God. What difference does it make which of these phrases is used? Why would the expression *al-ḥamdu li-'llāh* be preferable to the others ones?

To start with, all three of the above examples are verbal sentences—sentences that begin with verbs. On the other hand, *al-ḥamdu li-'llāh*—"All praise is due to God"—is a nominal sentence, a sentence that begins with a noun. In Classical Arabic, verbal sentences have the following limitations that nominal sentences do not have:

1. Verbs are bound by time. If you say "I praise God," you indicate that this is happening in the present, but not necessarily that it occurred in the past or will occur in the future. Likewise, if you say "I praised God" or "I will praise God," the act remains bound in the past or future, respectively. In contrast, the nominal sentence in Classical Arabic suggests timelessness, stability, and permanence. *Al-ḥamdu li-'llāh* suggests that God always was, is, and will be worthy of all praise.
2. Verbs are also bound to their subjects, that is, the person performing the action. On the other hand, *al-ḥamdu li-'llāh* is an objective statement that is not dependent on any specific person praising (or not praising).
3. The verbal sentence only indicates that someone is performing the act of praising, but it does not indicate whether that object is actually *deserving* of the praise. The use of this type of nominal sentence in Classical Arabic (with the particle *li-*) affirms that God is actually deserving of this praise. This meaning would not actually be conveyed in the other modes of expression.

In short, by using *al-ḥamdu li-'llāh*, the worshiper is declaring that no matter whom God is praised by, when He is praised, or whether anyone even praises Him at all, the fact is that He is deserving of praise.

al-Ḥamdu li-'llāh vs. Li-'llāhi 'l-ḥamd

Finally, let us consider the order in which the words of *al-ḥamdu li 'llāh* are arranged. An alternative ordering of these words occurs once in the Qur'an

(45:36), where the subject (*al-ḥamdu*) and the predicate (*li-'llāh*) are reversed: *li-'llāhi 'l-ḥamd* ("To God all praise is due"). This alternative phrase is also said during the Muslim holiday of Eid and during the Hajj pilgrimage. As we saw in chapter 5, "Other Subtleties of Style and Grammar," in Classical Arabic, a reversal of the normal sentence order—such as, in this case, placing the predicate or object before the subject—has at least one of four rhetorical effects. In this case, the effect is to convey exclusivity: "All praise is due *only* to God." This is even more powerful than simply saying *al-ḥamdu li-'llāh*. This again raises the question: why is the form *li-'llāhi 'l-ḥamd* not used in the Fatiha? Or, for that matter, why is it only used on a few specific occasions in Islamic devotion, and only once in the Qur'an?[92]

As with the use of *inna*, the reversal of the order of a sentence in classical Arabic is only done in special contexts. For example, Sura 45 is largely a debate against the polytheism of the Meccans. Similarly, during the Hajj, Muslims circle the Ka'ba in Mecca, which (according to Islamic tradition), although initially a symbol of monotheism, became corrupted when the Arabs transformed it into a center of idol worship. The phrase *li-'llāhi 'l-ḥamd* is appropriate in these instances because they involve contexts in which praise was devoted to others besides God. On the other hand, the beginning of the Fatiha and the many other mentions of *al-ḥamdu li-'llāh* in the Qur'an and Islamic devotion do not involve contexts that require the refutation of polytheism.

The first half of the Fatiha consists of simple but comprehensive statements about God, and the knowledge and faith the worshiper should have about Him. According to Islam, this understanding of God is in harmony with the inherent nature of human beings, which the Qur'an calls the *fiṭra* (see 30:30). Accordingly, polytheism and improper concepts of God are deviations from the pure human *fiṭra*, which affirms a basic and pure monotheism. In the Fatiha, this monotheism is expressed in a way that does not even indicate the existence of an alternative point of view because within the human *fiṭra*, there is none.

"The Lord of All Peoples"

Transliteration: rabbi 'l-'ālamīn

The individual words of this second part of the verse can be roughly translated as follows:

rabb: "Lord, Master"; etc.
al-'ālamīn: "(all) peoples"

---

92 The wording at the start of the Fatiha occurs many times in the Qur'an, including the start of suras 6, 18, 34 and 35.

Rabb ("Lord")

Besides the name "Allah," the most frequent title for God in the Qur'an is *Rabb*. The primary meaning of *rabb* is "master" or "lord." It is related to the Hebrew term "rabbi," which is commonly used to refer to a Jewish religious teacher, but literally means "my master." The word *rabb* also differs from other words in Arabic that have similar meanings—such as "owner" (*mālik*) or "one in charge" (*sayyid*)—in that it additionally includes the meanings of "caregiver" (*murabbī*), "maintainer" (*qayyim*), "manager" or "planner" (*mudabbir*), "giver of gifts" (*mun'im*), and "fixer" or "restorer" (*muṣliḥ*).[93] The use of the word *rabb,* therefore, indicates not only that God is the Lord or Master of all peoples, but that He is also their Caregiver, Planner, Maintainer, Provider, and Restorer.

al-'Ālamīn ("All peoples")

The word *al-'ālamīn* is usually translated as "the worlds," referring to all of creation: the world of human beings, the world of angels, the world of plant life, the world of the sea, the world of stars and planets—all types of existing things besides God. This translation derives from the fact that *'ālam* means "world" in this sense, while *-īn* is the plural ending. However, this translation of *al-'ālamīn* as "the worlds" is problematic. The normal plural of *'ālam* in Arabic is actually *'awālim*. When the Qur'an refers to God as the *Rabb* of all of creation, it calls Him *Rabb as-samāwāti wa-'l-arḍ*, "the Lord of the heavens and the earth"—"heavens and earth" being a phrase used for all of creation in the Semitic languages.[94] On the other hand, the plural ending *-īn* is generally used in the Arabic language for rational beings. *'Ālamīn* therefore literally means "worlds of people"—that is, "peoples" or "nations." The term *al-'ālamīn* encompasses human beings of every nation, generation, race, and social status. According to a narration from the Prophet's disciple Ibn 'Abbās (d. c. 688 CE), it also includes the beings known as jinn,[95] because these are the two species of beings granted free will; the Qur'an was sent to thinking beings, calling them to the worship of God alone. Other types of creation, by contrast, worship God by their very nature: "Whatever is in the seven heavens and the earth exalt

---

93 Ibn Manẓūr al-Anṣārī, *Lisān al-'Arab*, 2nd ed. (Beirut: Dār Ṣādir, 1993), 1:399-401. See the lecture "Beautiful Servitude" by Nouman Ali Khan on Youtube (www.youtube.com/watch?v=yJGTabeZlaY).

94 This idiom is found, for example, in the very first verse of the Hebrew Bible: "In the beginning when God created the heavens and the earth" (Gen. 1:1).

95 See the commentaries of aṭ-Ṭabarī and Ibn Kathīr on this verse. The jinn were explained in a footnote in chapter 1.

Him, and there is nothing that does not exalt Him with praise; but you do not understand their mode of exalting" (17:44).[96]

Based on the above observations it is clear that *Rabb as-samawāti wa-'l-arḍ* is more comprehensive than *Rabbi 'l-'ālamīn*, since the former includes all of creation while the latter only includes only rational beings. Why, then, is the latter used in this verse? The use of the word *rabb* subtly defines our relationship with God as that of slaves to a Master. This idea is actually the main theme of the Fatiha (and in fact the whole Qur'an), as we will see when we discuss the fourth verse,[97] which forms the center of the sura. Since the Fatiha is a discourse between human beings[98] and God, it is only right that God's relationship with humans is emphasized.

The Connection of "Praise" with "the Lord of All Peoples"

It is reasonable to say that, over the course of time, few slaves have adored their masters or cherished their relationships with them, since the "master" is usually an oppressive figure who cares little for the actual welfare of his slaves. Not only does the Fatiha identify God as the only one who truly has the right to claim slaves, making all human beings equally slaves of the same Master, but is also shapes this Master-slave relationship as radically different from its human counterpart. First, the worshiper's designation of God as his *rabb* only comes immediately after a genuine expression of adoration towards Him, "All praise (and thanks) are due to God." Second, the word *rabb* differs from other words for "Master" in Arabic (such as *sayyid* or *mālik*) in that it includes the meaning of "Caregiver," "Maintainer," and "Gift-Giver." Moreover, as we will see in the final chapter, where we continue our exploration of this sura, the very next verse highlights God's status as the Most Merciful.

---

96 Farrin, *Structure and Qur'anic Interpretation*, 3.
97 See Chapter 15.
98 Or more precisely, human beings and jinn.

PART II

Macro Literary Features

In chapters 9 through 15, we will study some of the "macro" literary features of the Qur'an, which are apparent on the level of large passages, entire suras, and in the structure of the Qur'an as a whole. In addition to a study of storytelling in the Qur'an (chaps. 9 and 10), Part II is largely concerned with the literary coherence and structure of the Qur'anic suras: how they form unified wholes and how their structure is key to their beauty and meaning. This includes a study of coherence within a sura (chap. 11), the phenomenon of ring composition in the Qur'an (chap. 12), a study of the structure and coherence of the longest sura (chap. 13), and the question of how the suras are ordered to form the scripture as a whole (chap. 14). This concludes with a study of word choice, grammatical devices, imagery, coherence, and structure in Sura 1, *The Opening* (*al-Fātiḥa*), and its placement as the very first sura of the Qur'an (chap. 15).

CHAPTER 9

Storytelling in the Qur'an I

The Qur'an presents itself both as a divine revelation continuous with those given to the Biblical prophets, and a source of moral and spiritual guidance for humanity. Given both of these roles, it should not be surprising that storytelling—especially featuring Biblical characters and themes—represents a core feature of the scripture. The stories of the Qur'an are not only rich in moral and spiritual lessons, but also in terms of literary qualities and narrative techniques. Mustansir Mir writes,

> the Qur'an possesses a rich literary repertoire of its own. Besides making a masterful use of language on the level of words and phrases, it contains figures of speech, satire, and irony; employs a variety of narrative and dramatic techniques; and presents characters that, is spite of the sparse personal detail provided about them, come across as vivid figures. For those who can read the Qur'an in Arabic, the all-pervading rhythm which, in conjunction with the sustained use of what may be called rhymed prose, creates in many surahs a spellbinding effect that is impossible to reproduce.[99]

Yet, until recently, an appreciation of the Qur'anic narratives has been held back by a number of trends among scholars and readers. First, within Muslim scholarship, theological, legal, and tradition-based approaches to the Qur'an—while certainly valuable in their own right—have overshadowed a literary approach to the scripture.[100] Second, for Western readers expecting sustained chronological narratives, the "fragmented" nature of the Qur'an's stories has presented a stumbling block. Rather than narrating a single story in full, the Qur'an tells and retells episodes of a traditional story in different

99 Mir, "Qur'an as Literature," 52.
100 Ibid., 49-52.

places. Different parts of the story may be told in different suras, a single sura may contain or allude to various stories, and the same story or episode may be told more than once. Finally, Western scholars trained in biblical and rabbinic studies have—until recently—concentrated on reducing the stories of the Qur'an to various Jewish and Christian sources, often accusing the Qur'an of "garbling," "mixing up," or "confusing" these stories, without appreciating the way they are retold and adapted in the scripture.

While an introduction to all of the features of Qur'anic storytelling would be beyond the scope of this book, in the next two chapters we will at least sample how recent scholarship has overturned some of these trends and has moved towards a greater literary appreciation of the Qur'an's stories. In this chapter, we will look at the suspenseful debate between Moses and Pharaoh, and the story of Joseph, paying special attention to dialogue and plot, respectively. In the next chapter, "Storytelling in the Qur'an II," we will explore the story of Adam, examining how the Qur'an retells a traditional story multiple times—each time with a different theme and context in mind—as well as how and why the Qur'anic story differs from that in the Bible.

Dramatic Dialogue: Moses vs. Pharaoh

The Qur'an uses dialogue effectively to bring out the intentions, emotions, and personality traits of its characters. The most common type of dialogue in the Qur'an is between prophetic messengers and their people. The messengers call on their people with a clear and consistent message: to worship only God, because it is He who created you and provides; to fear His punishment and seek His pleasure; and to repent from the immoral and oppressive practices that are rampant in each society.

The speeches of the messengers underscore their integrity, dedication, and tactfulness in communicating their message. However, time and again, their people—especially the wealthy and powerful among them—respond with stubborn denial, using diversions and insults to derail the message. The chiefs of Noah's people dismiss him and mock his followers, saying, "We see that you are only a human being like us, and it is clear to see that you are only followed by the lowliest among us" (11:27). The people of Thamud disparage their messenger Salih with: "O Salih, you were among us someone of promise before this!" (11:62). The people of Midian fail to grasp why Shu'ayb's personal religious devotion should motivate him to confront the corruption in his society, protesting, "O Shu'ayb, does your prayer tell you that we should abandon what our forefathers worshiped and refrain from doing whatever we please with our own property? Indeed you are a tolerant and sensible man!" (11:87). They likewise dismiss him saying, "We see you among us as weak. Were it not for your family, we would have stoned you. We see that you have no status or authority over us" (11:91).

The most sustained and dramatic example of this kind is the dialogue between Moses and Pharaoh in Sura 26, *The Poets* (*ash-Shu'arā*), in which Moses challenges Pharaoh's claim to divinity and demands the release of the enslaved Israelites.[101] In this dialogue, Pharaoh is distinguished for his clever rhetoric, as he tries to toy with Moses and back him into a corner. Moses has to skillfully navigate Pharaoh's ploys, while not allowing him to steer the conversation away from the message. Eventually, Moses's consistency and wit give him the upper hand.

The dialogue begins with a brief review of the end of Moses's historic conversation with God on Mount Sinai, which is told in full elsewhere in the Qur'an (20:9-48). God directs Moses, "Go to the wrongdoing nation, the nation of Pharaoh" (26:10-11). Pausing for a moment, we can imagine the fear and hesitation that must have seized Moses at this instant. Although Moses was an Israelite, he had been raised in the palace of the Pharaoh. But he fled Egypt, fearing the punishment of the Pharaoh, after the news spread that he had accidentally killed an Egyptian slave driver. Now, after many years, he is being commanded to go back and confront the very Pharaoh whose wrath he had fled.

Moses voices his concern about confronting the powerful Pharaoh and his court: "My Lord, I fear that they will call me a liar, that my chest will become tight [out of anxiety], and that my tongue will not be articulate." Besides his own self-doubt, Moses faces the threat of being indicted for murder: "And they have a shameful deed recorded against me, so I fear they will kill me." In response, God reassures Moses against these fears, and appoints his brother Aaron to accompany him as a spokesperson and fellow messenger. The message they must deliver to Pharaoh is captured in two brief sentences: "Both of you go to Pharaoh and say, 'We are messengers of the Lord of all peoples. Send with us the Children of Israel'" (vv. 16-17).

The Qur'an does not narrate Moses's journey back to Egypt, his reunion with Aaron, their entrance into the royal palace, or their demand from Pharaoh, but instead cuts straight to the Pharaoh's response. This technique of "fast forwarding" is a frequent device in Qur'anic storytelling: it passes over the parts of the story that are easily filled in by the reader—sparing needless details and giving the story a rapid pace—while zooming in on the key parts of the narrative.

---

101 This dialogue has been studied in Mustansir Mir, "Dialogue in the Qur'an," *Religion & Literature* 24:1 (1992): 12-16, on which this section is based.

Pharaoh simply ignores Moses's demand for the Israelites' freedom, as if declining to even acknowledge their existence. He instead tries to turn the tables on Moses, setting up a number of rhetorical traps:

> "Did we not raise you in our midst as a child, and did you not stay with us for many years of your life? Then you committed that act that you did—and you were ungrateful." (vv. 18-19)

Moses cannot deny that Pharaoh adopted, sheltered, and provided for his upbringing. Furthermore, Pharaoh has slipped in an allusion to Moses's crime, hinting that he could easily have him humiliated and disposed of, even though he has yet spared from doing so. And should Moses deny any of these favors, he will condemn himself as an ungrateful man.

Still, Moses refuses to be cornered. He first confronts the most serious issue, his crime of manslaughter. While he could make valid excuses, pointing out that the murder was an accident, that he had righteous intentions, and only fled for fear of being wronged by Pharaoh's judicial system, Moses already has God's guarantee that he will not be executed—and so he simply confesses his mistake. Yet he does so carefully, without exposing himself to the observers: "I did it while I was among the lost. Then I fled from you and I feared you" (v. 21). Note the past tense of "feared," suggesting that he fears the Pharaoh no longer. Moses has no need to beg for forgiveness, and so he uses his confession as an opportunity to bring the conversation back to his mission: "Then my Lord granted me wisdom and prophethood and made me a messenger." He also acknowledges Pharaoh's favor towards him, but then begins his own offensive, pointing out that this does not give Pharaoh the right to oppress the Israelites: "And is this a favor that you remind me of: that you have enslaved the Children of Israel?" (v. 22).

Once again, Pharaoh dodges Moses's question, this time scoffing at his claim to be sent from a divine authority: "And what is the 'Lord of all peoples'?" (v. 23). Moses gives no attention to Pharaoh's dismissive and sarcastic tone, but takes advantage of the chance to explain the message: "The Lord of the heavens and the earth and whatever is between them, if you should be certain." (v. 24). Pharaoh is presented with yet another challenge to his power and divinity. Disturbed by the silence of his courtiers, he turns to them, exclaiming, "Do you not hear?!" (v. 25). Moses calmly presses on, while Pharaoh—seeing that all of his tactics are failing to discourage Moses—becomes increasingly flustered:

> Moses: "Your Lord and the Lord of your forefathers." (v. 26)
> Pharaoh: "Indeed your 'messenger' who has been sent to you is mad!" (v. 27)

Moses: "The Lord of the east and the west and whatever is between them, should you all reason." (v. 28)
Pharaoh: "If you take a god other than me, I will surely imprison you!" (v. 29)

Moses's statements also appear to be precisely calculated to challenge the royal mythology of ancient Egypt. In v. 24, Moses stated that God is the Lord "of the heavens and the earth and whatever is between them." The pharaohs of this period (the New Kingdom Era) were regarded as the earthly incarnations of the supreme deity, the sun god Amon-Ra. However, Moses claimed both the sky and the earth for God. In v. 26, Moses closes in on Pharaoh, indicating that God has complete authority over him and his ancestors: "your Lord and the Lord of your forefathers." Finally, in v. 28, he states that God is the Lord "of the east and the west"—i.e., where the sun rises and sets—"and whatever is between them."

Now the ball is in Moses's court, and it is his turn to challenge Pharaoh. He offsets Pharaoh's threat to imprison him, asking, "Even if I brought you something to make the matter clear?" (v. 30). It is easy to imagine Pharaoh's skepticism: what could this man, who has lost his place in the royal palace and possesses little in the way of wealth or resources, possibly show one of history's most powerful and affluent rulers? Yet, the ambiguity and boldness of Moses's claim could only have provoked curiosity. "Then bring it," Pharaoh challenges, "if you are truthful" (v. 31).

Moses produces his two miracles, turning his staff into a live snake and making his hand glow white. Despite witnessing the clear miracles, Pharaoh dismisses the spectacles as magic and, further, accuses Moses of having dangerous political aims: "He wants to drive you out of your land with his magic!" (v. 35). Because of his protest against Pharaoh, Moses is now branded a threat to the nation's security—hardly a unique case of government propaganda.

Pharaoh calls upon the greatest magicians of the land for a public showdown against Moses. The story continues to build, and includes further snapshots of dialogue worthy of study, but this much should suffice to illustrate the depth and artfulness of dialogue as a narrative feature of the Qur'an.

Plot, Theme, and Irony in the Story of Joseph

Sura 12, *Joseph* (*Yūsuf*), is the only sura devoted entirely to a complete, chronological narrative. The narrative aspects of the story have gained attention in recent literature.[102] Mustansir Mir has highlighted the central role of irony—the reversal of expectations, either of the characters of the

102 For a bibliography, see Robinson, *Discovering the Qur'an*, 312, n. 13.

story or its audience—in the development of the plots and themes of the story.[103] We will look at the story of Joseph with special attention to how the Qur'an employs such irony, bringing out some of the particular instances in bold and then reflecting on its role in the story as a whole.

The story of Joseph opens immediately with a dialogue between the young Joseph and his father Jacob, which foreshadows some of the key events of the story. Joseph describes to his father a dream he experienced: "O my father, I saw eleven stars and the sun and the moon; I saw them prostrating to me" (v. 4). Jacob recognizes the dream as a sign that Joseph will be divinely favored with prophethood, just like Jacob himself, his father Isaac, and his grandfather Abraham, but warns Joseph not to tell his brothers, for fear that they may plot against him out of envy:

> He said, "My son, tell your brothers nothing of this dream, or they may plot to harm you—Satan is man's sworn enemy. This is about how your Lord will choose you, teach you to interpret dreams, and perfect His blessing on you and the House of Jacob, just as He perfected it earlier on your forefathers Abraham and Isaac: your Lord is Knowing and Wise." (vv. 5-6)

Already, the stage is set for both the conflicts of the story and its irony: we are alerted that Joseph's brothers will cause some sort of trouble, but that in the end God's plan will work out for Joseph. At the same time, the information we are given is vague enough to keep us wondering what Joseph's brothers will do, what exactly his dream signifies, and how it will eventually be fulfilled.

Despite Jacob's precautions, his older sons take notice of his special fondness for Joseph, and conspire to get rid of him:

> They said, "Joseph and his brother [Benjamin][104] are more dear to our father than us, even though we are a strong clan (*uṣba*). Our father is in clear error." [One of them said,] "Kill Joseph or banish him to another land. Your father's attention will be all yours, and after that you will be a righteous people." One of them said, "Do not kill Joseph, but cast him into the bottom of a well where some caravan will pick him up." (vv. 8-10)

Yet, as we will see, the brothers' scheme will accomplish the very opposite of what they had planned, as Jacob will only become more preoccupied by the thought of Joseph and further emotionally distanced from them.

---

103 Mustansir Mir, "Irony in the Qur'ān: A Study of the Story of Joseph," *Literary Structures of Religious Meaning in the Qur'ān* (Richmond, Surrey: Routledge, 2000), 173-87.

104 Joseph and Benjamin are the two youngest of Jacob's twelve sons and are full brothers, sharing the same mother, Rachel.

The brothers approach their father Jacob, claiming a desire to take Joseph out with them to have fun. Jacob is hesitant: "The thought of you taking him away with you worries me: I am afraid a wolf may eat him when you are not paying attention" (v. 13). Nonetheless, the brothers manage to convince Jacob, assuring him that they will keep Joseph under their care, saying, "If a wolf should eat him while we are a strong clan (*uṣba*), then truly we would be losers" (v. 14). Their response is highly ironic, because it will be the very chain of events that their scheme sets off that will reduce them to the status of losers.[105]

In another ironic twist, the very fear Jacob confessed is what gives the brothers the idea for staging Joseph's death. After casting their younger brother into a well, they return to Jacob from their outing with the following story:

> They said, "Our father, we went off racing one another, leaving Joseph behind with our things, and a wolf ate him. But you would not believe us, even if we were telling the truth!" And they showed him [Joseph's] shirt, stained with deceiving blood. (vv. 17-18)

The brothers' absentminded slip, "You would not believe us, *even if we were telling the truth*," is also rich with irony: for indeed, later in the story, they will come to Jacob with a true confession, but he will not believe them.

While Jacob distrusts his sons' claim, he realizes that there will be no way for him to get Joseph back, so he resigns himself to endure his loss with patience. Meanwhile, God inspires Joseph in the well, informing him of a time when he will encounter his brothers again, they will fail to recognize him, and he will surprise them by reminding them of their scheme against him. Some caravan travelers then come along and, just as one of the brothers had predicted (perhaps not seriously), they discover Joseph and pick him up. Because they do not value him highly, the travelers sell him off as a slave "for a reduced price" (v. 20). The travelers' indifference towards Joseph provides another instance of irony, since they are completely oblivious of the status he is destined to attain—both spiritually and politically. Moreover, it contrasts with the intense interest (welcome or unwelcome) shown to Joseph by virtually every other character in the narrative.

The events of the middle part of the story will be briefly summarized, and we will focus in on the story's climax and resolution. Joseph is acquired in Egypt by a powerful official, whom the Qur'an simply calls *al-ʿazīz*

---

105 Ibid., 180.

("minister," "governor," or "official"), but whom the Bible names as Potiphar. Each of the subsequent incidents of the story involves an ironic twist:

- While the caravan traders were completely indifferent towards Joseph, Potiphar's wife becomes utterly obsessed with him.
- Potiphar's wife attempts to seduce Joseph, but when he refuses her advances, she schemes to have him imprisoned. Although she is the guilty one, and her guilt is even exposed, it is nonetheless Joseph who is thrown into prison (vv. 23-35).
- While in prison, Joseph interprets the dreams of two of his prison-mates, informing one of them that he will be executed and the other that he will be released and restored to his position as the king's cupbearer. Joseph secures a promise from the latter that, upon his release, he will tell the king of Joseph's innocence. When he is released, however, the cupbearer forgets his promise, and Joseph remains in prison. Only several years later, when the king requests the interpretation of a dream, does the royal cupbearer remember Joseph (vv. 36-45).

Yet, an even more significant irony runs throughout this course of events, because it is precisely this string of apparent misfortunes that leads to Joseph's interpretation of the king's dream—the turning point of the story, which proves to have far-reaching significance. After several years, the cupbearer returns to Joseph with the king's request for the interpretation of his dream. Joseph explains that there will be seven years of harvest, followed by seven years of famine. He instructs that over the first seven years, the king's administration should mark out a portion of the harvest for the people to live on for the following seven (vv. 46-49). Grateful, the king orders Joseph's release, but Joseph first has his innocence proven, and Potiphar's wife confesses her guilt (vv. 50-53). The king then appoints Joseph to a high office with control over the storehouses of Egypt (vv. 54-57). Thus, in another key irony of the story, while Joseph entered prison as a slave, he exits it as one of the highest-ranking officials of the Egyptian government.

After seven years, a famine strikes, just as Joseph predicted. Canaan[106] is also affected, and the older brothers of Joseph travel to Egypt in search of food. They go before the minister of the storehouses, failing to recognize—even when they see him—that he is their brother. Surprisingly, Joseph decides for the time to maintain the secret of his identity, which

---

106 Canaan is the Biblical name for ancient Palestine, the land God promised to Abraham and his descendants, also known in the Bible as "the land of Israel." It is northeast of Egypt, across the Sinai Peninsula.

allows him to toy with them. Their resulting interactions (v. 58 onwards) are full of dramatic irony. Later, the brothers even make a demeaning comment about their younger brother Joseph to his face, not knowing that he is the one they are addressing (v. 77).

Hoping to get an additional camel-load of food, the brothers tell Joseph of their younger brother, Benjamin, whom Jacob has kept in Canaan. Joseph gives them the extra grain, but says that when they come the following year, they must bring Benjamin to prove their truthfulness, or else they will be denied further supplies. When the brothers return to Jacob, they tell him about the condition that Joseph gave them, but emphasize that if they fulfill it, they will obtain "an easy measure" (v. 65). Once again, their expectations are completely wrong: it will prove anything but easy.[107] Jacob, understandably, is distrustful of them, and only concedes after forcing them to take a solemn oath.

The brothers return to Joseph the following year with Benjamin. Joseph shares his identity with Benjamin, but maintains the secret from the other brothers. He provides them the grain and sends them all back, but not before—under God's direction (v. 76)—slipping one of the king's golden utensils into Benjamin's bag. As they set out to leave, an officer stops the brothers and finds the king's utensil in Benjamin's bag. The brothers swear, "we have not been thieves" (v. 73), and are brought before Joseph, unaware that the "theft" they are truly being held responsible before is the separation of Joseph from his father (cf. v. 77).[108] In what is now a sincere effort to prevent a similar thing from happening to Benjamin, the brothers volunteer to have one of them imprisoned in Benjamin's place. Joseph refuses; their offer is, or rather seems to be, a failure. They return to Jacob in grief and explain the story to him…

> "…and we are indeed speaking the truth." [Jacob] said, "Rather, your souls have enticed you. So beautiful patience. Perhaps God will bring them to me all together. Indeed, it is He who is the Knowing, the Wise." And he turned away from them and said, "Oh, my sorrow over Joseph!" and his eyes turned blind out of grief. They said, "By God, you will not stop remembering Joseph until you become gravely ill or die!" (vv. 82-85)

Here, the irony of the story has reached its climax:

- First, while the brothers had originally sought to rid of Joseph so that "the attention" (literally "face," *wajh*) of their father would be exclusively

107 Ibid., 181.
108 Ibid.

theirs (v. 9), it is now clear that it has only increased Jacob's longing for Joseph and further turned him away from them.[109] As a matter of fact, Jacob is now unable to even look at them.[110]

- Second, when the brothers had told Jacob their false story about Joseph being eaten by a wolf, they absentmindedly said, "You would not believe us, even if we speaking the truth" (v. 17). Now, when reporting to Jacob what had happened to Benjamin, they are actually speaking the truth, but he does not believe them.[111] Moreover, while the brothers had earlier succeeded in casting away their younger brother Joseph, in this case they have made the sincerest attempt to protect their youngest brother, Benjamin, but have failed. These ironic reversals display significant character development on part of the brothers, who now show a degree of integrity and loyalty that contrasts dramatically with their previous behavior.
- Finally, as Mir remarks, "In the former case, they consider[ed] themselves to be the masters of Joseph's fate—and [were] mistaken about it; in the latter, they are like pawns in the hands of Joseph—and are unaware of it."[112]

Jacob sends the brothers back to Egypt, where they plead desperately before Joseph. Joseph reminds them of how they had mistreated their two younger brothers, referring to himself and Benjamin. They suddenly come to realize that the minister they are pleading to is Joseph himself.

> They said, "Are you indeed Joseph?" He said, "I am Joseph and this is my brother. God has truly been gracious to us. Whoever is conscious of God and is patient—God does not let the reward of the good-doers go to waste." They said, "By God, certainly God has preferred you over us, and we have been sinners." He said, "There will be no blame on you this day. May God forgive you. He is the most merciful of the merciful. Take this, my shirt, and cast it over my father's face. He will come seeing. And bring your family all together." (vv. 90-93)

The shirt of Joseph was, towards the beginning of the story, presented to Jacob as a proof of Joseph's death, and embodied their loss and separation. But now, it plays exactly the opposite role, as a symbol of restoration and reunion.

---

109 Ibid., 178.
110 Ibid., 180.
111 Ibid., 180-181.
112 Ibid., 187.

The entire House of Jacob migrates to Egypt and is reunited with Joseph. Joseph's parents and eleven brothers bow down to him, and he exclaims to Jacob, "My father, this is the explanation of my dream from before!" (v. 100). Joseph then remembers God's blessings and realizes the wisdom in all the trials that happened to him.

We have drawn attention to particular layers of irony that surface as the plot of the story of Joseph unfolds, but now it is appropriate to reflect on the larger role of irony in the story. The entire plot is filled with irony: the very chain of events that appears at almost every step to spell misfortune—the brothers' scheme, Joseph being sold as a slave in a foreign land, the attempted seduction by Potiphar's wife, Joseph's imprisonment, and the cupbearer's failure to remember Joseph until the king's dream years later—is what actually leads to the Joseph's appointment as a high-ranking official, his ability to provide his family a haven in Egypt during the famine, and the fulfillment of the prophetic dream he had as a boy. It is the irony that brings out the theme of the story. To quote Mir:

> The essential irony of *Joseph* may be summed up in the statement that evil intended by human beings is turned into good by God. The very attempt of the brothers to consign Joseph to oblivion becomes a means of raising him to the pinnacle of fame and power. And those who conspire to dispose of Joseph are, in the end, thrown at his mercy.[113]

In close connection with this is another theme, that "God does not abandon those who resolutely place their trust in Him" (cf. vv. 67, 90).[114] These themes fit within a larger theological principle, which is stated by v. 21: "God is in complete control of His affairs, but most people do not know." As Mir again observes,

> That God is dominant and always fulfills His purposes is a theme that is not peculiar to *Joseph* but is expressed in many other places in the Qur'ān. What is peculiar to *Joseph* is the way in which the theme is brought home—through a sustained use of irony.[115]

These lessons would have had obvious relevance to the Muslims of the late Meccan period, who were suffering persecution from their own tribe, which showed no obvious signs of resolution. The story of Joseph signaled a divine promise of hope. We conclude with Mir's words:

---

113 Ibid., 176.
114 Ibid., 177.
115 Ibid., 176-177.

Muḥammad is identified with Joseph, and the tribe of Quraysh, to which Muḥammad belonged and which had turned hostile to him, with Joseph's brothers. In addition, the story predicts that just as Joseph finally triumphed over the obstacles put in his way by his brothers, so Muḥammad will eventually emerge a victor in his struggle against the Quraysh. When, in 630, Muḥammad conquered Mecca and the Quraysh anxiously waited for the verdict on their fate, Muḥammad addressed them, asking them how they expected him to treat his former enemies. Their plea for mercy was made in the form of praise: "You are a noble brother and the son of a noble brothers." Muḥammad issued a general amnesty, saying: *lā tathrība 'alaykumu 'l-yawm*, "No blame rests on you today." These words were taken from v. 92 of the twelfth sūra of the Qur'ān—*Joseph*. The story had worked itself out in history. And so had the irony.[116]

For further exploration:

For recorded talks by Nouman Ali Khan focused on bringing out the narrative aspects of the Qur'an's stories for audiences of all ages, see the "Story Night" series on Bayyinah TV (www.bayyinah.tv).

116 Ibid., 184.

CHAPTER 10

Storytelling in the Qur'an II

Retelling of a Story: The Story of Adam

Each sura of the Qur'an contains a unique combination of themes, which, as we will see in upcoming chapters, are subtly woven together in the sura to create a coherent and well-ordered discourse. As we saw in the previous chapter with the story of Joseph in Sura 12, *Joseph* (*Yūsuf*), the themes of a sura tend to reflect its historical context, because each sura addresses a distinct combination of problems, depending on where and when the sura was revealed. The Qur'an frequently narrates stories—usually to some extent familiar to members of its audience from Arab, Jewish, or Christian tradition—as a way of illustrating the themes and addressing the problems a given sura is concerned with.

In some cases, the Qur'an narrates different stories from the life of a prophet—such as Abraham or Moses—in different suras, in each case using a story relevant to the themes and purposes of a given sura. For example, Sura 6, *The Cattle* (*al-An'ām*), is largely an attack on polytheism and idolatry. Verses 74-82 narrate a story from the life of Abraham in which he argues against the divinity of the heavenly bodies that his people took as gods, concluding that worship should only be directed to a transcendent and always-present Creator. The story is used effectively to refute the idolatry of the Quraysh, both on rational and historical grounds, since the Quraysh also worshiped celestial deities and, furthermore, looked back to Abraham as their ancestor, boasting themselves the heirs of his legacy as the rightful custodians of the Ka'ba. Another Meccan sura, Sura 21, *The Prophets* (*al-Anbiyā'*), foreshadows the defeat of idolatry in Mecca (see 21:18, 43-44, 105). Verses 51-67 narrate a story in which Abraham demolishes the idols of the city temple as a sign foreshadowing the destruction of the idols at the

Ka'ba—an event that happened many years later, in the Conquest of Mecca.[117] Both of these stories about Abraham—which, although absent from the Biblical text, were widely celebrated in Jewish tradition—are used fittingly to address the concerns of their respective suras.

In other cases, however, the *same* essential story may be narrated in multiple suras, though each time retold differently to bring out the themes and lessons of a particular sura. In this chapter, we will consider some examples of this aspect of storytelling in the Qur'an with respect to the story of Adam, which is narrated a total of seven times in the scripture. We will look at three of these examples—2:30-39, 7:11-25, and 20:115-124—exploring how the story is retold each time in a way that is relevant to the themes and historical context of each respective sura. In the course of this chapter, we will also have the opportunity to see how the Qur'an, rather than simply reproducing the Biblical story of Adam and Eve, reshapes it to express its own distinctive message and worldview.

"Whoever follows My guidance..."

We will begin with the story of Adam found in Sura 2, *The Cow*, which mostly dates to the first two years of the Medinan period. The version of the story of Adam found in this sura is the last to have been revealed, but we will begin with it because it is the most comprehensive version and the first that the reader will encounter when reading the Qur'an in its arranged sequence. We will first look at the story by itself, and then examine the role it plays in the context of *The Cow*.

The story begins with God announcing to the angels that He will create on the earth a "*khalīfa*," that is, a representative appointed to act on behalf of God and given certain powers. Although this carries with it the responsibility to act according to God's moral will, it also implies that this new creation, the human being, will have a certain degree of freedom of choice.[118] The angels, aware that such freedom entails the ability to carry out great evils, are puzzled as to why God would create such a being:

> When your Lord said to the angels, "I will place on the earth a vicegerent," they said, "Will you place on it someone who will cause corruption and shed blood, while we celebrate your praise and sanctify you?" (2:30)

Readers familiar with the story of Adam and Eve in the Bible (Genesis 1-3) may be surprised by this element of the Qur'anic story, as it is absent from the

117 Mir, "The Qur'an as Literature," 59-60.
118 Mustansir Mir, *Understanding the Islamic Scripture*, 21.

Biblical account. It does, however, have a parallel in Jewish sources. The Babylonian Talmud states that when God wished to create man, He created a group of angels and asked their opinion, saying, "Is it your desire that we make a man in our image?" When the angels objected, God destroyed them with fire. A second group of angels offered the same reply and thus met the same fate. Finally, a third group of angels expressed approval, and God went on to create man.[119]

Notwithstanding, the Qur'anic version of this story is not a simple reproduction of its Jewish counterpart, but rather differs from it in significant ways. In the Qur'anic passage, God does not seek the approval of the angels, but rather carries out His own divine plan. More significantly still, He does not destroy them, but, anticipating their question, uses it to reveal a deeper wisdom:

> He said, "Indeed I know what you do not know." He taught Adam the names, all of them, and then He presented them to the angels and said, "Tell me the names of these ones if you are truthful." They said, "Exalted are you! We have no knowledge except what You have taught us. Truly it is you who are the Knowing, the Wise."
>
> He said, "Adam, tell them their names." When he told them their names, He said, "Did I not tell you that I know what is hidden in the heavens and the earth, and that I know what you manifest and what you conceal?" (2:30-33)

God responds to the angels' question not by providing a verbal explanation, but instead by giving a practical demonstration of the new creature's potential. He teaches Adam "the names, all of them," which many commentators interpret to mean the names of all things. The Arabic word generally translated as "names" (in accordance with the Biblical story, cf. Gen. 2:20) can also mean "qualities." On this view, what Adam demonstrates is the human being's distinctive capacity for language, and furthermore, his vast potential for knowledge and for learning the nature of things.

Yet, the word choice in the Arabic suggests something further. When the Qur'anic passage states that God "presented *them* (*araḍa-hum*) to the angels"; that He commanded the angels, "Tell me the names/qualities of *these ones* (*al-asmā'i hā'ulā'i*), if you are truthful"; and that He said, "Adam, tell them *their* names/qualities (*asmā'i-him*)," the Arabic pronouns used are *personal* pronouns, used specifically for people. This suggests that what God is displaying to the angels is in fact the human race—Adam's future descendants. This is supported by 7:172-173, which states that God extracted all of Adam's descendants from one another before they came into this world, and

119 Sanhedrin 38b, cited in Gabriel Said Reynolds, *The Qur'ān in Its Biblical Subtext* (London: Routledge, 2010), 47.

required them to testify to His Lordship, thereby leaving in the subconscious of every person a natural recognition and inclination towards God:

> When your Lord took out the offspring from the loins of the Children of Adam and made them bear witness about themselves, He said, "Am I not your Lord?" and they replied, "Yes, we bear witness." This was so that you would not say on the Day of Resurrection, "We were unaware of this," or, "It was our forefathers who, before us, ascribed partners to God, and we are only the descendants who came after them: will you destroy us because of falsehoods they invented?"[120]

This interpretation suggests that when God says to the angels, "Tell me the names/qualities of these ones," He is referring to a select group of Adam's virtuous descendants. It follows that what the angels had lacked knowledge of, and what Adam then reveals to them, is the identities and traits of Adam's virtuous descendants, who would faithfully carry out the role of God's representative that has been entrusted to them. God's response to the angels, "I know what you manifest and what you conceal," suggests that while the angels' question highlighted the atrocities that some human beings would carry out, it failed to acknowledge the great virtue that others would be able to attain.

Now that the angels have witnessed a glimpse of man's potential, they acknowledge his special status and prostrate to him in honor. However, Iblīs, a jinn who was among the company of the angels (18:50), refuses God's command:

> When your Lord said to the angels, "Bow down before Adam," they all bowed—but not Iblīs. He rebelled and was arrogant, and was one of the disbelievers. (2:31-34)

Elsewhere, the Qur'an quotes Iblīs justifying his refusal to prostrate to Adam on the basis that Adam was created from clay while he was created from fire (7:12; 38:76). This indicates that it was Iblīs's arrogance that led him to deny God's command, and to thereby expose himself as a disbeliever. Thereafter, Iblīs pledges to lead mankind astray (4:119; 15:39; 17:62; 38:82), thus becoming the Devil or Satan (*ash-Shayṭān*). In another example of the Qur'an's subtlety of word choice, the scripture consistently refers to Satan as "Iblīs" when referring to His rebellion against God, and "*Shayṭān*" (Satan) when describing his attempts to mislead human beings.[121]

---

120 The story of Adam and his descendants prior to their existence on earth finds further elaboration in the hadiths.

121 Reynolds, 38. Interestingly, this matches the original meaning of the word *sāṭan* in Hebrew: "adversary," from the verb "to plot against".

The episode of the angels' prostration to Adam, and Satan's refusal, is also absent from the Biblical account, but it is found in later Jewish and especially Christian interpretations of the story. While some of these sources say that the angels were commanded to "worship" Adam, however, the Qur'an avoids this impression, which would conflict with its emphasis on strict monotheism. It instead simply says that the angels were commanded to "prostrate" to Adam. Elsewhere in the Qur'an, when Joseph's family prostrates to him (12:4, 100), prostration occurs simply as a gesture of humility and respect.

The Qur'anic story continues:

> We said, "Adam, live you and your wife in the Garden. Both of you eat freely there as you will, but do not approach this Tree, lest you become wrongdoers." But Satan made them slip and removed them from the state they were in. We said, "Go down, enemies to each other! On the earth you will have a place to stay and livelihood for a time." (2:35-36)

Now, both Satan and Adam have sinned and fallen from their places in the heavenly Garden. Yet, there is a crucial difference between the two. While Satan's sin was out of an attitude of rebellion, arrogance, and denial of God's command, Adam's sin was no more than a mistake. Adam admits his wrong and strives for divine forgiveness, performing the first act of sincere repentance, and displaying profound spiritual growth:

> [Adam and Eve] said, "Our Lord, we have wronged ourselves. If you do not forgive us and have mercy on us, we will surely be among the losers." (7:23)

> Then Adam acquired some words from his Lord and He accepted his repentance: He is the Oft-Returning, the Merciful. (2:37)

The narrative continues:

> We said, "Go down, altogether! But if guidance comes to you from Me, then whoever follows My guidance, there will be no fear on them nor will they grieve. But those who disbelieve and deny Our signs shall be the companions of the Fire, and they will remain in it." (2:38-39)

Although Adam and Eve are still required to struggle and live on the earth, we recall that they were meant to be there all along: "I will place on the earth a vicegerent" (2:30). Earthly life, with its accompanying trials and with the freedom and temptation to choose evil over good, becomes the stage for human beings to develop their moral potential. Being a "vicegerent" of God means carrying out His moral will and exemplifying His attributes—such as knowledge (2:32), wisdom (2:32), mercy (2:37), and forgiveness (2:37)—in ways that other creatures are incapable. The story concludes with the promise that those who do so, following God's guidance, will return to their home in the heavenly Garden, where they will live in eternal peace and satisfaction. But those who imitate Satan's behavior, insisting on rebellion and denial, will have to meet the consequences of their actions.

Now we may look into the role of this narration of the story of Adam in the context of *The Cow*. The main theme of this sura is the establishment of a new faith community on the legacy of Abraham, based on consistent faith in all of God's messages, the sources of divine guidance.[122] The story of Adam appears in the sura's first section (2:1-39), which discusses the contrast between the attitudes and behavior of believers and disbelievers. Here, the story of Adam is retold in a way that especially brings out these themes.

In connection with the historical situation of the early Medinan period, the angels' doubts over the status of Adam as a representative reflect the hesitation of some of the Qur'an's audience concerning Muhammad's status as a prophet. Among them were people of sincerity and even God-consciousness, but who needed to learn more about the Qur'an and Muhammad before coming to certainty. The Qur'anic story suggests that once such people are given that knowledge and the truth becomes clear to them, they prove willing to submit to God in faith, just as the angels accepted Adam's status wholeheartedly once their doubts were answered: "They said, 'Exalted are you! We have no knowledge except what You have taught us. Truly you are the Knowing, the Wise'" (2:32).

On the other hand, despite God's assurance, Satan refused to acknowledge Adam's status out of arrogance, thereby exemplifying the attitude of the disbelievers whom the Qur'an repeatedly condemns: "they prostrated—but not Iblīs. He refused and was arrogant, and he was one of the disbelievers" (2:34). In the same way, the disbelievers and hypocrites of Medina, who at the highest levels consisted of formal tribal leaders, disbelieved out of their grudgingness to accept Muhammad's status as a higher source of authority. Moreover, it appears that one of the reasons the Jewish leadership in Medina rejected the Prophet and his community was because of their Gentile, or particularly Arab, origin (cf. 7:157-158; 62:2). This mirrors the fact that Iblīs disbelieved and rejected Adam because he felt he was of superior origin. The reciters of this passage may have recalled Satan's argument from earlier revelations: "He said, 'I am better than him. You created me from fire and created him from clay'" (7:12; 38:76). Elsewhere, Sura 2 indicates that the Jews of Medina disbelieved out of envy that God would choose Muhammad

---

122 See chapter 13, "The Coherence and Structure of Sura 2, *The Cow*."

and his community (2:90, 109), no longer uniquely privileging them, just as Iblīs disbelieved out of envy towards Adam. Finally, Satan's determination to undermine Adam and his wife parallels the determination of the disbelievers and hypocrites of Medina to undermine the Prophet and his followers.

The story of Adam in Sura 2 therefore depicts the situations of three kinds of people during the early part of the Medinan period: those who exhibit the qualities of faith, those who are willing to do so once they attain sufficient knowledge, and those who persist in disbelief out of arrogance and become determined to undermine the believing community.[123]

"We did not find him steadfast"

Sura 20, *Ṭā Ḥā*, a Middle Meccan sura, contains the first narration of the story of Adam to have been revealed in the Qur'an (vv. 115-123). The story is prefaced with a brief statement about the Qur'an's revelation and the following advice to the Prophet:

> Do not hasten (*ta'JaL*) the recitation before (*min qabl*) its revelation to you is completed. But do say, "My Lord, increase me in knowledge." (20:114)

The story of Adam is then narrated to the Prophet and his followers as a caution against hastiness:

> We had made a covenant with Adam from before (*min qabl*), but he forgot and We did not find him steadfast. When We said to the angels, "Prostrate to Adam," and then they prostrated—but not Iblīs (Satan): he refused. Then We said, "O Adam, truly this is an enemy to you and your wife, so do not allow him to remove you both from the Garden and make you suffer. It is for you not to go hungry in it or feel naked, and you will not be thirsty in it or suffer the heat of the sun."
>
> But Satan whispered to him, "O Adam, shall I show you the Tree of Immortality and of kingdom that never fades?" Then they both ate from it, and their nakedness became exposed to them, and they began to cover themselves with leaves from the Garden. Adam disobeyed his Lord and was led astray. (20:115-121)

The story begins with the mention of "a covenant" that God made with Adam, but states that Adam forgot and was not steadfast. What this covenant

123 Mustansir Mir, "Some Aspects of Narration in the Qur'an," in *Sacred Tropes: Tanakh, New Testament, and Qur'an as Literature and Culture*, ed. Roberta Sterman Sabbath (Leiden: Brill, 2009), 98-99.

was is then explained. While in the Garden, Adam and Eve were honored with a high status, and could enjoy being freely fed, clothed, and protected against harmful weather. In a moment of impulse and temptation, however, they "forgot" (20:115) the only condition on their end, which was not to obey Satan by eating from the forbidden Tree. Because they violated this condition, they became stripped of their heavenly garments and were removed from their place in the Garden. Although they became bound to a life of hardship on the earth, the story does not end on a note of despair, for it concludes:

> Then [Adam's] Lord chose him, turned to him in forgiveness, and guided him. He said, "...When there comes to you guidance from Me, then whoever follows My guidance will not go astray or fall into misery." (20:122-123).

Should a person fall into wrongdoing, the door of repentance and divine forgiveness always remains open.

This story is connected to the immediately preceding instruction to the Prophet by the shared phrase "(from) before" (*min qabl*) (20:114 and 115). This phrase draws a parallel between the Prophet's temptation to hasten the revelation of the Qur'an beyond what God has already determined, and Adam's temptation to secure the immediate gains he thought he would acquire by eating from the forbidden Tree. In essence, the story serves to caution: be steadfast and do not fall for the temptation to be hasty, lest you fall into the same type of error that Adam did before.

It is worth noting that the same lesson is also stressed in an earlier part of the sura, which narrates that Moses ascended Mount Sinai before the time God had appointed for him. God says to him, "What made you hasten (*a'JaLa-ka*) from your people, O Moses?" (20:83). Moses replies, "They are following in my footsteps. I hastened (*'aJiLtu*) to you, my Lord, so that you may be pleased" (20:84). Although Moses's intention was noble, God informs him that, in his absence, his people have taken to the worship of a Golden Calf (20:85). These stories encouraged the Muslims during the Meccan period to be steadfast in the face of their adversity and persecution, with the assurance that their patience will bring about the best outcome.[124]

"Their nakedness became exposed to them"

The story of Adam is told again in Sura 7, *The Heights* (*al-A'rāf*), verses 11-25, revealed at the end of the Meccan period. The first ten verses of the sura introduce some of the themes which the story then fleshes out. This

---

124 Ibid., 101-102.

introduction urges the audience to follow what their Lord has revealed to them and not to take up spiritual allies (*awliyāʾ*) apart from Him (7:3), warning of the destruction that comes upon those who do so in this world and the next (7:4-9). The warning against taking up allies apart from God is key, because the following version of the story of Adam will emphasize that although many people follow Satan's whispers, he is only an enemy to them. The prologue ends with God reminding the Quraysh of Mecca of His favors: "We have established you on the earth (*arḍ*) and gave you means of livelihood. Little are you grateful (*taSHKuRūn*)."

The story of Adam is then retold to express these themes. God's address to humanity, and especially to the Quraysh, continues,

> We created you, We gave you shape, and then We said to the angels, "Bow down to Adam." (7:10)

The shift from the plural "you" to "Adam" puts the audience in the place of Adam in the story. The narrative goes on to state,

> So they prostrated—but not Iblīs: he refused.

On one level, Satan's antagonism towards humankind is established and made clear. On another level, the Quraysh's refusal to believe in and obey the revelations is indirectly compared to Satan's attitude and associated with his legacy.

This version of the story then concentrates on Satan's vow to mislead mankind:

> Iblīs said, "Give me respite until the Day people are raised from the dead," and God replied, "You have respite." And then Iblīs said, "Because You have put me in the wrong, I will lie in wait for them all on Your straight path: I will come at them—from their front and their back, from their right and their left—and You will not find most of them grateful (*SHāKiRīn*)." God said, "Get out! You are disgraced and banished! I swear I shall fill Hell with you and all who follow you!" (7:15-18)

Satan's promise to prevent most of mankind from being grateful (*SHāKiRīn*) recalls the charge against the Quraysh at the end of the first set of ayas, "Little are you grateful (*taSHKuRūn*)." It is therefore implied that, at least in the case of the Quraysh, Satan has succeeded in his vow.

The story then goes on to describe in detail *how* Satan managed to lead the first human couple into error:

> [God said:] "But you and your wife, Adam, live in the Garden. Both of you eat whatever you like, but do not go near this Tree or you will become wrongdoers."
>
> Satan whispered to them so as to expose their nakedness, which had been hidden from them: he said, "Your Lord only forbade you this Tree to prevent you becoming angels or immortals," and he swore to them, "I am giving you sincere advice." He lured them with lies. Their nakedness became exposed to them when they ate from the Tree, and they began to put together leaves from the Garden to cover themselves.
>
> Their Lord called to them, "Did I not forbid you to approach that Tree? Did I not warn you that Satan was your sworn enemy?...Go down all together, enemies to one another. On the earth (*arḍ*) you will have a place of settlement and a provision for a time." (7:19-24)

Satan posed as a well-wishing advisor to Adam and Eve, but in reality only sought to demean them, disrobing them of their heavenly garments. While this element of the story existed in the earlier version (20:115-123), here it is given prominence by a subsequent address cautioning humanity from allowing Satan to lure them into exposing their nakedness shamelessly:

> Children of Adam, We have given you garments to cover your nakedness and as adornment for you; the garment of God-consciousness is the best of all garments—this is one of God's signs, so that people may take heed.
>
> Children of Adam, do not let Satan seduce you, as he did your parents, causing them to leave the Garden, stripping them of their garments to expose their nakedness to them. He and his forces can see you from where you cannot see them: We have made the devils allies (*awliyā*) to those who do not believe. (7:26-27)

The following aya sheds light on the historical relevance of this theme to the situation in Mecca. The Quraysh had instituted a custom for pilgrims of circling around the Ka'ba in a state of nudity. The Qur'an denounces this practice, denying that it was ever sanctioned by God:

> Yet when [these people] do something disgraceful, they say, "We found our forefathers doing this," and, "God has commanded us to do this." Say [Prophet], "God does not command disgraceful deeds. How can you say about God things that you do not know [to be true]?" (7:28)

In effect, the Qur'an counters their argument that they are imitating their forefathers, by recounting the cautionary example of humanity's earliest father, Adam, who was likewise stripped of his clothing as a result of heeding Satan's whispers. The story of Adam is therefore used in this sura to confront a specific practice of the pre-Islamic Arabs, as well as to provide a universal caution against indecency and obeying the whispers of Satan in place of divine command.[125]

Rewriting of Biblical Narratives

In the nineteenth and twentieth centuries, European orientalists who studied the Qur'an had the advantage of being equipped with thorough knowledge of the Bible, as well as extra-Biblical Jewish and Christian traditions. However, the attitude implicit in their methodology was to regard the Bible as the benchmark of religious textual tradition and to view the Qur'an as merely a derivative text. As a result, when a Qur'anic story differed in some respect from its counterpart in the Bible, these scholars assumed that the Qur'an had "garbled," "mixed up," or "confused" the Biblical tradition. With this approach, there was little attempt to undertake a literary appreciation of *how* the Qur'an makes use of these traditions.

Modern scholarship has largely moved past this approach, coming to recognize that the Qur'anic versions of Biblical (and post-Biblical) stories represent neither plain "borrowing" of these traditions nor "garbled" recollections. Rather, much like in the tradition of the Biblical prophets and writers themselves, the Qur'an reshapes these stories to its own vision of salvation history, ethics, and theology, investing them with original meanings that express its worldview and are relevant to its context.[126] Sidney Griffith writes,

> Hermeneutically speaking, one should approach the Qur'ān as an integral discourse in its own right; it proclaims, judges, praises, blames from its own narrative center. It addresses an audience which is already familiar with oral versions in Arabic of earlier scriptures and folklores. The Qur'ān does not borrow from, or often even quote from these earlier texts. Rather, it alludes to and evokes their stories, even sometimes their wording, for its own rhetorical purpose. The Arabic Qur'ān, from a literary perspective, is something new. It uses the idiom, and sometimes the forms and structures, of earlier narratives in the composition of its own distinctive discourse. It cannot be reduced to any presumed sources. Earlier discourses appear in it

---

125 Ibid., 99-101.

126 See Angelika Neuwirth and Nicolai Sinai, "Introduction," in *The Qur'ān in Context: Historical and Literary Investigations into the Qur'ānic Milieu*, ed. Angelika Neuwirth, Nicolai Sinai, and Michael Marx (Leiden: Brill, 2010), 4. They describe the Qur'an's adaptations of the biblical and postbiblical traditions as "functionally meaningful transformations."

> not only in a new setting, but shaped, trimmed and re-formulated for an essentially new narrative.[127]

Similarly, Michel Cuypers writes,

> There is of course no question of criticizing "borrowings," "imitations," or "influences" from apologetic or polemical intentions, as a certain Orientalism in bad taste has done, but rather recognizing that the Qur'an shares a phenomenon which is characteristic of Biblical writings—re-writing. The books of the Bible unceasingly re-appropriate earlier writings, reusing them and turning them to a new perspective which makes revelation advance. The Qur'an does no different, although it does so in a different way from the Bible...since it positions itself as the final revelation in the Judeo-Christian tradition, it has had to re-assume the earlier traditions while making its own mark on the texts it repeats in this way.[128]

To illustrate this aspect of the Qur'an's storytelling, we will revisit an example from the story of Adam, with a focus on how the Qur'an refashions Biblical tradition for its own literary purposes and to convey its own distinctive message.

"Immortality and kingdom that never fades"

Naturally, the Qur'an's telling of the story of Adam has a number of parallels with the account found in the Bible (Genesis 1-3). God created Adam from the dust of the earth, breathed life into him, and created for him Eve as a mate. God permitted them to eat freely from any tree of the Garden of Eden except one, but they were tempted by Satan (or in Genesis, a serpent) and ate from it. They stitched clothes to cover their nakedness, were admonished by God for their act of disobedience, and were banished from the Garden, having to live a life of toil concluding in death.

In many other respects, the Qur'an differs starkly from the Biblical account.[129] The Qur'an leaves out references that depict God in the manner of a human "walking in the Garden at the time of the evening breeze" (Gen. 3:8) or not knowing Adam and Eve's whereabouts (Gen. 3:8-9). Moreover, in the

---

127 Sidney H. Griffith, "Christian Lore and the Arabic Qur'an: The 'Companions of the Cave' in *Surat al-Kahf* and in Syriac Christian tradition," in *The Qur'ān in Its Historical Context*, ed. Gabriel Said Reynolds (London: Routledge, 2008), 116.

128 Michel Cuypers, *The Banquet: A Reading of the Fifth Sura of the Qur'an* (Miami: Convivium, 2009), 31.

129 For an insightful study of the differences between the Qur'anic and Biblical account of the creation story, see Muhammad Abdel Haleem, *Understanding the Qur'an: Themes and Style* (London: I.B. Tauris), 2011, 126-140.

Biblical account, the Tree that God prohibits to Adam and Eve is the "Tree of Knowledge of Good and Evil" (Gen. 2:9, 17). Their attainment of this knowledge, which is reserved for divine beings, happens contrary to God's plan. God banishes them from the Garden out of fear that they may also eat from the Tree of Immortality, and thereby acquire the divine quality of eternal life as well:

> Then the Lord God said, "See, the man has become like one of us, knowing good and evil; and now, he might reach out his hand and take also from the Tree of Life, and eat, and live for ever"—therefore the Lord God sent him forth from the Garden of Eden, to till the ground from which he was taken. He drove out the man; and at the east of the Garden of Eden he placed the cherubim, and a sword flaming and turning to guard the way to the Tree of Life. (Gen. 3:22-24)

In the Qur'anic story, the forbidden Tree is not associated with knowledge of good and evil. This has been pointed to as an example of the Qur'an's alleged "confusion" of the Biblical source, because the Qur'an elsewhere portrays Satan as enticing Adam and Eve with the claim that eating from the tree will cause them to become "immortal" (7:20; cf. 20:120) and "like angels" (7:20).[130] The claim is that the Qur'an confuses the Tree of Knowledge of Good and Evil with the Tree of Life.

Closer consideration, however, indicates that this is not a case of confusion. In the Qur'an, the Tree offers neither moral knowledge *nor* immortality, but is only forbidden as mankind's first test. God shows no interest in withholding moral knowledge; rather, the Qur'an suggests that moral knowledge was a part of man's design from the beginning (2:30 and 76:3, 90:10 and 91:8-10).[131]

Moreover, Satan's claims about the Tree in the Qur'anic narratives play distinctive functions. Let us start with 20:120, in which Satan claimed, "O Adam, shall I show you the Tree of Immortality and of kingdom that never fades?" This quotation occurs, as we have seen in the previous section, in a passage that serves as a caution to the Prophet and the believers to be steadfast and to avoid haste. Recall how the story in this passage is introduced:

> Do not hasten (*ta'JaL*) the recitation before (*min qabl*) its revelation to you is completed. But do say, "My Lord, increase me in knowledge." And We had taken a promise from Adam from before (*min qabl*), but he forgot and We did not find him steadfast... (20:114-115)

---

130 Abraham Geiger, *Judaism and Islam: A Prize Essay*, trans. F.M. Young (Vepery: M.D.C.S.P.C.K. Press, 1898), 79.

131 Abdel Haleem, *Understanding the Qur'an*, 132.

The Qur'an presents Satan's claim that the forbidden Tree will grant immortality and eternal kingdom as false advice, not as a description of the actual nature of the Tree. Against such temptations, the Qur'an is stressing just the opposite point: when a person disobeys God or acts out of haste, he does so in hopes of acquiring immediate gains or gratification. But such gains are an illusion and at best short-lived, occurring at the expense of benefits that are longer lasting, but which also require discipline and hard work. The Qur'anic story serves as a lesson that to attain what is *truly* "immortal" and "never fades" demands patience and steadfastness. It provides a warning not to follow the whispers of Satan by seeking immediate results, because it is in doing so that "Adam disobeyed his Lord and was led astray" (20:121).

Now consider Satan's other claim about the Tree: "Your Lord only forbade you this Tree to prevent you becoming angels or immortals" (7:20). We have seen in the previous section that the story here, viewed in context, serves as a warning not to take Satan as an ally by following his suggestions instead of God's commands. As in the previous case, Satan's claim here that the Tree will make Adam and Eve "immortal" and "like angels" is presented as an example of his false promises, and a warning to instead follow God's guidance. As a verse elsewhere in the Qur'an states, "Satan will say to them when the matter has been concluded, 'God promised you a true promise, and I promised you but I betrayed you'" (14:22).

Satan's promise in this passage also has a touch of irony. He swore to Adam and Eve that God only prohibited the Tree from them lest they become "like angels," whereas earlier in the story God had already awarded them a status higher than that of the angels, when He commanded the angels to prostrate to Adam.[132] Moreover, this also expresses an important difference with the Biblical account, in which God decided to prevent Adam and Eve from attaining the status of heavenly beings. In the Qur'anic story, by contrast, it is God's plan from the beginning to afford humanity with the opportunity to rise to a higher status than that of the angels. The differences with the Biblical story do not represent a confusion or garbling of it, but a reshaping of it to express the Qur'an's own distinctive teaching about God, and about man's purpose, salvation, and relationship with Him.

132 Mir, "The Qur'an as Literature," 57.

CHAPTER 11

The Coherence and Structure of the Qur'anic Sura

Before approaching any discourse, whether oral (such as a story, poem, song, or speech) or written (such as a book, essay, chapter, or article), we generally expect it to have an intelligible order and structure—a beginning, middle, and end. Even if the discourse addresses a variety of topics or issues, we expect that they will all relate in some way to a single main idea (or plot, in the case of a story) and that there will be meaningful connections between one topic and the next. If a story is not told in chronological order, a speaker fails to connect his points, or the pages of a book are read non-sequentially, making sense of the composition will usually be very difficult.

Readers approaching the Qur'an are often confused by what they perceive to be the scripture's lack of coherence, structure, and organization. This impression results from several factors. First, unlike the chapter of a book, a single sura is likely to address multiple topics and issues that may seem unrelated, while the discussion of a given topic is usually dispersed over several different suras. Moreover, the title of a sura usually does little to give the reader an idea of its contents or main idea, but serves only as a convenient label by which the sura has come to be known. Second, the suras are not arranged chronologically or classified by topic, but are arranged, very roughly, by length, with the longest suras (which tend to be chronologically later) at the beginning and the shortest suras (which tend to be among the earliest) at the end. Third, there are also the sudden shifts of person, number, and tense (analyzed in chapter 4, "Grammatical Shifts"), which the reader is likely to mistake for inconsistency or confusion in the scripture's narrative voice. These apparent signs of disorder led the nineteenth-century essayist Thomas Carlyle to complain, "I must say, it is as toilsome reading as I ever undertook. A wearisome confused jumble, crude, incondite; endless iterations, long-windedness, entanglements…"[133] The fact that Carlyle otherwise wrote sympathetically of Islam and its Prophet, defending them against the criticism of his European contemporaries, gives his harsh verdict added force.

This judgment was not unique to Carlyle. The German scholar Theodor Nöldeke (d. 1930) ascribed what he viewed as the Qur'an's "endless repetitions" and "long-winded" style to Muhammad—whom he assumed to be the author of the Qur'an—having been "an average stylist at best,"[134] while the gentler William Montgomery Watt (d. 2006) described the Qur'an as being "unsystematic," "disjointed," and generally lacking "sustained composition at any great length."[135] Such a perception led the British scholar Richard Bell (d. 1952) to theorize that the Qur'an's editors mistakenly stitched together originally separate passages that scribes had recorded on various fragments of material or on opposite sides of parchment. The impression that the Qur'an is disorderly has not only affected scholars and critics. As one observer has put it, "A lack of logical connection in the chapters of the Qur'ān has been felt by many Westerners and has often discouraged them from its perusal."[136] Modern Western readers, as well as even many traditional Muslim scholars, have maintained that the Qur'an displays no particular order or arrangement, due to the fact that it was revealed piece by piece and in response to a variety of audiences, issues, and situations.

On the other hand, some distinguished Muslim commentators have marveled at the wisdom and interconnections they found in the sequence of the Qur'an's verses and suras.[137] The commentator Fakhr ad-Din

---

133 Thomas Carlyle, *On Heroes, Hero-Worship, and the Heroic in History*, ed. Archibald MacMechan (Boston: Athenaeum, 1901), 74, qtd. in Farrin, *Structure and Qur'anic Interpretation*, xiii.

134 Theodor Nöldeke, Friedrich Schwally, Gotthelf Bergsträßer, and Otto Pretzl, *The History of the Qur'ān*, trans. Wolfgang H. Behn (Leiden: Brill, 2013), 117.

135 William Montgomery Watt, *Bell's Introduction to the Qur'an* (Edinburgh: Edinburgh UP, 1970), xi and 22. Quoted in Mir, *Coherence in the Qur'an*, 2.

136 John E. Merrill, "Dr. Bell's Critical Analysis of the Qur'ān," *Muslim World* 37.2 (1947): 134-48, qtd. in Mir, *Coherence in the Qur'an*, 2. Mir suggests, surely correctly, that this has been a major factor that has led to the interest among Western scholars in reconstructing the chronology of the revelations.

137 Standing out among them are Fakhr ad-Dīn ar-Rāzī (d. 1209), Niẓām ad-Dīn an-Nīsābūrī (d. 1327), Abū Ḥayyān al-Andalūsī (d. 1344), Burhān ad-Dīn al-Biqā'ī (d. 1480) and in more modern times Maḥmūd al-Ālūsī (d. 1854). Al-Biqā'i named his commentary *The Arrangement of Peals In the Connections of Āyas and Sūras* (*Naẓm ad-Durar fī Tanāsubi 'l-Āyāt wa's-Suwar*). Other famous "partisans of coherence" included Abū Bakr ibn al-'Arabī (d. 1148), Badr ad-Dīn az-Zarkashī (d. 1391), and Jalāl ad-Dīn as-Suyūṭī (d. 1505). See Mir, *Coherence in the Qur'ān*, 17-19; Mir, "The Sūra as a Unity: A Twentieth-century Development in Qur'ānic Exegesis," ed. Gerald R. Hawting and Abdul Kader A. Shareef, *Approaches to the Qur'ān* (New York: Routledge, 1993), 211-212; and Farrin, *Structure and Qur'anic Interpretation*, xi-xii.

ar-Razi (d. 1209) declared, "The majority of the subtleties (*laṭā'if*) of the Qur'an are embedded in its arrangement and connections."[138] He and later scholars devoted considerable attention to this aspect in their large commentaries of the Qur'an. Despite these advances, the approach of this school has been described as "linear-atomistic"—focusing almost exclusively on the connections between one verse or group of verses and the next, or the connections between the end of one sura and the beginning of the next, but giving little treatment to overall structure and thematic unity of a sura.[139]

Given such complaints, it is not surprising that the study of the Qur'an's ***naẓm***—its "arrangement," "composition," or more loosely, "coherence"—has achieved renewed interest in modern times. The Indian scholar Hamid ad-Din Farahi (d. 1930) devoted his research to the subject, producing original and sophisticated arguments for the coherent arrangement of individual suras and for the Qur'an as a whole. Farahi argued that the study of the Qur'an's *naẓm* does not simply bring out its subtleties and nuances is, in fact, an essential principle for the interpretation of the scripture. *Naẓm* brings out the themes and subject matter of the sura, provides each verse the proper context for its interpretation, and shows how the sura's themes and arguments are tied together.

Among Farahi's contributions was his emphasis on the unity and distinctiveness of each sura. He explored the question of what unites the contents of the sura from within, and distinguishes each sura from the others, making it a coherent, distinct, and self-contained composition. Farahi also offered an intuitive methodology for determining the coherence and structure of a sura. In essence, one reads a given sura until he is able to distinguish its individual thematic sections based on change in subject matter. Each section is then studied to discern the overall idea that unites the verses within it. Finally, one examines how the various sections relate and contribute to the development of the overall idea or argument that characterizes the whole sura.[140] While Farahi wrote commentaries of only fourteen suras, all of them relatively short and only one of them typically identified as Medinan, his student Amin Ahsan Islahi (d. 1997) wrote a full commentary of the Qur'an in Urdu, the official

138 This is quoted approvingly by as-Suyūṭī, *al-Itqān fī 'Ulūm al-Qur'ān*, vol. 2, 216.

139 Mir, "The Sūra as a Unity," 212. Some scholars have noted an exception in Abū Bakr al-Bāqillānī (d. 1013), who identifies a common central theme shared by suras 40 and 41, namely "the necessity of the Qur'an being a proof, and the indication of its miracle," which he says unites them from beginning to end. See Nevin Reda, "Holistic Approaches to the Qur'an: A Historical Background," *Religion Compass* 4.8 (2010): 497.

140 Mir, *Coherence in the Qur'ān*, 39.

language of his native Pakistan, with the aim of highlighting the *naẓm* of all 114 suras.[141]

While Farahi's and Islahi's contributions remained unknown to the Western world until they were introduced in Mustansir Mir's *Coherence in the Qur'an* in 1986, five years prior to that, the German scholar Angelika Neuwirth published her own breakthrough study, *Studien zur Komposition der mekkanischen Suren* (*Studies in the Composition of the Meccan Suras*).[142] Neuwirth observed that the bodies of the Meccan suras are composed of sections that can be distinguished based on changes in rhyme and other formal criteria. She found that, as a rule, each section deals with one of six key themes, which we will examine shortly. Furthermore, she showed that these thematic sections, or "building blocks," are well balanced and proportioned within the sura, proving that, contrary to Bell, each sura is crafted as a distinct and intentional literary unity.[143] Neuwirth's findings were taken significantly further by the British scholar Neal Robinson, who investigated how the different types of thematic sections relate to each other, and how they build on one another within a sura to form a coherent argument.[144] We will be exploring some of Robinson's contributions in the course of this chapter.

While Neuwirth showed that the Meccan suras form distinct unities, she did not depart from the prevailing view that some of the long Medinan suras are essentially miscellaneous patchworks of material. However, in addition to the work of Islahi, the newer research of other scholars, such as Mustansir Mir, Neal Robinson, Michel Cuypers, and Raymond Farrin, have shown that the suras of both the Meccan and Medinan periods display a far greater degree

---

141 Farahi's commentary in Arabic is published as 'Abd al-Ḥamīd al-Farāhī, *Tafsīr Niẓām al-Qur'ān wa Ta'wīl al-Qur'ān bi 'l-Qur'ān* (Azamgarh, India: ad-Dā'irat al-Ḥamīdiyya wa-Maktabatu-hā, 2008), and is also available in Urdu translation as *Majmu'ah-yi Tafāsīr-i Farāhi*, tr. Amīn Aḥsan Iṣlaḥī (*Lahore: Anjuman-i Khuddāmu 'l-Qur'ān, 1973*). *Islahi's commentary in Urdu is published as Tadabbur-i Qur'ān* (Lahore: Anjuman-i Markazi, Anjuman-i Khuddāmu 'l-Qur'an and Fārān Foundation, 1967-1980).

142 Angelika Neuwirth, *Studien zur Komposition der mekkanischen Suran: die literarische Form des Koran—ein Zeugnis seiner Historizität?* (Berlin: de Gruyter, 1981; 2nd ed., 2007).

143 In some cases, however, the search for symmetry leads Neuwirth to go as far as to propose significant emendations to the text. A study with an approach comparable to Neuwirth's was published in French the same year: Pierre Crapon De Caprona, *Le Coran: Aux Sources De La Parole Oraculaire, Structures Rythmiques Des Sourates Mecquoises* (Paris: Publications Orientalises De France, 1981). Caprona's focus on meter offers some useful methods and insights, but leads him to propose even more radical emendations. See Robinson's critique in *Discovering the Qur'an*, 183-188.

144 Robinson, *Discovering the Qur'an*, 97-195. Robinson also subdivides these six types of sections into smaller component parts, which he calls "formal elements," and provides an exhaustive and extremely valuable inventory of all of the formal elements of the Early Meccan suras.

of coherence and structure than is generally recognized.[145] As we will see over the next four chapters, this is found at all levels, from the individual passage, the section, the sura, and even the arrangement of the Qur'an as a whole.

Aspects of the Composition of the Suras

Medieval and modern scholars writing in Arabic have used the word *naẓm* to describe the arrangement of a sura, as well as the order of the suras of the Qur'an. The primary meaning of *naẓm* is "arrangement," "order," or "organization." It signifies the arrangement of individual parts into a coherent whole. For example, this word is used for stringing beads or pearls together to produce a beautiful necklace, or the arrangement of a set of wells into a uniform layout. They are also used to refer to the "contiguity" of a series of items, or how a group of items "stick" or "cohere" together.[146]

The word *naẓm* also signifies the "composition" of a verse, poem, or musical piece.[147] When speaking of literature, "composition" is perhaps the English term that most closely corresponds to the Arabic term *naẓm*. To say that a piece of writing lacks composition, or has poor composition, is to say that it lacks an orderly presentation of ideas. Similarly, when scholars such as Farahi or Islahi argue that the suras of the Qur'an, or the Qur'an as a whole, are characterized by *naẓm*, they mean that they are arranged in a coherent or logical fashion. To explain *naẓm* another way, we could say that it includes the notions of coherence and structure—**coherence** referring to how ideas are logically related and ordered, forming a unified whole, and **structure** referring to the overall form or pattern of their arrangement. From here onwards, we will use the terms "composition" or "coherence and structure" as English substitutes for the Arabic term *naẓm*.

The study of the composition of a sura involves several aspects. We will call the first aspect **linear coherence**, which concerns the linear flow, continuity or sequential arrangement of the Qur'an. In what way is one verse, topic, section, or even entire sura connected to the next one, if at all? Mustansir Mir has also referred to this as the "continuity" or "linkage" between verses or groups of verses.[148]

The second aspect is the **structure** of a sura. Through close study, one may be able to discern the individual sections of a sura. After doing so and

145 For more information, see Sharif Randhawa, "A Bibliography of Studies in English on the Coherence and Structure of the Qur'an's Suras," *Bayyinah Blog*, April 15, 2016, http://blog.bayyinah.com/nazm-bibliography.

146 Ibn Manẓūr, 12:578-579; Mustansir Mir, "Continuity, Context, and Coherence in the Qur'ān: A Brief Review of the Idea of *Naẓm* in *Tafsīr* Literature," *Al-Bayan* 11.2: 16.

147 Ibn Manẓūr, 12:578. The Arabic word for composition is *ta'līf*.

148 Mir, "Continuity, Context, and Coherence," 15.

studying the relationships between these sections, he might notice something distinctive about the sura's structure. For example, the studies of Meccan suras pioneered by Angelika Neuwirth have shown that their structure is finely balanced or proportioned. For instance Sura 51, *The Scatterers* (*adh-Dhāriyāt*), has the following structure in terms of its verse count:

Part I: 9 + 14
Part II: 14 + 9
Part III: 7 + 7

Part I consists of a section of 9 verses followed by a section of 14 verses. This is mirrored by part II, which consists of a section of 14 verses followed by a section of 9 verses. Finally, part III consists of two sections of equal size, each consisting of 7 verses. In addition to the verse count, the suras may also show balance when studied from the perspective of their rhyme or meter. Other studies of individual suras have found that they are often structured according to identifiable literary patterns, which we will see in the next chapter. In particular, we will focus on a pattern known as ring composition, in which the contents of a passage, section, or entire sura are organized symmetrically around a centerpiece (AB/C/B'A').

The third aspect of coherence is what we will call the **integrative coherence** of a sura. This is concerned with how different verses, passages, or sections within a sura, or even between separate suras, are interconnected by key terms, verbal roots, images, parallel expressions, or even sound patterns that they share. We will call these items **anchors**. Although this sort of study is already known more formally as the study of *intertextuality*, we will use the term "integrative coherence" to emphasize the role of these anchors in (1) integrating different parts of a section together, (2) linking separate sections of a sura, thereby helping to unify it, and (3) linking verses or passages from separate suras, such as suras that form a pair or group (see chapter 14, "The Order of the Suras").

Finally, each of these approaches contributes to understanding what we will call the sura's **holistic coherence**, how the sura is united into a consistent and distinct whole.[149] In this regard, one might be interested in identi-

149 The term "unity" is often used for this aspect. However, while some scholars (such as Farahi and Islahi) use the term to signify how the parts of a sura are united by a central theme, others use the term with a weaker meaning, such as how the sura forms a continuous whole through a connected flow of ideas from beginning to end, how it is unified by certain themes or motifs that recur throughout it, or how it is composed with balance and symmetry. Our use of the term "holistic coherence" implies a combination of all types of coherence, looking for a central theme, as well as perhaps even studying a sura in terms of its role in a broader sura pair, group, or the Qur'an as a whole. For a similar use of the term "holistic," see Reda, "Holistic Approaches to the Qur'an."

fying an overarching idea that unites and explains all of the sura's contents or components. In addition to seeing the unity of an individual sura and how each part of it fits into the scheme of the whole, one might also be interested in understanding the role of the sura in a broader sura pair or group, or in the Qur'an as a whole.

It should also be mentioned that both sound and rhythm play important roles in the coherence and structure of a sura. Often, an individual section within a sura is unified by a pattern of rhyme that occurs at the end of each of its verses, with a change in rhyme pattern signaling the start of a new thematic section. Additionally, as we will see in this chapter, a similar sound or end rhyme may function like an anchor, linking verses or sections in two different parts of a sura together. Finally, as noted above, in terms of rhythm or meter, when the number of syllables within the sections of a Meccan sura is counted, they often show a particular balance and symmetry. We will see how these features play out in our study of coherence within this chapter.

In this chapter, we will be looking in particular at the coherence and structure of an Early Meccan sura, Sura 79, *Those Pulling* (*an-Nāzi'āt*). We will also briefly look at a passage within another Early Meccan sura, Sura 75, *The Resurrection* (*al-Qiyāma*), to see how a passage that at first seems out of place proves, upon closer investigation, to be well integrated with the surrounding text. We will reserve our study of structural patterning for the next chapter, chapter 12, "Symmetry in the Qur'an." In chapter 13, we will combine all of these approaches in a study of Sura 2, *The Cow*, which is a Medinan sura and the longest sura of the Qur'an. Then, in chapter 14, we will turn to the question of the order of the suras in the Qur'an as a whole.

The Coherence and Structure of the Meccan Suras

Neuwirth has analyzed the forty-eight suras that Theodor Nöldeke assigned to the Early Meccan period, showing that all but five of them are composed of one or more discrete "sections" or "building blocks" of material dealing with six consistent themes:

- **Signs of God in nature:**[150] These point to phenomenon in nature such as the creation of the universe, the heavenly bodies, rainfall, the creation of animal and plant life, and the creation of the human being as "signs" (*āyas*) of God's mercy, power, and activity, and of His power to reward, punish, and resurrect the dead for judgment.

---

150 Neuwirth calls these "hymnic passages," but we will instead follow Robinson in describing these as "signs passages."

- **Polemic against the disbelievers**: These sections condemn the disbelievers for their arrogance, denial, and oppression of the less privileged, and debate their attitudes regarding monotheism, the revelation, and the afterlife.
- **Eschatology (descriptions of the end times and afterlife)**: These sections describe in powerful and vivid imagery the catastrophic end of the world, the Resurrection, the Judgment, Paradise, and Hell.
- **Stories or lessons from history**: These tell stories about past generations, usually centering on prophetic messengers from Biblical and Arabian tradition. In a common type of story, the "punishment story," the messenger calls his people to repent, worship God alone, and fix their corrupt practices. Despite the messenger's warnings of punishment from God, his people use various tactics to oppose him, and are consequently destroyed. These stories served as a warning to the people of Mecca, most of whom were resistant to Muhammad's preaching, but also provided assurances to the believers of God's justice and future deliverance. Some of the Middle and Late Meccan suras offer extremely rich and diverse stories, such as those of Adam, Abraham, Joseph, Moses, and Mary.
- **The status of the revelation**: These affirm the divine status, authenticity, and function of the revelation as guidance.
- **Words of encouragement to the Messenger**: These are addresses from God to Muhammad, most often referred to generically as "you." They provide words of consolation and instruction to him and his followers.[151]

Robinson has shown that the type of material found in each of these six categories is not entirely distinct, but that they are subtly interrelated, especially in the Middle and Late Meccan suras. For example, the punishment stories often contain strong elements of polemic against the Meccan disbelievers, may quote a past prophet drawing his audience's attention to God's signs, or may include verbal echoes of the sections in which God addresses Muhammad, drawing a direct parallel between the situation of Muhammad and the past prophet.[152] Even more significantly, thematic sections of one type may serve as a springboard for sections of another type. For example, signs passages, which draw attention to natural phenomena in this world, may open up eschatological passages concerning the next:

> In the signs section of Surah 78 [*The News, an-Nabā'*], the cosmos is depicted as a temporary edifice, a tent pitched by the Creator, thus preparing

151 Robinson, *Discovering the Qur'an*, 125.
152 Ibid., 159.

> the ground for the eschatological prelude in which the tent-pegs are removed and the celestial canopy opens up. In the signs section of Surah 55 [*The All-Merciful, ar-Raḥmān*], the catalogue of God's abundant provision for our needs in this world has its counterpart in the eschatological section, in the description of His even more lavish provision for us in the Hereafter. The signs controversy in Surah 56 [*The Inevitable Event, al-Wāqiʿa*] points to the transformations observable in nature as evidence that God is able to raise the dead in a new form. In Surah 75 [*The Resurrection, al-Qiyāma*], on the other hand, it is the creation of humankind from seminal fluid which is cited as proof of God's power to raise the dead.[153]

By being aware of these different types of material, the reader is able to break down the Meccan suras into smaller, more manageable chunks, and to recognize the logical connections between them. When studied in this way, the Meccan suras turn out to be marvelously structured, balanced, and coherent compositions.

In what remains of this chapter, we will summarize Robinson's observations on two short Meccan suras, both of which are normally attributed to the Early Meccan period.

"Has the story of Moses reached you?"

Sura 79, *Those Pulling* (*an-Nāziʿāt*), is a good candidate for the study of coherence in the short Meccan suras, because it consists of multiple thematic sections, and is one of the suras that Richard Bell used as an example to support his thesis that the sura sections were originally independent fragments, only joined by editors by mistake. Bell's view was based on the alleged discontinuity between the sections: an initial oath is followed by a seemingly unrelated discussion of Judgment Day, the story of Moses and Pharaoh, a description of God's signs in the creation, and then Judgment again. However, Neuwirth and especially Robinson have shown that the sections form a coherent and well-designed whole. Robinson's observations will be summarized here.[154]

The sura consists of three parts, each in turn consisting of multiple thematic sections:

> Part I. Eschatology (vv. 1-9) + Polemic (vv. 10-14)
> Part II. Narrative (vv. 15-26) + Signs (vv. 27-33)
> Part III. Eschatology (vv. 34-41) + Address to the Messenger (vv. 42-46)

---

153 Ibid.
154 This section owes to ibid., 177-188.

Robinson points out that the sura is acoustically symmetrical. Part I and Part III consist of rhyming verse patterns of 5 + 9 and 9 + 5 respectively. This is accentuated by the fact that the last verse in Part I and the first verse in Part III both begin with the phrase *fa-idhā* (meaning "and behold" and "but when" respectively).[155] The middle verse of Part II (v. 24), in which Pharaoh blasphemously claims "I am your Lord the Most High!" also occupies the center of the sura in terms of its rhyme count.[156] We will see additional ways in which the placement of this verse unifies the narrative (vv. 15-26) and signs (vv. 27-33) sections as the middle part of the sura.

Even a casual perusal of the sura will indicate that the main subject is the reality of the Judgment and Resurrection—a common theme of the Meccan suras. The question that we will be concerned with is how each section of the sura builds on the previous sections to develop this theme. We will offer a translation of each section before commenting on it. For the reader's convenience, we will print the English translation of the anchors or otherwise important words in bold, and will provide a transliteration of the original Arabic word in parentheses, with the root letters capitalized. We will also print the transliteration of the rhymed words at the end of each verse so that the reader can see the rhyme scheme that exists for each section in the original Arabic.

Part 1

1.1 Eschatology (vv. 1-9)

The sura begins with a rider oath, a type of divine oath in the Qur'an that depicts natural or personal forces moving in swift succession, and which is imitated by a consistent sound pattern (*al-fāʿilāti faʿlā*):

1. By those **pulling** to plunge! (*wa-'n-NāZiʿāti gharqā*)
2. And those moving briskly and energetically! (*wa-'n-nāshiṭāti nashṭā*)
3. And those **swimming** along, (*wa-'s-SāBiḤāti SaBḤā*)
4. then forging ahead, (*fa-'s-sābiqāti sabqā*)
5. then **managing the affair**! (*fa-'l-muDaBBiRāti 'AMRā*)[157]

The oath contains a consistent rhyme scheme and singles out three groups of entities, the first pulling and plunging with force and effort (v. 1); the second moving actively, rapidly, and energetically (v. 2); and the third gliding seamlessly ("swimming"), taking the lead, and performing the desired task

155 Ibid., 181.
156 Ibid., 184.
157 This is the translation given in ibid., 177-178.

(vv. 3-5). This particular oath is among the most ambiguous passages of the Qur'an, and commentators have offered a variety of interpretations. Most plausibly, however, Robinson suggests that it refers to three waves of marauding horsemen, charging in battle, or more specifically carrying out a dawn raid, just as in Sura 101, *The Chargers*.[158] (Robinson interprets the first verse as "By those pulling [*at the reigns*] to plunge [*into the fray*]!") Recall from chapter 7, "Divine Oaths," that Sura 101, *The Chargers*, uses the image of a dawn raid as a model to depict the scouring of the graves on the Day of Resurrection. The oath at the beginning of this sura functions in the same way.

Muslim commentators have also adduced other Qur'anic passages in which the same verbs used in this oath are found. For example, the verb "to pull" (*NaZaʿa*) is used in scenes of divine retribution in this world (54:20) and the Day of Judgment (19:69), in which natural forces (in the former case) and angels (in both cases) might be viewed as the agents carrying out the punishment by divine command (*ʿaMR*). The verb "swimming" (*yaSBaḤūn*) is used to describe the orbits of heavenly bodies (21:33; 36:40). Moreover, God is described as "managing the affair" (*yuDaBBiRu ʾl-ʿaMR*) of creation (10:3; 10:31; 13:2; 32:5), again possibly through the agency of natural forces and angels. While these usages do not provide sufficient evidence that the objects of the above oath mainly signify angels or heavenly bodies, as many commentators argue, they do underscore that the oath employs wording that has additional theological, cosmic, and eschatological meanings in the Qur'an. This may suggest a picture in which the angels, heavenly bodies, and forces of nature are all participating in the "cosmic raid" and upheaval of Judgment Day.

The complement of the oath (vv. 6-9) uses the established raid metaphor to now depict in more explicit terms what will happen on Judgment Day:

6. On the Day when what causes a commotion is set in motion (*rājifa*)
7. and another rides behind it in quick succession, (*rādifa*)
8. hearts on that Day will be palpitating (*wājifa*)
9. their looks downcast. (*khāshiʿa*)

The mention of "commotion," "motion," and "riding in quick succession" (vv. 6-7) recalls the waves of marauders depicted in the oath. This time, it is explicit that they are agents of God. The sense of fear upon this cosmic raid is captured by the images of hearts palpitating and gazes being downcast.

While vv. 6-9 are part of the same thematic section as vv. 1-5, they begin a new rhyme scheme that is continued in the next section (vv. 10-14). Hence

158 Ibid., 181-182.

in this case, the change in rhyme scheme does not coincide with the change in thematic register. There is a reason for this however, as this arrangement allows the "acoustic mirror-effect" noted earlier between Part I and Part III.[159]

1.2 Polemic (vv. 10-14)

Part I then turns to address the skepticism of the disbelievers, marking a polemic section:

> 10. They say, "Will we be restored to our first state (*ḤāFiRa*)
> 11. when we are decayed bones?" (*nakhira*)
> 12. They say, "That is a losing return!" (*khāsira*)
> 13. Yet there will be only a single cry (*wāḥida*)
> 14. and behold they will be wide awake! (*sāhira*)

The image of the raid is continued to describe Judgment Day. Robinson notes the irony of the disbelievers' use of the word *ḤāFiRa* ("first state"), which originally referred to the "ground dug by a horse's feet" (from the verb *ḤaFaRa*, "to dig"). The disbelievers' reference to Judgment Day as a "losing return" is exploited to invoke the scene of the victims of a raid returning to their campsite but finding nothing but loss. The mention of "a single cry" that arouses the dead "wide awake" continues the analogy of the dawn raid, in this case alluding to "the cry of the watchman rousing his sleeping fellow-tribesmen to face an imminent attack."[160]

Part 2

2.1 Narrative: Moses and Pharaoh (vv. 15-26)

The next section is marked off by a change in end rhyme and a shift to the topic of Moses' confrontation with Pharaoh:

> 15. Has the story of Moses reached you? (*mūsā*)
> 16. When his Lord called to him in the sacred valley of Tuwa, (*ṭuwā*)
> 17. "Go to Pharaoh. Indeed he has **transgressed**. (*ṬaGHā*)
> 18. So say, 'Is it for you to purify yourself? (*tazakkā*)
> 19. and that I should guide to your Lord so you may **fear** Him?'" (*taKHSHā*)
> 20. And he **showed** (*aRā*) him the **greatest** sign, (*KuBRā*)
> 21. but he denied and disobeyed, (*'aṣā*)

---

159 Ibid., 181.
160 Ibid., 183.

22. then **turned away** (*aDBaRa*) **striving**, (*yaS'ā*)
23. and he gathered and called, (*nadā*)
24. and he said, "I am **your Lord, the Most High**!" (*RaBBikumu 'l-a'Lā*)
25. So God seized him with the punishment of the hereafter and the first. (*ūlā*)
26. Truly in that there is an admonition for whoever **fears**. (*yaKHSHā*)

The story retold here is not disconnected from the previous sections, as Bell thought, but is a historical illustration of the theme of divine retribution. It warns the Quraysh that because Pharaoh refused to repent for his crimes and persisted in his disbelief even though a messenger was sent to him, God punished him in this world and the next.

Besides this general thematic connection, the story of Pharaoh's punishment is tied to the rider oath at the beginning of the sura. In v. 22, Pharaoh is said to have "turned away" (*aDBaRa*) from Moses' warning, ominously calling to mind the earlier description of God's agents "managing" (*muDaBBiRāt*) the affair of the raid, the two verbs sharing the same root in Arabic. Moreover, it was no less than the hurried pursuit of the Israelites by Pharaoh in a horse-pulled chariot, and in command of a horse-powered army, that led to his doom. While God's agents in the rider oath "plunge" (*GHaRQā*) into the fray and successfully execute His command, in contrast Pharaoh and his cavalrymen literally "drown" in the sea (another meaning of *GHaRQā*) in a vain attempt to fulfill his orders. Once again, the raid or battle imagery is invoked, warning the Quraysh that a similarly disastrous fate awaits them in this world and the next if they, like Pharaoh, do not take heed.

It is also significant that v. 24, which quotes Pharaoh as proclaiming, "I am your Lord, the Most High," occurs as both the midpoint of the rhyme count of the sura and the middle verse of the sura's middle part (Part II). The next section will play off of this central point.

2.2 Signs in Creation (vv. 27-33)

The next section describes God's signs in the creation:

27. Are you harder **to create** (*KHaLQan*) or the heaven? He built it. (*banā-hā*)
28. He raised its canopy and then **formed it**, (*SaWWā-hā*)
29. And He made dark its night and brought out its **morning brightness**, (*DuḤā-hā*)
30. And the earth after that, He expanded it. (*daḥā-hā*)
31. He **brought out** (*aKHRaJa*) of it its water and **its pasturage** (*maR'ā-hā*)
32. —and the mountains, He **fixed** them— (*aRSā-hā*)
33. As a provision for you and for **your herds**. (*aN'āMi-kum*)

Once again, the shift of topic does not suggest that this section is disconnected from the previous ones or the overall message of the sura. Its purpose is to provide a further line of evidence that the Resurrection is not a farfetched notion, but a feasible reality. The creation—given its vastness, organization, and suitability to human flourishing—testifies to the design and tremendous power of the Creator. If He is capable of fashioning the entire cosmos around you, it is implied, then it should be all the more within His power to recreate you.

This section also plays off of the central point that we saw in the previous section (vv. 15-26). Just like God's ability to crush the arrogant Pharaoh, this signs list demonstrates who *truly* is "your Lord, the Most High." Note the connections with the hymnic opening of Sura 87, *The Most High* (*al-A'lā*):

> Exalt the name of **your Lord, the Most High** (*RaBBi-ka 'l-a'Lā*), who **created** (*KHaLaQa*) and **formed** (*SaWWā*), and who measured and guided, and who **brought out the pasture** (*aKHRaJa 'l-maR'ā*). (87:1-4)

In both the narrative and signs section of *Those Pulling* and the opening of *The Most High*, the title of "your Lord, the Most High" (*RaBBu-ka/kumu 'l-a'Lā*) is associated with God's "creating," "forming," and "bringing out [the earth's] pasture."

The word "pasturage" (*maR'ā*) in particular serves as a key anchor to the story of Moses and Pharaoh, as the verb "to pasture" (*Ra'ā*) only occurs in suras that mention Moses (28:23, 38; 87:4). The sura from which we have just quoted, *The Most High*, concludes with an allusion to the "scrolls of Moses" (87:19). In Sura 28, when Moses arrives in Midian, he helps the young girls to water their flocks when the wells are hoarded by shepherds (*Ri'ā*) (28:23). Finally, Sura 20 narrates a longer version of Moses' confrontation with Pharaoh. In this scene, God inspires Moses with a signs list that is strikingly similar to 79:27-33 and 87:1-4. He then tells Pharaoh,

> "Eat and **pasture** (*iR'aw*) **your herds** (*aN'āMa-kum*)" (20:54)

It is therefore clear from these connections that the two sections of Part II, the narrative (vv. 15-26) and the signs sections (vv. 27-33), are closely tied together.

There are further subtleties in the other references to creations in this passage. The sky, its canopy, and the mountains are all highlighted as created entities that are vastly higher than Pharaoh, and discredit his claim to be "the Most High." The reference to the night followed by the morning is relevant to the image of the raid at dawn.[161] The reference to the earth's

161 Ibid., 184-185.

expansion calls to mind an idiom in the Arabic language (found in the Qur'an, 9:25, 118), "the earth became constricted upon him," an expression describing the state of a person whose attackers have closed in on him and who has nowhere to escape—again with obvious relevance to the raid symbol.[162] Finally, water is the force that brought about the demise of Pharaoh and his army. Embedded in this imagery is a warning that just as God has made the earth a vast habitation and has made the water a source of life-supporting pasture, He also has the ability to "constrict" the earth and make the water a source of destruction.

Part 3

3.1 Description of the Judgment and Afterlife (vv. 34-41)

The next section contains a description of the Judgment, contrasting the fates of "one who transgressed" and "one who restrained himself":

34. So when the **greatest** calamity comes, (*KuBRā*)
35. On the day when man will **remember** (*yataDHaKaRu*) what he **strived for**, (*Sa'ā*)
36. And Hell will be displayed to whoever **sees,** (*yaRā*)
37. Then as for one who **transgressed** (*ṬaGHā*)
38. and preferred the worldly life, (*dunyā*)
39. Then surely Hell—that is his refuge. (*ma'wā*)
40. As for one who feared standing before his Lord and restrained himself from desire, (*hawā*)
41. Then surely the Garden—that is his refuge. (*ma'wā*)

The basic thematic coherence of this section with the previous ones is straightforward: it depicts the Judgment and its outcomes. What is of particular note however is how the section is closely tied to the earlier narrative section on Moses and Pharaoh. It both resumes the rhyme scheme and rhythm of that section and contains several verbal anchors. The mention of the "greatest" (*KuBRā*) calamity (v. 34) and of Hell's display to whoever "sees" (*yaRā,* v. 36) recalls Moses' "showing" (*Ra'ā*) Pharaoh the "greatest" (*KuBRā*) sign. Man's remembrance of what he "strived for" (*Sa'ā*) recalls Pharaoh's turning away "striving" (*yaS'a*) in v. 22. Finally, the preparation of Hell for whoever "transgressed" (*ṭaghā*) harks back to Pharaoh's having "transgressed" (*ṭaghā*, v. 17) and his resulting fate. It should additionally be pointed out that the references to Hell (with pointed irony) and the Garden as places of "refuge," though

162 See Mir, *Verbal Idioms*, 215.

echoed elsewhere in the Qur'an, take on additional significance against the background of the raid image that dominates the sura.

3.2 Address to the Messenger (vv. 42-46)[163]

The sura concludes with an address to the Messenger:

> 42. They ask (*yas'alūna*) you about the **Hour** (*Sā'a*), "When is its **fixed time**?" (*muRSā-hā*)
> 43. What have you to do with **mentioning** it? (*DHiKRā-hā*)
> 44. With your Lord is its end. (*muntahā-hā*)
> 45. You are only a warner to whoever **fears** it. (*yaKHSHā-hā*)
> 46. It will be as if they, on the day they **see** it, (*yaRawna-hā*) only tarried a single evening or its **morning brightness**. (*ḌuḤā-hā*)

This section is linked to the section on God's signs in creation (vv. 27-32) by a shared rhyme scheme. Moreover, the meter of the two sections is precisely balanced, as they contain an almost identical number of syllables, short vowels, and long vowels.[164]

In terms of its content and grammatical structure however, it is closely related to vv. 10-14, which quotes and responds to the questions of the disbelievers. Both sections begin with a similar sounding verb ("they say," *yaqūlūna*/"they ask," *yas'alūna*), contain the word "only" as the first word of the penultimate verse (*innamā*: "there will only be a single cry"/"you are only a warner"), and contain the pronoun *-hum* as the third syllable of the last verse.[165]

The concluding section is linked to the previous sections by a number of anchors. The term "Hour" (*Sā'a*), referring to the commencement of Judgment Day, is of the same root as the word "striving" (*Sa'ā/yaS'ā*) in vv. 22 and 35, recalling that at that time "every man will remember what he strived for." The term "fixed time" (*muRSā*) recalls God's "fixing" (*aRSā*) of the mountains in v. 32, drawing the implication that the same God who put the mountains in place has determined the time of the Hour. The statement that the Prophet has not been given any knowledge of the future time of the Hour on the basis of which he could make "mention" (*DHiKR*) of it recalls that man will "remember" (*yataDHaKaRu*) on that Day what he had done in his past (v. 35). The Prophet's role is only that of a warner for whoever "fears it" (*yaKHSHā-hā*), just as Moses' mission was that of a warner inviting Pharaoh to "fear" (*taKHSHā*, v. 19).

---

163 The translation here is inspired by Robinson, *Discovering the Qur'an*, 180.
164 See Robinson's table in ibid., 187.
165 Ibid.

This final verse (v. 46) is especially noteworthy: "It will be as if they, on the day they see it (*yaRawna-hā*), only tarried a single evening or its morning brightness (*DuḤā-hā*)." That the disbelievers will "see" (*yaRawna*) that Day recalls that Moses "showed" (*aRā*, v. 20) Pharaoh the greatest sign and that Hell will be displayed to whoever "sees" (*yaRā*, v. 36). The term "its morning brightness" (*DuḤā-hā*) recalls that God was said in the previous section to have brought out "its morning brightness" (*DuḤā-hā*, v. 29).

Most significant, however, is how the verse brings the entire composition to a solemn close. It concludes the sura by evoking the times of day alluded to in the image of the dawn raid that the sura opened with. The raid commenced in the darkness of the early morning and was completed before the sky had become bright. The state of the disbelievers on Judgment Day is compared to the somber condition of a people who have just experienced a surprise attack and have been stripped of their valuables. At the end of this tragic incident, the entire experience of life has been reduced in their minds to the brief slumber of the previous night and the shock of what they had awakened to.

It should now be clear that far from being a random assemblage of material, Sura 79 is a remarkably well ordered and integrated discourse in which the main idea—the Judgment—is developed in a step-by-step fashion, with each section powerfully building on cues from the previous ones.

"So when We have recited it, follow its recitation"

A topic that may appear to be completely out of place in a sura may, upon closer inspection, prove to be well integrated with the rest of the sura through the use of various types of anchors. Before concluding this chapter, we will briefly study an example of this in Sura 75, *The Resurrection* (*al-Qiyāma*). In this case, the title of the sura provides an accurate summary of its contents, as the entire sura is a discussion of the Resurrection. The one exception appears to be a parenthetical passage in which God addresses the Messenger, telling him not to hastily move his tongue reciting the revelations in an effort to commit them to memory, as God will ensure their preservation. The passage (vv. 16-19) is translated below, along with its immediately preceding and subsequent context:

13. Man will be informed on that Day of what he put forth and kept back.
14. Rather, man is against himself a witness, (*baṣīra-h*)
15. Even if he lays out his excuses. (*ma'ādhīra-h*)
16. Do not move your tongue with it so that you may hasten (*ta'JaLa*) in reciting it.
17. Indeed upon Us is its collection (*JaM'a-hu*) and its recitation, (*qur'āna-h*)
18. So when We have recited it, follow its recitation. (*qur'āna-h*)

19. Then indeed upon Us will be its elucidation. (*bayāna-h*)
20. No indeed! But you (plural) love the Hastily-Fleeting, (*al-'āJiLa*)
21. and you (plural) leave behind the Hereafter. (*al-ākhira*)

Verses 16-19 may appear out of place with their surrounding context or with the rest of the sura, to the extent that one might suspect these verses of having been wrongly interpolated into the text. However, a closer study indicates that that is not the case. To begin, the passage is linked to its succeeding context by the verb "hasten" (*ta'JaLa*) in v. 16, which shares the same root as the word used in v. 20 to designate the present world, "the Hastily-Fleeting" (*al-'ĀJiLa*). While the former command is addressed to the Messenger and the latter admonition is to the disbelievers, the shared root underscores a connection, in Robinson's words, "between the unbelievers' love for the world which will quickly disappear and the reciter's temptation to recite too quickly."[166]

The passage is also integrated into the rest of the sura through several other anchors. For example, with the exception of v. 16, the passage is linked to the opening section of the sura (vv. 1-6) by a shared end rhyme scheme:

1. No! I swear by the Day of Resurrection, (*qiyāma*)
2. And I swear by the self-reproaching soul— (*lawwāma*)
3. Does man think that We will not assemble (*naJMa'a*) his bones? (*'iẓāma-h*)
4. Indeed, We are able to reshape his very fingertips. (*banāna-h*)
5. Yet man wants to deny what is ahead of him: (*amāma-h*)
6. He says, "So, when will this Day of Resurrection be?" (*qiyāma*)

Additionally, the word "collection" (*JaM'a-hu*) in v. 17 of the passage recalls the earlier mention here of God's "assembling" (*naJMa'a*) the bones of the deceased in v. 3. The implication is that the same God who will reconfigure the bodies of the dead will configure the Qur'an in the hearts of the Messenger and his followers by ensuring that it is memorized.

What is more, the reference to the Prophet's "tongue" in v. 16 of the passage is part of the larger motif in this sura of God's power over human body parts: "bones" (v. 3), "fingertips" (v. 4), "faces" (vv. 22-25), backs (alluded to by the word "backbreaking task," *fāqira*, in v. 25), "collar bones" (v. 26), the "leg" (v. 29), and allusions to seminal emission and the formation of the embryo (vv. 37-38).[167]

166 Robinson, "The Qur'ān as the Word of God," *Heaven and Earth: Essex Essays in Theology and Ethics*, ed. Andrew Linzey and Peter J. Wexler (Worthing: Churchman), 1986, 53.
167 Robinson, *Discovering the Qur'an*, 139.

Finally, the passage is integrated perfectly into the symmetry of the sura, which divides into two precisely equal halves (vv. 1-19 and 20-40). Each half consists of 66 metrical feet, 119 long syllables, and 108 short syllables, with 68 of the syllables of each half being accented.[168]

* * *

We have seen in the case of two Early Meccan suras that a careful reading shows them to be far more orderly, well-integrated, and complete compositions than is generally recognized. To appreciate the coherence and structure of a sura on the most general level, one must pay attention to the main themes that are developed in each section and discern how they are related. A close reading in the Arabic further reveals that the sections of a sura are interlinked by a network of verbal cues and other devices, which we have dubbed "anchors," that highlight the subtler thematic connections between the different parts of the sura. As the recent surge of interest in the subject might suggest, the coherence of the Qur'anic sura turns out to be a rich, impressive, and highly rewarding study. We will continue to explore further examples and aspects of this study in the remaining chapters.

168 Robinson, "The Qur'ān as the Word of God," 50, citing Crapon De Caprona, *Le Coran: Aux Sources De La Parole Oraculaire*, 311-341.

CHAPTER 12

Symmetry in the Qur'an

In the previous chapter, we explored several aspects of the coherence of the Qur'anic sura: how it unfolds in a logical sequence; how its discrete sections combine to form a thematically coherent whole; and how key themes, terms, lexical roots, and even ending sounds bring unity to its different parts. Now, we will turn to an exciting aspect of the Qur'an's composition that has only started to come to light in recent decades: the symmetrical patterning of ideas, known as **ring composition**. To give an idea of what ring composition is, why it is important, and why the Qur'an uses it, it is helpful to give a brief historical background of this discovery.

In the field of Biblical studies, most scholars over the last two centuries have concentrated on historical and textual criticism.[169] These disciplines address issues such as the historical context and setting of the books of the Bible, their authorship, how the stories and traditions within them developed, how they compare with archaeological discoveries, and how reliably these texts have been transmitted. However, some scholars have focused instead on a literary study of the books of the Bible, trying to understand their poetics, literary composition, narrative techniques, major themes, and other literary qualities. Literary approaches to the Bible have become increasingly prominent in recent scholarship.

What is important for our purposes is that, while historical-critical scholars have often found various books of the Bible to lack structure and narrative coherence—putting this down to poor compositional skills on part of the author(s), or to interference by multiple authors or editors—some

169 The term "criticism"—as in "historical criticism," "textual criticism," or "literary criticism"—is a scholarly term that simply means "analysis." It does not denote faultfinding.

literary scholars have found, on the contrary, that Biblical authors and editors employed considerations of *symmetry* as their key principles of composition. While modern Western readers expect a book to flow in a connected, sequential order (ABCD…), the ancient Biblical writers were often equally if not more concerned with composing their books according to symmetrical patterns, which would draw meaningful connections between different parts of the book. These considerations of symmetry could apply on a small scale (such as even a single sentence) or on a large scale (such as a whole book, or even a group of books).

These symmetrical patterns took two main forms. The first kind is parallelism, in which the parts of a composition are ordered on the pattern AB/A'B'. (The parallel sides can be added to, such as ABC/A'B'C'.) This was the main organizing principle of Hebrew poetry, such as the Psalms, and in fact continues to be a ubiquitous feature of poetry to this day. For example, take the following line of the Book of Isaiah:

He shall judge between the nations,	A B /
And shall arbitrate for many peoples. (Isa. 2:4)	A' B'

In this example, typical of Hebrew poetry, the relationships between A ("shall judge") and A' ("shall arbitrate") and between B ("the nations") and B' ("many peoples") is that of synonymy, similarity, or close association. However, the relationship between the parallel terms does not have to be one of similarity. They could also be direct opposites, as in the following quote from Malcolm X:

> A man who stands for nothing will fall for anything. A B / A' B'

Here "stands for nothing" and "will fall for anything" stand in a parallel relationship, but in this case the parallel terms—A ("stands") and A' ("will fall"), B ("nothing") and B' ("anything")—are opposites. The point is that the parallel terms must have some conspicuous relationship, whether it is a relationship of similarity or something else.

The Qur'an also contains many examples of parallelism. A simple example is 28:73:

> And from His mercy He made for you the night and the day, so that you may rest in it and pursue from His bounty.

In this case, "night" (A) is associated with "rest" (A'), and "day" (B) with "pursuing from His bounty" (B'). A more complex example occurs in the opening of Sura 91, *The Sun* (*ash-Shams*), which we looked at in chapter 7, "Divine Oaths." It is a divine oath consisting of a series of parallelisms:

> By the sun and its morning brightness,
> By the moon when it follows it,
>
> By the day when it displays it,
> By the night when it veils it,
>
> By the sky and how He built it,
> By the earth and how He spread it out. (91:1-6)

Parallelism is an extremely common device in poetics and rhetoric, because it is simple, intuitive, aesthetically appealing, and potentially moving.

The second type of symmetrical form may be called *inverted* parallelism: it is where the terms or ideas are presented in one order but then repeated in the *reverse* order. This follows the pattern AB/B'A', such as in Jesus's saying, "But many who are first will be last, and the last will be first" (Matt. 19:30), or in the Qur'an, "He brings out the living from the dead and brings out the dead from the living" (6:95). This type of pattern is also known by other names, such as chiasmus,[170] chiastic structure, or **mirror composition** (we will occasionally use the latter term, because of its simplicity). The term **ring composition** is used to describe such a structure when it contains a discrete center. It could either have a stand-alone centerpiece that connects the two halves (as in AB**C**B'A') or simply be a mirror composition on a large or complex scale, such as ABC/C'B'A', in which C/C' might be considered the center. This type of structure is very prominent in the Qur'an and forms the subject of this chapter. A brief example in the Qur'an is the beginning of Sura 18, *The Cave* (*al-Kahf*):

> All praise is due to the One who sent down on His slave the Scripture and did not place in it any crookedness—
>
> A. Straight, to warn of a severe calamity from Him.
>   B. And to give glad tidings
>   C. To the believers,
>   C'. Those who perform good deeds,
>   B'. That for them is a good reward, in which they will remain forever,
> A'. And to warn those who say, "God has taken a son." (18:1-4)

---

170 Pronounced *kai-az-muhs*, from a Greek phrase meaning "to make an X," because when the corresponding terms are connected they are imagined to form an X: $\begin{smallmatrix} A & & B \\ & \times & \\ B' & & A' \end{smallmatrix}$.

Diagram 1

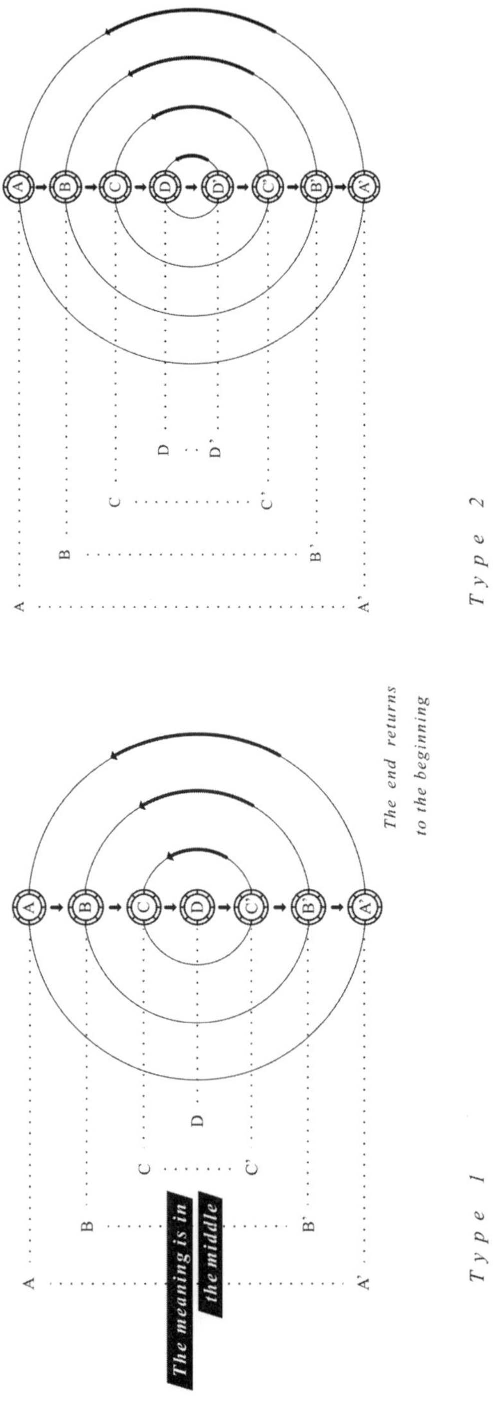

Diagrams of Ring Composition

Each segment, in some way, corresponds to and complements the segment directly opposite to it. The center, in this case, underscores faith and the performance of good deeds.

Several features are significant about ring composition. First, it may occur on a very large scale, even that of a whole book. Literary scholars of the Bible have found that various Biblical books are composed as ring structures. In some cases, a large-scale ring composition consists, in turn, of smaller rings. We will see an example of this in the Qur'an in chapter 13, "The Coherence and Structure of Sura 2, *The Cow*."

Second, ring composition was extremely widespread in the ancient world, and even up until modern times. After its discovery in the Hebrew Bible, scholars in other fields of literature have uncovered ring composition in such diverse works as Homer's *Iliad* in Greek; the Gathas, hymns attributed to the Iranian prophet Zoroaster in the Avestan language; Classical Arabic poetry; Chinese literature; the medieval Persian *Mathnawi* of Rumi; medieval European epic poems such as the Old English *Beowulf*, the French epic poem *chanson degeste*, and medieval German *Nibelungenlieder*; modern English poems such as John Milton's *Paradise Lost* and Ezra Pound's *Cantos*; and various genres of oral recital in different parts of the world.[171] Ring composition was ubiquitous in written and oral compositions throughout the ancient world, and continues to enjoy prominence in some cultures even into modern times. The discovery of ring composition is extremely important because works (especially from the ancient world) that scholars once regarded as "disorderly," "disjointed," "fragmented," "repetitive," "chaotic," "clumsy," "rambling," or "full of long digressions" have in fact turned out to be extremely coherent, structured, and well-organized.[172] This is certainly the case with the Qur'an.

Third, the ring form gives the composition potential to grow. For example, with appropriate additions, ABCB'A' can be expanded to ABCDC'B'A', or a linear composition can be made into a ring, such as ABCD becoming ABCDC'B'A'.[173] This may be relevant in the case of longer suras in the Qur'an

171 See Mary Douglas, *Thinking in Circles: An Essay on Ring Composition* (New Haven/London: Yale University Press, 2007), 4-12 and Raymond Farrin, *Abundance from the Desert: Classical Arabic Poetry* (Syracuse, NY: Syracuse University Press), 2011, xvii. On ring composition in Classical Arabic poetry, see Farrin, *Abundance from the Desert.*

172 Douglas, 9-11.

173 Thus, a pre-existing work can be expanded by its author or by later editors to either form a ring structure or expand an already existing ring. This may be the case with the Pentateuch or Torah (the first five books of the Bible), which some scholars have argued forms a ring composition, some adding the sixth Biblical book, the Book of Joshua, as well (see Douglas, xiii-xiv). This capacity for revision and addition was commonly utilized by live poets and folkloric reciters, who would recite a traditional story or poem but supply their own creative additions. In contrast to the Qur'anic memorizers and reciters, however, they were not concerned with word-for-word recall.

that exhibit ring composition, since at least some of them were revealed not all at once, but in piecemeal.

Finally, understanding ring composition is important for understanding the meaning of a composition. In a ring composition, usually "the meaning is located in the middle";[174] that is, the center of the composition literally underscores the central idea. The two halves of the composition may be seen as elaborations of that theme, and the beginning and ending segments (A and A') introduce and conclude that theme. Moreover, the ring structure points to common themes that underlie the two corresponding terms or segments on the opposite sides of the structure. In essence, the ring manifests the relationship between the parts and reveals the logic of the composition. It is important to add that the relationship between the two corresponding segments (e.g., B and B') does not always have to be immediately obvious. The discovery of a ring structure forces the audience to contemplate and uncover the relationship between the corresponding parts.[175]

The discovery and recent study of ring composition and other symmetrical patterns in the Qur'an owes especially to the work of Neal Robinson, Michel Cuypers, and Raymond Farrin.[176]

Short Passages

The Throne Verse

Muslim tradition regards 2:255, "The Throne Verse" (*Āyat al-Kursī*), as the most sacred verse in the entire Qur'an. It is a hymnic description of God's maintenance, sovereignty, and all-encompassing knowledge and awareness of the creation. Commentators have offered several different explanations of the word that we have translated as "throne" (*kursī*), but it is commonly recognized as a symbol of God's sovereignty. The verse is a beautiful example of a ring structure:

God, there is nothing worthy of worship but

A. He, the Living (*al-Ḥayy*), the Maintainer of Existence (*al-Qayyūm*).
  B. Neither drowsiness nor sleep overtakes Him.

---

174 Douglas, x.

175 Douglas writes, "When the reader finds two pages set in parallel that seem quite disparate, the challenge is to ask what they may have in common, not to surmise that the editor got muddled" (p. 36), and "We expect matching sections to be related by analogy, but the parallel is not always obvious. The reader who is puzzled can take it as a challenge to reflect further and to consider the seemingly obscure similarities the editors had in mind when they strung what we first see as two apparently dissimilar beads on the same rope" (p. 56).

176 See Randhawa, "A Bibliography of the Coherence and Structure of the Qur'an's Suras."

C. Whatever is in the heavens and whatever is on the earth is His.
D. Who can intercede before Him except by His permission?
E. He knows what is in front of them
E'. and what is behind them.
D'. They do not encompass anything of His knowledge except what He wills.
C'. His throne (*kursī*) extends over the heavens and the earth
B'. and their preservation does not burden Him.
A'. He is the Most High (*al-'Alīy*), the Great (*al-'Aẓīm*).

The opening and closing segments, A and A', both consist of the pronoun "He" and two names of God: the Living (*al-Ḥayy*) and the Maintainer of Existence (*al-Qayyūm*) (A), and the Most High (*al-'Alīy*) and the Great (*al-'Aẓīm*) (A'). The first two names relate to the contents of the rest of the verse because they highlight God's unfaltering maintenance of the entire creation. The divine name we have translated as "the Maintainer of Existence" (*al-Qayyūm*) is actually both intransitive (i.e., "the Self-Existent") and transitive (i.e., "the One who causes and maintains the existence of other things"). On the phonetic level, the names that are paired together display assonance: in A, *al-Ḥ**ayy*** and *al-Q**ayy**ūm*; and in A', *al-**'A**līy* and *al-**'A**ẓīm*. At the same time, the names that are directly opposite to each other on the ring terminate with the same letter-sound: *al-Ḥa**yy*** (A) and *al-'Ali**yy***[177] (A'); *al-Qayyū**m*** (A) and *al-'Aẓī**m*** (A').

B and B' both state that God's constant maintenance of the universe induces no strain or tiredness in Him. This is tied closely not only with His name *al-Qayyūm*, the "Maintainer of Existence," but also with His name "the Living" (*al-Ḥayy*), because sleep appears in the Qur'an and the hadiths as an analog of death. God's status as "the Living," whose life is perfect, therefore precludes Him from experiencing sleep or its onset. Similarly, God's maintenance of all creation indicates His majesty and greatness: "the Most High, the Great."

C and C' both affirm God's total ownership of creation, which follows from the fact that He is its cause and maintainer. The word *kursī* in C' may additionally signify God's knowledge, as the famous commentator aṭ-Ṭabarī (d. 923 CE) recorded, because it is mentioned immediately after His knowledge is described (E-D') and, furthermore, such knowledge is requisite for the complete ownership (C) and preservation (B') of the creation. Hence we see that the ring structure places each segment in relation to the one that comes immediately before it, the one that comes immediately after it, and

177 *'Aliyy* is an alternative way to transliterate *'Alīy*. In the Arabic, both *Ḥayy* and *Aliyy* end with a doubled 'y' or *yā'*.

the segment that mirrors it on the opposite side. It may also be added that God's knowledge presupposes His life and His awareness (A and B).

D and D' both concern the authority of God's will. Moreover, they also relate to His knowledge. In D, the allusion to God's knowledge is implicit: a person intercedes on behalf of another in order to *inform* the arbiter or judge of the goodness or innocence of that individual. Since God already has full knowledge of all that happens in the universe, who can plead a case for another in front of Him? Yet, even though God already has complete knowledge, He may permit certain exceptional persons to intercede on behalf of others, as a generous allowance on Judgment Day. D' refers to both God's will and knowledge explicitly: His knowledge encompasses all of creation, but His creatures can only grasp of that knowledge what He wills them to.

E and E' form the center, giving the central focus to God's knowledge, and thereby tying the surrounding parts together. This center refers to His knowledge of everything that is "in front of" and "behind" His creatures, both in space and in time. We have seen that the topic of God's knowledge underlies the surrounding segments. God's knowledge is also intrinsically related to each of the four divine attributes that frame the verse. First, God's attribute of being "the Living" (*al-Ḥayy*, A) implies, as we have already noted, that He is always awake and therefore always aware. Second, it is not only God's power but also His knowledge that qualifies Him to be "the Maintainer" (*al-Qayyūm*, A) of the universe and whatever is in it. Finally, His infinite knowledge is an aspect of His unlimited majesty, underlined by His names "the Most High" (*al-ʿAlīyy*) and "the Great" (*al-ʿAẓīm*) (A').

Through this first example, we can see that the ring structure of a composition can enhance its meanings by drawing semantic relationships between its different parts.

The Verse of Light

The "Verse of Light" (24:35) is another of the most treasured Qur'anic verses in Muslim devotion. We explored its meaning in chapter 6, "Figurative Language and Imagery," but without considering its structure, which is that of a ring:

A. God is the light of the heavens and the earth.
  B. The example of His light is like a niche in which there is a lamp. The lamp is in a glass, the glass as if it were a brilliant star.
    C. [The lamp] is lit from a blessed olive tree
      D. neither of the east
      D' nor of the west.
    C.' Its oil almost radiates even though a fire had not touched it.

B.' Light upon light.
A.' God guides to His light whomever He wills.

That "God is the light of the heavens and the earth" (A) signifies that He is both the source of physical light that manifests the beauty of creation and allows His creatures to see, as well as the source of spiritual light—guidance—that enlightens His creatures. God, as the source of this "light," is thus in the position to "guide to His light whomever He wills" (A').

B describes the lamp that gives off the light, part of which is intrinsic to it and part of which comes from an outside source. When the lamp inside the glass (i.e., the light contained within a pure heart) is ignited by a radiant flame (i.e., revelation), the effect is "light upon light" (B').

C describes the fuel of the lamp—the oil, which may be understood as a symbol for the pure human spirit. Because it derives from such a "blessed" source, the oil "almost radiates even though a fire had not touched it" (C'). That is, the pure human spirit possesses its own glow even before the light of revelation kindles it.

The center emphasizes that the source of the inner light of the human being is "neither of the east nor of the west." All human spirits originate from a single, non-terrestrial source. Therefore, pure human spirits are not confined to any geographical location, but are dispersed across the earth, regardless of direction. God does not restrict His guidance to any particular race, region, or nationality, but only requires that a person has kept his pure nature intact. It is when the light of revelation reaches such people that it ignites their spirits, producing the "light upon light" that illuminates the dark corners of the world.

Short Suras

Sura 101: The Crashing Blow (al-Qāriʿa)[178]

Sura 101, *The Crashing Blow* (*al-Qāriʿa*) is a brief but powerful description of the catastrophic breaking-in of Judgment Day. Its power derives from a combination of the mystery and suspense that it invokes, its imagery, its symmetry, and its patterns of sound. We have indicated the word at the end of each line, so that the reader can see the end rhyme that exists in the Arabic.

A. The Crashing Blow (*al-Qāriʿa*)!
  B. What is the Crashing Blow (*…al-Qāriʿa*)?

---

178 This is paraphrased from Michel Cuypers, "Semitic Rhetoric as a Key to the Question of the *Naẓm* of the Qur'anic Text," *Coherence in the Qur'an* 13.1 (2011): 7-9.

And what will convey to you what the Crashing Blow is? (…*al-Qāri'a*)

C. On a Day people will be like scattered moths, (…*mabthūth*) and the mountains will be like tufts of carded wool— (…*manfūsh*)

C'. Then as for one whose good deeds are heavy on the scales, then he will be in a pleasant life. (…*rāḍiya*).
But as for one whose good deeds are light, then his home will be the Abyss (…*hāwiya*).

B'. And what will convey to you what she [the Abyss] is? (…*mā hiya*)

A'. Blazing fire (*nārun ḥāmiya*).

The sura is a mirror composition in which the first half (ABC) describes the cosmic upheaval that will occur at the onset of Judgment Day, called *al-Qāriʿa*, while the second half (C'B'A') describes the outcome of the Judgment. Both of these descriptions are incomplete, suggesting that words alone can convey only a small glimpse of these realities. The very name *al-Qāriʿa* also carries a frightening air of vagueness: it is capable of various possible translations, including "the Crashing Blow," "the Calamity," and "the Crushing."

The sura is framed by two isolated terms: A, "The Crashing Blow" (*al-Qāriʿa*) and A', "Blazing fire" (*nārun ḥāmiya*). The former, as we have noted, alludes to the cosmic upheaval of Judgment Day, while the latter alludes to Hell. Their relationship as manifestations of divine judgment is underscored not only by their placement across from each other on the mirror, but also by their rhyme (*qār**iʿa**/ḥām**iya***).

B and B' both pose the question, "What will convey to you what X is?" ("*wa-mā adrāka mā* X?"), the former about "the Crashing Blow" and the latter about "the Abyss." Again, the answers that follow only offer warnings, and shy of attempting to convey a full grasp of these realities.

At the core of the sura are C and C', each containing a parallelism. C consists of two parallel similes that offer a partial glimpse of the "the Crashing Blow" of Judgment Day, one comparing the people on that Day to scattered moths and the other likening the mountains, apparently the most stable objects in nature, to tufts of wool being torn from their roots. C' concerns the outcome of the Judgment, containing two parallel but contrasting portraits of the fates of the righteous and the damned. In accordance with the overall tenor of the sura, the fate of the righteous is described vaguely, but assuredly, as "a pleasant life," while the "home" of the damned is referred to even more enigmatically as "the Abyss," evoking a sense of both mystery and despair. This sense of despair is heightened by a second, underlying image: the word used here for "home," *umm*, literally means "mother," and the word for the "Abyss," *hāwiya*, also denotes a woman bereft of her child.[179] The sense of mystery concerning what "the Abyss" is becomes heightened (B') and then only partially resolved—but the sense of anguish intensified—by its characterization as (or comparison to) "blazing fire" (A').

Sura 85: The Celestial Fortresses (al-Burūj)[180]

Sura 85, *The Celestial Fortresses* (*al-Burūj*), was revealed in the Meccan period, in the context of the violent persecution of the Prophet's followers. What follows is a literal translation of the sura, with a few notes added in parentheses. The sura is a ring composition, with the center emphasizing God's justice as it will be fully realized in the afterlife. An extended commentary should not be necessary to show the correspondences between each verse and its counterpart on the opposite side of the structure.

- A. By the heaven containing the celestial fortresses (*burūj*), (v. 1)
  - B. And by the Promised Day (i.e., "promised" in the Qur'an), (v. 2)
    - C. And by the witness and the witnessed: (v. 3)
      - D. Cursed be the Companions of the Trench, (v. 4)
        - E. The fire containing fuel, when they were sitting over it ("news" of their deeds) (*qu'ūd*) (vv. 5-6)[181]
          - F. While they were witnesses over what they did (*yaF'aLūna*) to the believers. (v. 7)
            - G. They only tormented them for believing in God, the Almighty, the Praiseworthy (*ḥamīd*). (v. 8)
              - H. To Him belongs whatever is in the heavens and the earth
                - I. And He is over everything a witness (*shahīd*). (v. 9)
                  - J. Indeed those who persecute the believing men and women and then do not repent, then for them is the punishment of Hell and for them is the punishment of burning. (v. 10)

---

179 See Sells, 24-26, 113, who highlights the psychological and emotional complexity that the sounds and images of the sura evoke.

180 This analysis is summarized from Robinson, *Discovering the Qur'an*, 312, n. 11, with some slight modifications.

181 The "Companions of the Trench" dug the trench and set it ablaze, executing the believers in its flames. The title "Companions of the Trench" has a certain irony: in the afterlife they will abide in the trenches of Hell. Commentators identify the event described here either as a specific incident, namely the massacre of the Christians of Najrān (also called "the Trench," *al-Ukhdūd*) by the South Arabian Jewish warlord Dhū Nuwās in c. 524 CE, or simply as a universal description of the persecution and massacre of believers throughout history.

J.' Indeed those who believe and do righteous deeds, for them are gardens underneath which rivers flow. That is the great victory. (v. 11)

I.' Truly the grip of your Lord is severe (*shadīd*). (v. 12)

H'. Truly He is the Originator and the Repeater (of creation). (v. 13)

G.' And He is the Forgiving, the Loving, Possessor of the Majestic Throne (*majīd*), (vv. 14-15)

F.' Doer (*Fa"āL*) of what He wills. (v. 16)

E.' Has the news of the armies reached you, of Pharaoh and Thamūd? (vv. 17-18)

D.' Indeed, those who disbelieve are in denial (v. 19)

C.' While God is encompassing them from behind. (v. 20)

B.' Indeed, this is a Majestic Qur'an (v. 21)

A'. In a Guarded (Heavenly) Tablet (*maḥfūẓ*) (v. 22)

The theme of the sura is the persecution and martyrdom of believers for holding on to their faith in one God, and in particular their reward with God and His retribution of their persecutors. The divine oath in the first verse invokes the "celestial fortresses" as a witness, and the motif of "witnessing" recurs as an anchor throughout the sura. The believers are assured—and the disbelievers warned—that their plight has been witnessed. The center emphasizes that those who hold onto their faith and good works while they are persecuted or martyred will attain "the great victory," even if they may seem to have lost everything in this world. In contrast, their persecutors—if they do not repent—will be treated to "the punishment of Hell...and burning." The various names and qualities of God invoked in this sura—"a Witness over everything," Owner of "the heavens and the earth," "Possessor of the Majestic Throne," "the Almighty," "the Praiseworthy," "Originator and Repeater" of creation, "the Forgiving," "the Loving," "the Executor of what He wills," and the "Encompassing"—all buttress the central message by reassuring the believers in the midst of their persecution.

A Medium-Sized Sura

Sura 12: Joseph (Yūsuf)

In chapter 9, "Storytelling in the Qur'an I," we explored the central role of irony in developing the plot and themes of the story of *Joseph* in Sura 12, the only sura devoted entirely to a complete, chronological narrative. Joseph was betrayed as a youth by his brothers and sold into slavery, but despite the trials and temptations that confronted him, he steadfastly maintained his moral integrity and trust in God. This trust was rewarded, as God used those very trials to make Joseph a great prophet, a hero of Egypt, and a member of high office, thereby saving his family from famine and reuniting them with him under prosperous conditions in Egypt. As Joseph states to his brothers at the end of the story, "Whoever is conscious of God and is patient—God does not let the reward of the good-doers go to waste" (v. 90). This theme is part of a wider theological teaching that "God is in complete control of His affairs, although most people do not know" (v. 21).

Recently, a number of scholars have observed that the narrative of Joseph is a ring composition, in which the conflicts of the story lead up to a central turning point—Joseph's interpretation of the king's dream—and are then resolved in the opposite order:[182]

A. Prologue (vv. 1-3)
  B. Joseph's vision (vv. 4-7)
    C. Joseph's disputes with his brothers: guile of the brothers towards Joseph (vv. 8-18)
      D. Joseph's relative promotion (vv. 19-22)
        E. Attempted seduction of Joseph by the woman (vv. 23-34)
          F. Joseph in prison, interpreter of the visions of both prisoners, and **prophet of monotheism** (vv. 35-42)
          F'. Joseph in prison, interpreter of the visions of the king (vv. 43-49)
        E'. Outcome of the woman's seduction: Joseph rehabilitated (vv. 50-53)
      D'. Joseph's definitive promotion (vv. 54-57)
    C'. Joseph's disputes with his brothers: Joseph's guile towards his brothers (vv. 58-98)
  B'. Fulfillment of Joseph's vision (vv. 99-101)
A'. Epilogue (vv. 102-111)

The center (F) contains a key passage, which is itself structured as a ring:

A. Joseph promises to interpret the dreams of his prison-mates (vv. 35-37)
  B. "'And I have followed the religion of **my fathers** Abraham, Isaac, and Jacob. **It was not appropriate for us to associate anything with God. That is from God's favor upon us and upon mankind, but most of mankind are not grateful** (*wa-lākin akthara 'n-nāsi lā yashkurūn*).'" (v. 38)

182 Of particular note are Mustansir Mir, "The Qur'anic Story Of Joseph: Plot, Themes, And Characters," *Muslim World* 76.1 (1986): 1-2, and Cuypers, "Semitic Rhetoric," 15-19. The outline I have presented is that of Cuypers.

C. "'O my two prison-mates! Are diverse lords better, or God the One, the Mighty?'" (v. 39)

B'. "'You do not worship besides him but names that you have named, you and **your fathers**, for which God has sent down no authority. **The decision is with God, and He commands that you do not worship other than Him. That is the upright religion, but most of mankind do not know** (*wa-lākin akthara 'n-nāsi lā ya'lamūn*)'" (v. 40)

A'. Joseph interprets the dreams of his prison-mates. (vv. 41-42)

In the center of this passage (C), Joseph invites his prison-mates to reflect on whether they should worship many deities or only serve the One who is characterized by unity and might. The reference to God as "the One" draws a parallel between Joseph and Muhammad, whose mission was to call his people to monotheism. It also recalls the historical background of the sura, the persecution of the Prophet and his followers by their own tribesmen—just as Joseph was persecuted by his own brothers—specifically on account of their monotheistic stance. The reference to God as "the Mighty" recalls the theme stated in v. 21, that "God is in complete control of His affairs," and therefore is fully capable of reversing the fortunes of those who persevere in the face of oppression and hardship, showing trust in Him and excelling in good works. God's attributes of unity and might, singled out for mention at the center of the sura, are key to the sura's themes and purposes.

* * *

In pre-modern times, ring composition was a highly valued way of structuring a text. It demands profound literary sophistication and ingenuity, endows the text with rich meaning and internal structure, is aesthetically impressive, and rewards the attentive reader with the excitement of discovery. It therefore makes great sense that it would occur as such a pervasive feature of a text like the Qur'an, which has been regarded throughout the ages as a miracle of literature and rhetoric. This feature becomes even more interesting when we consider examples of it on a larger and more complex scale. Thus, in the next chapter, we will see what roles ring composition and other aspects of coherence play in the largest and most complex sura of the Qur'an, *The Cow*.

CHAPTER 13

The Coherence and Structure of Sura 2, *The Cow*

After contemplating the brief and elegantly simple opening sura of the Qur'an (see chapter 15, "Sura 1, *The Opening*"), the reader turns the page and is confronted with the longest and one of the most complex suras of the entire scripture, Sura 2, *The Cow* (*al-Baqara*). The main themes and lessons of the sura are not difficult to grasp, but what challenges many readers—including seasoned scholars—is understanding the flow of the sura's discourse, the connections between its diverse topics, and its structure. To such readers, the sura seems to address a bewildering variety of issues, without obvious relevance to each other, and frequently shifts from one topic to the next and back to earlier ones. The reader encounters, in order, the following topics: believers and disbelievers; creation; Paradise, Hell, and Resurrection; the story of Adam; a lengthy and non-chronological review of the history of the Children of Israel; the story of Abraham's and Ishmael's construction of the Ka'ba; Jacob's (Israel's) testament to his sons; the religion of Abraham and the prophets among his descendants; the change in the direction of prayer from Jerusalem to the Ka'ba; the establishment of the new Muslim community; warnings of upcoming tests from God; pilgrimage to the Ka'ba; monotheism, idolatry, and disbelief; dietary regulations; righteousness; regulations concerning the crime of manslaughter, inheritance, fasting, pilgrimage, battle, spending in charity, marriage, and divorce; the Biblical story of Saul; God's attributes; the Resurrection; regulations about financial transactions; the Day of Judgment; and a concluding prayer—with some other topics addressed briefly in between. In the judgment of many readers and scholars, the sheer variety and supposed randomness of the sura's subject matter counter any attempt to view the sura as a unified composition.

As one of several long Medinan suras, *The Cow* also presents a number of challenges in terms of its form or structure that we did not encounter with the Early Meccan suras. Dividing the Medinan suras into smaller thematic sections is more difficult, as a single section may address a stream of issues, the rhyme scheme of the sura is more uniform, and the transition from one thematic section to another tends to be subtle. Accordingly, many scholars, Muslim and non-Muslim, have suggested that these suras are largely miscellaneous patchworks of revelation from different occasions, collected together without any meaningful structure or arrangement.

Given this state of affairs, it is all the more remarkable that recent studies have uncovered a stunning degree of unity, coherence, and organization in the long Medinan suras.[183] This is especially the case with *The Cow*. In this chapter, we will see how the diverse topics of the sura are presented in light of a central theme, how the topics are ordered in a meaningful sequence, and how the sura possesses a beautiful and intricate structure.

To explore the sura's coherence exhaustively would require an entire book. What we will instead aim to do in this chapter is to follow the linear flow of the sura's discourse, seeing how one discussion is connected to the next, how the sura consists of discrete and coherent sections, and how each section builds on those before it, resulting in a harmonious and beautifully structured whole. To prevent this chapter from becoming too long, we will explore only the first and final sections of the sura in detail, while providing just a summary look at the linear coherence of the intervening sections.[184] Nonetheless, we will still chart the structure of each section, and eventually look at the structure of the sura as a whole.

Our study of the coherence and structure of Sura 2 in this chapter builds on the work that has been done successively by a number of scholars, namely Amin Ahsan Islahi, Neal Robinson, A.H. Matthias Zahniser, Nevin Reda,

---

183 Suras 2-5, which are the longest and most complex Medinan suras, have received significant study. See Randhawa, "A Bibliography of Studies in English on the Coherence and Structure of the Qur'an's Suras."

184 For a more detailed summary of the contents each section and their linear and integrative coherence, see Robinson, *Discovering the Qur'an*, 203-223. Much of our description of the linear coherence of each section summarizes Robinson, especially for sections 5-7. Note however that our analysis of the number of sections in the sura and where they begin and end differs on some points from his.

and Raymond Farrin.[185] Our analysis of the structure of the sura is especially indebted to Farrin's work. However, we have contributed a substantially new analysis of the internal structure of most of the sections, in one case adjusting the border between two sections (sections 2 and 3) accordingly. We have also offered fresh observations about the integrative coherence between certain sections, particularly between the first two sections and between the first and last sections. A more complete exploration of the coherence of Sura 2, involving an in-depth look within each of its sections, calls for its own separate publication. For now, however, we will merely aim to provide an overview of how sophisticated the composition of the sura really is, and to inspire interest in the prospect of future studies of this kind.

Historical Background

To fully appreciate the discussions within *The Cow* and how they are related, it is important to bear its historical context in mind. Most of the sura was revealed over the course of the first year and a half of the Medinan period, after the Prophet's migration to Medina in the summer of 622 and before the Battle of Badr in March of 624. Most of the inhabitants of Medina had embraced the message of Islam, and they had invited the Prophet and his followers in Mecca to come settle in their city. As a result, in Medina, the Muslims no longer remained a small, persecuted minority, but became an autonomous community independent from the Quraysh of Mecca, regulated by the Qur'anic revelations, and with the Prophet as their political and judicial head. Moreover, they entered into a pact or covenant of solidarity with the city's Jewish tribes, which stipulated that in the event of an outside attack, they would all fight as one for the common defense.

The early Medinan period was not without serious challenges, however. Despite the pact, the leaders of the Jewish tribes became increasingly antagonistic towards the Prophet and the Muslim community, resulting in

185 Amīn Aḥsan Iṣlāḥī, *Tadabbur-e-Qur'ān: Pondering Over the Qur'ān, Volume 1: Tafsīr of Sūrah al-Fātiḥah and Sūrah al-Baqarah*, trans. Mohammad Saleem Kayani (Kuala Lampur: Islamic Book Trust, 2006), 526-527; Mustansir Mir, "The Sūra as a Unity: A Twentieth Century Development in Qur'an Exegesis" in *Approaches to the Qur'an*, eds. G. R. Hawting and Abdul-Kader A. Shareef, eds. (London: Routledge, 1993), 211–24; Robinson, *Discovering the Qur'an*, 201-223; A. H. Mathias Zahniser, "Major Transitions and Thematic Borders in Two Long Sūras: al-Baqara and al-Nisā'" in *Literary Structures of Religious Meaning in the Qur'an*, ed. Issa J. Boulatta (Richmond: Curzon, 2000); Raymond Farrin, "Surat al-Baqara: A Structural Analysis," *Muslim World* 100.1 (2010): 17-32; Nevin Rida El-Tehry, *Textual Integrity and Coherence in the Qur'an: Repetition and Narrative Structure in Surat al-Baqara* (PhD diss., University of Toronto, Toronto, 2010); Farrin, *Structure and Qur'anic Interpretation*, 9-21.

deep political and religious tensions. Along with members of the Jewish tribes, there were insincere converts within the Muslim community—especially former political or tribal leaders—who attempted to undermine the authority of the Prophet and the unity of the Medinan society. Moreover, the need for a unified and disciplined community was becoming increasingly urgent, as the Quraysh continued to be a hostile force and the prospect of war with the far more powerful pagan tribe was becoming imminent. Sura 2, *The Cow*, was revealed to address these audiences and circumstances.

Coherence within Section 1 (Faith and Disbelief, vv. 1-39)

Linear summary of section 1

> "*This is the scripture concerning which there is no doubt—a guidance for the God-conscious: those who believe in the unseen and establish the prayer and spend out of what We have provided them; those who believe in what was sent down to you and what was sent down before you, and in the afterlife they are certain. It is they who are upon guidance from their Lord and it is they who are the successful*" (vv. 2-5).

The first section of *The Cow* is a long introduction that presents the sura's main themes. It begins with a profile of three types of people in terms of their receptiveness to the guidance of the revealed scripture (vv. 1-20). The first two groups are diametrically opposed: they are "those who believe" or "the God-conscious" (vv. 2-5), and "those who disbelieve" (vv. 6-7). The believers are described as those who believe in and are conscious of "the unseen"—that is, realities that are beyond the reach of physical sight—who have consistent faith in all that God has revealed, and who establish the prayer and spend on righteous causes. In contrast, the disbelievers are described as those whose hearts, hearing, and vision are completely sealed off from faith and guidance, as they are people who insist on their disbelieving ways in spite of all warning. Already, in the first six verses, we are exposed to a variety of terms that embody the major themes of the sura, and which constitute key anchors that will recur throughout it: "scripture" (*kitāb*), "guidance" (*hudā*), "God-consciousness" (*taqwā*), "faith" (*īmān*), "establishing the prayer" (*iqāmat aṣ-ṣalāh*), "spending" (*infāq*), "disbelief" (*kufr*), and others.

The third group that is described (vv. 8-20) is, for all intents and purposes, a subgroup of the second. They are people who claim to be believers, but who are in fact disbelievers. Their descriptions in this passage are echoed in later verses about the Children of Israel, making it clear that this category refers historically to a segment of the Jewish community in Medina.[186] For convenience, we will refer to this group as the "pseudo-believers." Among their descriptions is that they have "purchased error in exchange for guidance (*hudā*), so their transaction did not profit them, nor were they guided" (v. 16). The description of guidance and misguidance through the metaphor of a financial transaction is a motif that runs throughout this sura, as we have already seen in chapter 6, "Figurative Language and Imagery." This motif in fact combines two of the major themes of the sura: spiritual guidance and spending of wealth. The descriptions of the pseudo-believers end in two parables about how God takes away their light and vision, leaving them in darkness. The second parable ends by mentioning that God is "powerful over all things" (v. 20).

The above profile of the three groups is followed by a short address encapsulating the main themes of the Qur'an (vv. 21-29)—in essence, a summary of the contents of faith. Humankind are first exhorted to worship God alone, who created them, made the world a habitable place for them, and gave them sustenance—physical proofs of God's "power over all things" mentioned immediately prior in v. 20. If they are in doubt about the divine origins of the revelation, they are challenged to try to "produce a sura like it" and to call upon witnesses who can testify that they have successfully met the challenge. This is followed up with a brief warning of Hellfire for the disbelievers if they fail to meet the challenge and persist in their disbelief, and a parable describing the rewards of Paradise for those who have faith and do righteous deeds. Following this, the disparaging attitude of the pseudo-believers towards God's parables is contrasted with that of true believers. It is stressed that although God both guides and misguides through His revelation, He only misguides through it the "defiantly corrupt"—those "who break God's covenant after contracting it" and "cause corruption on the earth," the latter description recalling one of the attributes of the pseudo-believers (v. 12). Finally, the disbelievers are asked how they can disbelieve in God, who created them, will resurrect them, and who created the heavens and earth.

The above address is directed in general terms to "mankind," begins and ends with the mention of God's creation of humanity (vv. 21, 29), and highlights the themes of faith and disbelief. It is therefore appropriate that what follows is an account of the story of the creation of mankind, the story of Adam (vv. 30-39), which is used in this context to further illustrate the contrasting attitudes of faith and disbelief. We have studied this account in chapter 10, "Storytelling in the Qur'an II," but we will summarize it again here. God announces to the angels His intention to create mankind, saying, "I will place on the earth a vicegerent"—that is, a representative appointed to act on behalf

186 Echoes of vv. 8-20 can been seen in vv. 41, 55, 60, 76-77, 79, 86, 90-91, 93, 100, 102-103, 108, 121, 170-171, 174-175, and 248.

of God and given discretionary power. The angels, understanding that this power will include the freedom and ability to commit great evils, question why God would create on the earth "one who will cause corruption on it and shed blood," while they worship God flawlessly. For the moment, God appears to merely assure them that He knows best. He then goes on to teach this new creature, Adam, "the names, all of them," which includes the names and traits of each member of the human race that will descend from him. When Adam displays this knowledge, and God showcases some of the righteous members of Adam's progeny to the angels, they glorify God's knowledge and wisdom. The angels, despite their initial doubts about Adam, came to show full conviction in his status as God's vicegerent once they were provided with the requisite knowledge. In this capacity, they represent those among the Prophet's audience who may at first have been uncertain about his prophetic status, but after acquiring the necessary knowledge fully embraced the faith.

On account of their newfound appreciation of his status, God commands the angels to prostrate to Adam. However, Iblīs (Satan) refuses God's command out of intent denial and arrogance, exposing himself as a disbeliever. Determined to undermine Adam and his wife, Iblīs tempts them to eat from a forbidden tree and to thereby become expelled from the heavenly Garden. While Iblīs only grows firmer in his disbelief and wrongdoing, Adam and his wife strive to correct themselves and to attain God's forgiveness, thereby demonstrating the human being's capacity for moral and spiritual growth. Although both humankind and Satan and his progeny are exiled to the earth, God promises that He will send guidance, recalling the description of the Qur'an at the very beginning of the section as "a guidance for the God-conscious" (v. 2). God assures that those who follow His guidance will, in the end, have nothing to fear or grieve, but also warns that those who deny His guidance will become inhabitants of the Fire. The story serves to highlight the essential differences between the God-conscious believer and the obstinate disbeliever, expanding on the thematic contrast presented at the very beginning of the section. Although believers and disbelievers may both fall into sin, the believer acknowledges his wrong, strives to amend himself, and implores God's forgiveness, while the disbeliever insists on his wrongdoing and refuses divine guidance.

Integrative coherence of section 1

The various parts of section 1 are linked together by a profusion of anchors. The list below is just a sample. Observe how even seemingly separate topics or discussions are integrated by the use of anchors, drawing thematic connections between them:

- "This is the scripture concerning which there is no **doubt** (*rayb*)" (v. 2); "if you are in **doubt** (*rayb*) about what We have sent upon Our servant, then produce a sura like it" (v. 23).
- "who believe in the **unseen** (*ghayb*)" (v. 3); "[God] said, 'Did I not tell you that I know the **unseen** (*ghayb*) of the heavens and the earth?'" (v. 33).
- "it is they who are the fools, but they do not **know** (*lā ya'LaMūn*)" (v. 13); "do not attribute rivals to God while you **know** (*ta'LaMūN*) (v. 22); "those who believe **know** (*ya'LaMūna*) it is the truth" (v. 26); "'Indeed I **know** (*a'LaMu*) what you do not **know** (*lā ta'lamūna*)'" (v. 30; cf. 29, 32-33); "and He **taught** (*'aLLaMa*) Adam the names, all of them" (v. 31).
- "who believe in what was **sent down** (*uNZiLa*) to you and what was **sent down** (*uNZiLa*) before you" (v. 4); "and He **sent down** (*aNZaLa*) water from the sky" (v. 22); "if you are in doubt about what We have **sent down** (*NaZZaLnā*) to Our slave…" (v. 23).
- "When it is said to them 'Do not **cause corruption on the earth** (*lā tufsidū fi'l-arḍ*)' they say, 'We are only reformers'" (v. 11); "who break God's covenant…and **cause corruption on the earth** (*yufsidūna fī 'l-arḍ*) (v. 27); "When your Lord said to the angels, 'I will place **on the earth** (*fī 'l-arḍ*) a vicegerent,' they said, 'Will you place on it one who will **cause corruption on it** (*yufsidū fi-hā*)…?'" (v. 30).
- "their **example** (*MaTHaL*) is like one who kindled a fire" (v. 17); "then produce a sura like it (*MiTHLi-hi*)" (v. 23); "God is not timid to present an **example** (*MaTHaL*)…but as for those who disbelieve, they say, 'What does God intend by this as an example (*MaTHaL*)?'" (v. 26).
- "their example is like one who **kindles** (*istaWQaDa*) a **fire** (*NāR*)" (v. 17); "fear the **Fire** (*NāR*) whose **fuel** (*WuQūD*) is men and stones" (v. 24); "those are the Companions of the **Fire** (*NāR*)" (v. 39).
- "they put their fingers in their ears…fearing **death** (*MaWT*) (v. 19); "how can you disbelieve in God when you were **lifeless** (*aMWāT*), then He gave you life, then He will **cause you to die** (*yuMīTu-kum*)" (v. 28).
- "and call your witnesses **if you are truthful** (*in kuntum ṣādiqīn*)" (v. 23); "[God] said, 'Tell me the names of these **if you are truthful** (*in kuntum ṣādiqīn*)'" (v. 31).
- "they will have **Gardens** (*JaNNāt*)…and they will have purified **spouses** (*aZWāJ*)" (v. 25); "We said, 'O Adam, dwell you and your **wife** (*ZaWJ*) in **the Garden** (*al-JaNNa*) (v. 35).
- "and they spend of what We have **provided** (*RaZQnā*) for them" (v. 3); "and brought thereby **fruits** (*THaMaRāt*) as a **provision** (*RiZQ*) for you" (v. 22); "whenever they are **provided** (*RuZiQū*) a **provision** (*RiZQ*) from its **fruit** (*THaMaRa*), they will say, 'This is what we were **provided** (*RuZiQnā*) before'" (v. 25).

This repetition of anchors shows that the section is a remarkably coherent network of overlapping terms and motifs, and serves to underscore subtle connections between seemingly disparate passages.

Symmetry of section 1

In addition to the linear flow and integrative coherence of the section, it is beautifully organized into five mirror or or ring compositions:

vv. 2-5: The believers	vv. 6-20: The disbelievers
A. (guidance) "This is the scripture concerning which there is no doubt—a **guidance** for the God-conscious ***(al-muttaqīn)***:	A. Whether you warn those who disbelieve or not, they will not believe; their hearts, vision, and hearing are sealed (6-7).
B. (faith) **those who believe in** the unseen	B. Among the people are those who say, "We believe," but do not really believe; they seek to deceive but only deceive themselves; they will be punished because they lie (8-10).
C. (action) and establish the prayer	C. When it is said to them, "Do not cause corruption," they say, "We are only reformers"—but it is they who are the corrupters (11-12).
C'. (action) and spend out of what We have provided them,	C'. When it is said to them, "Believe," they say, "Shall we believe as the fools believe?"—but it is they who are the fools (13).
B'. (faith) **those who believe in** what was sent down to you and what was sent down before you, and in the afterlife they are certain.	B'. When they meet the believers they say, "We believe," but when they go to their devils they say, "We were only mocking"; God mocks them; their transaction does not profit them (14-15).
A'. (guidance) It is they who are on **guidance** from their Lord and they who are the successful (***al-mufliḥūn***)."	A'. They are deaf, dumb, blind; they lit a fire but God took away its light; God takes away their sight (16-20).

vv. 21-29: God and creation, belief in the revelation, and resurrection
A. Mankind, worship your Lord who created you; who made the earth and sky for you and the earth's fruit; do not set up rivals to Him while you know (21-22).
B. Disbelievers and revelation (23-24).
C. Paradise for those who believe and do good deeds (25).
B'. Disbelievers and revelation (26-28).
A'. He gave you all life and will resurrect you; He created for you all that is on the earth and made the seven skies; He knows all things (28-29).

vv. 30-34a: Adam and the angels	vv. 35b-39: Adam and Satan
A. God announces to the angels that He will create a vicegerent (Adam) (30a).	A. Satan refuses to prostrate to Adam: he was one of the disbelievers (34).
B. The angels question; God responds, "I know what you do not know" (30b).	B. God tells Adam and Eve to dwell in the Garden (but not to approach a specified tree) (35).
C. God teaches Adam all the names; the angels are commanded to inform of them if they can (31).	C. Satan causes them to disobey; they are all commanded to "go down" (36).
D. The angels confess, "Exalted are you! We have no knowledge except what You taught us. Indeed it is You who are the Knowing, the Wise" (32).	D. "Adam acquired words from his Lord and He accepted his repentance. Indeed it is He who is the Returning, the Merciful" (37).
C'. Adam informs the angels of the names (33a).	C'. They are all commanded to "go down,"
B'. God says to the angels, "Did I not tell you I know the unseen of the heavens and the earth? And I know what you manifest and what you have concealed" (33b).	B'. but God assures, "Whoever follows My guidance, there will be no fear upon them nor will they grieve" (i.e., like the state of the inhabitants of the Garden) (38).
A'. God commands the angels to prostrate to Adam (34a).	A'. "But those who disbelieve and deny Our signs, they are the companions of the Fire, remaining in it" (39).

Looking horizontally, the two mirror structures at the beginning form complementary opposites ("the believers" vs. "the disbelievers"), as do the two at the end ("Adam and the angels" vs. "Adam and Satan"). Looking vertically, the two on the left side underscore the behaviors of the faithful ("the believers" and "the angels"), and the two on the right side underscore the behavior of disbelievers ("the disbelievers" and "Satan"). The ring in the center brings together the main themes of the Qur'an: monotheism and creation, faith and disbelief in the message, and the afterlife.

Take special notice of the messages that are highlighted by each of the mirror or ring structures. The first mirror structure (vv. 2-5) introduces the themes of guidance, faith, and righteous action (guidance itself consisting of faith and righteous action), while the second mirror structure (vv. 6-20) is concerned with the opposite characteristics. The third structure (vv. 21-29), which is at the center of the entire section, is a ring, outlining the contents, attitudes, and consequences of faith and disbelief. At its own center, and hence the central verse of the entire section, it draws attention to the rewards in store for those who have faith and do righteous actions.

The centers of the two bottom rings highlight the themes of faith and righteous deeds respectively. The quotation of the angels in the center of the bottom-left ring (v. 32) is an exclamation of *faith* (also note the emphasis on knowledge), and the names of God that are mentioned in the verse ("the Knowing" and "the Wise") underscore why a person should invest such faith. The allusion to Adam's repentance in the center of the bottom-right ring (v. 37) highlights the *action* of the believer, and the divine names that are mentioned here underscore why a person should engage in virtuous acts like repentance: namely, that God is "Returning" and "Merciful" towards those who do so.

Finally, the entire section is bracketed by the same key terms and themes, forming what is known as an *inclusio* or envelope structure:

Opening (vv. 2-7)

Those who follow guidance	Their outcome
"This is the scripture concerning which there is no doubt—a **guidance** (*HuDan*) for the God-conscious…It is they who are upon **guidance** (*HuDan*) from their Lord…"	"…and it is they who are the successful."
Those who disbelieve	**Their outcome**
"**Those who disbelieve** (*alladhina kafarū*), it is the same whether you warn them or do not warn them: they will not believe…"	"…they will have a tremendous punishment."

Conclusion (vv. 38-39)

Those who follow guidance	Their outcome
"If **guidance** (*HuDan*) comes to you from Me, then whoever follows my **guidance** (*HuDaya*)…"	"…there will be no fear on them, nor will they grieve."
Those who disbelieve	**Their outcome**
"**Those who disbelieve** (*alladhina kafarū*) and deny Our Signs…"	"…they will be the companions of the Fire, remaining in it."

Coherence between Sections 1 and 2

Linear summary of section 2: Criticism of the Children of Israel

Section 2 (vv. 40-121) is a lengthy discourse criticizing the Children of Israel, who identified as followers of Moses, but a significant portion of whom actually disbelieved (recall vv. 8-20). In its historical context, these criticisms were addressed to the Jews of Medina, who were becoming increasingly hostile to the Prophet and his followers, despite having agreed to an alliance with the rest of the Medinan community. By addressing the Jews as the "Children of Israel," the Qur'an emphasizes their connection to their forefathers in Biblical times: in this section, it compares their behavior to that of the rebellious and disbelieving Israelites during the time of Moses or later, while in the next section, it urges them to instead emulate their prophetic ancestors Abraham, Isaac, and Jacob (Israel). It is essential to bear in mind that the Qur'an's criticisms are not directed at all Jews, as it emphasizes in several places (vv. 62, 100, 121), but rather that it criticizes *tendencies* that it identifies within the Jewish and Christian communities. These are meant to dissuade the members of these communities from these tendencies and to warn the new Muslim community, in turn, not to adopt them.

Throughout the first third of the section, God personally addresses the Children of Israel, reminding them of His special favors on them and calling on them to fulfill their covenant with Him by believing in the revelation. The main message of this divine address is set forth in the opening verses of the section:

> O Children of Israel, remember My favor that I favored you with. Fulfill your covenant with Me, and I will fulfill My covenant with you. It is I you should fear. Believe in what I have sent down, confirming what is already with you, and do not be the first to disbelieve in it. And do not exchange My signs for a small price. It is I you should be conscious of. Do not mix the truth with falsehood and conceal the truth while you know. Establish the prayer, pay the poor-due, and bow down along with those who bow. (vv. 40-44)

The section goes on to provide an overview of the history of the Children of Israel, highlighting their repeated violations of the Covenant and acts of ingratitude and disbelief. God then turns to address the Prophet and the Muslim community, advising them not to have high hopes in the prospect of the Israelites joining with them in faith.

Among the crimes the Israelites are criticized for are: concealing or distorting revelation, urging others to piety while forgetting it themselves, taking the Golden Calf in worship, showing ingratitude to God despite the miraculous blessings given to them, violating the Sabbath, behaving irreverently towards Moses, slaying prophets who were sent to them, shedding each others' blood, preferring the worldly life over the afterlife, practicing sorcery and ascribing it to Solomon, and claiming that only they would enter Paradise. The overview of these incidents is not chronological, but it does unfold with a certain progression: the further one reads, the more severe are the crimes that the section highlights. The increasing intensity of these admonitions suggests a piecemeal revelation and a continuous lack of receptiveness on the part of the Medinan Jews.

This section also contains a unique parable, from which the sura acquires it name. When Moses tells the Israelites that God has commanded them to slaughter a cow, they attempt to defer the obligation by asking a series of questions about the type, age, and color of the cow. The more questions they ask, however, the more specific and complex the requirements become. As a result, in the end they just barely manage to sacrifice the cow, having made it all but impossible for themselves (vv. 67-71). Although the parable of the cow is not thematically central to the sura, its unique and memorable character made it a convenient hallmark to refer to the sura by.

Integrative coherence between sections 1 and 2

The history of the Children of Israel that is presented in section 2 offers a historical study of the themes introduced in section 1, such as guidance, God-consciousness, faith in God's revelations and messengers, remembrance of God's favors, disbelief, punishment, and even resurrection. However, there are also more subtle connections between the two sections:

Section 1: Introduction (vv. 1-39)	Section 2: Criticism of the Israelites (vv. 40-121)
Section 1 metaphorically describes the pseudo-believers as being overtaken by "a rainstorm from the sky, in which there is darkness, thunder, and lightning. They put their fingers in their ears against the **thunderclaps** (*ṢawāʿiQ*) in fear of **death** (*MaWT*)…Had God willed, He could have taken away their hearing and their sight" (vv. 19-20).	Section 2 narrates that when the Israelites told Moses that they would not believe in God until they saw Him directly, "**a thunderbolt**" (*Ṣāʿiqa*) literally struck them dead (v. 55). It would have ended them for good had God not "revived [them] after [their] **death** (*MaWT*) so that perhaps [they] would be grateful" (v. 56).
Section 1 warns the disbelievers to "fear the Fire, whose fuel is men and **stones** (*ḤiJāRa*)" (v. 24). The mention of stones indicates the intensity of the Hellfire, since it is able to consume solid rocks.	Section 2 narrates that when Moses prayed for water for his people, God told him, "Strike the **rock** (*ḤaJaR*) with your staff." Moses did so, and twelve springs gushed out from the rock, one for each tribe (v. 60). Later, section 2 states that the hearts of the Israelites became harder than rocks: "Then your hearts became hardened after that, being like **stones** (*ḤiJāRa*) or even harder" (v. 74). The connection one may infer between v. 74 and v. 24 is that some hearts are so hard that only the Hellfire can melt them.

	However, even hard hearts are not all the same, for "indeed, there are **stones** (*ḤiJāRa*) from which rivers gush forth, and there are some that split open and water comes out, and there are some that fall down out of fear of God" (v. 74). That is, even some hardened hearts do contain good, or the potential for good, deep inside them. This parable uses imagery familiar to the Israelites from their experience of wandering with Moses in the desert, using stones to symbolize hearts and water to symbolize goodness and faith.
Recall that in section 1, the angels asked God why He would place on the earth "one who will **cause corruption on it** (*yuFSiDu fi-hā*) and **shed blood** (*yasSFiKu 'd-DiMā'*)" (v. 30). In section 2, the Israelites are charged with exactly these crimes. Moses scolds them, "do not transgress **on the earth causing corruption** (*fī 'l-arḍi muFSiDīn*)" (v. 60; cf. 17:4).	Similarly, even though God commanded them in the Torah, "Do not **shed each other's blood** (*lā taFSiKūna DiMā'a-kum*)," they did so anyway (vv. 84-85). The Israelites therefore appear to confirm the angels' apprehensions.
Nonetheless, in section 1 God replied to the angels, "I **know** (*a'LaMu*) what you manifest and what you **conceal** (*taKTuMūn*)" (v. 33).	In section 2, He says to the Israelites, "and do not mix the truth with falsehood and **conceal** (*taKTuMū*) the truth while you **know** (*ta'LaMūn*)" (v. 42). (The word "conceal" is an anchor that occurs ten times in the sura.)
God commanded the angels to "**prostrate** (*uSJuDū*) to Adam" and "they **prostrated** (*SaJaDū*)—but not Iblīs" (v. 34).	The Israelites were commanded, "Enter the gate **prostrating** (*SuJJāDan*)" (v. 58).
God told Adam and his wife, "**Eat from it [the Garden] plentifully wherever you wish** (*kulā min-hā raghadan ḥaythu shi'tumā*), but do not approach this tree!" (v. 35).	God told the Israelites, "**Enter this town and eat from it wherever you wish plentifully** (*kulū min-hā ḥaythu shi'tum raghadan*)" (v. 58).
Despite having the entire Garden to eat from, the first human couple coveted a single tree that was not allotted for them, and therefore disobeyed God's command. As a result God ordered them, "**Go down** (*ihbiṭū*) [from the Garden]!" (vv. 36, 38).	Despite being miraculously saved and provided for, some of the Israelites complained and demanded the food items they had while slaves in Egypt. As a result, Moses told them, "Go down (*ihbuṭū*) to the countryside!" (v. 61).

After his mistake, Adam was given "**words**" (*kalimāt*) of repentance, and he used them (v. 37).	When the Israelites were given a **word** of repentance ("*ḥiṭṭa*," meaning, "put down from us our sins"), they altered it and fell further into disobedience (v. 58)—replicating the attitude of Iblīs rather than of Adam.

From these parallels, which are only a few among many, it should be clear that section 2 builds on and is closely connected to section 1.[187]

Symmetry of section 2

Structurally, section 2 is arranged into a mirror composition and a ring composition:

- A. Address to the Israelites: Believe and be faithful (40-46).
  - B. Address to the Israelites: Beware the Day of Judgment; God will not save you from the consequences of your own deeds as He saved you from the Pharaoh's persecution (47-50).
    - C. Address to the Israelites: You worshiped the Golden Calf, but God was willing to turn to you in forgiveness (51-54).
      - D. Address to the Israelites: You repeatedly disbelieved and violated the covenant (55-74).
      - D'. Address to the believers: Do you have hope that the Israelites will believe when they repeatedly disbelieved and violated the covenant? (75-91).
    - C'. Address to the Israelites: You disbelieved by worshiping the Golden Calf (92-93).
  - B'. Address to the Messenger: The disbelieving Israelites covet this world and are merely stalling their punishment in the afterlife (94-96).
- A'. Address to the Messenger: Most of the Israelites disbelieve (97-103).

- A. Faith vs. disbelief in the messengers and revelations (104-106a).
  - B. God owns and has power over all things (106b-107).
    - C. Exchange of faith for disbelief; People of the Scripture wish they could turn you from your faith; establish prayer and give alms (vv. 108-110).
      - D. They say no one will enter Paradise except for Jews or Christians (111).
        - E. Rather, whoever submits to God will have their reward with Him (112).

187 For other examples of anchors linking passages in section 2 to section 1, see Robinson, *Discovering the Qur'an*, 206-208.

D'. The Jews and Christians accuse each other of having nothing to stand on; God will judge between them (113).
C'. Who is more unjust than those who try to prevent God's name from being mentioned in places of worship? (114).
B'. God owns and has power over all things (115-117).
A'. Faith vs. disbelief in the messengers and revelations (118-121).

Keep in mind how, throughout the sura, the centers of the rings repeatedly emphasize the themes of faith in and submission to God.

Linear and Structural Overview of the Rest of *The Cow*

We will now overview the rest of the sura, showing how it divides into thematically coherent sections, how each section builds on the previous ones to further develop the ideas of the sura, how the topics within each section unfold in a logical order, and the structure of each section.

Section 3: The legacy of Abraham (vv. 122-141)

> *"Who would be averse to the religion of Abraham except one who makes a fool of himself? We had chosen him in this world and he will indeed be among the righteous in the afterlife. Remember when his Lord said to him, 'Submit (aS-LiM).' He said, 'I have submitted (aSLaMtu) to the Lord of all peoples'" (vv. 130-131).*

The previous section on the Children of Israel leads to a new section on Abraham, the physical ancestor of both the Israelites, who included the Jews of Medina, and the Ishmaelites, who included the Prophet, his Meccan followers, and the disbelievers of the Quraysh. What is more important, however, is Abraham's spiritual legacy. The story of Abraham in this section is introduced with the following words:

> Remember when Abraham was tested by His Lord with commands, and he fulfilled them. [God] said, "I will make you a leader for mankind." (v. 124)

In the original Arabic, the wording and sentence structure of God's promise to Abraham recall His earlier declaration to the angels, "I will place on the earth a vicegerent." The connection that seems to be implied is that it is Abraham, above others, who fulfilled this cosmic role, and that God therefore appointed him as the spiritual role model *par excellence* whom the rest of humanity should strive to follow. This applies all the more to his own descendants, the Israelites and Ishmaelites, who both take great pride in their lineage from him. Yet, so far the Israelites and Ishmaelites have both largely failed to live up to their father's legacy, the Israelites repeatedly violating their covenant with God, and the Ishmaelites succumbing to the worship of idols. In this section, both of them are called back to the Abrahamic legacy and to fulfill the spiritual role of vicegerents of God on the earth. As we will see, however, it is the fledgling Muslim community who will be newly elected to that role.

The Qur'an goes on to narrate Abraham and Ishmael's prayer upon completing the construction of the Ka'ba. They ask God to make the location "a secure city," and to raise among the Ishmaelites a prophet who will bring them back to the path of monotheism after they stray—"who will recite to them your verses, teach them the Scripture and wisdom, and purify them" (v. 129)—and thus make them "a submitting (*muSLiM*) community." The section then emphasizes that the fathers of both the Israelites and the Ishmaelites—Abraham, his sons Ishmael and Isaac, Isaac's son Jacob (Israel), and Jacob's twelve sons (the ancestors of the twelve tribes of Israel)—all shared a common faith in one God and a common religion of *islām*, or submission to Him. Accordingly, the Qur'an summons both the Israelites and Ishmaelites to be *muslims* and to believe in all of the prophets of Abraham's line.

The Abraham Lineage of the Israelites and Ishmaelites

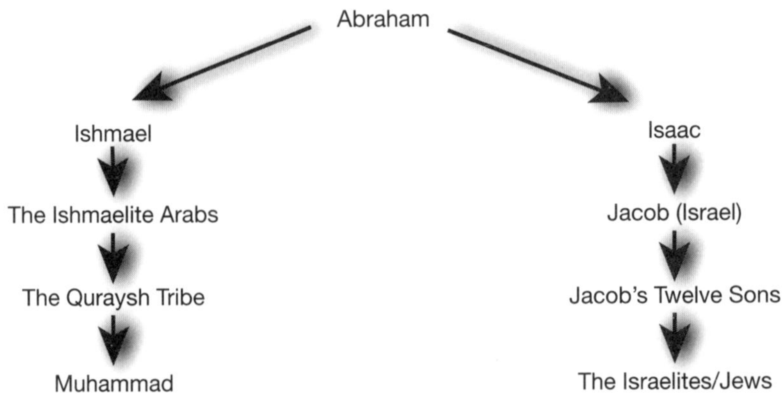

This section reveals the following symmetrical structure:

A. God addresses the Israelites: Remember My special favor on you and beware of Judgment Day (vv. 122-123).
   B. Abraham's Lord tested him with unique tests, and he fulfilled them completely; God tells Abraham He will make him a leader for mankind (v. 124a).

C. Abraham asks about his descendants, but God states that His covenant will not cover wrongdoers (v. 124b).

D. God makes the Ka'ba a sanctuary and commands Abraham and Ishmael to purify it (v. 125).

E. Abraham asks God to make Mecca "a secure city" and to "provide fruits" for the believers among its inhabitants; God responds that He will provide for both those who believe and those who disbelieve, but that in the afterlife He will drive those who disbelieve into Hell (v. 126).

D'. Abraham and Ishmael raise the foundations of the Ka'ba (v. 127).

C'. Abraham and Ishmael ask God to raise among their descendants a Messenger who will bring them back to the way of Abraham and make them a submitting (*muslim*) nation (vv. 128-129).

B'. Only a fool would turn away from the religion of Abraham; God chose him; when God told him "submit," he said, "I submit to the Lord of all peoples" (vv. 130-131).

A'. Like Abraham, Jacob (Israel) and his sons were on the way of *islām*, or submission to God (vv. 132-133).

A. "That is a community that has passed on. It will have what is has earned, and you will have what you have earned, and you will not be asked about what they used to do" (v. 134).

B. They say: 'Be Jews' or 'Be Christians.' Say: We follow the religion of Abraham, plain monotheism (v. 135).

C. "Say: We believe in God and in all of what was revealed to us and to Abraham, Ismail, Isaac, Jacob and the tribes, Moses and Jesus, and the prophets, and it is to Him that we submit (*wa-naḥnu la-hu muslimūn*)."

D. If they believe in what you believe in, then they are guided, but if they turn away, then God is sufficient for you.

C' [Say:] "Ours is the dye of God. And whose dye is better than God's?[188] And it is Him that we worship (*wa-naḥnu la-hu 'ābidūn*)" (vv. 136-138).

B'. Say: Do you argue about God while He is our Lord and yours? Do you say that Abraham, Ismail, Isaac, and Jacob and the tribes were Jews or Christians? They conceal a testimony from God, and God is All-Knowing (vv. 139-140).

---

188 Christian writings of the ancient Near East attest to the notion of God "dying" or "coloring" a person at baptism, transforming him and marking him for salvation. The Qur'an seems to be turning this metaphor on its head, implying that what is truly the "dye of God," qualifying a person for salvation, is the natural monotheism and submission to God exemplified by Abraham. See Sean Anthony, "Further Notes on the Word *Ṣibgha* in Qur'an 2:138," *Journal of Semitic Studies* 59.1 (2014): 117-129. We have followed Anthony's translation here.

A'. "That is a community that has passed on. It will have what is has earned, and you will have what you have earned, and you will not be asked about what they used to do" (v. 141).

Section 4: The change of prayer direction & the establishment of a new nation (vv. 142-152)

> *"Thus We have made you a middle nation, so that you may bear witness [to the truth] before mankind and so that the Messenger may bear witness [to it] before you. We only made the prayer direction the one you used to face in order to distinguish those who follow the Messenger from those who turn on their heels: that test was hard, except for those God has guided. God would never let your faith go to waste, for God is most compassionate and most merciful towards people" (v. 143).*

In keeping with the emphasis on Abraham's legacy, the Qur'an proclaims that the direction of prayer has shifted from the former site of the Holy Temple of Jerusalem to the Ka'ba in Mecca. The believers are now clearly established as a new religious community distinct from the People of the Scripture, the Jews and Christians, and as one that more faithfully represents the balanced way of Abraham and his family: "Thus We have made you a middle nation" (v. 143). Just as Abraham was made "a leader for mankind," the new community is supposed to "bear witness for mankind"—that is, carry the divine message through word and example. The Prophet, in turn, functions as a witness over the community (v. 143), reciting to them God's verses, purifying them, and teaching them the Scripture and wisdom (v. 151), thus fulfilling Abraham's prayer after building the Ka'ba in the previous section (v. 129). The audience is also informed that the change of prayer direction is only a test to distinguish those who are sincere in their religious commitment from those who are merely clinging to tradition. What really matters is not the direction of prayer *per se*, but sincere submission to God's command. Finally, in words that echo God's earlier addresses to the Children of Israel (vv. 40, 47, 122), the new community is told, "It is so that I may complete My favor upon you" (v. 150) and are instructed, "Remember Me and I will remember you. Be grateful to Me and do not disbelieve in Me" (v. 152).

This section has the following structure:[189]

A. Regarding change of prayer direction: God guides whoever He wills; message to Muslim community: the Prophet is a witness over you; change in prayer direction is a test of faithfulness (142-143).
    B. Command to the Prophet: turn your face in the direction of the Sacred Mosque (the location of the Ka'ba) (144-146).

---

189 This is reproduced from Farrin, "Surat al-Baqara," 24, with very slight modification of wording.

C. Adjuration: the truth (regarding the prayer direction) is from your Lord, so do not doubt; each community has its own direction, so race to do good and God will bring you together (147-148).

B'. Command to the Prophet: turn your face in the direction of the Sacred Mosque; command to Muslims: turn your faces in the direction of the Sacred Mosque (149-150).

A'. Message to the Muslim community: We have sent a Messenger of your own among you, instructing you in the Scripture and wisdom; do not reject faith (151-152).

Section 5: Restoring Abraham's legacy (vv. 153-177)

> *"O you who have believed, seek help through patience and prayer: indeed God is with the patient. Do not say that those who are killed in God's cause are dead; they are alive, though you do not realize it. We will certainly test you with something of fear and hunger, and loss of wealth, lives, and fruits. But give glad tidings to those who are patient—those who say, when afflicted with a calamity, 'We belong to God and to Him we will return.' Those are the ones who will receive blessings and mercy from their Lord, and it is they who are the rightly guided" (vv. 153-157).*

Although God has just honored the new Muslim community, He now addresses them with a serious message. Restoring Abraham's legacy is no easy task, for just like their father Abraham, they are about to be heavily tested (v. 155). This test will involve "fear and hunger, and a loss of wealth, lives, and fruits," but those who exhibit patience will be awarded "blessings and mercy from their Lord" (v. 157). A disclaimer that those who are martyred are not dead but alive (v. 154) and a subsequent reference to the pilgrimage to the Ka'ba in the Sacred Mosque (v. 158) further signal that the community must ready themselves for upcoming battles: as the spiritual community of Abraham, they should be prepared to fight the Quraysh and, ultimately, liberate the Ka'ba.[190] The reference to pilgrimage at the Ka'ba is followed by a stern warning to those who disbelieve by concealing what God has revealed in scripture (vv. 159-162)—an allusion either to the polytheists, who obscured the Abrahamic faith by placing idols in the Sacred Mosque, or to the Israelites, who are charged with concealing the scriptural evidence in their possession concerning the Abrahamic status of the Ka'ba.[191]

The reference to concealing what God has revealed leads into a discussion of faith and disbelief, which we have seen are major themes of this sura. First, God's exclusive right to worship is affirmed and substantiated with signs in

190 For a fuller discussion of fighting in the Qur'an, see the appendix, "Jihad in the Qur'an."

191 Verse 146 in the previous section states that "those to whom We gave the Scripture know it like they know their own sons," apparently referring to the status of the Ka'ba, but that "a faction among them conceals the truth while they know."

creation. This serves to remind and emphasize that the aim of liberating the Ka'ba is ultimately to allow people to worship God in the Sacred Mosque, free from idols or other deities (vv. 163-164). True devotion to God is then contrasted with polytheism and disbelief, both of which include rejecting what God has revealed in favor of ancestral custom—an accusation probably aimed at both the Jews and polytheists.

Within the discussion of monotheism, polytheism, and disbelief, several verses occur that address the topic of pure and impure foods. Although this topic may seem unrelated, it is in fact connected in several ways with the surrounding material about monotheism, polytheism, and disbelief. The passage about monotheism had emphasized that among God's signs is that He "spreads on [the earth] every kind of beast" (v. 164). It is accordingly that God urges mankind to "eat from the earth what is lawful and pure" (v. 168). In connection with polytheism, impure foods include "that which is dedicated to other than God" (vv. 168-173). In connection with disbelief, the disbelievers are accused of "saying about God what [they] do not know" (v. 169) and, again, "concealing what God revealed in the Scripture for a small price"—thereby "consuming into their bellies only fire" (v. 174). These verses probably allude to the invention of complex dietary rules by the Israelites, and their concealment of the fact that God "only prohibited for you carrion, blood, the flesh of swine, and that which has only been dedicated to other than God" (v. 173; cf. 3:93).[192] Finally, the topic is also connected with the preceding verse about the pilgrimage and the Sacred Mosque, since the pilgrimage rites involve sacrificing animals and distributing them as food.

Contrasting with the Israelites' ritual formalism and tendency to "urge people to piety while forgetting [them]selves" (v. 44), the section concludes with a summary of what true "piety" entails:

> It is not piety that you turn your faces towards the east or the west, but piety is in whoever has faith in God, the Last Day, the angels, the Scripture, and the prophets; who give wealth in spite of love for it to kinsfolk, the orphans, the needy, the traveler, those who ask, and for the freeing of slaves; who establish the prayer and pay the prescribed alms; who fulfill their promises [literally "covenants"] when they make them; and who are patient in poverty and hardship and during battle. Those are the ones who have proven truthful, and it is they who are the God-conscious. (v. 177)

This verse, known as the "Verse of Piety" (*Āyat al-Birr*), emphasizes to the Muslims that, despite the recent change God has ordained in the direction of prayer, what is important is not the direction itself but the

192 Robinson, *Discovering the Qur'an*, 212-213.

sincere willingness to follow God's commands. Readers of this sura who fear being overwhelmed by its variety and intricacy should take special note of this verse, as it provides a highly systematic and practicable summary of the entire sura's contents. The only theme from this verse that has not yet been discussed in detail in the sura is the theme of spending in charity, but it will form one of the major themes of the upcoming sections.

Section 5 has the following structure:[193]

A. Exhortation to believers: Seek help through patience and prayer; God will test you with adversity and a loss of lives and wealth, but give glad tidings to the patient; "Those are the ones who will receive blessings and mercy from their Lord, and it is they who are the rightly guided." (153-157).
  B. Safa and Marwa are symbols of God and part of the pilgrimage; those who conceal the Scripture and do not repent will be punished in the Hellfire (158-162).
    C. Monotheism/faith and polytheism/disbelief (163-172).
  B'. Those who conceal the Scripture will be punished in the Hellfire (174-176).
A'. Exhortation to believers: Piety is in faith, spending one's wealth on the needy, prayer and the poor-due, fulfilling promises, and being patient in times of poverty, adversity, and war; "Those are the ones who have proven truthful, and it is they who are the God-conscious" (177).

It should also be noted that the center, C, is internally structured as a parallelism:[194]

A. Monotheism and signs of God (163-164).
  B. People follow their ancestors in worshipping rivals to God; they will be punished severely (165-167).
    C. Injunction: Eat what is good and lawful from the earth (168-169).
  B'. Disbelievers say, "we follow the ways of our fathers", but their fathers were not guided. (170-171).
    C'. Injunction: eat of the good God has provided you; God has only forbidden carrion, pig, blood, and animals over which any other name than His has been invoked (172-173).

Section 6: Laws for the new Muslim nation (vv. 178-242)

"And among the people is one who sells himself, seeking the pleasure of God, and God is most kind to His servants. You who believe, enter wholeheartedly into submission to God and do not follow in Satan's footsteps, for he is your sworn enemy. If you slip back after clear proof has come to you, then be aware that God is almighty and wise (vv. 208-209)."

---

193 This is reproduced from Farrin, "Surat al-Baqara," 26, with modifications.
194 Reproduced from ibid., though we have added segment A here.

Before the newly founded community can engage in battle, it is in need of laws. The concluding statement of the last section, the Verse of Piety, sets the ethical tone for the body of legislation that will follow it. This begins with regulations that concern the sanctity of human life (vv. 178-179) and property (vv. 180-182), two essential pillars of a peaceful and just society. These verses have a number of anchors that parallel the beginning of the previous section (vv. 153-155): "those killed" (*al-QaTLā*), "mercy" (*RaḤMa*), "life" (*ḤaYā*), "God-consciousness" or "self-protectiveness" (*TaQWā*), "death" (*MaWT*), and "fear" (*KHaWF*). Since respect for the life and property of others requires self-restraint, the practice of fasting in the sacred month of Ramadan is enjoined to nurture this quality (vv. 183-187). This also thematically relates to the previous section's emphasis on keeping from unlawful foods and on being patient in times of hunger (v. 155). Fasting also removes greed, hence v. 188 prohibits bribery and the unlawful consumption of other people's wealth.

The theme of self-discipline also provides a basis for a discussion of pilgrimage and fighting in battle, which were already linked together in the previous section (vv. 153-158). Since battle requires funding, these verses also have a direction connection to the previous verse about unlawful consumption or uses of wealth (v. 188). The issues of pilgrimage and fighting subsequently raised several questions in the believers' minds. These included questions about pre-Islamic superstitions related to the pilgrimage (v. 189) and on whether it is permissible to fight in the area of the Sacred Mosque or in the sacred months, should they be attacked (vv. 191-195). The questions are sometimes quoted ("They ask you concerning...") before they are answered, indicating that they were revealed over time, as the issues were brought up. The fact that they still show a logical arrangement is therefore especially noteworthy.

Further instructions concerning pilgrimage (vv. 196-199) lead into a discussion of people who only perform the religious rites for worldly gain (vv. 201-202) and of the associated problems of hypocrisy and disbelief, which are then contrasted with full and sincere submission to God (vv. 203-214). The conversation then returns to the subject of problems that arise during times of battle. Verse 219 tackles the issues of alcoholic drinks and gambling, two habits that men out at war are especially prone to. The same verse then directs people to spend their excess wealth instead on God's cause.[195] A pre-Islamic Arab practice provides a further link between the topics of drinking, gambling, and giving one's wealth. During times of famine, the Arabs would hold gatherings in which they would become intoxicated, sacrifice a camel, and gamble over its meat. Following this, each participant would distribute what he won of the meat to the poor.[196]

---

195 Robinson, *Discovering the Qur'an*, 214.
196 Iṣlāḥī, 526-527.

Chief among the problems of warfare is that of orphans (v. 220) and widows. Marriage is a means of solving the problem of widows. Accordingly, the rest of section 6 provides regulations concerning marriage and divorce (vv. 221-241). However, one brief passage appears towards the end of the section that appears disconnected from the surrounding discussion of divorce and widows:

> Guard the prayers, especially the middle prayer, and stand before God in devout obedience. And if you fear [an enemy], then [pray] on foot or while riding. Then when you are secure, remember God, as He taught you what you did not know. (vv. 238-239)

Since divorce is the severing of one of the most emotionally involving of human relationships, the instruction to "guard the prayers (*ṢaLaWāt*), especially the middle prayer (*aṣ-ṢaLāt al-wusṭā*)" (v. 238) reminds individuals in the process of divorce not to forget the most important relationship, which is one's relationship with God. This instruction also recalls the earlier instruction, at the beginning of section 5 ("The new nation will be tested"), to "seek help" in times of adversity "through patience and prayer (*aṣ-ṢaLāt*)"—a piece of advice that is relevant in times of divorce (hence v. 238) and which was also revealed concerning the context of war (hence v. 239). Moreover, the instruction in v. 239, to pray on foot or while on horseback "if you fear (*KHiFtum*)" an enemy (v. 239), also recalls the beginning of section 5: "We will test you with something of fear (*KHaWF*)" (v. 155). Additionally, the instruction in v. 239 to "remember God (*fa-'DHKuRū 'llāh*), as He taught you what you did not know" recalls the command repeated throughout earlier parts of the sura, and especially in this section, to "remember God" (vv. 152, 198, 200, 203) and to "remember [His] favor" (vv. 40, 47, 122, 231).

The parallels we have just noted between the end of section 6 and the beginning of section 5 connect the two sections together, as if they were a single, continuous section. Indeed, when these sections are read together, a number of interesting literary patterns emerge. We will just mention one of them here. Section 5 contained a discussion on the topics of monotheism (vv. 163-164), polytheism (vv. 165-167), and dietary regulations (vv. 168-169 and 172-173). This was followed shortly after, in the beginning of section 6, with regulations concerning the sanctity of human life and the crime of manslaughter (vv. 178-179). Robinson observes that this sequence of topics parallels material in section 2:

> The Children of Israel were commanded to revere the One God (cf. v.40), but they fell into idolatry and worshipped the calf (cf. vv. 51-54). Their

idolatry led them in turn to be discontent with the food with which God provided them (cf. v. 61) and to commit manslaughter (cf. v. 72).[197]

It should also be pointed out that the word *taqwā*, which denotes cautious restraint and most often occurs with the meaning of "God-consciousness," is a major anchor throughout the sura (it appears as early as v. 3), but is especially prominent in this section. The distribution of the word throughout the section provides an underlying theme that unites all of the laws: wine, gambling, and consuming others' wealth, laws for fasting and pilgrimage, and regulations on battle, marriage, and divorce. Maintaining prayers is emphasized both at the beginning of section 5 and towards the end of section 6 as a means of building this pious restraint (vv. 153, 238). Even the casual reader of section 6 will notice that the wider ethical principles that underlie the laws are stressed throughout, so that it is not merely a dry collection of commands and prohibitions, but a flowing moral discussion.

Finally, section 6 is also organized symmetrically:

A. Legal retribution for murder; inheritance and wills (vv. 178-182).
- B. Fasting and regulations about marital relations (vv. 183-187).
  - C. Consuming others' wealth unjustly (v. 188).
    - D. Answers to questions about superstitions (v. 189).
      - E. Fighting (vv. 190-194).
        - F. Spending; pilgrimage, sacrifice and charity, seeking God's bounty (vv. 195-203).
          - G. Hypocrisy (vv. 204-206).
            - H. Enter into peace and submission wholeheartedly (207-208).
          - G'. Deviation and disbelief (209-214).
        - F'. Spending (215).
      - E'. Fighting (217-218).
    - D'. Answers to questions about wine and gambling (219a).
  - C'. Spending, orphans (219b-220).
- B'. Marital relations (221-226).

A'. Divorce and compensation; children; death and widows (227-242).

Section 7: The struggle of the believers against the disbelievers (vv. 243-286)

"When [Saul] crossed [the river] with those who had kept faith, [those who had little faith] said, 'We have no strength today against Goliath and his warriors.' But those who knew that they were going to meet their Lord said, 'How often a

---

197 Robinson, *Discovering the Qur'an*, 213. Nevin Reda, *Textual Integrity*, 169-170, also lists a variety of anchors between our sections 5 and 6 and sections 1 and 2.

> *small force has defeated a large army with God's permission! God is with the patient.' And when they met Goliath and his warriors, they said, 'Our Lord, pour patience on us, make us stand firm, and help us against the disbelieving people,' and so with God's permission they defeated them. David killed Goliath, and God gave him sovereignty and wisdom and taught him what He pleased. If God did not drive some back by means of others the earth would be completely corrupt, but God is bountiful to all" (vv. 149-151).*

The final section concludes a number of key topics of the sura: faith versus disbelief, and in particular the struggle to liberate the Ka'ba from the disbelievers; God's power over the creation and to resurrect the dead; the Day of Judgment; and laws regarding financial dealings. Once again, we will see how such apparently unconnected topics are, in fact, closely intertwined.

The section begins with the mention of a people who left their homes in the thousands, fearing slaughter. God caused them to die and then resurrected them. In light of vv. 55-56, this likely refers to the Israelites who fled Egypt during the Exodus. In a similar fashion, the believers left their homes in Mecca to escape persecution, and just as the Israelites were to conquer the Promised Land, it is implied that the believers should prepare to conquer Mecca. Moreover, just as God struck the Israelites dead when they refused to obey Moses, but subsequently revived them (v. 55-56), the Muslims should obey the Prophet's military orders, because God will likewise resurrect them and hold them to account.[198] Those who do so can expect that God will repay their loan many times over on the Day of Judgment (v. 245). The themes of battle, resurrection, the Day of Judgment, and financial transactions are thereby connected.

The section then goes on to retell the Biblical story of the Israelites' battle against the Philistines and their struggle to retrieve the Ark of the Covenant (vv. 246-251), which parallels the situation of the Muslims in their struggle to liberate the Ka'ba. We will look at this story in a little more detail shortly, but a number of connections with the previous material should be noted here. First, as we will see, the story contains another warning about not obeying the Prophet's authority in battle. Second, it emphasizes that "God gives His kingdom to whomever He wills; He is Extensive (*Wāsi'*), Knowing" (v. 247). We will encounter verbal echoes of this statement shortly. Third, the story contains an episode in which Saul, Israel's first king, tests which of his troops are disciplined enough for battle by forbidding them from drinking more than a handful of water from a river. This episode reinforces the connection between fasting and combat in the previous section.[199] The

198 Robinson, *Discovering the Qur'an*, 215-217.
199 Ibid., 218.

story concludes with divine affirmation of Muhammad's prophetic authority and a statement about the previous messengers and peoples' differing responses to them (vv. 252-253).

Following this, the believers are instructed to spend in God's cause before a day comes in which "there is no transaction (*tijāra*), no friendship, and no intercession" (vv. 254), again tying the themes of battle, transactions, and the Day of Judgment. The grammatical form of the negation in the Arabic is not categorical, but rather allows for exceptions. The exception to "no intercession" is spelled out in the next verse, the Throne Verse (v. 255), which contains a beautiful description of God's power, sovereignty, and knowledge. It says, "Who is the one who can intercede with Him *except by His permission*?" The verse also states that God's throne "extends (*WaSiʿa*) over the heavens and the earth," echoing the earlier mention of God as "Extensive" (*WāSiʿ*). In both cases, this prevents the misconception that God's presence is localized in the Ark of the Covenant or the Kaʿba.[200] The next several verses declare that there shall be no compulsion in religion, for God has made truth clear from error; state that God is the ally of the believers; and emphasize the consequences of serving false gods (vv. 256-257).

Verses 258-260 contain three stories pertaining to God's total power over the creation and to resurrect the dead. The first story involves a king who disbelieved after God had "given him kingship (*ʾāTā-hu ʾllāhu ʾl-mulk*)," echoing the earlier statement that "God gives His kingdom (*wa-ʾllāhu yuʾTī mulka-hu*) to whom He wills" (v. 247). Moreover, the references to God's ability to "give life" (*iḤYāʾ*) in all three stories echo a reference to God as "the Living" (*al-ḤaYY*) in the Throne Verse.

The section then turns to a discussion on giving in charity (vv. 261-274), the evil of dealing in interest (vv. 275-281), and rules for writing down transactions in which one believer incurs debt from another for a fixed period (vv. 282-283). In the section on charity, God is described twice more as "Extensive (*WāSiʿ*), Knowing" (vv. 261, 268), just as in the story of Saul earlier in the section. Additionally, when believers are told to give up what is owed to them of interest, they are warned of a Day when every soul will be "paid in full for what it has earned" (v. 281)—once more using the transaction metaphor to describe Judgment Day.

Verses 284-286 bring the sura to a close. The audience is told that God will "bring [them] to account" for whatever they reveal or conceal, using the transaction metaphor one last time. The believers are said to accept all of God's messengers, angels, and revelations without distinction, and when the word of revelation comes, they say, "We hear and we obey." They pray for

200 Ibid.

forgiveness, for God not to overwhelm them with burden—"like those before us," alluding to how the Israelites were given increasingly difficult laws because of their disobedience—and for "victory over the disbelieving people," echoing the prayer of the believers in the story of Saul (v. 250).

As a whole, the section has the following symmetrical structure:

A. To God is the return; aid against the disbelieving people; faith in all of God's messengers (243-253).
  B. Spending for the sake of God; be conscious of a Day of no friendship, bargaining, or intercession (254).
    C. God's attributes and unfaltering maintenance of the creation (255).
      D. God guides whom He wills; He helps believers (256-257).
    C'. Resurrection, tied to God's control over creation (258-260).
  B'. Spending properly (261-283); be conscious of a Day you will be returned and every soul will receive what it has earned (281).
A'. To God is the return; aid against the disbelieving people; faith in all messengers (284-286).

The central message (E) assures the believers that, despite their small numbers and resources in comparison to the disbelieving Quraysh, God is able to give them victory.

Inside this ring structure are two smaller ring structures. The first is the Throne Verse, already discussed in the previous chapter. The second is embedded in A (vv. 243-253):

A. God saved the thousands who fled their homes in fear of death by causing them to die and reviving them; "God is full of bounty to people, but they are not grateful" (v. 243).
  B. Encouragement to fight in God's cause (vv. 244-245).
    C. The Israelite elites' claim that they would fight was proven false (v. 246).
      D. God makes Saul king (v. 247a).
        E. "God gives His kingdom to whom He wills. God is Extensive, Knowing" (v. 247b).
      D'. A divine sign of Saul's kingship, the return of the Ark of the Covenant (v. 248).
    C'. Most of the Israelites fail Saul's test of discipline and do not participate in battle (v. 249).
  B'. The believing soldiers pray for victory of the disbelieving people (v. 250).
A.' God gave them victory; "God is full of bounty to all peoples" (v. 251).

Note how the centerpiece reinforces a message similar to the one in the larger ring.

In addition to the ring structures, Reda observes that the section is a mosaic of alternations between various themes and methods of narration. For example, the content of this section switches between the themes of spending and God's power over life and death:[201]

243–244	245	246–253	254	255–260	261–283	284–286
God as master of life and death; fighting	Spending	God as master over life and death; fighting	Spending	God as master over life and death	Spending	*Epilogue*

Additionally, there is alternation between the themes of faith and action:

243	244–245	246–253	254	255–260	261–283	284–286
Faith: In God's power over life and death	Action: Fighting and spending	Faith: In God's power to give victory	Action: Spending	Faith: The Throne Verse; Parables about God's power to resurrect	Action: Spending	*Epilogue*: Faith: Summary

Finally, there is alternation between narrating a story and mandating laws or other forms of instruction:

243	244–245	246–253	254–257	258–260	261–283	284–286
Story: People who left their homes; God caused them to die and resurrected them	Injunction to fight and spend	Story: Samuel and the chiefs; Saul and his troops	Injunction to spend; Throne verse	Story: Three short stories on God's power to resurrect	Injunctions on spending	*Epilogue*

201 These charts are adaped from Reda, *Textual Integrity*, 119. We have added to Reda's descriptions for the readers' benefit.

The interested reader may consult a translation of the Qur'an to further examine how these alternations play out.

The Overall Symmetry of *The Cow*

The Structure of The Cow

As far as the structure of the sura is concerned, we have looked at the mirror or ring compositions *within* each section. Now we may direct our attention to the *overall* structure of the sura, which is itself a grand ring composition:

- A. **Faith and Disbelief (vv. 1-39)**: Believers and disbelievers; God created and will resurrect.
  - B. **Criticism of the Israelites (vv. 40-121)**: Moses delivers law to Children of Israel; Children of Israel fail to submit.
    - C. **Abraham's legacy (vv. 122-141)**: Abraham was tested; Ka'ba built by Abraham and Ishmael; prayer that descendants will return to monotheism and submit to God.
      - D. **The change of prayer direction to the Ka'ba (vv. 142-152)**: the new Muslim community is established as a "middle nation" who believe and compete in doing good works.
    - C'. **Restoring Abraham's legacy (vv. 153-177)**: Muslims will be tested; instructions about pilgrimage to Mecca; warning not to take ancestors or their gods as rivals besides God.
  - B'. **Laws for the new Muslim nation (vv. 178-242)**: Prophet delivers law to Muslims; Muslims exhorted to submit wholeheartedly.
- A'. **The struggle of the believers against the disbelievers (vv. 243-286)**: Believers in struggle against disbelievers; God's power over creation and to resurrect; laws of financial dealings.

The sections opposite to each other (A and A', B and B', and C and C') closely correspond in content. We will see this especially as we take a more detailed look at the connections between sections A and A' shortly.

It is also significant how the two panels of the sura, ABC and C'B'A', mirror each other and are brought together in the center by D. The first panel of the sura (ABC) is largely concerned with the Children of Israel, and while it introduces the themes of faith and disbelief, the theme of disbelief is discussed in more detail:

- In section A, while the believers and their qualities are described briefly (vv. 2-5), it is the attributes of the disbelievers, particularly the pseudo-believers, that are described in detail (vv. 6-20). In the subsequent sections, we learn that the latter descriptions relate to people from within the Children of Israel.

- Section B opens with the first address from God directed to a specific religious community, which are not the Muslims, as one might expect, but the Children of Israel: "O Children of Israel, remember My favor that I favored you with…" (v. 41). The entire section goes on to scrutinize the history of the Children of Israel and to highlight their failure to keep the faith and submit to the divine commandments.
- Section C opens with a similar address to the Israelites—"O Children of Israel, remember My favor that I favored you with and that I privileged you over all peoples" (v. 122)—and calls especially on them to return to the way of Abraham.

In direct contrast, the second panel of the sura (C'B'A') focuses entirely on the new Muslim community. The panel begins with a divine address to the new Muslim nation—"O you who have believed…" (v. 153)—just as sections B and C of the first panel began with a divine address to the Israelites. While the panel focusing on the Children of Israel highlighted their lapses into disbelief and acts of rebellion, and hence their failure to maintain the legacy of Abraham, this panel focuses on the believers' faith and submission to God, and their newly designated role as the heirs of the Abrahamic legacy.

Section D forms the central turning point of the sura, around which the sura could be said to "revolve." Fittingly, it concerns the shift of the direction of prayer to the Ka'ba, which believers literally turn to in prayer and collectively revolve around during the pilgrimage. What is more, in v. 143, the numerical center of the sura—which consists of 286 verses—God formally announces the establishment of the Muslim community as "a middle nation." Hence, it is with the change of prayer direction from Jerusalem to the Ka'ba, and the revelation of this section, that marks the formal establishment of the Muslims as the new divinely selected religious community or nation (*umma*), taking the place of the Children of Israel in this role. This is made even more clear in v. 150, in which God declares, "It is so that I may complete My favor upon you and so that you may be guided" (cf. 1:5-6), recalling the earlier mentions of God's "favor upon" the Children of Israel (vv. 40, 47, 121). This section therefore provides a very fitting transition from panel ABC to panel C'B'A'. Finally, it is in this central section that we discover an overarching theme of the sura, namely *the establishment of the new Muslim nation to restore Abraham's legacy, a community based on submission to God and consistent faith in all of God's messengers and revelations* (in contrast with the previous religious community, the Children of Israel). Each section and topic within the sura fits neatly within this central overarching theme, and contributes to its overall development.

The Motifs of Election, Instruction, and Test

Additionally, Nevin Reda has drawn attention to a recurring pattern in the sura, which involves a combination of the topics of *election*, *instruction*, and *test*.[202] "Election" refers to the divine appointment of a person or group to a special role and position. "Test" refers to a test of the obedience of a person or group. "Instruction" refers to God's provision of guidance in the form of a command or counsel. In each case, it is God who does the electing, testing, and instructing of human beings. These motifs appear throughout the sura in varying combinations:

- In section 1, Adam, representing the human race, is divinely **elected** to the position of God's representative on the earth. He is then **tested** with the command not to approach the forbidden Tree. Finally, when he "slips" and eats from the Tree, God provides Adam **instructions** on how to obtain His forgiveness.
- Section 2 alludes to the Israelites' **election** to the position of God's chosen nation (vv. 40, 47). The section refers to the **instructions** they were given in the form of the Covenant (the Torah). However, they were repeatedly **tested** and failed the tests, eventually resulting in their loss of their elected position.
- In section 3, the story of Abraham is told. Abraham is **tested**. As a result of passing these tests, he is **elected** to the position of being "a leader for mankind." Finally, he is **instructed** to build and purify the Ka'ba.
- In section 4, the people of Medina—including both the Muslims and Jews—are **tested** with the change of prayer direction and **instructed** to pray towards Mecca. The Muslims obeyed the command, and were thus **elected** as the new divinely chosen nation, taking over the position the Israelites previously held.
- In section 5, the community is warned that, because of their **election** to this role, they will face upcoming **tests**, which will involve a loss of lives and fruits. However, they are given various **instructions** to prepare them for these tests, which extend all the way through sections 6 and 7.

Reda observes that while the idea of *election* was central to sections 1-3—the stories of Adam, the Children of Israel, and Abraham respectively—the idea of *testing* is central to sections 5-7, which are addressed to the new Muslim nation.[203] Our above analysis also reveals another interesting pattern:

---

202 Reda, *Textual Integrity*, 161-163, 165-166, 177-178. However, our analysis of how these motifs are ordered in the different sections differs from Reda's.

203 Ibid., 177.

The elected, tested, and instructed individual or group	The order of election (E), testing (T), and instruction (I)
The story of Adam (section 1)	**ETI**
The Children of Israel (section 2)	EIT
The story of Abraham (section 3)	**TEI**
The change of prayer direction (section 4)	TIE
Address to the Muslim nation (sections 5-7)	**ETI**

Notice that the first and last examples, "the story of Adam" and the "address to the Muslim nation," display an identical pattern: *election, test, instruction*. Then, in the second and second-to-last examples, "the Children of Israel" and "the change of prayer direction," these occur in opposite order: *election, instruction, test* and *test, instruction*, and *election*. Finally, and very appropriately, in the center is "the story of Abraham," which is characterized by its own unique pattern of *test, election, instruction*.

Integrative Coherence Between Sections A (vv. 1-39) and A' (vv. 243-286)

In an earlier part of this chapter, we looked at how two consecutive sections of the sura, the first and second sections (A and B), are connected. Now we will look into the relationship between two sections that mirror each other—being located directly opposite to each other on the ring—the first and final sections of the sura (A and A').

To briefly review section A, its main themes are faith (vv. 2-5, 25) and disbelief (vv. 6-20, 23-24, 26-28) in the messengers and the revelation, and also in the Last Day (vv. 4, 8). These are followed by the themes of God's creation and His power over it (vv. 20-22, 28-29). The creation story is told as a practical illustration of the contrasting attitudes of the believer (Adam, or Adam and the angels) and the disbeliever (Satan). The final two verses wrap up the section, concluding with the message—thematically echoing the beginning of the section—that those who follow God's guidance will have nothing to fear or grieve, but those who reject it will abide in the Fire. The theme of God's knowledge (vv. 29, 30, 32, 33) and the knowledge (or lack thereof) of His creatures (vv. 13, 22, 26, 30, 32) also recurs throughout the section. The topic of resurrection also occurs in v. 28, where it is tied with God's original creation: "How can you disbelieve in God when you were lifeless and He gave you life, and He will cause you to die, then He will revive you, and then to Him you will return?" Although the themes of section A reappear in some form throughout the rest of the sura, recall that they have special prominence in the immediately following section, B, especially through the use of anchors. As we will now see, this is even more the case between section A and the the section that mirrors it, A'.

First, looking at A' thematically, this concluding section shares the same major themes as the introductory section (A): faith (in everything that God has sent down and in the Last Day), disbelief, and God's power over the creation and to resurrect the dead. Yet this section also contains several important variations on both of these themes. First, it concentrates on the *physical* struggle of the believers against the disbelievers—the implied context being to defend against the disbelieving Quraysh and to liberate the Ka'ba from them. Second, while the first section had focused more on creation than resurrection, this section focuses more on resurrection than creation. Third, the theme of spending or making a transaction, which occurs in the first section more briefly (vv. 3, 16), is significantly expanded on in this section.

In addition to sharing the same essential themes, the concluding section is connected to the beginning section by an extensive overlap of anchors:

Section A': Conclusion (vv. 243-286)	Section A: Introduction (vv. 1-39)
The phrase "**fearing death**" (*ḥadhara 'l-mawt*) occurs in the first verse of this section (v. 243), describing the flight of a people (probably the Israelites) from their homes.	This phrase only occurs one other time in the Qur'an, in a parable about the pseudo-believers in section A of the sura (v. 19). The connection highlights the pseudo-believers' fear of fighting, due to their lack of belief that God will give them victory or reward them in the afterlife.
God is described as "**giving life**" (*aḤYā/yuḤYī*/etc.) after "**causing death**" (*MaWT/yuMīT*/etc.) in vv. 243, 258, 259, 260.	This echoes v. 28: "How can you disbelieve in God when you were **lifeless** (*aMWāT*) and He **gave you life** (*fa-aḤYā-kum*), and He will **cause you to die** (*yuMīTu-kum*), then He will **revive** (*yuḤYī-kum*) you, and then to Him you will return?"
Verse 245 describes the "**goodly loan**" of the believers who fight justly in God's path, which God will pay them back many times over (see also the parable of one who gives in charity in v. 261).	This is the direct opposite of the "**transaction**" of the pseudo-believers, in which they have "**purchased error for guidance**" and which "**did not profit them**" (v. 19).

Verse 246 introduces the story of the battle between the Israelites, under the leadership of Saul, and the Philistines (vv. 246-251). This story illustrates the themes of **faith** and **disbelief** that were presented in the first section of the sura (vv. 2-20), but this time in the context of the physical struggle between the believers and the disbelievers. This Biblical story is retold in a way that directly compares with and comments on the situation of the

Muslim community in Medina. The Children of Israel—who fled their homes in Egypt, settled in the Promised Land, and became a unified society under the leadership of a prophet—serve as a prototype of the situation of the Muslim community.

In the story, the mighty and numerous Philistines have attacked the Israelites and taken hold of their sacred Ark of the Covenant. The Philistines represent the disbelievers of the Quraysh, who aggressed against the Muslims, dwarfed them in terms of both power and number, and held control over the Ka'ba. Despite these enormous disadvantages, God promises the Israelites in the story that they will retrieve the Ark—signaling a guarantee to the Muslim audience that they will defeat the Quraysh and liberate the Ka'ba (v. 248).

Faced with the prospect of battle, the chiefs of the Israelites swear to their prophet, named in the Bible as Samuel, that they would surely fight in God's cause and in defense of their people if only God would give them a king (v. 246). This is not only a veiled attempt to acquire power among their own ranks, but also an implicit rejection of their prophet's leadership as a political head and military commander. However, when God appoints Saul as Israel's first king, they show their true colors, refusing to fight and contesting Saul's authority: "How can he have authority over us while we are more entitled to authority than he, and he has not been granted an abundance of wealth?" (2:247). In all of this they resemble the pseudo-believers and the hypocrites, who respectively included people of leadership in the Jewish and Arab tribes in Medina before the Prophet had become the leader of the city. These groups only claimed allegiance to the Prophet in order to make political and social gains, while they at the same time tried to undermine his religious and political authority and refused to fight for the defense of the Medinan community.

In direct contrast to these groups, the believing soldiers in the story display strong faith. When tested with the difficult and even baffling command not to drink more than a handful of water from a river, they comply, showing trust in and obedience to Saul. This test recalls the connection between fasting and fighting in the previous section, fasting being a means of inculcating patience and discipline. Through this test, Saul effectively sorts out his loyal and disciplined soldiers from those who will lack the obedience and discipline required to fight. Subsequently, when the Israelites who are lacking in faith cry out, "There is no power for us today against Goliath and his soldiers!" Saul's faithful soldiers calmly respond, "How many a small company has overcome a large company by God's will—and God is with the patient" (v. 249). These soldiers exemplify the attitude of the believers, who show faith in God's promises to them and readily obey His Prophet's commands.

Some of the remaining connections between the rest of the concluding section and the introductory section are as follows:

Section A′: Conclusion (vv. 243-286)	Section A: Introduction (vv. 1-39)
The above story concludes with the moral, "Had God not repelled some people by means of others, the earth would have been corrupted (*la-FaSaDati 'l-'aRḌu*)" (v. 251), providing an ethical basis for fighting against aggression and persecution.	The crime of "causing corruption on the earth" (*iFSāD fi'l-'aRḌ*) was mentioned three times in the first section of the sura (vv. 11, 27, 30).
The phrase "O you who have believed, **spend out of what We have provided for you** (*aNFiQū mim-mā razaqnā-kum*)" occurs in v. 254. The word spending (*iNFāQ*) also occurs in vv. 261, 262, 264, 265, 267 (twice), 270, 272 (three times), 273, and 274, all in the context of charity.	This echoes the description of the believers as those who "**spend out of what We have provided them** (*yuNFiQūna mim-mā razqnā-hum*)" in v. 3.
The Throne Verse emphasizes God's unlimited knowledge ("He **knows** (*ya'LaMu*) what is before them and what is ahead of them") as well as the dependency and limited scope of the knowledge of His creatures ("and they do not encompass anything of His **knowledge** (*'iLM*) except what He has willed"). God is also described as "Knowing" (*'alīm*) in this section in vv. 246, 256, 257, 261, 265, 268, 273, 282, 283.	The same theme is stressed throughout section A (vv. 13, 22, 26, 29-33). Of particular note is the angels' declaration in section A, which forms the center of a ring, "'Exalted are you! We have no **knowledge** (*'iLM*) except what You have **taught** (*'aLLaMta*) us. Indeed it is You who are the Knowing (*al-'ALīM*), the Wise" (v. 32).
Verse 257 states that the false gods of the disbelievers take them "from **light** (*nūr*) to **darkness** (*ẓulumāt*)" and that they are "the companions of the **Fire** (*nār*)" (v. 257).	This echoes the comparison of the pseudo-believers to "someone who kindled a **fire** (*nār*), but when it illuminated what was around him, God took away their **light** (*nūr*) and left them in **darkness** (*ẓulumāt*)" (v. 17).
Verses 282-283 mandate that when believers enter into a transaction in which one of them contracts a debt from another for a fixed time, they should "**write** it down" (*f-aKTuBū-hu*) or call a "**scribe"** (*KāTiB*) to do so. If the one who owes the debt is unable to reliably dictate the debt to the scribe, such as if he is "feeble-minded" (*SaFīH*), his guardian should dictate it and they should call "**witnesses**" (*shuhadā'*) to oversee its recording. This will ensure that they "do not **doubt**" (*lā taRtāBū*, from *RayB*). All parties involved should "be conscious of God" (*wa-'TTaQū/wa-'l-yaTTiQi*).	In v. 2, it was stated that the Qur'an is the "**scripture** (*KiTāB*) concerning which there is no **doubt** (*rayb*), a guidance for the **God-conscious** (*muTTaQīn*)." In v. 23, skeptics are told that if they "are in **doubt** (*rayb*) about" the Qur'an, they should produce a sura of its like and "call upon **witnesses** (*shuhadā'*)"—except "if **transaction** (*tijāra*) is immediate." Additionally, it was said about the pseudo-believers that "it is they who are the **feeble-minded** (*SuFaHā'*)" (vv. 13) and that "their **transaction** (*tijāra*) did not benefit them" (vv. 16).

The concluding verses (vv. 285-286) state that the believers have faith in all of what God has revealed and include a final prayer by the believers for victory over the disbelieving people.	This recalls the beginning of the sura, which describes the believers as "those who have faith in what was revealed to you and what was revealed before you" (v. 4) and contrasts them with the disbelievers (vv. 6-20).

The above list, which has been reduced somewhat for the sake of concision, should suffice to show how closely the first and final sections of the sura are connected, further reinforcing the overall ring composition of the sura.

* * *

In chapter 11, "The Coherence and Structure of the Qur'anic Sura," we opened the question of the coherence and structure of the suras by noting the confusion and dissatisfaction among many Western readers of the scripture, who have judged it to be inferior literature. We have made the case that this perception is due to a lack of appreciation of the ancient, Near Eastern, and Classical Arabic rhetorical styles and methods that the Qur'an excels in. Recent scholarship has begun to overturn this tendency, increasingly shedding light on these techniques and the effectiveness with which they are used in the Qur'an. In the case of *The Cow*, until recently regarded as the most chaotic of the suras, we have seen that a careful study reveals a beautiful and intricate structure, as well as profound logic and coherence. In the next chapter, we will turn to the question of the sequence in which the suras of the Qur'an are arranged, which seems to have no real precedent, even in the literature of the ancient Near East.

CHAPTER 14

The Order of the Suras

It should now be clear that the Qur'anic sura is a far more coherent and well-designed composition than is usually appreciated. We will now turn to the question of the structure of the Qur'an as a whole. The reader approaching the Qur'an for the first time is often surprised and even dismayed to find that its suras are neither ordered chronologically nor arranged into discrete topics. To grasp all that the Qur'an says of a particular subject, or how its discussion of that subject developed over the course of its revelation, requires a careful study of the scripture as a whole.

On the other hand, the key themes and morals of the Qur'an are repeated throughout, and the reader is bound to encounter them, regardless of where he starts to read or which sura he is listening to. This feature of the Qur'an can be understood by the fact that it is primarily intended to be experienced in the life of the individual and the community as an oral recitation, whose varied revelations are encountered in the daily prayers, in times of private devotion, or even simply during periods of leisure. As Michael Sells writes,

> The Qur'anic experience is not the experience of reading a written text from beginning to end. Rather, themes, stories, hymns, and laws of the Qur'an are woven through the life stages of the individual, the key moments of the community, and the sensual world of the town and village...The experience is a nonlinear repetition through recitation. The actual stories, which may seem fragmented in a written version, are brought together in the mind of the hearer through repeated experiences with the text.[204]

---

204 Sells, *Approaching the Qur'an*, 12.

Still, it cannot be denied that the Qur'an also refers to itself as a written "Book" or "Scripture" (*kitāb*), and if one chooses to read the Qur'an (or a translation) in its received order, it may be unsatisfying to assume that there is no meaningful sequence to its suras. It may easily be observed that the suras are arranged very roughly according to length, so that the longest suras occur at the beginning of the Qur'an and the shortest suras at the end, but is there any deeper significance to the structure of the Qur'an? As the reader finishes one sura and turns to the next, is there any kind of connection that places them in relationship to one another? Does the Qur'an as a whole exhibit the kind of order and coherence that we found upon an examination of its individual suras?

In this chapter, we will explore several aspects of the Qur'an's structure that have been uncovered by scholars over the centuries and continue to be of interest to researchers to this day. While the subject is yet to be exhausted, what has been discovered so far is surprising, especially given how the revelations appeared over time in a much different order and originally functioned mainly as oral communications.

Dovetailing Between Suras

From the twelfth century CE, some Muslim scholars have noticed that, in their received order, consecutive suras of the Qur'an appear to have interconnections (what we have called "anchors") in which a key word, phrase, or image that occurs towards the end of one sura also appears at the beginning of the next, thereby linking them together. Neal Robinson refers to this phenomenon as "dovetailing," and lists thirty examples, while other researchers have attempted to chart the connections between the beginnings and endings of all 114 suras.[205] To illustrate this feature, we will list examples of dovetailing only between the first twelve suras:

Sura #s	End of Sura	Beginning of Next Sura
1 & 2	Sura 1 ends with a prayer for guidance: "Guide us (*iHDi-nā*)…" (1:6-7).	The beginning of Sura 2 presents the rest of the Qur'an as an answer to that prayer: "This is the Scripture concerning which there is no doubt, a guidance (*HuDan*) for the God-conscious" (v. 2).

205 See Robinson, *Discovering the Qur'an*, 266-269; Hussein Abdul-Raof, *Consonance in the Qur'an: A Conceptual, Intertextual and Linguistic Analysis* (Munich: Lincom, 2005); Muḥammad Fārūq az-Zayn, *Bayān an-Naẓm fī al-Qur'ān al-Karīm* (Dimashq: Dar al-Fikr, 2004); as-Sāmarrā'ī, *Kitāb at-Tanāsub Bayna 's-Suwar fī 'l-Muftataḥ wa'l-Khawātīm* (Dammam: Dār Ibn al-Jawzī, 2011); aṣ-Ṣuyūṭī, *Tanāsuq ad-Durar fī Tanāsub as-Suwar*, A.M. ad-Darwīsh (ed.), 2nd ed. (Bayrūt: 'Ālam al-Kutub). See also the commentaries of ar-Rāzī, al-Biqā'i, Farāhī, and Iṣlāḥī.

2 & 3	The last section of Sura 2 contains the statement "God, there is nothing worthy of worship but He, the Living, the Maintainer of Existence" (v. 255).	This statement is reproduced word-for-word in 3:2, occurring nowhere else in the Qur'an.
3 & 4	The end of Sura 3 contains a promise from God, "Truly I will never allow the work of any worker among you go to waste, *male or female*" (v. 195).	In 4:1, God mentions the creation of both "men and women."
4 & 5	The last verse of Sura 4 lays out the division of the inheritance of a person who has no living descendants or ascendants (v. 176), highlighting the theme of social equity and fulfillment of social obligations.	Sura 5 opens with the command to "fulfill all binding contracts" (v. 1), highlighting the same themes.
5 & 6	Sura 5 ends with the declaration, "To God belongs the kingdom of the heavens and the earth" (v. 120).	Sura 6 opens with the statement, "All praise is due to God, who created the heavens and the earth" (v. 1).
6 & 7	Towards the end of Sura 6, there is a discourse about revelation (vv. 154-157) containing four instances of the word "Scripture" (*kitāb*) and three instances of the verb "sent down" (*anzala/unzila*). This includes the phrase "This is a scripture We have sent down."	Sura 7 begins with the words, "A.L.M.Ṣ. A scripture (*kitāb*) sent down (*unzila*) to you…"
7 & 8	The last three verses of Sura 7 explain how the believer should respond to God and His revelation. They say, "When the Qur'an is recited, listen to it and pay attention, so that you may receive mercy"; urge the individual, "remember (*uDHKuR*) your Lord to yourself in humility and fear"; and state that the believers "are not too arrogant to worship Him, and they exalt Him and prostrate to Him" (vv. 204-206).	8:2-3 says, "The believers are those who, when God is mentioned (*DHuKiRa*), their hearts become fearful, and when His verses are recited to them, it increases them in faith, and they only rely upon their Lord; those who establish the prayer…"
8 & 9	The end of Sura 8 refers to the "emigration" of the believers from Mecca, their "fighting" in God's cause, explains that the disbelievers violated their peace treaties with the believers, and clarifies that "the believers are allies to one another" while "those who disbelieve are allies to one another" (vv. 71-75).	Sura 9 opens sternly with, "A disavowal of God and His messenger with those whom you made a treaty with among the polytheists!" (v. 1). It permits the Quraysh to "travel freely across the land" of Mecca for four months (v. 2), but states that if they stay after that, the believers will fight them for their crimes.

		One of the main crimes listed is the disbelievers' repeated violations of their treaties, but the believers are required to maintain their treaties of peace with whoever has not violated them (vv. 1-6ff).
9 & 10	The last verse of Sura 9 refers to God as "the Lord of the Tremendous Throne" (v. 129) located above the heavens.	10:3 states that after the creation of the heavens and the earth, God "established Himself on the Throne."
10 & 11	The last verse of Sura 10 commands the Messenger, "Be patient until God judges (*yaḤKuMu*), for He is the best of judges (*ḤāKiMīn*)" (v. 109).	Sura 11 begins, "ALR. A scripture whose verses are made decisive (*uḤKiMat*) in the presence of One who is Wise (*ḤaKīM*)" (vv. 1-2).
11 & 12	The end of Sura 11 refers to "Everything We narrate upon you (*naQuṢṢu 'alay-ka*) from the stories of the messengers" (v. 120).	12:3 states, "We narrate upon you (*naQuṢṢu 'alay-ka*) the best of narratives."

Dovetailing continues to occur throughout the Qur'an, though it becomes less common with the suras at the end of the scripture, which are too brief, in most cases, to allow this feature. (Nonetheless, we will see that they are arranged according to other considerations.) This demonstrates that the Qur'anic suras are actually not ordered randomly, but that their received order is a large-scale feature of the scripture's composition. For further instances of dovetailing, selected from various parts of the Qur'an, the reader is encouraged to consult Robinson's list in *Discovering the Qur'an*, 266-269.

Sura Pairs and Groups

The dovetailing of the ends and beginnings of consecutive suras provides one clue to their order. But classical scholars interested in the Qur'an's arrangement observed that even more fundamental connections exist between neighboring suras, for suras that share strong commonalities in structure, subject matter, and style appear to be grouped together. In the last century and a half, further studies of the Qur'an's overall structure have been carried out by Hamid ad-Din Farahi and his student Amin Ahsan Islahi.[206] They argued that the whole Qur'an consists of several large-scale sura groups (seven on Islahi's view) in which each group is distinguished by a focus on a particular theme.[207] Islahi further expanded on this concept, maintaining that each of the seven groups

206 See the introduction of chapter 11, "The Coherence and Structure of the Qur'anic Sura."
207 Islahi's seven groups are suras 1-5, 6-9, 10-24, 25-33, 34-49, 50-66, and 67-114. On Islahi's sura groups, see Mir, *Coherence*, 85-98.

consists of at least one Meccan sura and at least one Medinan sura, with the Meccan suras always preceding the Medinan sura inside the group.

Islahi also contributed the concept of the "sura pair," contending that most of the Qur'anic suras form a pair with the sura either immediately before or after it. The suras within a pair may complement each other in any of the following ways: what one sura states in brief, the other explains in detail; what one sura states as a principle, the other illustrates through example; what one sura lays out as a premise, the other uses to argue for a conclusion; they may address the opposite sides of an issue, such as monotheism and polytheism, or faith and disbelief; they may discuss the same issue with different points of emphasis; or they may argue towards a common conclusion using different lines of evidence.[208] Among contemporary researchers, Islahi's observation that the suras tend to form complementary pairs has received support from Michel Cuypers and Raymond Farrin.[209]

One does not have to accept all the details of Islahi's scheme to recognize that many of the suras of the Qur'an form complementary pairs or that the Qur'an as a whole does appear to consist of sura groups—perhaps even on multiple levels. In this section, we will explore the connections between suras that form pairs or groups. We will begin with a medium-sized sura pair, and then explore the last ten suras of the Qur'an as a group, while also drawing attention to a couple of the small sura pairs within it.

A Medium-Sized Sura Pair: The All-Merciful & The Inevitable Event

Sura 55, *The All-Merciful* (*ar-Raḥmān*) may be an exceptional case in that it can be argued to form a pair with either Sura 54, *The Moon (al-Qamar)*, or Sura 56, *The Inevitable Event (al-Wāqi'a)*. We will come to the connections between suras 54 and 55 at the end of this chapter. In this section, we will direct our attention to how suras 55 and 56 display the same themes, but in reverse order, forming a mirror or ring composition. Positioned between the two halves is a description of the judgment and the division of humankind into three classes, each of which will receive a different treatment on Judgment Day.

Sura 55, *The All-Merciful* (*ar-Raḥmān*)

Introduction: "The All-Merciful" (*ar-Raḥmān*)" (v. 1):

A. "He taught the Qur'an" (v. 2);
  B. Wonders of creation (vv. 2-25);

208 On Islahi's theory of sura pairs, see Mir, *Coherence*, 75-84.
209 Farrin, *Structure and Qur'anic Interpretation*, 22. For a bibliography of Cuypers' work in French on symmetric coherence in the last thirty suras, see ibid., 146.

C. Judgment and punishment (vv. 26-45);
D. Lower level of Paradise (vv. 46-61);
E. Higher level of Paradise (vv. 62-78);

End praise: "Blessed is the name of your Lord, Owner of Majesty and Honor" (v. 79)

Sura 56, *The Inevitable Event* (*al-Wāqi'a*)

Introduction: The "inevitable event" (i.e., the Judgment) and the division of humanity into the three groups (vv. 1-10).

E'. "Those who are brought near" (vv. 11-26);
D'. "People of the right hand" (vv. 27-40);
C.' "People of the left hand" (vv. 41-56);
B.' Wonders of creation (vv. 57-75);
A.' The Qur'an (vv. 76-82);

Latch: Concludes the pair with a final description and warning of the afterlife (vv. 83-95);
End praise: "So exalt the name of your Lord, the Most Great" (v. 96).

To start, the two suras share similar endings: "Blessed is the name of Your Lord, Owner of Majesty and Honor" (55:78) and "So exalted is the name of Your Lord, the Most Great" (56:96). The divine titles "Owner of Majesty and Honor" and "the Most Great" also both occur earlier in their respective suras (55:27; 56:74).

After Sura 55 introduces God as "The All-Merciful," from which the sura takes its name, it goes on for twenty-four verses listing the All-Merciful's favors on mankind and jinn. The very first favor listed is that "He taught the Qur'an" (A). Sura 56 contains a corresponding section about the Qur'an (A', vv. 76-82), in which God swears that "it is a noble recital (*qur'ān*)" (56:77) and "a revelation from the Lord of all peoples" (56:80). The swearing of the oath "by the places of the stars" and the references to the heavenly tablet and angels underscore that the Qur'an is a gift from the creator of the universe.

Sections B of Sura 55 (vv. 2-25) and B' of Sura 56 (vv. 57-75) list some of the wonders and blessings of God's creation. Both lists include the creation of man (55:3, 14; 56:57-62), the growth of crops (55:11-12; 56:63-67), water (the sea, 55:19-22, 24; rain, 56:68-70), a mention of fire (55:15; 56:71), and trees (55:6; 56:72-73).

C (55:26-45) and C' (56:41-46) describe the impending judgment and punishment. In C', the criminals who will receive the punishment are labeled "the people of the left hand," because they will receive their books of deeds in their left hand (cf. 69:25). Both sections mention the criminals' "denial" (55:43, plus the refrain "which of the favors of your Lord will you deny?"; 56:51) and the punishment of "scalding water" for them (55:44; 56:42, 54).

D (55:46-61) describes a level of Paradise characterized by two gardens, which will surround the inhabitant from both sides as he enters them.[210] D' (56:27-40) portrays the rewards of the "companions of the right hand," people who will have passed the examination on Judgment Day, receiving their books of deeds in their right hands (cf. 17:71; 69:19; 84:7). The rewards listed in the two sections closely correspond:

D (55:46-61): "two gardens" for "one who feared standing before His Lord"	**D' (56:27-40): rewards for "the companions of the right hand"**
"shading branches" (55:48)	exotic trees and "extended shade" (56:28-30)
"two springs, flowing" (55:50)	"constantly flowing water" (56:31)
"every fruit, in two kinds" (55:52)	"abundant fruits, unfailing, unforbidden" (56:32-33)
"beds lined with brocade" (55:54)	"beds raised high" (56:34)
maidens "limiting their glances," "untouched," and "like rubies and coral" (55:56, 58)	maidens "specially created" and "virginal, loving, and of matching age" (56:35-37)

E (55:62-78) depicts two more gardens. Most commentators argue that these are of a lower rank compared to the previous pair of gardens, since they are introduced as being *min dūni-himā*—a phrase that can mean "below them"—and because the rewards described in these two gardens are less impressive in quality. Nonetheless, the phrase *min dūni-himā* can also simply mean "besides them," and there is a case that the descriptions of this second pair of gardens would have actually had the greater appeal to the pre-Islamic Arabs:

The previous gardens were described as having "shading branches." These gardens, on the other hand, are described as being "dark green" (*mudhāmatān*), a word used nowhere else in the Qur'an and which suggests abundant leaves and foliage as well as profound beauty, uniqueness, and mystery.

The previous gardens were said to have two springs that are "flowing." In contrast, these gardens have two springs that are "gushing," which is a more powerful image.

---

210 Abdel Haleem, *Understanding the Qur'an*, 181. This "pairing" is a motif that runs throughout Sura 55. The sura has a rhyme scheme in which most of the verses end in *-ān*, which is also the dual suffix in Arabic. The rhyme scheme therefore allows this motif to be repeatedly expressed throughout the course of the sura.

These gardens are said to contain "fruit, date palms, and pomegranates." Although the previous gardens were said to contain "every fruit, in two kinds," the specific mention of "date palms" and "pomegranates" in association with these gardens suggests that their fruits are catered to the highest tastes of the Arab audience, while the unqualified mention of "fruit" may be intended to encompass the two kinds of every fruit mentioned of the previous gardens and even more.

While the maidens of the previous gardens were described as "limiting their glances," the maidens of these gardens are described more exquisitely as being "sheltered in pavilions." While the beauty of the maidens of the previous gardens was expressed by their comparison to "rubies and coral," the beauty of the maidens of these gardens is first stated in general terms and then given a more concrete but tantalizing example in their description as "houris" (*ḥūr*), women distinguished with beautiful eyes that are marked by a deep contrast of white and black.

The previous gardens were said to contain beds and the quality of their lining was described. In the case of these gardens, it is the quality of their cushions that is highlighted, cushions being a greater symbol of luxury. These gardens are further described as having "beautiful carpets," which are *'abqarī*—a word signifying exquisite design and craftmanship, and which additionally carries a sense of mystery and otherworldliness, being an ascription to a fabled land of the jinn, in pre-Islamic Arab folklore.

Likewise, E' (56:11-26) describes the "gardens of bliss" reserved for "the foremost" or "those brought near" (56:10-12), therefore indicating the highest level of Paradise. In this section the gardens are described as including ornamented thrones, eternally youthful servants, wine pured from a spring into various kinds of vessels, fruits and fowl of any choice, houris, and greetings of peace from God Himself.

56:1-10 describes the judgment and identifies the three classes of people whose fates are described in each of the two halves. Thus, it not only serves as an introduction to Sura 56 but also summarizes the majority of Sura 55 (vv. 26-78).

Sura 56 concludes with a latch (vv. 83-95), a feature of some ring structures similar to an epilogue and reaffirms the central idea or ideas of the composition. This latch provides a final summary, listing again the three kinds of people and their destinations, and concluding with the statement, "Indeed, this is the certain truth" (56:95).

Sura Groups: The Last Ten Suras

In addition to the sura pairs, both modern and classical scholars have recognized that the suras in their arranged order appear to form groups that have thematic and stylistic commonalities. In this section, we will explore a small sura group consisting of the last ten suras of the Qur'an.[211] These suras are as follows:

105. The Elephant (*al-Fīl*)
106. Quraysh
107. Small Kindnesses (*al-Mā'ūn*)
108. The Abundance (*al-Kawthar*)
109. The Disbelievers (*al-Kāfirūn*)
110. The Help (*an-Naṣr*)
111. The Flame (*al-Lahab*)
112. Purity (*al-Ikhlāṣ*)
113. Daybreak (*al-Falaq*)
114. Mankind (*an-Nās*)

These suras, in their received order, progressively develop and establish a single theme: the restoration of Abrahamic monotheism to (and through) its capital in Mecca.[212] To begin, we must turn once more to Abraham's prayer in Sura 2. The prayer opens with the following request:

> When Abraham said, "My Lord, make this a secure city (*baladan 'āMiNan*), and provide its people with fruits—whoever among them believes in God and the Last Day." God said, "As for whoever disbelieves, I will give him enjoyment for a little while, and then I will force him into the punishment of the Fire (*nār*). What a terrible destination!" (2:126)

Abraham and his son Ishmael then ask God to raise a messenger from their descendants who will call them back to his monotheistic legacy so that they will be "*muslims*," people submitted to God:

> When Abraham was raising the foundations of the House, and Ishmael: "Our Lord, accept from us. Truly You are the Hearing, the Knowing.
>
> Our Lord, make us submitters to you and make from our descendants a nation submitted to you. Show us our rites and accept our repentance. Truly You are the Returner, the Merciful.
>
> Our Lord, send them a messenger from among them who will recite your verses, teach them the Scripture and wisdom, and purify them. Truly You are the Almighty, the Wise." (2:127-130)

---

211 Some argue view these as two sura groups, consisting of 105-108 and 109-112, with 113-114 forming a supplementary conclusion. For our purposes we will treat them as a single cohesive group.

212 These observations mostly owe to the commentaries of Hamid ad-Din Farahi and Amin Ahsan Islahi.

Now we are in a position to see how the last ten suras of the Qur'an fit together and are placed in a meaningful order.

As we have just seen, Abraham opens his prayer by asking God to grant his city the two conditions essential for a functioning society—peace and prosperity: "My Lord, make this a secure city (*baladan 'āMiNan*), and provide its people with fruits." The answer to this prayer is exemplified in the first two suras of this group, *The Elephant* (s. 105), which highlights God's miraculous protection of the city, and *Quraysh* (s. 106), which concerns the city's economic success. These are also among the earliest suras revealed and form a small pair, noticeably complementing each other.

Sura 105, *The Elephant* (*al-Fīl*), refers to God's protection of Mecca in the sixth century from the assault of Abraha, an Ethiopian Christian ruler over South Arabia. Arabic sources tell us that Abraha led an attack on Mecca with an army that included one or more war elephants, with the intention of destroying the Ka'ba and rerouting the traffic of pilgrims to a massive church he had built in the Yemeni capital of Sana'a. However, the attack was thwarted when the army was pelted with a barrage of stones from the sky:

1. Have you not seen how Your Lord dealt with the Companions of the Elephant?
2. Did He not make their plot go astray?
3. And He sent upon them birds in flocks,
4. Pelting them with stones of baked clay,[213]
5. And then He made them like straw eaten up.

The sura demonstrates how God made Mecca "a secure city" (*baladan 'āMiNan*), just as Abraham requested in his prayer.

Sura 106, *Quraysh*, similarly reminds that tribe how God gave them provision and protection in their caravan trade journeys in the winters and summers, which (along with the traffic of Arab pilgrims to the Ka'ba) brought them economic success:

1. For the keeping of the Quraysh
2. Their keeping in the caravan journeys of the winter and summer:

---

213 If one assumes that the addressee is the individual member of the Quraysh, another translation is possible: "*You* were pelting them with stones of baked clay." On this interpretation, the subject of "pelting" is not the birds, as usually assumed, but the individual member of the Quraysh, and the birds were merely birds of prey preparing to feast on the carnage. This view was argued by Farahi and his student Islahi on the basis of pre-Islamic poetry and other lines of evidence. See Mir, "Elephants, Birds of Prey, and Heaps of Pebbles: Farāhī's Interpretation of Sūrat Al-Fīl," *Journal of Qur'anic Studies* 7.1 (2005): 33-47.

3. Let them worship the Lord of this House,
4. Who fed them against hunger and secured them (*'āMaNa-hum*) from fear.

The sura's reference to God having "secured" (*'āMaNa*) the Quraysh from fear once again recalls Abraham's prayer. This time, however, the sura draws special attention to how God's protection of them led to their economic prosperity, thereby answering the second part of Abraham's prayer: "and provide its people with fruits."

While *Quraysh* describes how God provided the tribe of Quraysh with food and wealth, the next sura scolds its leaders for refusing to do the same for the poor and needy under their authority, to the point that they would not give even the "smallest kindnesses." Sura 107, *Small Kindnesses* (*al-Mā'ūn*), says:

1. Have you seen the one who denies the Recompense?
2. That is the one who pushes away the orphan
3. And does not urge the feeding of the poor.
4. So woe to those who pray—
5. Those who are heedless of their prayers,
6. Those who are all show
7. And refuse small kindnesses.

The next four suras (108-111) are logically connected. They represent, respectively: a divine promise of victory and of the enemy's destruction; the contrast between the religion of monotheism and the religion of the enemy; the victory of the religion of monotheism; and the destruction of the enemy. As we will see, it is also likely that these suras logically represent four stages of the Prophet's career: the low point, the turning point, the final victory, and the enemy's demise.

Sura 108, *The Abundance* (*al-Kawthar*), is the shortest sura of the Qur'an. Most scholars regard it as Meccan, viewing it as a consolation to the Prophet during the low point of his career, when he and his followers were weak, powerless, and small in number, and faced with the powerful opposition of the Quraysh leadership. Early commentators have further related that the Prophet's infant son had died, leaving him without a male heir—a terrible humiliation in Arabian tribal society. As a result, his enemies—including none other than his own uncle Abu Lahab—made fun of his situation, boasting that his legacy was "cut off" and that his efforts to reform his society were doomed to failure.

The sura is a small ring structure, consisting of only three short verses. In the first verse, God assures the Prophet that He has already given him full success and victory in this world and the next: he just has to wait to see it. In the last verse, God also informs him that it is his enemies who are truly "cut off" from all good, for they will be defeated and will have to suffer the consequences of their actions in the next life. In the center, the Prophet is commanded to express his gratitude to God through prayer and sacrifice—the two modes of worship most directly associated with the legacy of Abraham—just as the Quraysh were ordered to "worship the Lord of this House" in Sura 106.

1. Truly We have given you the Abundance,
2. So pray to your Lord and sacrifice.
3. Truly your enemy is the one who is cut off.

The fulfillment of these prophecies is illustrated in the next three suras. However, let us pause to consider the connection of this sura with the previous one, *Small Kindnesses*. The commentator Fakhr ad-Dīn ar-Rāzī observed that in *Small Kindnesses*, four qualities are listed of "the one who denies the Recompense":

1. He is exceedingly miserly: "That is the one who pushes away the orphan and does not urge the feeding of the poor."
2. He prays inattentively: "So woe to those who pray and are heedless in their prayer."
3. He only prays to show off: "Those who are all show."
4. He is unwilling to give even the smallest amount from his wealth or food: "And refuse small kindnesses."

The Abundance mentions four exactly opposite qualities in the same order:

1. God is extremely giving: "Truly We have given you the Abundance."
2. The Prophet is commanded to pray: "So pray."
3. He is commanded to do it sincerely: "to your Lord," which can also be translated as "for your Lord."
4. He is commanded to sacrifice an animal, which involves expending money and giving out the meat of the animal to others: "and sacrifice."

As the two suras show such close symmetry, their placement side-by-side cannot be regarded as accidental, but as an intentional part of the Qur'an's design.

The next sura—109, *The Disbelievers* (*al-Kāfirūn*)—marks the end of the Prophet's attempts at inviting the leaders of the Quraysh to Abrahamic monotheism in Mecca:

1. Say: "O disbelievers,
2. I do not worship what you worship,
3. And you are not worshipers of what I worship,

4. Nor will I be a worshiper of what you worship,
5. And nor will you worship what I worship.
6. To you be your religion (*dīn*), and to me be my religion (*dīn*)."

This disavowal of the Quraysh would lead to the Prophet's departure from Mecca (the Hijra, 622 CE), which would end up being a major turning point in his mission—to the extent that the Islamic calendar used to this day begins with it. Were it not for the disavowal put forward by this sura, the Muslims would never have been able to form an independent community in Medina and the political and military confrontations between the Muslims and the disbelievers of the Quraysh could not have taken place.

It follows neatly from this that the next sura—109, *The Help* (*an-Naṣr*)—describes the victory of the Prophet and his community over the Quraysh, foreshadowed by the first verse of *The Abundance*. This victory was the Conquest of Mecca (629 CE) and the entry of most of the tribes of Arabia into Islam:

1. When the help of God comes and the Conquest,
2. And you see the people entering the religion (*dīn*) of God in droves,
3. Then exalt your Lord with praise and ask for his forgiveness. Truly He is the Returner.

Additionally, the word for "religion," *dīn*, which the previous sura ended with—"To you be your *dīn*, and to me be my *dīn*"—is picked up again in this sura, where it is made clear which of the two *dīns* is the victorious and divinely-aided one. This sura represents the fulfillment of Abraham's prayer to raise among his descendants a *muslim* nation: "Our Lord, make us submitters to you and make from our descendants a nation submitted (*muslim*) to you. Show us our rites and accept our repentance. Indeed you are the Returner, the Merciful."

The next sura graphically illustrates the prophecy in the last verse of *The Abundance*: "Truly your enemy is the one who is cut off." Sura 111, *The Flame* (*al-Lahab*) (also called *The Palm Fiber*, *al-Masad*) concerns 'Abd al-'Uzza ibn 'Abd al-Muttalib, who was the most vicious leader of the Quraysh in his hostility against the Prophet, despite being his uncle. 'Abd al-'Uzza was known by the nickname "Abu Lahab," "Father of the Flame," because of the bright, ruddy complexion of his face. His wife supported him in his hatred: it was said that while carrying firewood, she would cast thorns bound with twisted palm fiber into the Prophet's path. The sura prophesies Abu Lahab's destruction and then satirically describes the couple's punishment in the afterlife:

1. The hands of Abu Lahab will perish and he will perish;
2. His wealth and gains will not avail him.
3. He will burn in a fire (*nār*) of flame (*lahab*).
4. And his wife, the firewood-carrier:
5. Around her neck is a rope of twisted palm fiber (*masad*).

According to Muslim sources, Abu Lahab died a gruesome death. Shortly after the Battle of Badr (624 CE), in which the Muslims won their first victory, Abu Lahab became sick with the plague. He was quarantined and no one approached him until days after he died. The smell of his decomposing body was so off-putting that his sons had to hire laborers to dispense of his body. *The Flame* serves as a commentary of God's response to Abraham's prayer: "As for whoever disbelieves, I will give him enjoyment for a little while, and then I will force him into the punishment of the Fire (*nār*). What a terrible destination!" The same word for "fire" is also used in this sura.

Suras 105-111 played out the fulfillment of Abraham's prayer in a logical sequence. The next sura—112, *Purity* (*Ikhlāṣ*)—recaps the purpose of the Prophet's entire mission: the restoration of monotheism. The title of the sura, *Purity*, calls to mind Abraham's prayer that God may raise among his descendants a messenger who would "purify them" (*yuzakkī-him*). Interestingly, this sura also picks up the end rhyme that the previous sura ended in.

1. Say, "He is God, One (*aḥad*),
2. God, the Eternal (*ṣamad*),
3. He does not beget, nor is begotten (*yūlad*),
4. And there is nothing comparable to Him (*aḥad*)."

Finally, the sura group, and the Qur'an as a whole, concludes with two suras which form a pair. Both of these suras are prayers, so that just as the Qur'an began with a prayer (Sura 1, *The Opening*), it ends with prayers. The first of these—Sura 113, *Daybreak* (*al-Falaq*)—is a prayer of refuge from human and supernatural agents who may seek to externally harm a person and his commitment to God:

1. Say: "I take refuge in the Lord of Daybreak
2. From the evil of whatever He has created,
3. And from the evil of the darkness when it overtakes,
4. And from the evil of those who blow on knots [i.e., practicing sorcery],
5. And from the evil of the envier when he envies.

Sura 114, *Mankind* (*an-Nās*), is a prayer of refuge from human and supernatural agents who may seek to lead a person away from the Straight Path by casting inside of his heart doubts or messages, referred to as "whispers," and then retreating:

1. Say: "I take refuge in the Lord of mankind,
2. The King of mankind,
3. The God of mankind,
4. From the evil of the slinking whisperer,
5. Who whispers into the hearts of mankind,
6. From among jinn and mankind.

The two suras form an obvious pair. They each consist of two parts, the first part beginning with "Say: 'I take refuge in the Lord of...'" and the second part beginning with "From the evil of..." Moreover, the two suras mirror each other. The first sura lists one attribute of God and three threats, while the second lists three attributes of God and one threat.[214]

Additionally, we will see in the next chapter that the final sura also returns back to the first one, mirroring it thematically, structurally, and verbally.

The Symmetry of the Whole Qur'an?

We have seen that the individual suras of the Qur'an exhibit both linear coherence and symmetry. We have also observed linear coherence between the suras. Do the suras, taken altogether, also exhibit symmetry? Could the Qur'an as a whole be a symmetrical structure, such as a ring composition?

While it is probably too early in the study of the Qur'an's composition to claim anything about its structure as a whole with certainty, Farrin has proposed that the entire Qur'an consists of two "systems" of sura groups, each forming a discrete ring structure:

---

214 Farrin, *Structure and Qur'anic Interpretation*, 24, citing Fakhr ad-Dīn ar-Rāzī, *Mafātīḥ al-Ghayb*, ed. 'Imad al-Bārūdī (Cairo: al-Maktaba al-Tawfīqiyya, 2003), 16:200.

Diagram 2

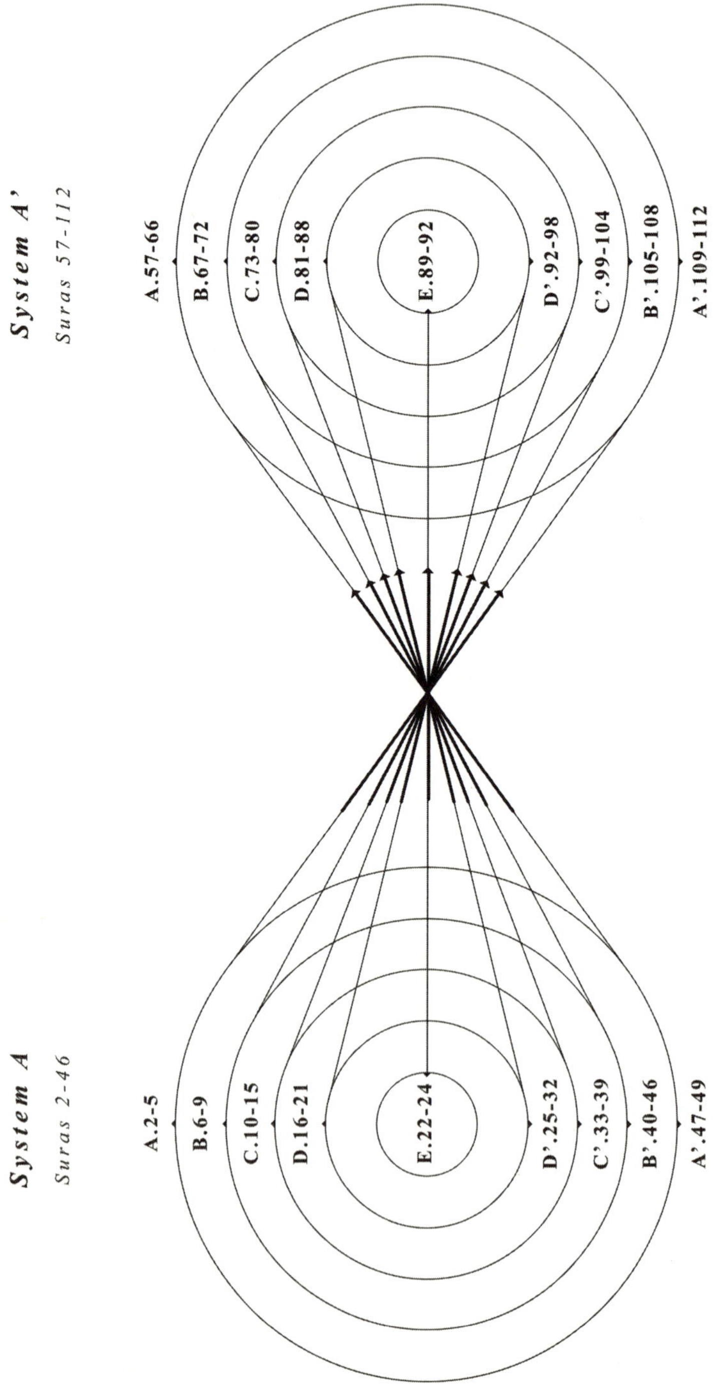

The Quran as Two Interlocking Ring Compositions

For example, to just look within system A:

- Groups A (ss. 2-5) and A' (ss. 47-49) contain the only references to Mecca by name ("Bakka" in 3:96, "Makka" in 48:24); contain a call to the Muslims in Medina to perform the Hajj (Group A, 2:196) and discuss the Treaty of Hudaybiyya, which they made during their attempted pilgrimage (Group A', s. 48); and emphasize unity within the Muslim community (Group A, 3:103; 49:10) and God's creation of different racial, ethnic, and religious communities (Group A', 2:148; 49:13).
- Groups B (ss. 6-9) and B' (ss. 40-46) contain exclusive reference to Mecca as the "Mother of Cities" (*Umm al-Qurā*) and contain special references to God's forgiveness, even in the titles of the suras (Sura 9, *Repentance*; Sura 40, *The Forgiver*).
- Groups C (ss. 10-15) and C' (ss. 33-39) inform that on Judgment Day it will be exclaimed, "All praise is due to God, the Lord of all peoples!" (10:10; 39:75). Both groups also refer to the story of Jonah, though one emphasizes that Jonah's people were saved from punishment when they repented (s. 10, *Jonah*, v. 98) and the other emphasizes that Jonah was saved from the whale when he repented (37:139-148).
- Groups D (ss. 16-21) and D' (ss. 25-32) contain suras named after insects (s. 16, *The Bee*, s. 27, *The Ant*; cf. s. 29, *The Spider*). One group records the accusation that the Prophet is a poet (21:5) and the other contrasts the character of the Prophet with that of the poets of Arabia (s. 26, *The Poets*).

Farrin also argues that the two systems are linked together by a central sura group (ss. 50-56, which thematically concentrate on the afterlife), uniting the entire Qur'an as a single vast ring composition, with Sura 1 and Suras 113 and 114 forming prayers that surround the structure:

Diagram 3

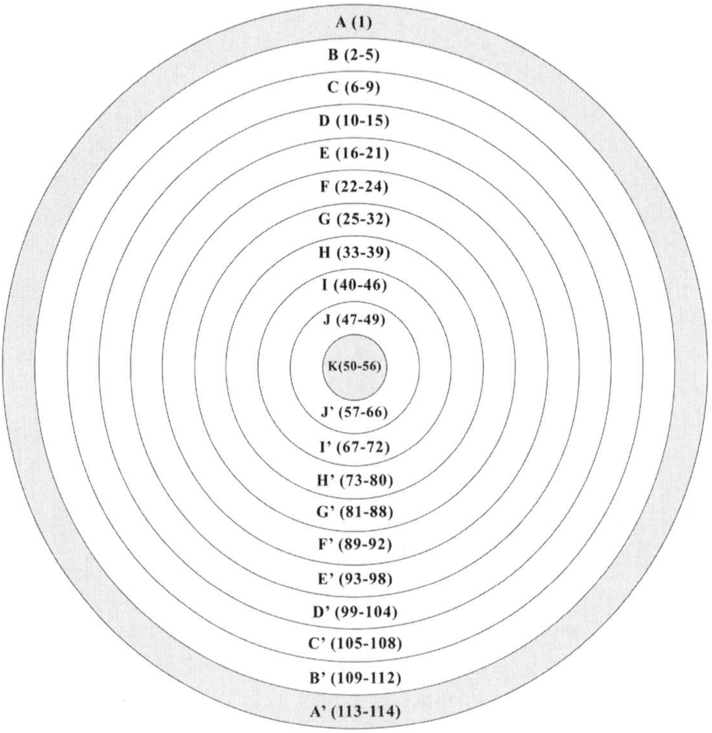

The Whole Quran as a Ring Composition

The first system consists of long suras, the second of short ones. Some of the anchors that Farrin points out between the groups include the following:

Group E (ss. 16-21)	Group E’ (ss. 93-98)
Moses prays to God, “My Lord, **expand for me my chest** (*iSHRāḤ lī ṢaDR-ī*), **ease** (*YaSSiR*) for me my task…and appoint for me a **helper** (*WaZīR*) from my family” (20:25-26, 29).	God asks the Prophet, “Did We not **expand for you your chest** (*naSHRāḤ laka ṢaDRa-k*)? And We removed from you your **burden** (*WiZRa-k*)” (94:1-2), and assures him, “Truly with every hardship comes **ease** (*YuSR*)” (94:5-6).
Says, “**The angels and the Spirit descend with His command**” (16:2), and commands the Prophet to say, “The Holy Spirit **brought it [the Qur’an] down from Your Lord** in truth” (16:102).	Describes the Night of Power (s. 97, *The Power*) as the night in which God “**sent it [the Qur’an] down**” (97:4) and in which “**the angels and the Spirit descend** by their Lord’s permission **with every command**” (97:1).

Group H (ss. 33-39)	Group H' (ss. 73-80)
Refers to the Qur'an as "the tremendous news" (*an-naba' al-'aẓīm*, 38:67).	Uses the same name to designate the Day of Judgment (s. 77, *The News*, v. 2).
Sura 37 is called *Those Who Line Up in Rows* (*aṢ-ṢaFFāt*), which is used as a description of the angels in the sura (*aṢ-ṢaFFāti ṢaFFan*, v. 1; *aṣ-ṢāFFūn*, v. 165).	The Day of Judgment is described as "a day in which the Spirit and the angels stand up in rows (*ṢaFFan*)" (78:83), though note that a similar but briefer reference occurs in 89:22.
Refers to the "**Day of Sorting**" (*yawm al-faṣl*), which the disbelievers "used to deny (*tuKaDHDHiBūn*)" (37:21).	Says, "...for the **Day of Sorting** (*yawm al-faṣl*). And what will convey to you what the **Day of Sorting** (*yawm al-faṣl*) is? Woe that day to the **deniers** (*al-muKaDHDHiBīn*)" (77:13-15).

Group I (ss. 40-46)	Group I' (ss. 67-72)
Narrates an account about a group of jinn testifying to the Qur'an's authenticity (46:29-34).	Narrates a similar account in s. 72, *The Jinn*, vv. 1-15.
Two of the five instances of the word *ḥamīm* with the meaning of "intimate friend" occur in this group (40:18; 41:34).	Two of the other instances of this occur in this group (69:35; 70:10).

In the very middle of the central group lie two suras, Sura 54, *The Moon* (*al-Qamar*)," and Sura 55, *The All-Merciful* (*ar-Raḥmān*). The two suras appear to form a pair, but the former deals mainly with God's judgment in the next life, emphasizes God's might, and invokes fear, while the latter highlights God's blessings in this life, emphasizes God's mercy, and invokes hope. Moreover, we will observe in the next chapter that this sura pair has two significant connections with the very first (s. 1) and last suras (ss. 113 and 114).

The reader who is further interested in the evidence Farrin uses for this analysis, the correspondences he finds between the groups on opposite sides of the ring compositions, and his study of the central group, can consult his *Structure and Qur'anic Interpretation*, 48-69. While it may, at this point, best be treated as a hypothesis, Farrin's theory raises the potential prospect of further study and possible refinement.

* * *

Through a study of select portions of the Qur'an, we have seen that the order of its suras turns out not to be arbitrary after all, but an intricate part of its design. It is striking that several independent criteria appear to come together in the arrangement of the suras: the overall pattern of decreasing length, the dovetailing between consecutive suras, the configuration of the suras into sequential pairs and groups, and possibly even the symmetry of the Qur'anic text as a whole. The interconnections that have been found between consecutive suras at least largely appear to be an intrinsic part of their designs, rather than the result of later compilation by editors. The surprising and fascinating nature of the discoveries so far about the Qur'an's overall design provides a strong incentive for further investigation. Only time and further study will reveal what other secrets lie behind the scripture's composition.

For further exploration:

Mustansir Mir, *Coherence in the Qur'an*, 75-103.
Neal Robinson, *Discovering the Qur'an*, 256-283.
Raymond Farrin, *Structure and Qur'anic Interpretation: A Study of Symmetry and Coherence in Islam's Holy Text.*

CHAPTER 15

Sura 1, *The Opening*

In chapter 8, we examined the first verse of Sura 1, *The Opening* or the Fatiha (*al-Fātiḥa*), which functions like an introduction and summary of the rest of the Qur'an. In this chapter, we will explore the remainder of the sura, to see what treasures are embedded in its language, structure, and placement in the Qur'an.

The sura can be translated as follows:

In the name of God, the All-Merciful, the Ever-Merciful:[215]

1. All praise is due to God, the Lord of all peoples,
2. The All-Merciful, the Ever-Merciful,
3. Owner of the Day of Recompense.
4. You alone we worship and You alone we ask for help.
5. Guide us along the Straight Path,
6. The Path of those whom You have favored,
7. Not of those who have earned wrath, nor of the astray.

Verse 1: "All praise is due to God, the Lord of all peoples."

Transliteration: *al-ḥamdu li-'llāhi rabbi 'l-'ālamīn*

al-ḥamd: "(all) praise" and "(all) thanks"

li-'llāh: "to/for Allah" ("Allah" is shortened for grammatical reasons)

rabb: "Lord"

215 See n. 1 of chapter 8. Because we take the position that the opening formula "In the name of God, the All-Merciful, the Ever-Merciful" is not counted as one of the verses of the Fatiha, the numbering of the verses will appear differently here than in most editions and translations of the Qur'an.

al-ʿālamīn = "all peoples"

Though we have already explored this verse in chapter 8, a brief review should be helpful. The phrase *al-ḥamdu li-'llāh,* "all praise is due to God," is an expression of both sincere praise and thanks to God by the worshiper. In fact, the attribution of "all praise" to God—and specifically by the name "Allah," as opposed to His other divine names—affirms His perfection in all respects, and without singling out any of His attributes and excluding others. Similarly, the expression is a complete acknowledgement of all of one's blessings as coming from God.

The phrase *rabbi 'l-ʿālamīn,* "the Lord of all peoples," affirms God's authority over people of every race, ethnicity, nationality, generation, religion, and social status—as well as over both humankind and jinn—and implies that all people are equally slaves of God. The word translated as "Lord" (*rabb*) also includes the meanings of "Maintainer" (*qayyim*), "Caregiver" or "Nurturer" (*murabbī*), "Manager" (*mudabbir*), and "Gift-Giver" (*munʿim*), highlighting God's creation, provision, care, and upbringing of every person. Moreover, the Master-slave relationship between God and man is completely different from the norm of human societies. The recognition of God as "Lord" is coupled with the slave's exclamation of *al-ḥamdu li-'llāh*, indicating that this is a relationship of care and compassion on God's part and sincere and willing service on the part of the slave. This is point is further underscored by the next verse.

Verse 2: "The All-Merciful, the Ever-Merciful."

Transliteration: *ar-Raḥmāni 'r-Raḥīm*

Vocabulary breakdown:

ar-Raḥmān: "the All-Merciful"

ar-Raḥīm: "the Ever-Merciful"

Verse 2 describes God with two more divine names, *ar-Raḥmān* and *ar-Raḥīm*. These names come from the Arabic word *raḥma*, which is most commonly translated as "mercy." As a result, these names might be translated as "the All-Merciful" and "the Ever-Merciful." However, it is important at this point to mention the limitations of the word "mercy" as a translation of *raḥma*.

In English, the word "mercy" tends to be used in situations that involve the possibility or expectation of harm or punishment. The *Oxford Advanced Learner's Dictionary* lists the definitions and some usages of the word "mercy" as follows:

1. a kind or forgiving attitude towards somebody that you have the power to harm or right to punish
    - to ask/beg/plead for mercy
    - They showed no mercy to their hostages.
    - God have mercy on us.
    - The troops are on a mercy mission (= a journey to help people) in the war zone.
2. an event or a situation to be grateful for, usually because it stops something unpleasant.
    - It's a mercy she wasn't seriously hurt. His death was a mercy (i.e. because he was in great pain).[216]

While the word *raḥma* includes these meanings, and "mercy" is therefore an appropriate translation in some cases, the English word does not always capture the full scope or the deep emotional meanings that the Arabic word contains. The word *raḥma* comes from *raḥim*, or "womb," and therefore evokes the sense of loving care and compassion that a mother deeply feels and expresses towards her child. This is the closest analogy to understand God's *raḥma* towards His creatures. This is emphasized in a hadith, which reports that a woman, upon finding her lost child, took the child to her chest and nursed him. The Prophet then asked his companions, "Do you think this woman would throw her child into a fire?" The companions replied, "No, by God, as long as it was in her power not to." The Prophet then said, "God is even more compassionate (*arḥam*) towards His servants than this woman is to her child."[217]

What, then, are some alternatives to the translation of "merciful" for the divine names that come from the word *raḥma*? Alternative English translations include "compassionate," "kind," and "beneficent." The word "compassion" better conveys the emotional sense of the word *raḥma*, but it again has the connotation of pity or concern particularly in the case of someone who is suffering. Moreover, while it highlights the emotional state of care or concern for others, it does not necessarily imply the active performance of acts of kindness and giving that the divine names suggest. The word "kind" is too simple and fails to convey the impact of the Arabic words. Words such as "benevolent" or "beneficent" might better capture the scope of the word *raḥma*, but they are quite unfamiliar to many modern readers, and this limits

---

216 "Mercy," *Oxford Advanced Learner's Dictionary*, www.oxfordlearnersdictionaries.com (accessed April 8, 2016); cited in Adnan Majid, "Rahmah - Not Just 'Mercy,'" *Muslim Matters*, December 3, 2012, http://muslimmatters.org/2012/12/03/rahmah-not-just-mercy/.

217 *Ṣaḥīḥ al-Bukhārī*, no. 5999; *Ṣaḥīḥ Muslim*, no. 2754.

their potential to convey the meanings of these divine qualities. In the end, we maintain that no English word offers a fully satisfying equivalent for *raḥma* and its derived adjectives. As a result, in this book we have settled for the common translations "mercy" and "merciful." Nonetheless, the reader should keep in mind that the word *raḥma* and the divine names that are derived from it indicate a sense of nurturing and loving care, compassion, and bounty—more than just the quality of being relenting or pitying.

Now that we have a fuller grasp of the meaning of the word *raḥma*, we are in a position to consider the two names of God stated in this verse that derive from it. Both *Raḥmān* and *Raḥīm* are nouns or adjectives that mean "one who is characterized by *raḥma*," and can be translated as "compassionate" or "merciful." But what qualities distinguish these two names from each other?

The first of these divine names, *ar-Raḥmān*, is among the most unique names of God in the Qur'an, because while most of the names of God are adjectives that can be used to also describe created beings—such as "merciful" (*raḥīm*), "king," (*malik*), or "wise" (*ḥakīm*)—the word *Raḥmān* is used *exclusively* for God in the Qur'an and the Arabic language, just like the name "Allah" or the title "Lord of all peoples." Prior to the revelation of the Qur'an, "*Raḥmān*" was already used by the Jews and Christians of South Arabia as a personal name or title of God.[218] It is used in the same way in numerous Qur'anic passages:

> Say: "Call upon 'Allah' or call upon 'the All-Merciful (*ar-Raḥmān*).' Whichever you call, His are the most beautiful names." (17:110)

To give an analogy from English usage, the terms "the Lord" and "the Almighty" are used specifically for God and have unmistakable divine connotations. They are also used interchangeably with the word "God," and therefore may occur in contexts that do not specifically highlight God's qualities of "lordship" or "might." In the same way, *ar-Raḥmān* is also sometimes used as a name or title referring to God even in contexts that do not seem to specifically highlight His mercy and compassion, but which nonetheless refer clearly to the divine:

> They say, "The All-Merciful (*ar-Raḥmān*) has taken a son." How terrible is this thing you assert: it almost causes the heavens to be torn apart, the earth to split asunder, the mountains to crumble to pieces, that they attribute a

---

218 An accessible study of this divine title in South Arabian Jewish and Christian is "Raḥmānān (RḤMNN)—An Ancient South Arabian Moon God?," *Islamic-Awareness*, March 28, 2009, http://www.islamic-awareness.org/Qur'an/Sources/Allah/rhmnn.html (accessed October 6, 2015).

> son to *ar-Raḥmān*. It does not befit *ar-Raḥmān* [to have offspring]: there is none in the heavens or earth who will not come to *ar-Raḥmān* as a servant. (19:88-93)

Other times, however, such as in the Fatiha, the name *ar-Raḥmān* is used in clear connection to God's mercy. In these contexts, the mercies that are highlighted are consistently those which are connected to God's unique status as the divine, majestic, and profoundly generous Creator and Caregiver of all things:

> The All-Merciful (*ar-Raḥmān*): He taught the Qur'an. He created man and taught him clear expression. The sun and the moon follow their calculated courses; the stars and the trees prostrate to Him. He has raised up the sky. He has set the balance so that you may not exceed in the balance: weigh with justice and do not fall short in the balance. He set down the Earth for His creatures, with its fruits, its palm trees with sheathed clusters, its husked grain, and its fragrant plants. (55:1-12)

> It is He who created the heavens and earth and what is between them in six Days, and then established Himself on the throne—He is the All-Merciful (*ar-Raḥmān*). (25:59)

> You do not see in the creation of the All-Merciful (*ar-Raḥmān*) any inconsistency. (67:3)

> Do they not see the birds above them, spreading and folding [their wings]? None holds them up except All-Merciful (*ar-Raḥmān*). He watches over everything. (67:19)

Because of the unique way that this divine name is used, it is even more difficult to translate into English.[219] We have opted for "the All-Merciful," to highlight its universality.

While the word *Raḥmān* is a title used only for God, *raḥīm* is more simply the Arabic word for "merciful," used both for God and for people. However, the form of the word in Arabic suggests mercy as an inherent and permanent quality of God, hence our translation, the "Ever-Merciful." In contrast to *ar-Raḥmān*, *ar-Raḥīm* occurs throughout the Qur'an in the context of special gifts that God provides to His servants. For example, it occurs most frequently paired with God's name "the Forgiving," His forgiveness being primarily for those who sincerely repent after committing wrong:

219 Abdel Haleem's rendering, "the Lord of Mercy," is good in that it captures its divine and majestic undertones.

> Say, "My slaves who have transgressed against themselves, do not despair of God's mercy. Indeed God forgives all sins; indeed it is He who is the Forgiving, the Ever- Merciful (*ar-Raḥīm*)." (39:53)

> You who have believed, be conscious of God and believe in His Messenger: He will give you a double portion of His mercy, provide for you a light by which you may walk, and forgive you. God is Forgiving, Ever-Merciful (*Raḥīm*). (57:28)

Similarly, *ar-Raḥīm* occurs in contexts that highlight God's special love, support, deliverance, and reward for His servants who do good:

> We saved Moses and those with him altogether, and then We drowned the others. Truly in that is a lesson, but most of them were not believers. Truly it is your Lord who is the Mighty, the Ever-Merciful (*ar-Raḥīm*). (26:65-68)

> The Companions of the Garden today are happily occupied, they and their spouses, seated on couches in the shade. There they have fruit and whatever they ask for. "Peace"—a word from an Ever-Merciful (*Raḥīm*) Lord. (36:55-58)

> A Day when no friend can take another's place. No one will receive any help except for those to whom God shows mercy: He is the Mighty, the Ever-Merciful (*ar-Raḥīm*). (44:41-42)

In short, while both divine names mean "the Compassionate" or "the Merciful," the name *ar-Raḥmān* highlights the bounties that God gives His creatures as the divine and universal Creator and Caregiver, while *ar-Raḥīm* is associated with special graces that God gives to His sincere servants.

Verse 3: "Owner of the Day of Recompense"

Transliteration: *Māliki Yawmi 'd-Dīn*

Vocabulary breakdown:

Mālik: "Owner"

Yawm: "the Day"

ad-Dīn: "Judgment"; "counting, calculation, reckoning"; "compensation, recompense, requital"

The previous verse described God as merciful and highlighted various aspects of that mercy. Even so, if God *only* ever acted with mercy, there would be no moral accountability. The third verse of the Fatiha addresses this problem by drawing attention to God's justice. It does so not by merely describing God's attributes of justice (*al-ʿadl*) or judgment (*al-ḥukm*) in abstract terms, but by drawing attention to how they are implemented, with reference to a definite time in which God's justice will be dealt out. It is significant that while the previous verse singled out God's compassion and mercy, this verse does not single out or even explicitly mention God's vengeance or punishment, but rather underscores God's justice, which includes both reward and punishment. While God's mercy stands on its own and He may distribute it freely, any punishment that He executes is only a function of His more fundamental attribute of justice, and He does not punish outside of the bounds of that justice. A person can be subject either to God's mercy or to His justice; there is no third possibility.

Punishment for bad deeds is only one aspect of justice; reward for good deeds and compensation for harms unduly suffered are no less a part of it. The word *dīn* here captures all of these aspects. One meaning of this word is "judgment"; another is "reckoning," "counting," or "calculation"; while another still is "compensation," "recompense," or "requital." Mercy towards the innocent and towards good doers is also a crucial part of the Day of Judgment. Despite the alarming descriptions of Judgment Day in the Qur'an and the hadiths, one famous hadith indicates that God's mercy will ultimately be in excess to His justice:

> When God completed His creation, He inscribed in His book, which is with Him above the Throne, "Indeed My mercy prevails over My wrath."[220]

Another hadith similarly highlights the relationship between God's mercy and Judgment Day:

> On the day God created the heavens and the earth, He created one hundred portions of mercy. From it, He placed on the earth one portion, by virtue of which the mother shows compassion to her child, and the beasts and the birds show compassion to each other. And God has kept back ninety-nine portions of mercy. When the Day of Resurrection comes, He will complete the distribution of this mercy.[221]

This hadith explains that all of the mercy and goodness that exist in the present world combined amount to only a grain of the mercy that God actually has in store. This world is the realm of tests and trials, through which people will be admitted into various levels of God's mercy in the next

220 *Ṣaḥīḥ al-Bukhārī*, no. 3194; *Ṣaḥīḥ Muslim*, no. 2751.
221 *Ṣaḥīḥ al-Bukhārī*, no. 6000; *Ṣaḥīḥ Muslim*, no. 2752, 2753.

life. It is on the Day of Recompense that the innocent, the sincere, the righteous, and the innocently suffering will encounter the full extent of God's mercy and compassion, which will far exceed the best of what has been experienced in this world.

God's judgment is presented in deliberately unusual and thought-provoking terms in this verse. The "ownership" of a period of time is a strange notion for humans to grasp. Human beings cannot even own a second, since we do not have full control over the flow of time and, even more importantly, over everything that happens within it. God's "ownership" over the Day of Judgment signifies His full authority on that Day over every matter and decision that occurs.

A second, less common but equally accepted reading of this verse describes God as the "King" or "Sovereign" (*Malik*) of the Day of Judgment—in place of the more common reading of "Owner" (*Mālik*). What added significance does this reading provide? Kingship or sovereignty refers to authority on a massive scale: someone may be the king of a country or an empire. But this authority does not necessarily apply on a smaller scale: the king does not *own* every grain of food, article of clothing, or item of furniture in his kingdom. (We would not describe someone as the "king" of a pencil or a chair!) Conversely, ownership involves more complete authority but occurs on a smaller scale. A person may be described as the owner of a car or a house, but not of a country or kingdom. Both readings (*Mālik* or *Malik*) complement each other and fill in what the other is missing. The description of God as the "Owner" (*Mālik*) of the Day of Reckoning credits Him with full authority over even the smallest of calculations and judgments, while His description as the "King" (*Malik*) of that Day points to His authority on the grandest scale.

Verse 4: "You alone we worship, and You alone we ask for help"

Transliteration: *Iyyā-ka na'budu wa-iyyā-ka nasta'īn*

Vocabulary breakdown:
iyyā-ka: "You"
na'budu: "We worship; serve, enslave ourselves to"
wa-: "and"
nasta'īn: "We implore, ask for help"

Each of the previous verses expressed key truths about God—that He is perfectly deserving of praise and gratitude; that He is the Master and Caregiver of all people; that He is extremely compassionate and merciful; and that He will also reward or punish each person depending on his actions.

These facts are expected to move the reciter or listener to worship God. Hence, there is a sudden grammatical shift from talking *about* God in the previous verses to talking directly *to* Him in this verse, in order to express that urge to worship Him. In fact, the verb *na'BuDu* (translated as "we worship"), from *'iBāDa* ("worship"), entails more than just religious adoration. It also comes from the word *'uBūDiyya*, meaning "slavery."

We have already seen how the concept of slavery to God signals a radical departure from the human concept of slavery. Now, it is important to consider how the concept of slavery is tied with worship. A worshiper (*'āBiD*) may pray to God at certain times of the day or perform rites on certain holidays, but outside of those times conduct himself however he wants. On the other hand, a slave (*'aBD*, in Arabic) cannot simply be a slave during certain times of the day or year; he is a slave at all times. Similarly, the expression *iyyā-ka na'budu*—meaning both "you alone we worship" *and* "you alone we enslave ourselves to"—indicates a willingness not only to worship God, but to try to live one's life at *all* times in service to Him and within the bounds of what He has permitted. The verb *na'budu* includes acts of religious worship, as well as the timeless condition of slavery.

The verb *nasta'īN*, "we ask for help," comes from the word *'awN*, which denotes help for someone who is struggling. The form *nasta'īn* means to seek or ask for *'awn*. It is an admission that one is already struggling to serve God, but cannot do it by himself and needs God's help. This indicates that a person does not have the right to ask for help until he has already taken up the effort himself to do it—a formula that occurs throughout the Qur'an: first one expresses the willingness to serve God, and then he may rightfully ask for help.

The grammar of these two clauses is also significant. In chapter 5, "Other Subtleties of Style and Grammar," and chapter 8, "'All praise is due to God, the Lord of all peoples,'" we explained that Classical Arabic has a standard sentence order, and that when this order is changed, it produces a rhetorical effect, such as singling out the object. This is the case with *iyyā-ka na'budu* and *iyyā-ka nasta'īn*. The normal sentence order would be to mention the subject and verb first (*na'budu*, "we worship," and *nasta'īn*, "we ask for help") and the object (*-ka*, "you") second. Instead, in both phrases, the object, referring to God, is placed first—*iyyā-ka*. (The word *iyya* merely serves as a chair for the attached pronoun, in this case *-ka*, when there is nothing else for it to attach to.) This has two rhetorical effects. One is that it gives the object, God, more importance in the sentence. The other is that it makes God the exclusive object: "It is You *alone* that we worship and enslave ourselves to." The same applies in the case of *wa-iyyā-ka nasta'īn*: "and it is You *alone* that we ask for help." In making this statement, the reciter declares himself free from slavery to and dependence on all things other than God.

Also notice that the subject is plural: "You alone *we* worship" rather than "You alone *I* worship." This underscores that the worshiper is not alone, but is part of a greater community of worshipers. As we will see in the next verse, the use of the first-person plural remains even as the Fatiha transitions into a prayer for guidance, making the prayer a collective one.

A lot could be said about the order of these two clauses, but two observations should suffice here. First, it is logical that the primary task (worship and slavery) is mentioned before the secondary one (asking for help). Put another way, the goal (properly serving God) is stated before the means (asking His help). Second, the worshiper becomes conscious that his duty before God is more worthy of being given first mention, while his plea for his own benefit should only be mentioned afterwards. What is God's due is mentioned first, while what is for the worshiper is mentioned second.

Verse 5: "Guide us along the Straight Path"

Transliteration: *Ihdinā 'ṣ-Ṣirāṭa 'l-Mustaqīm*

Vocabulary breakdown:
Ihdi: "Guide"
-nā: "us"
aṣ-Ṣirāṭ: "the Path, the Way"
al-Mustaqīm: "Straight"

In verse 5, the worshiper asks for guidance for himself and on behalf of other worshipers. This guidance is specified with the term *aṣ-Ṣirāṭa 'l-Mustaqīm*, "the Straight Path."

The word *ṣirāṭ* means "road," "path," or "way." It resembles the word "street" in English, because both words have a common origin in the Latin *strāta*, meaning "paved way." By making the word *ṣirāṭ* definite, "*the* Straight Path," this verse indicates that there is only one path of guidance, as opposed to the many and countless paths of misguidance. In fact, the word *ṣirāṭ* is used in the Qur'an chiefly to refer to "the Straight Path" and is never used in the plural. (According to many authorities on Classical Arabic, *ṣirāṭ* does not even have a plural, and therefore signifies the *only* path to a given destination.) This is in contrast to its frequently used near-synonym *sabīl*, which also means "path" or "way," but which does occur in the plural. In one famous hadith, the Prophet's student Ibn Mas'ūd reported,

> The Prophet (may God's peace and blessings be upon him) drew a line for us and said, "This is God's Straight Path." Then he drew lines to its right and left and then said, "These are other paths [*subul*, plural of *sabīl*]. Upon every

> one of them there is a devil calling towards it." Then he recited, "This is My Path (*ṣirāṭ*), which is Straight, so follow it. Do not follow other ways (*subul*): they will lead you away from it" (6:153).[222]

This analogy depicts the "Straight Path" as the one path that God has chosen and which leads to Him. The Straight Path is surrounded on both sides by alternative paths, as if it is positioned centrally between two extremes.[223] As we will see, the last verse of the Fatiha classifies all of these alternative paths into two groups, which might be thought of as representing two opposite extremes.

Although the "Straight Path" that leads to God is one, this does not mean that it is narrow or excludes diversity. The Qur'an indicates that the Path is timeless, wide, and includes many sub-paths, which might be compared to the different lanes of a wide highway. These sub-paths include religious laws that God has given to previous religious communities (5:48). It also suggests the many different ways individuals may choose to serve God in their own lives, within the wide boundaries of this Straight Path:

> There has come to you from God a light and a clear scripture, whereby God guides whoever seeks His pleasure to paths (*subul*) of peace, and brings them from darknesses[224] to light by His permission, and guides them to a Straight Path. (5:15-16)

One individual might excel in acts of ritual worship or charitable spending, another might strive to serve God by becoming a doctor and helping the sick, another by becoming a teacher or educator, and still another by raising children who will contribute positively to society.

The adjective *mustaqīm*, translated as "Straight," has two basic meanings. First, it means "straight" in the physical sense. This entails that this Path leads in one direction, towards God, and is clearly distinguished from the other paths, which deviate and lead their travelers astray. The second meaning of *mustaqīm* is "right," "correct," "sound," or "proper," thus distinguishing this Path as the one right course.

---

222 *Musnad Aḥmad*, no. 4142; *Ṣaḥīḥ Ibn Ḥibbān*, no. 6; authenticated by al-Albānī and Aḥmad Shākir.

223 The early commentator Mujāhid (d. 722) astutely commented that the Straight Path is positioned between two extremes, which he characterized as "extremism and negligence." Recall that in 2:143, God refers to the newly established Muslim society in Medina as "a middle nation."

224 The Qur'an uses light and darkness as symbols of guidance and misguidance respectively. In every instance, light is used in the singular (*nūr*, occurring 33 times) but darkness is used in the Arabic plural (*ẓulumāt*, occurring 23 times), once again highlighting the unity and singularity of guidance against the diverse and extensive paths of misguidance.

In normal cases, the verb *ihdi-nā* ("guide us") would be followed by a preposition, such as "Guide us *to* the Straight Path" or "Guide us *on* the Straight Path." Here, any such preposition is left out. This omission has the rhetorical effect of suggesting that no preposition can actually capture the extent of what the asker is requesting. He is requesting guidance *to* (*ilā*) the Straight Path, guidance *on (fī)* the Straight Path, guidance *by means of* (*bi-*) the Straight Path, and guidance all the way to the very end of the Straight Path. In translation, we have chosen the preposition "along" to convey a fuller sense of what the verse implies.

The imagery of guidance and misguidance in the Qur'an deserves notice, as it employs the rich imagery of a desert journey. Commenting on the word *ṣirāṭ*, Walid Saleh writes,

> The Qur'an weaves a matrix of words around the concept of journeying, guidance, path, and destination. It speaks of finding one's way, of getting lost, of roaming the earth, of straight paths and crooked paths (Q 7:86); it speaks of lurking near highways to ambush, it speaks of stampeding on a highway; it speaks of darkness lit by lightning through which one attempts to walk, only to halt again as the skies darken, thus recreating day and night in an instant, guidance and bewilderment in the flash of a moment, while the believers have their light guiding them on the way. It depicts believers wondering as to where one should face when in need of guidance, only to be answered that direction is meaningless, for God's face is everywhere. Lost in the desert, a human being rushes to a mirage only to find God waiting there.
>
> Indeed the vocabulary is so rich and so varied, the imagery so complex and adroit that one has to take this imagery as fundamental in the message of the Qur'an as to how it understands guidance, and hence salvation.[225]

Verse 6: "The Path of those whom You have favored"

Transliteration: *Ṣirāṭa 'lladīna an'amta 'alayhim*

Vocabulary breakdown:

Ṣirāṭ: "path, way, road" (see above)

alladīna: "those, those people"

---

225 Walid A. Saleh, "The Etymological Fallacy and Qur'anic Studies: Muhammad, Paradise, and Late Antiquity," *The Qur'ān in Context: Historical and Literary Investigations into the Qur'ānic Milieu*, ed. Angelika Neuwirth, Nicolai Sinai, and Michael Marx (Leiden: Brill, 2011), 666.

an'amta = "you favored, you blessed"
'alayhim = "upon them"

In verse 6, the path of guidance is further defined, this time with reference to those who who have already travelled it. These people are described as those whom God has favored. Three points should be noted here. First, the word for "favor" (*ni'ma*), stems from the same root as *nu'ūma*, meaning "softness," "tenderness," or "smoothness." This suggests that although traveling this path requires struggle and patience, it is still the path in which one will find the greatest source of peace and spiritual comfort, and that God will eventually make it smooth and easy for those who choose to travel it (cf. 87:8; 92:7). Second, this favor is credited to God, indicating that a human being cannot reach the end of the path except with God's help. Finally, the expression "those whom you have favored" is in the past tense, indicating that the worshiper should look back at history for examples of role models who took this path. Many of these examples are recorded in the Qur'an itself, in the stories of past prophets and believers.

Verse 7: "Not of those who have earned anger, nor of the lost"

Transliteration: *Ghayri 'l-maghḍūbi 'alay-him wa lā 'ḍ- ḍāllīn*

Vocabulary breakdown:
ghayr: "not; unlike"
al-maghḍūbi 'alay-him: "those who anger/wrath is upon"
wa: "and"
lā: "not"
aḍ-ḍāllīn: "the lost, the astray"

The previous verse described the Straight Path in positive terms, with reference to those who adhere to it. In the final verse, verse 7, it is described in negative terms, contrasting it from the paths of two other kinds of people.

The first of these groups are *al-maghḍūbi 'alay-him*—literally "those whom anger is upon." It is often translated as "those who have earned *Your* anger," but the subject of "anger" is left unspecified in the Arabic, unlike in the previous verse, "the Path of those who *You* have favored." There are two likely reasons for this. First, it is as if God, who revealed this prayer, is distancing Himself from this group of people, to the point that He does not even want to be mentioned in connection to them. Second, the subject is left open so that it may include not only God, but also angels and other human beings (cf. 2:159). The second category of people mentioned in this verse is *aḍ-ḍāllīn*, meaning "those who are lost" or "those who are astray."

The grammar of the verse indicates that these are two different groups. Who are they, and what distinguishes them from each other? A hadith of the Prophet gives the example of "those who have earned anger" as the Jews, and the example of "the astray" as the Christians.[226] This hadith must be understood in the context of Qur'anic teachings. The Qur'an recognizes the existence of upright Jews and Christians (2:62; 3:110, 113-114, 199; 5:69, 82; 7:159), and therefore does not include all of them in its criticisms, but rather points to tendencies that have appeared within these religious communities in order to discourage against them and warn the new Muslim community from falling into the same errors. The Qur'an suggests that the Israelite community in particular had knowledge of divine revelation (e.g., 2:42, 75, 144, 146), but acted in direct violation of that knowledge, provoking God's anger.[227] The category of "those who have earned anger" therefore suggests the quality of defiance in action. On the other hand, the term "the astray" (*aḍ-ḍāllīn*) has the connotation of becoming lost in error or being unable to find one's way, suggesting the quality of confusion in belief.[228] In connection with this, Qur'an identifies the source of error within the Christian community as a lack of grounding in true knowledge (e.g., 4:157; 10:68; 18:5, 15), that is, knowledge rooted in authentic revelation. In putting forth these criticisms, the Qur'an's major concern is to call all three communities—Jewish, Christian, and Muslim—to guidance. The commentator Ibn Kathīr (d. 1373) summarized the Qur'an's criticisms by saying, "The Jews did not have [proper] action, and the Christians did not have knowledge, and because of that the Jews had acquired anger (*al-ghaḍab li-'l-yahūd*), and the Christians went astray (*aḍ-ḍalāl li-'n-naṣāra*)." Once again, these descriptions do not apply to all Jews or Christians, nor do they exhaust these two categories, but the Qur'an points to trends within these communities as cautionary examples of how people can fall away from the Straight Path, even after receiving the gift of revelation.

What is significant here is that the verse divides all people who fail to be guided into two categories. The first earn God's anger because of

---

226 Authenticated by al-Albānī, *as-Silsila aṣ-Ṣaḥīḥa*, no. 3263.

227 2:61, 90; 7:152; 20:81, 86; 42:16. See also 7:150 and 154, where Moses becomes angry with his people. Also, in a different context, 4:93 associates God's anger with committing a grave offense "with intent" (*mutta'amid*). 42:14-16 and 58:14 associates God's anger with those who commit an offense knowingly. Similar implications are found in other verses that mention God's wrath (*ghaḍab*).

228 The Qur'an therefore also uses this term to describe the idolaters and the Muslims before they were guided (e.g., 2:198; 6:77; 23:106; 26:86; 37:69; 56:51, 92).

wrongful actions, and the second go astray due to *lack of knowledge*. From this we can infer that *guidance consists of sound knowledge (or sound belief) and sound action*. This is captured in the oft-repeated Qur'anic formula, "those who have faith and do righteous deeds." The Fatiha is itself a remedy for both of these problems. It provides key knowledge about God, drawing attention to the human necessity to worship and pray to Him alone, while at same time serving as an example of those very actions of worship and prayer.

The Structure and Balance of the Fatiha

We have explored the Fatiha verse by verse, but have yet to look at its overall composition. The Fatiha is a ring composition with the following structure:

All praise is due to God

A. The Lord of all peoples,
  B. The All-Merciful,
  B'. The Ever-Merciful,
A'. The Owner of the Day of Recompense.

C. You alone we worship
C'. and You alone we ask for help.

D. Guide us along the Straight Path,
  E. the path of those whom You have favored,
  E'. not of those who have earned wrath,
D'. nor of the astray.

The brackets indicate the two halves of the sura. Notice that the first half, culminating in the statement "*You alone we worship*," in fact consists entirely of words of *worship of God*. Likewise second half, beginning with "*You alone we ask for help*," consists entirely of a *prayer for God's help*—specifically guidance. Together, these two statements—"*You alone we worship* and *You alone we ask for help*—form the middle verse and the center of the composition.[229] The central theme of the Fatiha is the realization of the relationship between the worshiper and God, the slave and the divine Master. In fact, this is the central theme of the whole Qur'an, of which Fatiha is the summary. Highlighting this central point, there is a saying among the earliest generations of Muslims that the contents of all the revealed scriptures were sum-

229 This placement is also highlighted by the grammatical shift to the second person, where God begins to be addressed directly as "You."

marized in the Qur'an, the contents of the Qur'an were summarized in the "Mother of the Scripture" (the Fatiha), and the Fatiha was summarized in the verse "You alone we worship and you alone we ask for help."[230]

The structure of the Fatiha, as just described, is referred to in a famous hadith of the Prophet, which says:

> God, may He be exalted, said: "I have divided the prayer [i.e., the Fatiha] into two halves between Myself and My slave; *half of it is for Me and half is for My slave*, and for My slave is what he asks for."

The hadith continues that when the worshiper recites each of the first three verses of the Fatiha, God responds in turn, "My slave has praised Me," "My slave has extolled Me," and "My slave has glorified Me," personally acknowledging the worshiper's words of devotion. When the worshiper recites the central verse, "You alone we worship and You alone we ask for help," God replies, "This is *between Me and My slave*, and for My slave is what he asked." Finally, when the worshiper completes the last three verses, the prayer for guidance, God responds, "*This is for My slave*, and for My slave is what he asked."[231]

Now, let us look within each half of the Fatiha. Each contains a mirror composition on the pattern ABB'A'. Consider the first half:

All praise is due to God	*al-ḥamdu li-'llāhi*
A. The Lord of all peoples	*rabbi 'l-'ālamīn*
B. The All-Merciful,	*ar-raḥmān*
B'. The Ever-Merciful,	*ar-raḥīm*
A'. The Owner/King of the Day of Recompense.	*māliki/maliki yawmi 'd-dīn*
C. You alone we worship	*iyyā-ka na'budu*

Observe how the segments within the mirror composition are placed in relationship to each other:

- A and A': "The Lord of all peoples" (A) is matched by "The Owner/King of the Day of Recompense" (A'). The words "Lord" (*rabb*) and "Owner" (*mālik*) or "King" (*malik*) are synonyms, *mālik* and *malik* each being one of the meanings of the word *rabb*.[232] The two segments are also grammatically

230 Taqī al-Din Aḥmad Ibn Taymiyya, *Majmū al-Fatāwa*, ed. 'Abd al-Raḥmān b. Muḥammad b. Qāsim and Muḥammad b. Abd al-Raḥmān b. Muḥammad b. Qāsim (Cairo: Dār ar-Raḥma), 2:456, 14:7. In 14:7, Ibn Taymiyya attributes this to the famous early scholar and ascetic al-Ḥasan al-Baṣrī.

231 *Ṣaḥīḥ Muslim*, no. 395.

232 See Ibn Manẓūr, 1:399.

parallel, both being genitive constructs (*iḍāfas*), nominal phrases on the pattern "the *x* of *y*."

- B and B': "The All-Merciful" (B) and "The Ever-Merciful" (B') are obviously related because they are both names of God describing His mercy (*raḥma*).
- A and B: "The Lord of all peoples" (A) and "The All-Merciful" (B) are positioned next to each other. This is fitting, as they both concern God's status as the Lord, Caretaker, and Provider of all people. Yet, in another way, they also counterbalance each other. "The Lord of all peoples" underscores God's total authority over His creatures, while "the All-Merciful" emphasizes that His conduct towards them is characterized by compassion and love.
- A' and B': "The Ever-Merciful" (B') and "The Owner of the Day of Recompense" (A') are positioned next to each other. Unlike the name "the All-Merciful," we have seen that the name "the Ever-Merciful" is used with reference to mercies that God particularly gives to His sincere servants, such as reward, support, forgiveness, and salvation. These all relate directly to "recompense" (*dīn*). Moreover, these are mercies that become fully and permanently realized not in the present world, but on the Day of Recompense itself. Hence there is a saying among some commentators, although not entirely precise, that God is "*ar-Raḥmān* in this world and the afterlife and He is *ar-Raḥīm* in the afterlife."

  Just as with AB, there is also an element of mutual balance. The divine title "Owner of the Day of Recompense" also implies complete authority and, in this case, justice. But this is again counterbalanced by its connection to "the Ever-Merciful," which stresses God's compassionate and forgiving nature as well. Once again we find that the divine names stated in A' and B' are closely connected and balanced, and are therefore appropriately placed next to each other.
- C: The worshipers' acknowledgement of God and reflection on His divine attributes in ABB'A' culminates in their confession of worship: "You alone we worship." Put a slightly different way, the *knowledge* of God given in ABB'A' is supposed to lead to the *action* of devoting one's worship to God alone.

Now consider the second half of the Fatiha:

C'. and You alone we ask for help.	*wa iyyā-ka nasta'īn*
D. Guide us along the Straight Path,	*ihdi-nā 'ṣ-ṣirāṭa 'l-mustaqīm*
E. the path of those whom You have favored,	*ṣirāṭa 'lladhina an'amta 'alay-him*
E'. not of those who have earned wrath,	*ghayri 'l-maghḍūbi 'alay-him*
D'. nor of the astray.	*wa-lā 'ḍ-ḍāllīn*

- C': "You alone we ask for help" begins the second half of the Fatiha, which as we have noted actually functions as a prayer for help, and particularly for guidance.
- D and E, and E' and D': The relationships that stand between these segments are most apparent, so they will be briefly stated first. D and E describe those who are on the path of guidance, while E' and D' describe the two types of people who are away from the path.
- D and D': "Guide us (*iHDi-nā*) along the Straight Path" (D) is matched by "nor of the astray (*aḌ-ḌāLLīn*)" (D') because guidance (*HiDāya*) and being astray (*ḌaLāL*) are direct opposites.
- E and E': "The path of those whom You have favored (*aN'aMta 'alay-him*)" (E) and "not of those who have earned wrath (*al-maGHḌūBi 'alay-him*)" (E') are also parallel opposites, having parallel grammatical structures in Arabic (a passive participle + *'alay-him*). Yet, in this case, they are not *direct* opposites. The direct opposite of "favor" (*Ni'Ma*) in Arabic is not *GHaḌaB* ("anger"), but *niqma* ("retribution, punishment"), while the direct opposite of *ghaḍab* is *riḍā* ("satisfaction, pleasure"). The contrast of *almost*-opposites is a literary device used in the Qur'an to create a four-way comparison. In this case, it implies that those who have God's favor (*ni'ma*) also have His pleasure and satisfaction (*riḍā*), while those who have earned His wrath (*ghaḍab*) have also earned His punishment (*niqma*).

As a ring composition, the end of the Fatiha also returns to the beginning. The first verse described God as the "Lord of *all peoples*." The last three verses in turn classify *all people* into three categories: those whom God has favored (*alladhina an'amta 'alay-him*), those who have earned wrath (*al-maghḍūbi 'alay-him*), and those who are lost and astray (*aḍ-ḍāllīn*).

The Placement of the Fatiha

Connection to Sura 2

We have seen that the second half of the Fatiha is a prayer by the worshiper requesting guidance: "Guide us (*iHDi-nā*) along the Straight Path…" (1:5). This dovetails with the next sura, *The Cow*, which opens, "This is the Scripture concerning which there is no doubt, a guidance (*HuDan*) for the God-conscious" (2:2). The rest of the Qur'an is thus presented as the answer to the prayer for guidance.

We have also seen that the Fatiha concludes by classifying people into three groups with respect to guidance:

1. Those whom God has guided—"Guide us (*iHDi-nā*) along the Straight Path";

2. "Those who have earned anger" (*al-maGHḌūBi 'alay-him*);
3. "The astray" (*aḍ-ḌāLLīn*).

Similarly, *The Cow* opens by mentioning three groups of people with respect to guidance:

1. "The God-conscious";
2. "Those who disbelieve" (*alladhīna KaFaRū*);
3. The pseudo-believers.

The three groups mentioned at the end of the Fatiha correlate with the three groups mentioned in the beginning of *The Cow*:

1. The first group mentioned in *The Cow*, "the God-conscious," are described as being "on guidance (*HuDan*) from their Lord" (2:5), thus identifying them with the first group in the Fatiha, those who are guided along the Straight Path.
2. Concerning the second group in *The Cow*, "those who disbelieve (*alladhīna KaFaRū*)," a later verse in the sura says,
   How evil is that for which they sold themselves, that they would disbelieve (*yaKFuRūna*) in what God has sent down…They have earned anger upon anger (*bi-GhaḌaBin 'alā GhaḌaB*), and the disbelievers (*al-KaFiRīna*) will have a humiliating punishment. (2:90)
   Hence they are tied to the second group in the Fatiha, "those who have earned anger" (*al-maGHḌūBi 'alay-him*).
3. Finally, the third group in *The Cow*, the pseudo-believers, are described as having "purchased error (*aḍ-ḌaLāLa*) in exchange for guidance" (2:16), and are therefore included in the third group in the Fatiha, "the astray" or "those lost in error" (*aḍ-ḌāLLīn*).

We have also seen that in the Fatiha, guidance consists of two ingredients: sound belief or knowledge and sound action (guidance = right belief + right action). The same formula is reflected in the ring structure of 2:2-5:

Verses 2-5: The believers

A. (guidance) "This is the scripture concerning which there is no doubt—a **guidance** for the God-conscious (***al-muttaqīn***):
   B. (faith) **those who believe in** the unseen
      C. (action) and establish the prayer
      C'. (action) and spend out of what We have provided them,
   B'. (faith) **those who believe in** what was sent down to you and what was sent down before you, and in the afterlife they are certain.

A'. (guidance) It is they who are on **guidance** from their Lord and they who are the successful (***al-mufliḥūn***)."

Additionally, every term that occurs in the first-second-person address in the Fatiha has one or more anchors in *The Cow*:[233]

The Fatiha (Sura 1)	*The Cow* (Sura 2)
"You alone we worship (*na'BuDu*)" (1:4a)	Mankind is called to "worship (*u'BuDū*)" their Creator (2:21); God takes a covenant from the Israelites, "do not worship (*ta'BuDūna*) except God" (2:83); Jacob's sons promise, "We will worship (*na'BuDu*) your God, the God of your fathers…" (2:133); the Muslims are commanded to announce that they are "worshipers" of God (2:138); they are told, "be grateful to God if it is He that you worship (*ta'BuDūn*)" (2:172).
"You alone we ask for help (*nasta'īN*)" (1:4b)	The Israelites and later the Muslims are told, "seek help (*ista'īNu*) in patience and prayer" (2:45, 153).
"Guide us (*iHDi-nā*) along the Straight Path (*aṣ-Ṣirāṭa 'l-Mustaqīm*)" (1:5)	This prayer is answered, "This is the scripture concerning which there is no doubt—a guidance (*HuDan*) for the God-conscious" (2:2); and later, "He guides (*yaHDī*) whom He wills to a Straight Path (*Ṣirāṭin Mustaqīmin*)" (2:142, 213); and the anchor *HuDan* recurs throughout the sura.
"of those whom You have favored (*aN'aMta 'alay-him*)" (1:6)	God thrice reminds the Israelites of "My favor (*Ni'Matī*) that I favored you with (*aN'aMtu 'alay-kum*)" (2:40, 47, 122), but later tells the Muslims to turn their faces in a new direction of prayer and fear only Him, so that "I may complete My favor upon you (*ni'MaTī 'alay-kum*) and you may be guided (*taHtaDūn*)" (v. 150).
"those who have earned anger (*al-maGHḌūBi 'alay-him*)" (1:7a)	The Israelites provoked God's anger (*GHaḌaB*) for their rebellion and disbelief (2:61, 90).
"the astray (*aḌ-ḌāLLīn*)" (1:7b)	The pseudo-believers and those who conceal God's revelations have "purchased error (*aḌ-ḌaLāLa*) at the price of guidance (*al-HuDā*)" (2:16, 175); pilgrims participating in the Hajj are told to remember God, "as He guided you (*HaDā-kum*), and you were indeed before that astray (*aḌ-ḌāLLīn*)."

Finally, not only is *The Cow* immediately *preceded* by a prayer by the believers in the first-person plural ("we") to God in the second person ("you") (1:4-7), it also *concludes* with such a prayer:

233 These observations come from Neal Robinson, "The Dynamics of the Qur'anic Discourse: Tradition and Redaction" in Bert Broeckaert, Stef Van Den Branden, and Jean-Jacques Pérennès (eds.), *Perspectives on Islamic Culture: Essays in Honour of Emilio Platti* (Leuven: Peeters, 2013), 3-18.

> We hear and obey. Grant us Your forgiveness, our Lord. To You we all return!...Our Lord, do not take us to task if we forget or make mistakes. Lord, do not burden us as You burdened those before us. Lord, do not burden us with more than we have strength to bear. Pardon us, forgive us, and have mercy on us. You are our Protector, so help us against the disbelieving people. (2:285-286)

The believers' prayer to God not to "burden us as You burdened those before us" is an allusion to the Israelites, who were the previous religious community to be given a divine law, but failed to live up to its mandates. This parallels the believers' prayer in the Fatiha that God not let them be among "those who have earned anger, nor of the astray."[234]

The relationship between the Fatiha and the concluding prayer of *The Cow* is mentioned in a hadith. It states that once, while the Archangel Gabriel was accompanying the Prophet, a gate opened in heaven that had never been opened before, and an angel descended from it. The angel delivered the following message to the Prophet: "Rejoice in the good news of two lights given to you, the like of which has not been given to any prophet before you: the Opening (Fatiha) of the Scripture, and the concluding verses of *The Cow*. You will never recite a word from them without being given the blessings they contain."[235]

Connection to Sura 114

As the first sura, the Fatiha is not preceded numerically by any other sura. However, if one were to read the Qur'an in its received order, he would end with Sura 114, *Mankind* (*an-Nās*), and then return to the start of the Qur'an with the Fatiha. Sura 114 actually dovetails with the Fatiha, as if the Fatiha were the next sura. The Qur'an could be seen both as a linear text with a beginning and end (Suras 1 and 114), or as a circle, with Sura 114 connecting back to Sura 1, directing the reader or reciter to venture through the scripture again and again, each time finding new treasures within it. Put another way, the entire Qur'an might be seen as a ring with the first sura and the last sura closely connected.

Mankind reads as follows:

> Say: I take refuge in the Lord of mankind,
> The King of mankind,
> The God of mankind,

---

234 Ibid.

235 *Ṣaḥīḥ Muslim*, no. 806.

From the evil of the slinking whisperer,
Who whispers into the hearts of mankind,
From the jinn and mankind.

Mankind has the following traits in common with the Fatiha:

- It is a prayer to God.
- It consists of two contrasting halves, the first listing attributes of God, and the second listing attributes of certain kinds of people.
- The three divine attributes mentioned in the first half correspond to divine attributes referred to in the first half of the Fatiha. The sura begins with the divine title, "The Lord of Mankind" (*Rabbi 'n-Nās*, 114:1), just as the Fatiha begins with the divine title, "The Lord of all peoples" (*Rabbi 'l-'Ālamīn*). The next divine title mentioned is "King of Mankind" (*Maliki 'n-Nās*, 114:2). This corresponds to "The Owner/King (*Mālik/Malik*) of the Day of Recompense" in the Fatiha (1:3). The third divine title, "The God of Mankind" (*Ilāhi 'n-Nās*, 114:3), corresponds to "You alone we worship" (1:4),[236] both statements concluding the first half of their respective suras.
- The last verse mentions two kinds of people in negative terms—whisperers "from jinn and from mankind" (114:6)—just as in the last verse of the Fatiha: "not of those who have earned anger nor of the astray" (1:7).

In other respects, the suras form complementary opposites. For example:

- The Fatiha is a collective prayer, while *Mankind* is an individual prayer.
- The tone of the Fatiha is positive—a prayer for guidance; the tone of *Mankind* is negative—a prayer of refuge from harm. The first verse of the Fatiha establishes the sura's positive tone with praise and thanks (*ḥamd*) to God: "All praise is due to God." Moreover, this positive declaration is objective and permanent. On the other hand, the first verse of *Mankind* establishes its negative tone with the statement, "I take refuge in the Lord of mankind." However, this statement is a verbal sentence in the Arabic, and this negative tone is limited by considerations of time: soon, the servant of God will be safe from the devilish influences he is seeking refuge from.
- The Fatiha mentions God's names "the All-Merciful" and "the Ever-Merciful," which have purely positive associations. The absence of these two names from *Mankind* contributes to its negative tone.

---

236 A basic definition of "god" (*ilāh*), given in classical lexicons, is "that which is worshiped" (*ma'būd*).

- The Fatiha highlights a positive category of people, "those whom You have favored," whom it contrasts with two negative categories of people. *Mankind* only mentions two negative categories of people, the whisperers from the jinn and mankind, again in tune with its negative tone.
- In the Fatiha, the petitioners ask God to exclude them from "those who have earned anger" and "the astray," which are both collectives. In *Mankind*, the single petitioner asks God for refuge from the jinn whisperer and the human whisperer, which are both represented as individual forces.

When the reader returns from *Mankind* to the Fatiha, he finds an answer to his prayer of refuge: he should find refuge from the individual whisperers in a wider community of worshipers who are also, like him, in constant pursuit of guidance.

To cap this all off, the very last verse of the Qur'an, "From the jinn and mankind" (114:6), returns to the very first, "All praise is due to God, the Lord of all peoples" (1:1), since "all peoples" here refers to the two kind of personal beings who are recipients of guidance: jinn and mankind.[237]

Connection to Suras 54 and 55

In the previous chapter, "The Order of the Suras," we drew attention to Raymond Farrin's argument that the sura groups of the Qur'an are arranged to form a grand ring composition, with Suras 54, *The Moon*, and 55, *The All-Merciful*, at the center of this scheme. Each of these two suras seems to share a notable element in common with the Fatiha and *Mankind*.[238]

First, recall that the Fatiha referred to God as "Owner" (*MāLiK*) of the Day of Recompense (1:3), and *Mankind* referred to Him as "King" (*MaLiK*) of mankind (114:2)—two related words in Arabic. *The Moon* ends with a praise of God as "Sovereign" (*MaLīK*), a third divine name with the root *m-l-k*, which is found nowhere else in the Qur'an.[239]

Second, as we have seen, the first verse of the Fatiha refers to "all peoples" and the last verse of *Mankind* alludes to them, as "jinn and mankind." *The All-Merciful* contains the refrain, "So which of the bounties of the Lord of you both (*rabbi-kumā*) will you deny?" (55:13, passim), which commentators identify as being addressed to mankind and jinn respectively, both of whom are referred to within the sura (55:3, 14-15).

If Farrin's scheme is correct, the first (s. 1), middle (ss. 54 and 55), and last (s. 114) suras of the Qur'an are connected, firstly by the use of divine names

237 Farrin, *Structure and Qur'anic Interpretation*. See the discussion of "*al-'ālamīn*" in chapter 8, "'All praise is due to God, the Lord of all peoples.'"

238 Ibid., 66.

239 Ibid., 69.

built on the root *m-l-k*; and secondly by reference to God's Lordship over both jinn and mankind—possible signs of the Qur'an as a grand ring structure.

* * *

In one hadith, the Prophet Muhammad is said to have sworn, "By the One in Whose Hand is my soul, God has not revealed the likes of [the Fatiha] in the Torah, the Gospel, the Psalms, or [the rest of] the Qur'an."[240] In other hadiths, the Prophet distinguished the Fatiha as the *Umm al-Kitāb*, the "essence (or 'summary') of the scripture." From what we have seen, one could make a persuasive argument for the Fatiha as the ideal summary of the Qur'an. The word choice of each verse appears fine-tuned to convey the greatest depths of meaning in the most concise way, with each element placed most suitably in a way that underlines its relationship to the whole, building the sura into an elegant and meaningful symmetry, while also maintaining harmony of rhythm, rhyme, and sound.

The central concern of the Qur'an, the relationship between God and man, is underscored by the symmetry of the sura. The first half concerns God (vv. 1-4a), the second half concerns man (vv. 4b-7), and the two are brought in proper relationship to one another in the central verse: "You alone we worship and You alone we ask for help" (v. 4). Man renders to God exclusive worship and servitude, while God answers his needs and offers guidance and salvation. The Fatiha itself exemplifies this relationship: its first half, ending with "You alone we worship," consists wholly of words of worship, while its second half, beginning with "You alone we ask for help," consists wholly of a prayer for help.

The knowledge of God conveyed in the first half of the Fatiha includes God's perfection and divinity ("all praise is due to God"), His authority over all people ("Lord of all peoples"), His bountiful mercy to all of creation ("the All-Merciful"), His special mercy towards His sincere servants ("the Ever-Merciful"), and His complete justice ("Owner of the Day of Recompense"). These are the key attributes of God that concern His relationship with mankind. The arrangement of the divine titles into a mirror composition, with mercy emphasized twice in the center, both underlines their connections and places them in balance. The symmetry is fittingly prefaced by the statement "All praise is due to God," and the acknowledgement of these at-

240 *Musnad Aḥmad*, no. 9345; *Sunan at-Tirmidhī*, no. 2875; *Sunan an-Nasā'ī*, no. 914. Authenticated by Ibn Ḥibbān, no. 775; Ibn Khuzayma, no. 500; and al-Albānī, no. 5560 (Abū Rumaysah, *The Spiritual Cure: An Explanation to Sūrah al-Fātiḥah*, Birmingham: Daar us-Sunnah, 2006, 30).

tributes culminates in the worshipers' statement, "You alone we worship and You alone we ask for help."

Here the Fatiha transitions to the subject of the human being, who calls upon God for guidance in life and its diverse aspects ("Guide us..."). This guidance is depicted as a single but broad, timeless, and well-trodden path ("...along the Straight Path"), which is identified with a single spiritual community spanning all ages of human history ("the Path of those whom You have favored"). They are differentiated from two other kinds of people, those who refused righteous conduct in spite of having knowledge ("not of those who have earned anger"), and those who have lost their way on account of a lack of knowledge ("nor of the astray"). It follows that proper guidance involves the combination of sound beliefs, or knowledge, and sound action. Further subtleties emerge from the arrangement of these items into a symmetry, structurally parallel to the symmetry in the first half of the Fatiha. The two symmetries (vv. 1-3) and (vv. 5-7) are in turn unified by the central verse into a single overarching symmetry (v. 4), bringing God and man together.

Postscript

This book is only a small effort to inspire further interest in the literary study of the Qur'an, and to make the scripture and some of the discoveries of contemporary scholarship accessible to a wider audience. In the course of our exploration, we have achieved a taste of the nuances of the Qur'an's language and word choice; its use of Classical Arabic grammatical and rhetorical devices; its use of imagery, figures of speech, and parables; the function of oaths as literary devices; some aspects of its narrative style; and the structure and coherence of its suras and of the scripture as a whole. In the process, we have also occasionally touched on the role played by meter, rhyme, and other aspects of sound in the beauty, structure, and meaning of the text.[241]

The literary study of the Qur'an is important for both Muslims and non-Muslims. Muslims look to the Qur'an for guidance and revere it as a literary miracle, an Arabic scripture of inimitable style and unrivaled excellence, appearing on the tongue of a merchant who was known to have had no education or expertise in literature, poetry, or scripture.[242] Yet this book challenged and transcended the rich literary tradition of Arabia, and in only two decades transformed a people boasting of no civilization, divided into perpetually warring tribal factions, and devoted to a pantheon of deities into a monotheistic civilization, which in only a century would become the largest and most prosperous in the medieval world, stretching from Spain to India, and distinguished for its religion, scholarship, and advancement in the arts and sciences. The Qur'an continues to have a defining impact on the lives of more than one-fifth of the world's population today.

The literary approach to the Qur'an is also important for those who have no prior theological commitments to the scripture, but who wish to understand

---

241 For a more focused treatment of this aspect of the Qur'an, see Michael Sells, *Approaching the Qur'an.*

242 Otherwise, the Qur'an could hardly have made the claim that "you did not read before it any scripture, nor did you transcribe one with your hand; in that case, those who follow falsehood might have doubted" (29:49), nor could it have described Muhammad as *ummī*, or "unlearned" (7:157-158; 62:2), without being easily falsified.

the message, beauty, and power of what that stands as the most read and revered book in the world, having an incalculable impact on history, but which also tends to pose a challenge to contemporary readers due to its complexity and the distinctiveness of its structure and discourse.

Thankfully, a renaissance is underway in the literary study of the Qur'an, which shows great promise of further advances in unveiling and making accessible the depth and power of the Qur'an. Below, under "Further Resources for the Literary Study of the Qur'an," the reader can survey some of the most recent literature on the Qur'an. We hope that this book is just one step towards the goals we have put forth here, and that there will be many more to come.

APPENDIX

Jihad in the Qur'an

Introduction

Given the political landscape of the world today, the topic of what the Qur'an says about fighting or jihad is an important one. Unfortunately, it is precisely this question that both extreme militant Muslim groups and opponents of Islam fail to give due care and consideration. Both groups share a common approach of quoting isolated statements of the Qur'an while disregarding the historical context and restrictions that are clearly spelled out by the surrounding text. It usually only requires drawing attention to this context to dispel these misinterpretations and to show that the concept of jihad in the Qur'an is conditioned by a clear ethical focus. Professor M.A.S. Abdel Haleem of the School of Oriental and African Studies in London has done this in a fairly recent study of jihad in the Qur'an. We will summarize his observations here, but the reader interested in further detail is encouraged to consult his work.[243] For the sake of brevity, we will focus on the most crucial passages for this topic: those which legislate fighting, describe the justifications for war, lay down the rules for fighting, and those which are most frequently cited out of context.

The word jihad (*jihād*) means "to struggle" or "to exert effort," or more precisely, "exerting effort in the face of an exertion by something or someone else."[244] Within the Qur'an and the hadiths of the Prophet Muhammad, there

243 M.A.S. Abdel Haleem, "Qur'anic '*jihād*': A Linguistic and Contextual Analysis," *Journal of Qur'anic Studies* 12.1-2 (2010): 147-66. Abdel Haleem also presents a slightly abridged version of his study in his popular book, *Understanding the Qur'an: Themes and Style*. For a more detailed study, see also Louay Fatoohi, *Jihad in the Qur'an: The Truth from the Source* (Birmingham: Luna Plena, 2009).

244 Abdel Haleem, "Qur'anic *jihād*." 147.

are several types of jihad. They include speaking out against evil or oppression (jihad of the tongue), resisting one's desires or temptations to commit wrong (jihad of the self), spending one's wealth in support of a just cause (jihad of wealth), and physical or military jihad.[245] In this essay, we will focus exclusively on physical *jihād*, also known as "fighting" or "combat" (*qitāl*).

The Justification for Fighting

Over the course of the Meccan period (610-622 CE), the Muslims made up a small minority, consisting chiefly of the disadvantaged classes of society: the poor, orphans, women, and slaves. They lacked the numbers or resources to defend themselves against violent persecution and most of them had no means of social protection. The Qur'an required them to patiently bear the persecution, promising that despite all appearances, God would soon alleviate their situation and give them victory over their oppressors, and that they would have a bountiful reward with Him in the afterlife. The Prophet directed many of them to flee to Ethiopia, where they could practice their religion in safety.

In 622, the Prophet and his remaining followers in Mecca emigrated to Medina, leaving their homes and most of their possessions behind. The natives of Medina embraced the fledgling faith in large number and appointed the Prophet as the political and judicial head of the city. Notwithstanding, the Meccan leaders continued to conspire against the Muslim community. In about 624, the Qur'an gave them permission for the first time to fight in defense of their rights and possessions. Note the many qualifications and restrictions that the Qur'an lays down, which we have printed in bold:

> **Those who are attacked** are permitted to take up arms **because they have been wronged**—God has the power to help them—**those who have been driven unjustly from their homes** only for saying, "Our Lord is God."
>
> If God did not repel some people by means of others, **many monasteries, churches, synagogues, and mosques, where God's name is much invoked, would have been destroyed**.
>
> **God is sure to help those who help His cause—God is strong and mighty—those who, when We establish them in the land, keep up the prayer, pay the prescribed alms, command what is right, and forbid what is wrong**: God controls the outcome of all events. (22:39–41)[246]

---

245 The word jihad occurs in the Qur'an with other meanings as well. See ibid., 147-148.

246 The translations in this appendix are mostly adopted from Abdel Haleem's essay or his translation of the Qur'an, sometimes with modification.

Observe that the Qur'an does not simply permit the Muslims to fight, but emphasizes the circumstances that justify fighting. This entails that war is not the desired norm but may only be permitted under morally and religiously justified conditions. The justification is highlighted multiple times: the Muslims have been "attacked," "wronged," and "driven unjustly from their homes," and therefore have the right to defend themselves. This is buttressed by the argument that if God did not allow some people to repel the aggression of others, there would be much destruction of places in which people worship God—and by extension the lands in which they are located. Note that these places of worship include not only mosques, but also churches and synagogues. Hence the passage allows fighting in defense of the safety, property, and religious freedom—not only of Muslims, but also (at the very least) of Jews and Christians as well.[247] Finally, the Muslims are told that God will only support those who, when given dominance, act virtuously and forbid injustice.[248] As Abdel Haleem writes,

> Permission to fight, then, is not given in the form of a simple instruction to 'Go forth and fight', but is couched in justifications, restrictions and reminders of God's power and the believers' duty to Him. This nuanced approach to the issue of 'taking up arms' is one that is too often unacknowledged in discussions on *jihād* by academics, let alone by the media and propagandists, which only leads to consolidating the popular image of *jihād*.[249]

Later revelations would add the permission and encouragement for Muslims to fight not only for their own rights, but also to defend others who are oppressed:

> Why should you not fight in God's cause and for those oppressed men, women, and children who cry out, "Lord, rescue us from this town whose people are oppressors! By Your grace, give us a protector and give us a helper!"? (4:75)

Even in this case, however, Muslims are prohibited from violating their treaties:

> if they seek help from you against persecution it is your duty to assist them, except against people with whom you have a treaty: God sees all that you do (8:72)

---

247 Mustansir Mir, "Islamic, Qur'anic," in *Encyclopedia of Religion and War*, ed. Gabriel Palmer-Fernandez (New York: Routledge, 2004), 207.

248 Abdel Haleem, "Qur'anic *jihād*," 150.

249 Ibid., 150.

Statements emphasizing the just causes of war are found consistently throughout Qur'anic discussion of jihad.

Guidelines for Fighting

The Qur'an did not merely give the Muslims permission to fight for their rights, but also provided strict guidelines and instructions for how the fighting may be waged. Again, note the many restrictions, printed in bold:

> Fight in God's way **against those who fight you, but do not overstep the limits: God does not love those who overstep the limits**. Kill them wherever you encounter them, and **drive them out from where they drove you out**, for persecution (*fitna*)[250] is more severe than killing. **Do not fight them at the Sacred Mosque unless they fight you there**. If they do fight you, kill them—this is what such disbelievers deserve—but **if they stop, then God is most forgiving and merciful. Fight them in order to put an end to persecution**, and so that [your] worship is devoted to God [without fear].[251] **If they cease hostilities, there can be no [further] hostility, except towards aggressors**. A sacred month for a sacred month: violation of sanctity [calls for] fair retribution. So if anyone attacks you [in a sacred

---

250 Because the term *fitna*, translated here as "persecution," has a variety of meanings (such as "trial," "temptation," or "sedition"), some translators and commentators have provided other interpretations, such as that it refers to idolatry or disbelief. The argument for this is that the verse says, "if they stop, God is most forgiving and merciful," whereas God's mercy and forgiveness is only promised to those who give up idolatry and disbelief. However, as Abdel Haleem (ibid., 153) notes, this phrase is most plausibly directed towards the believers, urging them to "overlook and forgive what their enemies have done, remembering that God is forgiving and merciful" (see parallels to this in 4:149 and 24:22). The translation of "persecution," which is adopted by most English translations, fits best with the verse's context, as the very next verse says, "if they stop, there can be no [further] hostility, except towards aggressors" (2:193). The word *fitna* also occurs with the meaning of persecution in 10:83, 16:110, and 85:10. The phrase "persecution is more severe than killing" therefore indicates that fighting against oppressors is the lesser evil, because otherwise the persecution will not cease but will only grow more intense.

251 This phrase has also given rise to misinterpretation. As Abdel Haleem observes,

> Dawood translates this as fight them until there is no more idolatry and God's religion reigns supreme. We have already dealt with his translation of *fitna* as idolatry, but we have here another issue: how to read the word *dīn*. *Dīn* is often (as here) translated as 'religion' but the word has many meanings in Arabic...The meanings that fit here are 'worship' or 'obedience': thus, 'if persecution stops, you will be able to worship God without oppression or concealment'. It has nothing to do with fighting until God's religion (i.e. Islam) becomes supreme as this has no relation to the beginning or end of the passage, *fight those who attack you ... whoever attacks you, attack him*, and it goes against such Qur'anic statements as, *most people will not believe* (Q. 12:103) and *they will always be different* (Q. 11:118). (ibid., 154)

> month], attack him **as he attacked you**, but **be mindful of God, and know that He is with those who are mindful of Him. Spend in God's cause**: do not contribute to your destruction with your own hands, **but do good, for God loves those who do good**. (2:190–195)

Several comments about this passage are in order.

First, the passage again repeatedly emphasizes the justifications for fighting. The Muslims are only told to fight "those who fight you," to drive out "those who drove you out," and to attack "those who attacked you." The explicit grounds for fighting are "to put an end to persecution." It is clear that the objective here is defensive: it is so that the Muslims may regain their lost land and possessions.

Second, these verses repeatedly stipulate the qualifications and restrictions of fighting. In Abdel Haleem's words, they

> contain many restrictions and are couched in restraining language that appeals strongly to the conscience: in them we find four prohibitions; seven restrictions (one 'until', four 'if's, two 'those who fight you'); as well as such cautions as '*in God's way*', '*be mindful of God*', '*God does not love those who overstep the limits*', '*He is with those who are mindful of Him*', loves '*those who do good*', and '*is most forgiving and merciful*'. Restrictions abound from beginning to end.[252]

Muslim jurists and exegetes such al-Baydawi (d. 1286) explained that the prohibition of "overstepping the limits" forbids the Muslims from:

> "initiation of fighting, fighting those with whom a treaty has been concluded, surprising the enemy without first inviting them to make peace, destroying crops or killing those who should be protected."[253]

Third, the phrase "kill them wherever you encounter them" is one of the phrases most frequently quoted out of context by polemicists against Islam in order to prove that the faith is inherently violent. By taking this phrase out of its context, they present it as if the pronoun "them" refers generically to non-Muslims and that the command lays down a general rule for how Muslims are required to interact with them. It is obvious when read in context that "them" refers back to "those who fight you"—that is, those who drove the Muslims out of their homes and committed persistent aggression against them.

The phrase "*wherever* you encounter them" is misconstrued in a similar fashion. Commentators such as Fakhr ad-Din ar-Razi (d. 1209) have noted

---

252 Ibid., 152.

253 Quoted in Abdel Haleem, *Understanding the Qur'an*, 66.

that the verse was revealed to allay the Muslims' fear that if the Meccans attacked them while they were performing the Hajj, they would be violating the sanctity of the holy city by fighting back to defend themselves. The Qur'an gave them permission "to kill their attackers wherever they encountered them, inside or outside the sacred area."[254] The same meaning applies to the statement, "for persecution is more severe than killing": the Muslims are being assured that if they are attacked in the sanctuary, they are allowed to fight back, because the severity of their enemies assaulting them in the sanctuary is greater than their killing them to defend themselves against the attack. This is in the same connection that the passage, a few verses later, allows the Muslims to fight in the sacred months if they are attacked (2:194; cf. 9:36). This given further confirmation by 2:217, in which the same issue is addressed and the same response is given:[255]

> They ask you [Prophet] about fighting in the sacred month. Say, "Fighting in that month is a great offence, but to bar others from God's path, to disbelieve in Him, prevent access to the Sacred Mosque, and expel its people, are still greater offences in God's eyes: *persecution is worse than killing*."

Subsequent revelations pertaining to jihad further emphasize that the Muslims are bound to maintain peaceful relations with non-Muslims and are only permitted to fight so long as they are under the threat of attack:

> So if they withdraw and do not fight you, and offer you peace, then God gives you no way against them. (4:90)

> But if they incline towards peace, you must also incline towards it, and put your trust in God: He is the All Hearing, the All Knowing. (8:61)

> There is no cause to act against anyone who defends himself after being wronged, but there is cause to act against those who oppress people and transgress in the land against all justice—they will have an agonizing torment—though if a person is patient and forgives, this is one of the greatest things. (42:41-43)

> He does not forbid you to deal kindly and justly with anyone who has not fought you for your faith or driven you out of your homes: God loves the just. But God forbids you to take as allies those who have fought against you for your faith, driven you out of your homes, and helped others to drive you out. (60:8-9)

---

254 Abdel Haleem, "Qur'anic *jihād*," 151.
255 Ibid., 151-153.

Furthermore, the subsequent revelations continue to emphasize that even in the case of justified war, Muslims are not permitted to be disproportionate in their response or transgress the bounds of justice:

> Do not let your hatred for the people who barred you from the Sacred Mosque induce you to transgress: help one another to do what is right and good; do not help one another towards sin and aggression. Be mindful of God, for His punishment is severe. (5:2)

> You who believe, stand firm for God as witnesses with justice: do not let hatred of others cause you not to act equitably, but act equitably, for that is nearer to God-consciousness. Be mindful of God: God is well aware of all that you do. (5:8)

> So, you who believe, be careful when you go to fight in God's way, and do not say to someone who offers you a greeting of peace, 'You are not a believer,' out of desire for the chance gains of this life– God has plenty of gains for you. You yourself were in the same position [once], but God was gracious to you, so be careful: God is fully aware of what you do. (4:94)

Similarly, the Qur'an repeatedly obliges Muslims to honor their treaties with non-Muslims (e.g. 8:72; 9:4, 7) and categorically prohibits converting people to Islam by force, declaring, "There is absolutely no compulsion in religion" (2:256; cf. 10:99; 18:29; 42:48; 109:6; etc.).

The Conquest of Mecca

One of the missions of the Prophet was to purify the holy city of Mecca from idolatry and to restore it as the center of Abrahamic monotheism, dedicated to the exclusive worship of God. Throughout the course of the Meccan period, the Prophet's role was only that of a messenger, reciting the Qur'anic revelations and trying to persuade the inhabitants of the city to abandon their idolatry. There was initially no question of fighting or conquest. As we have seen, it was only after the Muslims had suffered repeated aggression by the Quraysh and were able to establish an independent polity in Medina that the Qur'an allowed them to fight back. Only at this point were they permitted to engage in combat in hopes of recovering their homes and property and to liberate Mecca from the idolaters of the Quraysh.

In the following years, the Muslims won a number of significant battles against the Quraysh, and in 628, the Quraysh agreed to a ten-year truce known as the Treaty of Hudaybiyya. The following year the Quraysh violated the treaty by assisting a particularly violent attack against one of the tribes allied to the Muslims. In December of 629, the Prophet led an army of ten thousand men, composed largely of tribes who had had newly embraced Islam, in a march on

Mecca. The Quraysh surrendered and, despite all of the crimes they had committed over the years, the Prophet forgave them, quoting the words of Joseph to his brothers, "No blame rests on you today" (12:92). The Conquest of Mecca was peaceful: no one was harmed except for a few criminals specifically marked for execution, and a small band who had picked up arms against the Muslims. The Prophet circled the Ka'ba on his camel, knocking down each of the idols that contaminated it, and restoring it as a shrine dedicated exclusively to God. The entire Quraysh tribe accepted Islam, including its leader Abu Sufyan, who had previously led armies against the Muslims in a number of battles but now became one of the Prophet's close companions.

The "Sword Verse"

Following the Conquest of Mecca, some of the remaining pagan tribes in Arabia continued to act belligerently against the Muslim community. This occasioned a revelation (9:1-37) containing some of the most austere instructions in the whole Qur'an on the topic of fighting. Frequently cited out of context to support militant agendas or to show that Islam is an intrinsically violent faith is the so-called "Sword Verse":

> When the [four] forbidden months are over, wherever you find the polytheists, kill them, seize them, besiege them, ambush them. (9:5)

Yet as with the previous examples, this statement of war is qualified by conditions, concessions of peace, and indications of historical context that clearly demonstrate that it is not a universal directive for fighting non-Muslims.

First, the surrounding verses state multiple times that the "polytheists" referred to are only those who repeatedly violated their treaties and engaged in acts of aggression against the Muslim community and its allies. For example, the verse immediately before the "Sword Verse" says:

> As for those who have honored the treaty you made with them and who have not supported anyone against you: fulfill your agreement with them to the end of their term. God loves those who are mindful of Him. (9:4)

This is followed a few verses later by the command:

> But as for those with whom you made a treaty at the Sacred Mosque, so long as they remain true to you, be true to them; God loves those who are mindful of Him. (9:7)

The crimes of the idolaters whom fighting is mandated against are further detailed in vv. 8-10 and 12-13. As Abdel Haleem summarizes,

> They continuously broke their agreements and aided others against the Muslims, they started hostilities against the Muslims, barred others from becoming Muslims, expelled Muslims from the Holy Mosque and even from their own homes. At least eight times the passage mentions their misdeeds against the Muslims.[256]

It is stated in v. 12 that the goal of fighting the "heads of disbelief" is so that "they might desist" from their acts of aggression. All of this is consistent with the rest of the Qur'anic injunctions about war, which oblige the Muslim community to be faithful to their treaties and to only fight those who have engaged in acts of belligerence or persecution.

Second, the perpetrators of these crimes are offered several warnings and concessions. They are a given a four-month period of respite (9:2, 5) to either consider embracing Islam or to leave the Arabian Peninsula. The Prophet is instructed to grant protection to any of the polytheists who request it, so that they may consider the message of the Qur'an without fear of harm (9:6). Otherwise, they may leave the Arabian Peninsula and will not be harmed. The stern declaration of war in the "Sword Verse" will only come into effect should they insist on maintaining their presence after the four-month period of respite. It is an important historical note that each of the polytheistic tribes took advantage of these provisions, most of them embracing Islam and joining the Muslim community. Hence, as a result of these provisions, the fighting came to an end, the tribes of Arabia were united for the very first time in history, and no blood was actually shed on account of the "Sword Verse."

In summary, the surrounding verses contextualize the "Sword Verse" and indicate that it was a stern threat revealed in response to the crimes of the polytheistic tribes of Arabia who had repeatedly conspired against the Muslim community, in violation of their peace treaties. Even in this case, they were given a period of respite and several peaceful concessions were offered to them, which effectively averted any further conflict. As Abdel Haleem observes, "The whole of this context to v. 5, with all its restrictions, is ignored by those who simply isolate one part of a sentence to build their theory of war in Islam on what is termed 'The Sword Verse', even when the word 'sword' does not occur anywhere in the Qur'an."[257] It should also be clear that the above passage does not negate the Qur'anic peace imperative, which requires Muslims not to harm anyone who maintains peace with them, but that the passage was specifically revealed in order to put an end to attacks from the hostile pagan tribes of Arabia against the Muslim community.

---

256 Abdel Haleem, *Understanding the Qur'an*, 67-68.
257 Ibid., 68.

Further Resources for the Literary Study of the Qur'an

Bayyinah online resources

- For dozens of examples rhetorical subtleties in the Qur'an's word choice and grammar, explained in easy language, see Nouman Ali Khan's "Amazed by the Qur'an" series on the Bayyinah Institute YouTube channel (www.youtube.com/user/BayyinahInstitute).
- Bayyinah TV (www.bayyinah.tv)—A rich online resource continuously updated with programs and seminars on the Qur'an, the Arabic language, and Islamic history. Although Bayyinah TV requires a paid subscription, free gift subscriptions are also available.

Translations of the Qur'an

Abdel Haleem, M.A.S. *The Qur'an: A New Translation*. New York: Oxford University Press, 2005.

- A smooth, elegant, and readable translation of the Qur'an for general audiences, with an informative introduction and occasional footnotes. This translation is also distinguished in that it divides the text into paragraphs rather than verse form.

Bewley, Abdalhaqq and Aisha. *The Noble Qur'an: A New Rendering of Its Meaning in English* (Norwich: Bookwork, 2005).

- A lucid, accurate, and elegant translation, but with minimal introduction and commentary.

Droge, A.J. *The Qur'ān: A New Annotated Translation*. Bristol, CT: Equinox Publishing, Ltd. 2013.

- For more academically inclined readers, this is an elegant and accurate translation of the Qur'an, with fairly extensive footnotes that guide reading, define important words, provide historical context, and supply helpful intertextual references to the Bible. It also contains useful supplements, such as a guide to academic works on the Qur'an in English, a map of the Qur'an's historical setting, a timeline of events relevant to the Qur'an, and a glossary.

Books

Abdel Haleem, Muhammad. *Understanding the Qur'an: Themes and Style.* London: I.B. Tauris, 2011.

- A rich, engaging, and highly readable study of select topics, stories, and suras of the Qur'an.

Ernst, Carl. *How to Read the Qur'an: A New Guide, with Select Translations.* UNC Press, 2011.

- Introduces and explores the Qur'an from a literary and historical point of view. This book adopts a chronological approach to the Qur'an, providing studies of passages in the context of their periods of revelation: Early Meccan, Middle to Late Meccan, and Medinan. It provides a good introduction to European language scholarship on the Qur'an, especially for more academically inclined readers.

Farrin, Raymond. *Structure and Qur'anic Interpretation: A Study of Symmetry and Coherence in Islam's Holy Text.* Ashland, OR: White Cloud Press, 2014.

- A highly readable account of the role of symmetry in the structure of the suras of the Qur'an, including discussions of ring composition, sura pairs, sura groups, and the possible symmetrical structure of the Qur'an as a whole.

Mir, Mustansir. *Understanding the Islamic Scripture: A Study of Selected Passages from the Qur'ān.* New York: Pearson Longman, 2008.

- This is one of the most rewarding books on the Qur'an in English, offering rich literary commentaries of 37 diverse and representative passages of the Qur'an, including the most famous and celebrated ones.

Robinson, Neal. *Discovering the Qur'an: A Contemporary Approach to a Veiled Text.* 2nd ed. Washington, D.C.: Georgetown UP, 2003.

- Since its first publication in 1996, *Discovering the Qur'an* has had a significant impact on English-language scholarship on the Qur'an. It includes detailed studies of how the Qur'an is experienced by Muslims;

the chronology of the revelations; an exhaustive account of the formal elements of the Early Meccan suras; the structure of the Meccan suras; studies of the coherence and structure of suras 2, 78, and 79; the role of sound and intertextuality in the coherence of the suras; the narrative perspective of the Qur'an and its grammatical shifts; and the order of the suras. This book is suited for academic students of the Qur'an.

Sells, Michael. *Approaching the Qur'an: The Early Revelations*. 2nd ed. Ashland, Oregon: White Cloud Press, 2007.

- Provides beautiful translations and brief commentaries of the short, hymnic, Early Meccan suras, focusing on qualities often neglected in academic studies and introductions, such as sound, gender, and spirit. The book comes with audio recordings of Qur'anic recitations to accompany the reading, providing direct access to the rhythm, rhyme, and other sounds qualities of the suras.

Essays

- A treasure of essays by Mustansir Mir related to the literary study of the Qur'an may be accessed on Youngstown.academia.edu/MustansirMir

Academic volumes

- Boullata, Issa J., ed. *Literary Structures of Religious Meaning in the Qur'ān*. Richmond, Surrey: Routledge, 2000.
- Rippin, Andrew, ed. *The Blackwell Companion to the Qur'ān*. Oxford: Blackwell, 2006.
- Neuwirth, Angelika, Nicolai Sinai, and Michael Marx, eds. *The Qur'ān in Context: Historical and Literary Investigations into the Qur'ānic Milieu*. Leiden: Brill, 2010.

For a bibliography of studies on the composition of the suras of the Qur'an, see Sharif Randhawa, "A Bibliography of Studies in English on the Coherence and Structure of the Qur'an's Suras," *Bayyinah Blog*, April 15, 2016 (http://blog.bayyinah.com/nazm-bibliography).

Glossary of Arabic Terms

Āya: Literally, "sign," "communication," or "lesson," referring in the Qur'an to (1) signs of God in history and nature and (2) the verses or revelations of the Qur'an and of previous scriptures.

Fatiha: Literally, "The Opening," referring to the first sura of the Qur'an. The Fatiha is recited by Muslims in each unit of the ritual prayer and is considered to be a summary of the Qur'an's teachings.

Hadith: A "report" or "account" of the sayings or deeds of the Prophet Muhammad.

Hijra: "Emigration," the departure of Muhammad and his followers from Mecca to Medina in the year 622 CE, marking the establishment of the Muslims as an independent community.

Islam: Literally "submission" to God's will. Islam is a monotheistic faith in the Abrahamic tradition of Judaism and Christianity, regarded by its adherents as the final revealed religion, communicated by God through the Prophet Muhammad. The sacred scripture of Islam is the Qur'an. Islam is the world's second largest faith, claiming over 1.5 billion adherents.

Jinn: A kind of creation the Qur'an mentions who, like humans, are intelligent, have free will, and are morally accountable. They have some supernatural abilities—such as the ability to possess humans, quickly traverse long distances, and sometimes manipulate objects—equivalent to the spirits or demons mentioned in the Bible (e.g. 1 Kings 22:21-23; Matt. 9:36) and found in other cultures and belief systems.

Ka'ba: The sacred shrine of Mecca, which pre-Islamic Arab and Islamic tradition regard as having been built by Abraham.

Mecca: A city in the western Arabian Peninsula where the Prophet Muhammad was born and preached for thirteen years, from 610 until 622 CE, when he and his followers emigrated to the city of Medina. According to Arab tradition and the Qur'an, Mecca was founded by Abraham. Muhammad conquered Mecca at the end of the year 629 CE.

Medina: A city in the western Arabian Peninsula to which Muhammad and his followers emigrated in 622 CE, where they became an independent community. The Medinan period of Muhammad's prophetic career lasted ten years, from 622 to his death in 632 CE.

Muslim: An adherent of the religion of Islam, literally "one who submits" to God's will.

Quraysh: The chief tribe of Mecca, to whom the Prophet Muhammad belonged. The Quraysh were descendants of Abraham through his son Ishmael, and took custodianship of the Ka'ba. Most of the leaders of the Quraysh bitterly opposed the Prophet's message, and are frequently addressed in the Qur'an.

Qur'an (or Quran): The sacred scripture of Islam, viewed by Muslims as God's final revelation to humanity in the Arabic language, revealed to the Prophet Muhammad in Arabia roughly 610 to 632 CE.

Sura: A "portion" of the Qur'an, often (but problematically) translated as "chapter." The Qur'an consists of 114 suras, arranged very roughly in order of length, with the longest suras placed at the beginning and the shortest at the end.

Glossary of English Terms

Coherence: How ideas in a literary composition are logically related and ordered, forming a unified whole.

Eschatology: The aspect of religion concerned with the "last things"—death, the end times, judgment, and final reward and punishment.

Imperfect tense: The verb tense that indicates an action that is not complete. It may be going on at the moment, as with the progressive tense in English ("I am/was driving my car"); it may be recurring, as in the present tense in English ("I drive my car"); or it may not have happened yet, as in the future tense in English ("I will drive my car").

Literary: Having to do largely with the artistic form, techniques, and devices of a composition, such as wordplay, metaphor, allegory, rhythm, rhyme, narrative techniques and styles, coherence and structure, and so on.

Near East: The term historians use to denote what roughly corresponds to the modern Middle East in ancient times. It includes Egypt, the Arabian Peninsula, the Levant, Asia Minor, Mesopotamia, and Persia.

Rhetoric: The art of eloquent and effective speech, with a focus on its persuasive, aesthetic, and emotional impact. (In Arabic this is known as *balāgha*.)

Ring composition: A literary pattern in which a series of ideas are presented in one order, and then in an opposite order, with a discrete centerpiece in between. A variant of ring composition without the centerpiece is known as "mirror composition" or more commonly as a "chiasmus" or "chiastic structure."

Perfect tense: The verb tense that indicates a completed action, such as in "I drove this car." This is usually, but not always, equivalent to the past tense in English.

Polemic(s): A *polemic* is a strong attack on an opposing view or party. *Polemics* is also another term for debate or argumentation.

Selected Bibliography

Abdel Haleem, M.A.S. *The Qur'an: A New Translation*. New York: Oxford University Press, 2004.

—— "Qur'anic 'jihād': A Linguistic and Contextual Analysis." *Coherence in the Qur'an* 12 (2010): 147-66.

——*Understanding the Qur'an: Themes and Style*. London: I.B. Tauris, 2011.

Abū Rumaysah. *The Spiritual Cure: An Explanation to Sūrah al-Fātiḥah*. Birmingham: Daar us-Sunnah, 2006

Brown, Jonathan A.C. *Muhammad: A Very Short Introduction*. Oxford: Oxford UP, 2011.

Cuypers, Michel. "Semitic Rhetoric as a Key to the Question of the Naẓm of the Qur'anic Text." *Coherence in the Qur'an* 13.1 (2011): 1-24.

——*The Banquet: A Reading of the Fifth Sura of the Qur'an* (Miami: Convivium, 2009).

Douglas, Mary. *Thinking in Circles: An Essay on Ring Composition*. New Haven/London: Yale UP, 2007.

Ernst, Carl W. *How to Read the Qur'an: A New Guide, with Select Translations*. Chapel Hill: University of North Carolina Press, 2011.

Farrin, Raymond. *Abundance from the Desert: Classical Arabic Poetry*. Syracuse, NY: Syracuse UP, 2011.

——*Structure and Qur'anic Interpretation: A Study of Symmetry and Coherence in Islam's Holy Text*. Ashland, Oregon: White Cloud Press, 2014.

Geiger, Abraham. *Judaism and Islam: A Prize Essay*. Trans. F.M. Young. Vepery: M.D.C.S.P.C.K. Press, 1898.

Griffith, Sidney H. "Christian Lore and the Arabic Qur'an: The 'Companions of the Cave' in *Surat al-Kahf* and in Syriac Christian tradition." Ed. Gabriel Said Reynolds. *The Qur'ān in Its Historical Context*. London: Routledge, 2008.

Hoyland, Robert G. *Arabia and the Arabs: From the Bronze Age to the Coming of Islam*. London: Routledge, 2001.

Ibn Kathīr. *Tafsīr al-Qur'ān al-Karīm*. Amman: Royal Aal Al-Bayt Institute for Islamic Thought, n.d. *Altafsir.com*. Web.

Ibn Manẓūr. *Lisān al-'Arab*, 2nd ed., 15 vols. Beirut: Dār Ṣādir, 1993.

Ibrahim, M. Zakyi. "Oaths in the Qur'ān: Bint Al-Shāṭi"s Literary Contribution," *Islamic Studies* 48 no. 4 (2009): 475-98.

Iṣlāḥī, Amīn Aḥsan. *Tadabbur-e-Qur'ān: Pondering Over the Qur'ān, Volume 1: Tafsīr of Sūrah al-Fātiḥah and Sūrah al-Baqarah*. Trans. Mohammad Saleem Kayani. Kuala Lampur: Islamic Book Trust, 2006.

Kaylānī, 'Abd ar-Raḥmān. *Mutarādifāt al-Qur'ān ma'a al-Furūq al-Lughawiyya*. Lahore: Maktabat as-Salām, 2009.

Mir, Mustansir. *Coherence in the Qur'an*. Indianapolis: American Trust Publications, 1986.

—— "The Qur'anic Story Of Joseph: Plot, Themes, And Characters." *The Muslim World* 76.1 (1986): 1-15.

—— "The Qur'an as Literature," *Religion & Literature* 20 no. 1 (1988): 49-64.

—— *Verbal Idioms of the Qur'ān*. Ann Arbour: University of Michigan, 1989.

—— "The Qur'ān's Oaths: Farāhī's Interpretation," *Islamic Studies* 29 no. 1 (1990): 5-27.

—— "Dialogue in the Qur'an." *Religion & Literature* 24 no. 1 (1992): 12-16.

—— "The Sūra as a Unity: A Twentieth Century Development in Qur'an Exegesis." Ed. G. R. Hawting and Abdul-Kader A. Shareef. *Approaches to the Qur'an*. London: Routledge, 1993. 211–24

——"Irony in the Qur'ān: A Study of the Story of Joseph." *Literary Structures of Religious Meaning in the Qur'ān*. Richmond, Surrey: Routledge, 2000. 173-87.

—— "Language." Ed. Andrew Rippin. *The Blackwell Companions to the Qur'ān*. Malden, MA: Blackwell, 2006. 88-106.

——"Some Figures of Speech in the Qur'an." *Religion & Literature* 40 no. 3 (2008): 31-48.

——*Understanding the Islamic Scripture: A Study of Selected Passages from the Qur'an* (N.p.: Pearson Education, 2008).

—— "Some Aspects of Narration in the Qur'an." Ed. Roberta Sterman Sabbath. *Sacred Tropes: Tanakh, New Testament, and Qur'an as Literature and Culture*. Leiden: Brill, 2009. 93-106.

Neuwirth, Angelika. "Images and Metaphors in the Introductory Sections of the Meccan Suras." Ed. G. R. Hawting and Abdul-Kader A. Shareef. *Approaches to the Qur'an*. London: Routledge, 1993. 3-36.

Nöldeke, Theodor, Friedrich Schwally, Gotthelf Bergsträßer, and Otto Pretzl. *The History of the Qur'ān*. Trans. Wolfgang H. Behn. Leiden: Brill, 2013.

Robinson, Neal. *Discovering the Qur'an: A Contemporary Approach to a Veiled Text.* 2nd ed. London: SCM Press, 2003.

—— "The Qur'ān as the Word of God." *Heaven and Earth: Essex Essays in Theology and Ethics.* Ed. Andrew Linzey and Peter J. Wexler. Worthing: Churchman, 1986. 38-54.

—— "The Dynamics of the Qur'anic Discourse: Tradition and Redaction." *Perspectives on Islamic Culture: Essays in Honour of Emilio Platti.* Ed. Bert Broeckaert, Stef Van Den Branden, and Jean-Jacques Pérennès. Leuven: Peeters, 2013. 3-18.

Reda, Nevin. "Holistic Approaches to the Qur'an: A Historical Background." *Religion Compass* 4.8 (2010): 495-506.

——*Textual Integrity and Coherence in the Qur'an: Repetition and Narrative Structure in Surat al-Baqara.* PhD diss. U of Toronto, 2010.

Rāzī, Fakhr ad-Dīn. *at-Tafsīr al-Kabīr.* Amman: Royal Aal Al-Bayt Institute for Islamic Thought, n.d. Altafsir.com. Web.

Reynolds, Gabriel Said. *The Qur'ān and Its Biblical Subtext.* London: Routledge, 2010.

Saleh, Walid A. "The Etymological Fallacy and Qur'anic Studies: Muhammad, Paradise, and Late Antiquity." Ed. Angelika Neuwirth, Nicolai Sinai, and Michael Marx. *The Qur'ān in Context: Historical and Literary Investigations into the Qur'ānic Milieu.* Leiden: Brill, 2011.

Sells, Michael. *Approaching the Qur'an: The Early Revelations.* 2nd ed. Ashland, Oregon: White Cloud Press, 2007.

as-Sāmarrā'i, Fāḍil Ṣāliḥ. *Lamasāt Bayyāniyya fi Nuṣūṣ min al-Tanzīl.* 3rd ed. Amman: Dar al-'Ammār, 2003.

——*al-Ta'bīr al-Qur'ānī.* 4th ed. Amman: Dar al-'Ammār, 2006.

Ṭabarī, Abu Ja'far aṭ-. *Jāmi' al-Bayān fi Tafsīr al-Qur'an.* Amman: Royal Aal Al-Bayt Institute for Islamic Thought, n.d. *Altafsir.com.* Web.

Qadhi, Abu Ammar Yasir, *An Introduction to the Sciences of the Qur'aan.* Birmingham: Al-Hidayah, 1999.